The Writings of Martin Buber

THE
WRITINGS
OF
MARTIN
BUBER

Selected, Edited, and Introduced
by WILL HERBERG

A MERIDIAN BOOK

NEW AMERICAN LIBRARY
TIMES MIRROR

Acknowledgments

For permission to include copyright material in this volume, acknowledgment is gratefully made to the following publishers:

Charles Scribner's Sons: Sections of *I and Thou;* a section of *Good and Evil,* copyright © 1952, 1953 by Martin Buber.

The Macmillan Company: Section of "The Question to the Single One" from *Between Man and Man;* section of *The Prophetic Faith;* chapters from *Paths in Utopia.*

Harper & Brothers Essay "God and the Spirit of Man" from *The Eclipse of God.*

Farrar, Straus and Cudahy, Inc.: Material drawn from *Moses,* from *At the Turning,* and from *Israel and Palestine,* all published by East and West Library and distributed by Farrar, Straus and Cudahy, Inc.

Schocken Books, Inc.: The following material from *Israel and the World,* translated by Olga Marx and Greta Hort, copyright © 1948 by Schocken Books, Inc.: "The Love of God and the Idea of Deity"; "And If Not Now, When?"; "The Faith of Judaism"; "The Two Foci of the Jewish Soul"; "Nationalism"; "The Land And Its Possessors"; "On National Education"; "Teaching and Deed"; "Biblical Leadership"; "Plato and Isaiah"; "The Man of Today and the Jewish Bible"; "Hebrew Humanism."

MERIDIAN TRADEMARK REG. U.S. PAT. OFF. AND FOREIGN COUNTRIES
REGISTERED TRADEMARK—MARCA REGISTRADA
HECHO EN FORGE VILLAGE, MASS., U.S.A.

SIGNET, SIGNET CLASSICS, MENTOR, PLUME, MERIDIAN and NAL BOOKS are published by The New American Library, Inc.
1633 Broadway, New York, New York 10019

FIRST PRINTING/WORLD PUBLISHING COMPANY, FEBRUARY, 1956

FIRST PRINTING/NEW AMERICAN LIBRARY, OCTOBER, 1974

4   5   6   7   8   9   10   11

PRINTED IN THE UNITED STATES OF AMERICA

Preface

The purpose of this volume is to present, within the available space, a selection of the writings of Martin Buber that will communicate to the reader something of the power and relevance of the thought of one of the most profound religious philosophers of the century. Selection is no mechanical operation, and the selection I have made more or less obviously reflects my convictions as to what aspects of Buber's thinking are of particular significance amidst the problems and perplexities of our time. These convictions are made even more explicit in the introductory essay, where exposition is supplemented by an attempt at criticism and evaluation.

Selections are taken exclusively from Buber's writings already available in English. The translations indicated in the sources have been employed; although here and there, in the interests of clarity, I have permitted myself certain modifications upon comparison with the original.

I desire to express my gratitude to Professor Buber for his encouragement and for his approval of the selection I have made, and to Maurice S. Friedman, for his advice and criticism. Neither, of course, is in any way responsible for my interpretations and conclusions, which are entirely my own.

WILL HERBERG

Contents

The Writings of Martin Buber

Introduction by WILL HERBERG

MARTIN BUBER:
PHILOSOPHER OF RELIGIOUS EXISTENCE

Martin Buber is one of the great creative forces in contemporary religious thought. Of his classic *I and Thou,* a small book
of some hundred pages first issued in 1923, J. H. Oldham said
twenty years after its appearance: "I question whether any book
has been published in the present century the message of which,
if it were understood, would have such far-reaching consequences for the life of our time." [1] Buber is easily the outstanding Jewish thinker of today, but the impact of his teaching has
been felt far beyond the limits of the Jewish community. Every
important Christian theologian or religious philosopher of the
past generation shows the signs of his seminal influence. And
not only theologians and philosophers; men of achievement in
every walk of life—scholars, educators, and writers, poets and
artists, psychologists and sociologists, physicians, psychothera-
pists, and social workers—have testified to what Buber the man
and the thinker has meant to them. [2] Few men of the spirit have
left so profound a mark on the best thinking of their time as
has this unforgettable Central European Jew, who now at seventy eight, is professor emeritus of social philosophy at the Hebrew University in Jerusalem.

I.   Martin Buber is one of those men whose life and teaching
are so fused that each in its own way bears authentic witness to
the other. He was born in Vienna in 1878, but until the age of

fourteen was brought up in the Galician home of his grandfather, Solomon Buber, a distinguished scholar. There he received a thorough Jewish education in the traditional style, and first came into contact with Hasidism, which was to become one of the great formative influences of his life and thought. At the universities of Vienna and Berlin, he pursued "secular" studies, particularly philosophy and the history of art, with great distinction.

While still a student in his early twenties, he joined the emerging Zionist movement, and in 1901 became editor of the Zionist periodical *Die Welt*. Buber's Zionism, however, soon revealed its basic differences with the purely political Zionism associated with the name of Theodor Herzl. His Zionism was cultural and spiritual, involving primarily an effort to encourage a renascence of total Jewish existence. *Der Jude,* which he founded and edited from 1916 to 1924, was the protagonist of this idea, and quickly became the leading organ of German-speaking Jewry. From 1926 to 1930, he published, jointly with the Catholic theologian, Joseph Wittig, and the Protestant physician and psychotherapist, Viktor von Weizsäcker, the journal *Die Kreatur,* devoted to social and pedagogical problems in relation to religion.

Meanwhile, Buber was pursuing his philosophical, cultural, and religious studies. His thinking at first had a decidedly mystical cast, and indeed some of his early writing was devoted to presenting and interpreting the classics of mysticism, Western and Oriental. Gradually, however, his outlook shifted, and the change was speeded, according to Buber's own account,[3] by a shattering experience which completed the conversion from the "mystical" (Buber calls it the "religious") to the "everyday." In *Daniel,*[4] published in 1913, a distinctively existential view comes to the fore. Men, Buber finds, are capable of a twofold relation to their experience and environment—"orientation" and "realization." "Orientation" is the "objective" attitude that orders the environment for knowledge and use; "realization" is the approach that brings out the inner meaning of life in intensified perception and existence (what German philosophy was beginning to call *Existenz*). The first draft of *I and Thou* was, according to Buber, made in 1916, though he did not, he says, attain "decisive clarity" until 1919. In *I and Thou,* as published in 1923, the existential has already given way to the dialogical approach, which governs all of Buber's subsequent work. Basically, each of the stages is transcended and subsumed in its successors: one aspect of the mystical reappears in the existential, and the existential is fulfilled and deepened in the dialogical.[5]

Soon after the first world war, Buber became acquainted with Franz Rosenzweig, with whom he collaborated in a fruitful series of literary and educational enterprises that have left their mark on a generation of German Jews. The most important of these joint ventures was the Buber-Rosenzweig translation of the Hebrew Bible[6] and the Freies Jüdisches Lehrhaus (Jewish Academy) in Frankfort, a unique institution that achieved an enduring intellectual influence. For a decade after 1923, Buber was professor at Frankfort. After the triumph of the Nazis, he took over direction of the educational activities of the hard-pressed Jewish community, and strove mightily to build up its inner strength and spiritual resources.

In 1938, at the age of sixty, Buber left for Palestine to become professor of social philosophy at the Hebrew University. His new life was no more sheltered and academic than his old life in Germany had been. His brand of religio-cultural Zionism had all along been frowned upon by the "politicals" in the Zionist movement, and now in Palestine itself he developed a viewpoint which threw him into sharp opposition to the dominant ideology. Along with Judah L. Magnes, Ernst Simon, and others, he advocated a program of Jewish-Arab understanding on the basis of a bi-national state. The movement made little headway in the heavily charged atmosphere of the Jewish community, but it did at least raise another and dissident voice against the prevailing orthodoxy. In 1951, upon his retirement at the age of seventy three, Buber visited the United States, lectured at many universities and seminaries, and made a profound impression upon large segments of the American intellectual community. Until three years ago, he directed the Institute for Adult Education, which he had founded in 1949, for the training of teachers who would work in the immigration camps to help integrate the vast numbers of new arrivals into the life of the community.

From early manhood, Buber has been a socialist of the "communitarian" (small community) school, poles apart from Soviet communism and West European centralist "state" socialism alike. Buber's social philosophy is closely linked with his basic religious teaching and the enduring interests of his life.

These few bare facts do no justice whatever to the creativity, the unity of thought and action, of commitment and performance, that characterizes Martin Buber's life. Everything he has done has enriched his thought, and every new departure in his thinking has found expression in some social or cultural activity. Though rarely possessed of overt power, he has wielded an influence—as much by the wholeness and integrity of his being as by the profound impact of his teaching—that is quite without parallel in our time. His audience always consisted of men of all professions and all types of formal belief open to a new word; today it is the world.

II.   Martin Buber's thinking, especially in its later phases, falls in with the general movement of religious existentialism—indeed, he is one of the main contemporary sources of the movement—but the particular direction he has given it unquestionably reflects the profound originality of his mind as well as the specifically Jewish sources of his spirituality. The "message," the heart of Buber's teaching, is that "real life is meeting." [7] Recalling the difference of "orientation" and "realization" in *Daniel,* Buber makes a radical distinction between the two basic attitudes, the two fundamental types of relation, of which men are capable, expressed in the "primary words" I-Thou and I-It (understood as referring not to the object of the relation, but to the nature of the relation itself). The "primary word I-Thou points to a relation of person to person, of subject to subject, a relation of reciprocity involving "meeting" or "encounter," while the "primary word" I-It points to a relation of person to thing, of subject to object, involving some form of utilization, domination, or control, even if it is only so-called "objective" knowing. The I-Thou relation, which Buber usually designates as "relation" par excellence, is one in which man can enter only with the whole of his being, as a genuine person. It is a relation, incidentally, which Buber feels it is possible for men to have not only with human beings, but also with nature and "intelligible forms" (art), thus recalling William James' comment that the "religious man" sees the universe as a "Thou," [8] and bringing upon Buber the not altogether unmerited charge of mysticizing. The I-It relation, on the other hand, is one that man enters not with the wholeness of his being, but only with a part of it;[9] in this relation, he is not really a person but an individual (this distinction is very similar to Jacques Maritain's). The "I" in the two relations is thus not really the same: "the I of the primary word I-Thou is a different I from that of the primary word I-It." [10] There is still another distinction of importance:

in the I-Thou relation, the relation itself is primary and underived; not so in the I-It relation, where the components, so to speak, precede the relation, and the relation is secondary.

There are phrases here and there in Buber which might suggest, to one so inclined, a kind of "personalist" ontology. "[The Thou] does not help to sustain you in life," Buber says, "it only helps you to glimpse eternity," [11] from which one might infer, in a quasi-Kantian mood, that whereas the I-It attitude gives access only to the world of appearance, the I-Thou gives access to the world of reality. Certain epistemological conclusions would also seem to follow. "From Buber's basic premise, 'As I become I, I say Thou,'" Maurice Friedman states, "it follows that our belief in the reality of the external world comes from our relation to other selves." And he refers to Viktor von Weizsäcker, who "sets forth a 'medical anthropology,' which begins with the recognition of the difference between the objective understanding of some*thing* and the 'transjective' understanding of some*one*." [12] These distinctions are real and valuable, but, along with Friedman, I do not think that they add up to a full-blown ontology, particularly in view of Buber's sustained emphasis on the "dramatic" character of the I-Thou encounter.[13] Certainly, there is no justification whatever for assimilating Buber's "metaphysics" to the "process philosophy" of Whitehead and his followers, as has been attempted on utterly inadequate grounds.[14] Buber's ontology—and in some sense, of course, every basic outlook implies an ontology—is altogether secondary to the immediacy of the I-Thou meeting.

It is in the I-Thou relation that the person in his authentic personality—what Kierkegaard calls the "Single One" —emerges: "Through the Thou a man becomes an I." [15] The primal reality, in which man achieves his real being, is the *Zwischenmenschliche,* the "between man and man." The self is "social" by nature; its very "essence" is interpersonal. Here Buber shows affinities and differences with Søren Kierkegaard, on the one side, and such "social humanists" as George Herbert Mead, on the other. Like Mead, with whom he has been compared,[16] Buber thinks of the self as "social" and involved in dialogue, but unlike Mead, he does not think of this dialogue as primarily an "I-Me" meeting within the self;[17] and unlike Mead again, he refuses to limit the interpersonal relation simply to relations among human beings, to the exclusion of God. Buber's attitude to Kierkegaard is much more complex. He stands firmly with Kierkegaard in the latter's insistence on being a "Single One" (person) and refusing to be swallowed up in the "crowd." Man realizes the "image of God" "through having become a Single One. . . . A man can have dealings with God only as a Single One, only as a man who has become a Single One . . . Only the man who has become a Single One, a self, a real person, is able to have a complete relation of his life to the other self." [18] But he refuses to limit the dialogue to the self with itself and God. As against Kierkegaard's assertion that "everyone should be chary about having to do with 'the others,' and should essentially speak only with God and with himself," Buber insists that the fundamental relation is *triadic*—the self, God, and the "other." "Real relationship with God cannot be achieved on earth if real relationships to the world and mankind are lacking," [19] but real relationship with other human beings is possible only in terms of a real relationship to God. (The triadic relation of K., the Castle, and the Village in Kafka's *The Castle* will occur to the reader.) What is more, Buber points out, Kierkegaard's "joining of the 'with God' with the 'with himself' is a serious incompatibility that nothing can mitigate . . . Speaking with God is something *toto genere* different from 'speaking with oneself'; whereas, remarkably enough, it is not something *toto genere* different from speaking with another human being." [20] Buber refers Kierkegaard to Jesus, who when he linked the two "great commandments"—the commandment to love God with all one's heart and the commandment to love one's neighbor as oneself—made it clear that the "absolute" relation to God is as inclusive as it is exclusive: while barring all other "absolute" relations, it not only makes room for but demands an authentic relation to one's fellow men.[21] "He who enters on the absolute relation . . . , [for him] everything is gathered up in the relation." [22]

Man's dialogue brings him into the "between man and man," but also into the "between man and God." For God is the Eternal Thou in whom "the extended lines of relation meet." "Every particular Thou is a glimpse through to the Eternal Thou; by means of every particular Thou, the primary word addresses the Eternal Thou." [23] God is the center of the circle of existence, the apex of the triangle of life.

In the dialogic meeting, man becomes and transcends himself. It is entering into relation that makes man really man; yet it is "in virtue of its dialogical character," that "human life touches upon absoluteness," and acquires "absolute meaning" that overpasses its "own conditioned nature." [24] The dialogic relation is the matrix of man's "finite infinity."

Authentic human existence—the dialogic life—is existence in the I-Thou. But such is the world that one cannot remain permanently in the I Thou relation. To survive, we need to know, control, and use things, and what is much more important, even human beings; in other words, to survive, we must engage in depersonalizing and dehumanizing our fellow men. This is a poignant expression of the "wrongness," of the "broken" character, of actual existence in this world. Yet, however inescapable, the I-It relation must remain subordinate; it is the predominance, not the mere existence, of the I-It that is the source of evil. "Without It," says Buber, "man cannot live; but he who lives with It alone is not a man . . . All real living is meeting." [25] As against the "thingification" of men and the world involved in I-It, there is the self-giving love of genuine relation, which does not, Buber emphasizes, by any means imply the suppression of the self: "It is not the I that is given up, but the false self-asserting instinct . . . There is no self-love that is not self-deceit . . . , but without being and remaining oneself, there is no love." [26]

Buber's thinking is profoundly religious, for he sees man as essentially oriented to God, and life as "a summons and a sending." Every man has his unique being as a gift from God, and it is his responsibility to realize it in its wholeness. "In the world to come," so runs a celebrated saying of the Hasidic rabbi Zusya, "they will not ask me, 'Why were you not Moses?' They will ask me, 'Why were you not Zusya?'" ("The great thing," Kierkegaard once remarked, "is not to be this or that, but to be oneself . . .") Such authenticity of being is possible only in the dialogic life in which man meets God and his fellow man in the fullness of the I-Thou. The divine demand is not heteronomous, not something imposed from without, running counter to man's being; nor is it simply man giving the law unto himself in the sheer self-will of false autonomy. It is, Buber insists, in a vein that brings to mind Paul Tillich's recent writings, a "true autonomy [which] is one with true theonomy . . . The law is not thrust upon man; it rests deep within him, to waken when the call comes." [27] The call comes in the midst of life. "God speaks to man in the things and beings he sends him in life. Man answers through his dealings with these things and beings." [28] Religious man is dialogical man, the man "who commits his whole being in God's dialogue with the world, and who stands firm throughout this dialogue." [29] It is a dialogue in which "God speaks to every man through the life which he gives him again and again . . . [and in which] man can only answer God with the whole of life, with the way in which he lives his given life." [30]

This wholeness of response in the dialogue is the "good" of man. Buber's understanding of evil comes, at least in great part, from his dialogic philosophy. Evil he sees as emerging in two stages. In the first, which he finds typified in the stories of Adam and Eve and Cain, evil—sin, in man—is *decisionlessness,* directionlessness, something that cannot be done with the whole being, something that falls under the shadow of the predominance of the I-It. For "only he who knows relation and knows about the presence of the Thou is capable of decision, [and] he who decides is free." [31] In the I-Thou, there is direction, wholeness, *kavvanah.* In the second stage, typified in the story of the Tower of Babel and the Iranian myth of Yima, evil, sin, is *wrong decision,* decision in self-sufficiency against God; "it is the existential lie against being in which man sees himself as self-creator." [32] Again, it is the "primal guilt" of "remaining with oneself," [33] but it is a much more sinister form of it. For in this second stage, the evil becomes obsessive and demonic. "Sin is not an undertaking which man can break off when the situation becomes critical, but a process started by him, the control of which is withdrawn from him at a fixed moment." [34] "If we may compare the occurrence of the first stage to an eccentric whirling movement, the process of the freezing of flowing water may serve as a simile to illustrate the second." [35] Man's self-assertion against God leads to his utter enslavement.[36]

In the end, evil remains a mystery with no answer. "The abyss which is opened by this question advances on to the darkness of the divine mystery even more dreadfully than the abyss opened by Job's question." [37] But however much of a mystery evil remains, one thing Buber insists upon throughout: it must not be attributed to a metaphysical or ontological dualism, which sees good and evil as substantive entities or powers. Such a dualism would, in effect, be a ditheism, and against every ditheism Buber repeats the words of the Lord to the prophet Isaiah: "I am the first and the last, and beside me there is no God" (Is. 44:6).

It is obvious that Buber's God, the God who meets us as the Eternal Thou in the dialogic life, is not the God of the philosophers or of the mystics. It is not a God that can be "inferred in anything—in nature, say, as its author, or in history as its master, or in the subject as the self that is thought in it. Something else is not 'given' and God then elicited from it . . . God is the Being that is directly, most nearly, and lastingly over against us , . . nearer to me than my I." [38] But neither is God the mystic's "divineness" with which the self is to be united in undifferentiated being.[39] Our encounter with God is intensely personal, and remains personal to the very end. In the last analysis, the God to whom Buber bears witness, who is of course, the God of the Bible, the God of Jewish-Christian faith, is a God that "may properly be addressed, not expressed," a God that may be "met," but not sought.[40]

Nor is Buber's religion, in any sense, a cult of reassurance. All thought of final security in religion, whether such security is philosophical, social, psychological, moral, or even religious, is repugnant to him. He preaches instead a "holy insecurity," life on the "narrow ridge." "O you secure and safe ones," he exclaims, "you who hide yourselves behind the ramparts of the law [or of theology or of ethics] so that you will not have to look into God's abyss! Yes, you have secure ground under your feet, while we hang suspended looking out over the endless deeps. But we would not exchange our dizzy insecurity and poverty for your security and abundance . . . Of God's will we know only the eternal; the temporal we must command for ourselves, ourselves imprint his wordless bidding ever anew on the stuff of reality . . . In genuine life between men, the new world will reveal itself to us. First, we must act; then we shall receive—from out of our own deed." [41] "Woe to the man so possessed that he thinks he possesses God!" [42]

Buber's whole outlook is existential and situational. The dialogic man is the man who thinks "existentially," that is, the man "who stakes his life on his thinking";[43] for him, "faith is . . . the venture pure and simple." [44] Buber agrees with Kierkegaard's statement that "the truth for the Single One only exists in his producing it himself in action." "Human truth is bound up with the responsibility of the person. . . . Man finds the truth to be true only when he confirms it" (*sie bewährt*, "makes it true").[45] "Any genuine life relationship to Divine Being— that is, any such relationship effected with a man's whole being

—is a human truth, and man has no other truth. The ultimate truth is one, but it is given to man as it enters, reflected as in a prism, into the true life relationships of the human person." [46]

Buber's ethic is a situational ethic of responsibility, and he uses this term in its precise sense. "Genuine responsibility exists only where there is real responding," real answering.[47] But this responsibility, this answering, "presupposes one who addresses me primarily, from a realm independent of myself, and to whom I am answerable." [48] "Our answering-for-ourselves is essentially our answering to a divine address." [49] Responsibility is thus, in the last analysis, readiness to respond in the dialogue with God which takes place in the "lived moment" of existence. It means hearing the unreduced claim of the hour and answering it out of the fullness of one's being. Many are the ways in which the self tries to evade its responsibility in the existential dialogue of life, but they all add up in the end to the erection of some protective structure of fixed and final general rules (ideas, programs, values, standards, etc.) to stand between the individual person and the concrete here-and-now which makes its demand upon him, so that it is not he who is deciding, but the general rule that decides for him. "No responsible person remains a stranger to norms. But the command inherent in a genuine norm never becomes a maxim, and the fulfillment of it never a habit . . . What it [the command] has to tell him is revealed whenever a situation arises which demands of him a solution of which till then he had perhaps no idea . . . [The situation] demands nothing of what is past; it demands presence, responsibility: it demands you." [50]

III. Buber's protest against depersonalization and "thingification," through the dominance of the I-It at the expense of true "relation," takes on particular relevance for our time in his social philosophy. True community, Buber holds, emerges out of the I-Thou. Just as the individual becomes a person, a "fact of existence," "insofar as he steps into a living relation with other individuals," so does a social aggregate become a community "insofar as it is built out of living units of relation . . . Only men who are capable of truly saying Thou to one another can truly say We with one another." [51] And just as the I of authentic personality emerges only in the dialogic "meeting" with God to which every other Thou points, so does the authentic We of community come forth only out of the relation of the individual members of the group to the transcendent.

"The true community does not arise through people having feelings for one another (though indeed not without it), but first, through their taking their stand in living mutual relation with a living Center, and second, their being in living mutual relation with one another. The second has its source in the first, but is not given when the first alone is given . . . The community is built up out of living mutual relation, but the builder is the living effective Center." [52] It is this radial relation to the living Center that makes true community.

In his affirmation of true community, Buber rejects both atomistic individualism and totalitarian collectivism. "Individualism understands only a part of man, collectivism understands man only as a part: neither advances to the wholeness of man. Individualism sees man only in relation to himself, but collectivism does not see man at all; it sees 'society'." [53] These false social attitudes reflect more fundamental existential attitudes which men assume in the face of life's demands. "Man as man is an audacity of life, undetermined and unfixed; he therefore requires confirmation." [54] This confirmation, which is a source of what Tillich calls the "courage to be," he may seek either in himself, in an attitude of defiant autonomy, or through his becoming part of some collective—which may well be spiritual, as in mysticism—in an attitude that can be defined only as heteronomy. Both of these types of confirmation are illusory: confirmation is by its very nature a reciprocal process, hence cannot be achieved in an attitude of stark autonomy; on the other hand, "confirmation through the collective . . . is pure fiction," [55] since the self that is to be "confirmed" is actually lost in the collectivistic submergence. In their social dimension, on the level of social life, these two false forms of "confirmation" appear as individualism and collectivism.

As against individualism, which he seems to identify with capitalism, and collectivism, which he sees not only in Soviet communism, but to a mitigated degree, also in West European "state" socialism, Buber raises the vision of an "organic community," a "community of communities," built out of "small and ever smaller communities," the basic cell of which is the "full cooperative," best exemplified in the Israeli kibbutz.[56] Thus Buber's religious socialism falls in with the "communitarian" ideas that have played so large a part in Catholic social radicalism, and with some trends in recent Protestant social thinking as well. But establishing true community seems to Buber a preeminently Jewish task, which the Jew can adequately cope with only under conditions of economic and political autonomy in the land appointed for the work: this is the ground of Buber's religio-social Zionism.

In his passionate plea for the "communitarian" idea, Buber tries to avoid utopian illusions. He knows that whatever may be true for Palestine, one cannot reorganize a large-scale economy, such as the American, along kibbutz lines; he insists that what he is presenting is not a blueprint, but, as he puts it, a direction and a goal. Much more serious is the challenge to the very desirability of the kind of "full cooperation" Buber envisages; there are those who charge, and a good deal of Israeli experience would seem to bear them out, that the very "fullness" of the "full cooperative," embracing the "whole life of society," carries within itself the seeds of totalism, and constitutes a threat both to personal privacy and to true community.[57] This grave question does not seem, so far, to have aroused Buber's concern. Nor does he appear to have seen the sinister possibilities of kibbutz-socialism as a secular substitute-faith. He notes, with no apprehension whatever, "the amazingly positive relationship— *amounting to a regular faith*—which these men have to the inmost being of their commune" [58] (emphasis added). The history of our time would seem to give ground for greater concern.

In his social ethics, Buber attempts to keep to the "narrow ridge" of responsibility, and to avoid falling into utopian "idealism" on the one side or amoral "realism" on the other. He is not a pacifist or an anarchist, as some have tried to make him out to be. He is indeed deeply suspicious of the centralized state, and sometimes tends too simply to identify the "social" principle with "free fellowship and association" and the "political" principle with "compulsion and coercion"; [59] but basically he recognizes that "in all probability, there will never, so long as man is what he is, be freedom pure and simple, and there will be State, that is, compulsion, for just so long." [60] He warns against using evil means for good ends, particularly violence to achieve peace—"If the goal to be reached is like the goal which was set, then the nature of the way must be like the goal; a wrong way, that is, a way in contradiction to the goal, must lead to a wrong goal" [61]—but he recognizes that living entails doing injustice, that "in order to preserve the community of man, we are compelled to accept wrongs in decisions concerning the community." [62] In particular, against the cult of pacifism and "nonviolence" he declares: "If there is no other way of preventing evil destroying the good, I trust I shall use force and give myself up to God's hands." [63] Not doctrinaire formulas to relieve one of the necessity of decision, but responsibility in the concrete situation is Buber's teaching. "What matters is that in every hour of decision we be aware of our responsibility and summon our conscience to weigh exactly how much is necessary to preserve the community, and accept just so much and no more." [64] As Ernst Simon has put it: "What he [Buber] seeks is the 'demarcation line' between the unconditional demand and the always only conditional realization." [65] Buber, perhaps, does not formulate the "cruel antithecalness of existence" [66] in all its tragic depth, but there can be no doubt that he understands and feels the bitter contradiction at the heart of a broken, unredeemed world.

In a famous polemic with Friedrich Gogarten, written during the early days of the Nazi regime and published in Germany in 1936, Buber tries to define the political implications of human sinfulness. Gogarten, following a pseudo-Lutheran line, justifies the authoritarian state on the ground that man is "radically and irrevocably evil, that is, in the grip of evil," and therefore must be kept in rigorous control by the state. Buber denies this conclusion, and points out that even in Gogarten's own theology, man stands in "radical evil" only before God, because "God is God and man is man and the distance between them is absolute." Over against his fellow men and society, however, "man cannot properly be described as simply sinful because the distance is lacking which alone is able to establish the unconditional." Gogarten's justification of the authoritarian state is, therefore, invalid; indeed, Buber generalizes, "no legitimate use can be made in politics or political theory of the concept of human sinfulness." [67]

One can only admire the skill and courage of Buber's polemic against the Nazi state carried on in the shadow of the Nazi power, and one must grant the validity of his refutation of Gogarten's attempt to provide a theological justification of the totalitarian police state. But Buber's generalization—that "no legitimate use can be made in politics or political theory of the concept of human sinfulness"—is surely open to doubt. Indeed, the whole theological vindication of democracy rests, at least in part, on the conviction that no one, no matter how good or wise he may be, is good enough or wise enough to be entrusted with unrestrained or irresponsible power over others[68]—and this is obviously equivalent to an assertion of universal sinfulness. By too hastily removing political theory from any relation to the sinfulness of man, Buber runs the danger of withdrawing it from the actualities of social existence, in which the insidious involutions of human sinfulness are to be detected on every level.

Buber's existential approach and social philosophy have given him a strong sense of the peril of collectivism in our time. Collectivism he holds to be the "last barrier raised by man against a meeting with himself" and therefore with God.[69] The great task of our day is "to be a person again, to rescue one's real personal self from the fiery jaws of collectivism, which devours all selfhood." [70] The ravages of the heteronomous spirit of collectivism—rampant not only in totalitarian societies, but in different and mitigated form, in the mass societies of the West as well—have undermined truth as well as personality. "The person has become questionable through being collectivized. . . . The truth has become questionable through being politicized." [71] What is needed in the face of this double danger, Buber feels, is a reassertion of personal authenticity without falling into irresponsible individualism, and of an authentic existential relation to truth without falling into a doctrinaire absolutism. The way of man in true community is along the "narrow ridge."

Yet one cannot help but recognize that true community as Buber understands it is not an historical possibility. It is a vision of the "original rightness" of man, a transcendent norm, and an eschatological promise, but it is not something that can be achieved within history. For every effort within history to institutionalize group relations—and without extensive institutionalization no society could survive—depersonalizes the I-Thou relation of true community and replaces it by "social" relations, even "interpersonal" relations, that belong to the world of I-It. No; true community is not a real historical possibility, but it is that for which man is intended, and it remains relevant—not as an "ideal," but as a reality—to every actual situation. Buber's emphasis is one for which we, in this country, should be particularly grateful since we are all tempted to think of the centralized and highly politicized "welfare state," resting on a large-scale, highly industrialized mass-production economy, as the last word in social achievement.

IV. Buber sees his entire dialogical philosophy grounded in the faith of the Bible, and he naturally tends to interpret biblical faith in terms of his dialogical philosophy. The extraordinary fruitfulness of this interpretation, the insight it affords into the deeper meaning of the biblical story, would seem to suggest that there is indeed the inner harmony between the dialogical philosophy and the essential structure of biblical faith that Buber claims.

Buber sees the Bible as essentially a dialogue between "the 'I' of the speaking God and the 'Thou' of the hearing Israel." [72] Despite all its multifariousness, the Bible "is really one book, for one basic theme unites all the stories and songs, sayings and prophecies, contained within it. The theme of the Bible is the encounter between a group of people and the Lord of the world in the course of history . . ." [73] "The basic doctrine which fills the Hebrew Bible is that our life is a dialogue between the above and the below." [74] The dialogic relation, which Buber has found to be the underlying reality in human existence, is here stated to be the very foundation of biblical faith—with one difference. Here, in biblical faith, God is no longer man's Eternal Thou corresponding to the human I; here God is the I, and man the Thou whom he addresses. Here it is God who speaks first and man who responds, though it should be emphasized that this response is genuine and not the mere gestures of a God-operated puppet. This shift from the divine Thou to the divine I is very significant, but it does not destroy the relevance of the dialogical philosophy to biblical faith.

The Bible to Buber is neither an infallible God-written document, nor merely the "folk literature" of Israel; it is taken in full seriousness as the continuing witness of the believing community to its encounter with God, and it is therefore taken as essentially, and in every part, both human and divine. How Buber is able to take the Bible seriously without taking it as a collection of inerrant statements about all sorts of things; how, in short, he is able to get to the heart of biblical faith, may be seen to best advantage in his two outstanding works of biblical scholarship, *Moses* and *The Prophetic Faith*.[75] For our purpose, it will be most convenient to summarize the thesis developed in the latter work.

The prophetic reality, which provides the underlying pattern of biblical religion, is presented as a divine-human encounter not in the abstract realm of a "sacred upper story," but in the full existential context of life, and that means history. Beginning with the Song of Deborah in Judges 5, which he takes to be the first text that scholarly criticism will grant comes out of the time it deals with, Buber moves backward to the Shechem assembly (Josh. 24:1-28), to Sinai, and to the patriarchs, and then forward to the settlement of Canaan and the rise and development of prophetism. At every stage, he asks the question: "What was the faith of Israel in that age?" And from Abraham to Deutero-Isaiah, he finds that faith to be essentially one, consisting of "three great articles": God's *ruah*-government (total sovereignty over all areas of life), the people's "loving" allegiance, and the demand for decision. Though the faith is one through the ages, it emerges only in concrete historical situations, and Buber is at pains to reconstruct the particular historical contexts in which the confrontations between God and man in the various crises of Israel's *Heilsgeschichte* took place. Yet the historical factor is not final, for the existential encounter at the core of the prophetic faith is always contemporaneous and thus transcends historical conditioning.

Thinking in such terms, Buber naturally finds irrelevant many of the problems which biblical scholars have long been concerned with. "The old controversy among scholars, whether the Hebrews who wandered from Egypt to Canaan were 'polytheists' or 'monotheists,' is," he insists, "an unreal question." [76] It is unreal because what is crucial in biblical faith is not philosophical opinions as to the nature of God, but total commitment to YHVH as absolute Lord. Was Deutero-Isaiah the "first monotheist in Israel," as some writers have maintained? What difference does that make, once we realize that both Abraham and Deutero-Isaiah stood in the same crisis of decision, shared the same ultimate commitment, and recognized the same absolute divine claim upon them? This is the prophetic faith.

Against the background of this interpretation of the meaning of the prophetic faith of the Bible, Buber develops his understanding of the biblical convictions on God and man and the great biblical themes of creation, revelation, and redemption.

God and man stand in dialogic relation, and it is dangerous abstraction to try to separate them so as to study their "essence." The God of the Bible is, indeed, the "wholly Other," the *"mysterium tremendum"*; but he is also the "wholly Present, . . . nearer to me than my I." [77] God's "presentness" in the meeting with man does not overcome his "absolute distance," nor does it mitigate his "absolute demand." "God is wholly Other and yet requires a total commitment: it is just this that gives the commitment a hazardous character which no subsequent intellectualization can wholly remove." [78]

Buber is particularly careful to emphasize the "personalness" of God in the Bible. God is the Absolute Person, who becomes person in order to "meet" man. But that is no mitigation of God's absoluteness; it is rather a testimony to his abounding love. "It is indeed legitimate to speak of the person of God within the religious relation and its language; but in so doing we are making no statement about the Absolute which reduces it to the personal. We are rather saying that it enters into the relationship as the Absolute Person whom we call God. One may understand the personality of God as his act. It is, indeed, even permissible for the believer to believe that God became a person for love of him, because in our human mode of existence the only reciprocal relation with us that exists is the personal one." [79] It has been argued that such a view implies belief in a non-personal "Godhead" beyond the "personal" God; but this Buber would categorically deny: for him there is no God beyond the God of the divine-human encounter.

This God makes his absolute demand upon man in the totality of life and being. For man, in the Bible, "stands created a whole body, ensouled by his relation to the created, enspirited by his relation to the Creator." [80] He stands also responsible to God not merely in the "religious" sphere, but in all areas of life. "YHVH as God of Israel does not become the lord of a cultic order of faith, shut up within itself, but the lord of an order of people, embracing all spheres of life—that is to say, a *melek*, and a *melek* taken authentically and seriously. . . ." [81] Indeed, the distinction between the "religious" and the "nonreligious" is ultimately unreal: "there are no such separate fields at all here [in the community of Israel at Sinai], but only one as yet undifferentiated common life. . . ." [82]

Confronting God's total demand upon him, man must answer, and he may answer in one of two ways: like Abraham with a "Here am I" (Gen. 22:1), or like the man and woman in the garden who ran away and "hid themselves" (Gen. 3:8). "To God's sovereign address, man gives his autonomous answer; if he remains silent, his silence too is an answer." [83] Whichever it is, it is an answer that man gives with his life and deeds, both the individual and the corporate group.

As man confronts this God who comes to "meet" him, he confronts him in fear, in love, in an unresolved and unresolvable tension of the two. Buber has no patience with the self-deluding sentimentalists who would like to conjure away all that is fearful in the divine. A God that is not feared is idolatrous; "the real God . . . is, to begin with, dreadful and incomprehensible," [84] for he is the God who shatters all the self-sufficiencies and securities of our existence. Only through the "gateway" of fear do we come to the love of God, and realize that both his blessings and his curse flow from his love. "The biblical concept of holiness," Friedman well summarizes Buber's teaching, "is that of a power capable of exerting both a destructive and a hallowing effect. The encounter with this holiness is therefore a source of danger to man. The danger is turned into a grace for those who, like Abraham, and Jacob, and Moses, stand the test." [85]

The love of God—God's love of man and man's responsive love of God—is the source of our power to love our neighbor, that is, the source of the biblical ethic of human relations. "The man who loves God," who lives in the grateful consciousness of God's love, "loves also him whom God loves." [86]

The fear and love of God combined give man his true autonomy in the world. "Those who know YHVH dare dread no earthly power"; [87] "since Israel is the 'peculiar property' of YHVH, no person in Israel can, properly speaking, be the slave of any other person in Israel. All belong to God, and are therefore free to make their own decisions." [88] The grounding of man's real autonomy in the theonomy of God's kingship is central to the biblical teaching.

By entering into relation, man responds to God in the "meeting." Refusal to enter into relation, turning away from the address in self-will and self-sufficiency, is sin in the biblical sense. We each reenact Adam's "fall," which "continually happens here and now in all its reality." [89] But God does not forsake the sinner. Even in the dark hour of his guilt and sin, "man is not abandoned to the forces of chaos. God himself seeks him out, and even when he comes to call him to account, his coming is salvation." [90] Yet man is not reduced to passivity by God's redemptive will: "God wishes to redeem us, but only by our own acceptance of the redemption with the turning of the whole being." [91]

This "turning" (*teshubah*) is of crucial importance in Buber's entire interpretation of biblical faith. It is the category in which repentance and grace are genuinely combined and preserved from the falsity that comes from the isolation of one from the other. Buber has a strong sense of the paradox involved in the divine power of grace. Grace is free and uncontrolled—"He bestows his grace and mercy on whom he will" [92]—and yet man's deeds count. Without grace there is nothing, and yet man must make the "beginning." Grace concerns us absolutely, but it can never become the object of our acquiring. Our freedom is real, yet grace is "prevenient": "The person who makes a decision knows that his deciding is no self-delusion; the person who has acted knows that he was and is in the hand of God." [93] These multiple paradoxes are subsumed and expressed, not resolved, in the "turning."

The "turning" is "something that happens in the immediacy of the reality between man and God." It has its "subjective" and psychological aspects, of course, but essentially it is "as little a 'psychic' event as is a man's birth or death; it comes upon the whole person, is carried out by the whole person. . . ." [94] All of life, individual and corporate, depends on the "turning"—the "turning" and the "re-turning"—of man to God. "For the sake of the 'turning,'" the Hasidic masters have said, "was the world created."

Creation, revelation, and redemption are the three crucial themes in the dialogue between heaven and earth. "The creation itself already means communication between the Creator and the created," [95] and in the creation which continues into the here-and-now, man is called upon to be a partner and "lovingly take part in the still uncompleted work." [96] Here creation touches upon redemption, just as in another phase it touches upon revelation.

Revelation is the "supreme meeting" of the people or the individual with God. It is dialogical, hence essentially divine-human. It is neither experience nor knowledge, and comes not with a specific content of any sort, but as the self-communication of "Presence as power," which embraces the "whole fullness of real mutual action," the "inexpressible confirmation of meaning," and the call to confirm ("make true") this meaning "in this life and in relation with this world." [97] Emil Brunner's *Wahrheit als Begegnung* ("Truth as Meeting") [98] is an authentic characterization of what Buber understands by revelation.

Revelation comes to the individual and the community; it comes through nature and history. [99] But does revelation have a fixed midpoint? Buber denies this, as far as Judaism is concerned. "The Jewish Bible does not set a past event as a midpoint between origin and goal. It interposes a movable, circling midpoint which cannot be pinned to any set time, for it is the moment when I, the reader, the hearer, the man, catch through the words of the Bible the voice which from earliest beginnings has been speaking in the direction of the gaol. . . . The revelation at Sinai is not this midpoint, but the perceiving of it, and such perception is possible at any time." [100] Cullmann agrees with Buber that Judaism knows no fixed midpoint in its *Heilsgeschichte,* and like Buber makes this absence of fixed midpoint a basic distinction between Judaism and Christianity in their understanding of biblical faith.[101]

Yet despite Buber's very welcome emphasis on the existential appropriation of revelation in the here-and-now, despite too the formidable authority of both Buber and Cullmann, the denial of a fixed midpoint in the Hebrew Bible cannot be accepted. Surely there is such a fixed midpoint of revelation in Exodus-Sinai. In the Hebrew Bible, Exodus-Sinai is the divine-human encounter par excellence, illumining and setting the pattern for all other encounters before and after; it is the crisis of crises in the history of Israel, the focal point in terms of which all earlier redemptive events are understood and from which all subsequent divine disclosures take their orientation. "I am the Lord thy God who brought thee out of the land of Egypt . . ." (Ex. 20:2, Deut. 5:6) is the introductory formula that gives redemptive relevance to God's call to Israel in the "dialogue between heaven and earth" to which the Bible bears witness.[102] Buber's unwillingness to see this has wider implications for his thinking.

Like creation and revelation, redemption concerns man in his wholeness and in the entirety of his life. "The redemption must take place in the whole corporeal life. God the Creator wills to consummate nothing less than the whole of his creation; God the Revealer wills to actualize nothing less than the whole of his revelation; God the Redeemer wills to draw into his arms nothing less than the all in need of redemption." [103] The eschatological hope is not the "abrogation and supersession [of creation] by another world completely different in nature," but the renovation and "consummation" of this.[104] The former picture Buber attributes to apocalyptic; the latter, the authentic biblical one, to prophecy. God's redeeming power he sees "at work everywhere and at all times," but a state of redemption, he believes, "exists nowhere and at no time." [105] This insistence that "there are no knots in the mighty cable of our messianic belief, which, fastened to a rock on Sinai, stretches to a still invisible peg anchored in the foundations of the world" [106] Buber makes into another point of distinction between Judaism and Christianity. Here the point may be more readily granted than in the case of the distinction about the fixed midpoint of revelation, yet even here is it quite accurate to see Christianity as affirming an entirely "realized" (consummated) eschatology and Judaism an entirely "futuristic" one? After all, the Christian yearns for the "return" of Christ, and the New Testament ends on the intensely futuristic note of "Come, Lord Jesus!" (Rev. 22:20), while the Jew must affirm that a great and unique act of redemption has already occurred in the "deliverance" of Israel from Egypt and the constitution of the holy people. Buber himself once stated: "He who does not himself remember that God led him out of Egypt, he who does not himself await the Messiah, is no longer a true Jew." [107] No better formulation of both the "realized" and the "futuristic" elements in the eschatology of the Hebrew Bible in their unity and tension could be desired.

The development of the messianic theme is perhaps the most exciting part of *The Prophetic Faith*. Buber sees messianism in its connection with the kingship and prophecy. "The way of the kingship is the way from failure to failure in the dialogue between the people and God." As the failure of the Judge leads to the King, and the failure of the King to the Prophet, so the failure of the Prophet in his opposition to the King leads to new types of leader who will set the dialogue aright—the Messiah of YHVH and the 'suffering servant of the Lord'." [108] In Isaiah, the Messiah is seen as the king of the remnant, from which the people will renew itself; in the "servant" of Deutero-Isaiah, the righteous one who suffers for the sake of the "God of the sufferers," the righting of the dialogue reaches its highest phase. It is laid on this "servant" to inaugurate God's new order of life for the world. "This is what the messianic belief means, the belief in the real leader, in the setting right of the dialogue, in God's disappointment coming to an end. And when a fragment of an apocryphal gospel has God say to Jesus: In all the prophets have I awaited thee, that thou wouldst come and I rest in thee, for thou art my rest,' this is the late elaboration of a truly Jewish conception." [109]

The messianic faith, Buber emphasizes, is a hope and a promise, but it is something more: it is a power and vision in the here-and-now. "A drop of messianic consummation must be mingled with every hour; otherwise, the hour is godless, despite all piety and devoutness." [110]

The faith of the Bible defines faith in the biblical sense. Faith in the biblical sense Buber holds to be *emunah,* "trust in the everlasting God." "The German philosopher Franz Baader," he feels, "did justice to the depth of Israel's faith relationship when he defined faith as 'a pledge of faith, that is, a tying of oneself, a betrothing of oneself, an entering into a covena..t.' " [111] Faith in this sense is not something that can be transferred from idolatrous gods to the true God with simply a change of object, for the faith is of a different kind. Man "cannot serve two masters—not even one after the other; he must first learn to serve *in a different way.*" [112]

Faith in the biblical sense is always being threatened by pseudo-religious substitutes, which have manifested themselves perennially through the ages. There is first "conjuration," or magic, an attempt to control the absolute through secret arts of manipulation. There is next "gnosis," in which the control of the absolute and the dissipation of the mystery are attempted through its "unveiling" by means of secret knowledge. Jung is often referred to by Buber as a modern gnostic, but Buber does not overlook others closer to home. "In many theologies [and philosophies] also," he says, "unveiling gestures are to be found behind the interpreting ones." [113] Finally, there is the pseudo-religious threat of "subjectivization," or religion as "religious experience." Here "the assailant is consciousness, the overconsciousness of this man here that he is praying, that he is *praying,* that *he* is praying." [114] On another level, all forms of objectivization constitute a threat to faith. "Centralization and codification, undertaken in the interests of religion, are a danger to the core of religion, unless there is the strongest life of faith, embodied in the whole existence of the community, and no relaxing of its renewing activity." [115] This renewal comes in the ever new confrontation of God and man in the dialogic encounter of faith.

"In Israel, all religion is history." [116] Buber repeatedly emphasizes that biblical faith is *Heilsgeschichte,* redemptive history, and that the "teaching" is itself "nothing other than narrative history." [117] History, for biblical man, is the texture of reality, the texture of the divine-human encounter, the texture of revelation and redemption. It has stamped nature with its mark, and in the "consummation" it will finally overcome and absorb it.[118] Biblical faith is a "history faith" in every fundamental sense.

It is in the grand framework of biblical *Heilsgeschichte* that Buber envisages the destiny of Israel. Israel is the covenanted people of God; only as such can it "come into being and remain in being." [119] Its vocation is to serve as God's instrument of redemption. "[The time of the patriarchs] is the peculiar point in biblical history where God, as it were, narrows down his original plan for the whole of mankind and causes a people to be begotten that is called to do its appointed work towards the completion of the creation, the coming of the Kingdom." [120] This people Israel is a corporate body through which the individual Israelite gains his standing before God,[121] yet the commands addressed to it are addressed to each individual who cannot lose himself in the collectivity.[122] It is a folk, yet it is a "religious category," not to be simply identified with the "actual people," with "that which the prophet who harangues the people sees assembled around him." "The religious character of the people consists emphatically in that something different is intended for it from what it is now, that it is destined for something different—that it should become a true people, the 'People of God.' " [123] Thus, it is a "holy people," and yet must forever strive to make itself such. "Both Moses and Korah desired the people to be the people of YHVH, the holy people. But for Moses this was the goal. In order to reach it, generation after generation had to choose again and again between the roads, between the way of God and the wrong paths of their own hearts, between 'life' and 'death' (Deut. 30:15)." [124] Because Korah saw Israel as already sufficiently "holy," thus shutting off the dialogue of demand and realization, he had to be extirpated from the community: in this his interpretation of the biblical story in Numbers 16, Buber defines his conviction as to the election and vocation of Israel which he sees as "a summons and a sending."

The dialogical character of the redemptive history of Israel is a clue to the dialogical character of all history. Buber rejects Gogarten's undialectical notion that "history is the work of God";[125] it is the work of God and man together, for man's response to God's call, whatever that response may be, is real and cannot be brushed aside as of no effect. The understanding of history, too, takes place within the dialogue, for the understanding of history takes place in terms of its personal appropriation. "If history is a dialogue between Deity and mankind, we can understand its meaning only when we are the ones addressed, and only to the degree to which we render ourselves receptive. . . . The meaning of history is not an idea which I can formulate independent of my personal life. It is only with my personal life that I am able to catch the meaning of history, for it is a dialogical meaning." [126]

V. In *Drei Reden über das Judentum,* a small but highly influential work published in 1911,[127] Buber undertakes to define what he believes to be the meaning of Jewishness. Jewishness, he says, is "a spiritual process which is documented in the inner history of the Jewish people and in the works of great Jews." [128] "The spiritual process of Jewishness expresses itself in history as a striving after an ever more perfect realization of three interrelated ideas: the idea of unity, the idea of deed, and the idea of the future." [129] These "ideas," and the "spiritual process" they reflect, Buber traces, as was his wont in those early years, to the "folk character" of the Jews and to the "specific gifts" with which they are endowed. Then he proceeds to examine each of the "ideas." The "idea of unity," not yet fully distinguished from the yearning of the mystic for union in undifferentiated being, is seen to have assumed two forms in the millennia of Jewish experience, an "exalted" and a "vulgar" form—an "exalted" form in the prophet's "great desire for God," and a "vulgar" form in the "petty play of concepts" of rabbinism. So with the "idea of deed": it too possesses its "exalted" form in the "unconditioned demand" which prophetism proclaims, and its "vulgar" form in the "panritualism" of the rabbis. The "idea of the future," finally, assumes its "vulgar" form in the well known Jewish concern for the next generation, and its "exalted" form in messianism, the "idea of the absolute future which confronts the actuality of past and present as the true life." [130]

Perhaps under the spur of criticism,[131] certainly with the development of his thought, Buber soon dropped overt reference to the quasi-Hegelian folk romanticism in which his concept of Jewishness was originally enveloped. But throughout his life to the present day, he has retained his conviction that Jewishness means the striving for realization expressed in the Jewish orientation toward unity, the deed, and the future. With the increasingly biblical direction of his thinking, what was at first essentially a manifestation of the alleged Jewish "folk character" became an expression of the vocation of Israel, the "elect" convenant people of God.

The "renewal" of Jewishness, which Buber proclaimed in those early days and which has remained the abiding concern of his life, he regards as of universal import. "The shaping of the new world feeling and the renewal of Jewishness are two sides of one and the same process. 'For salvation is of the Jews': the basic tendencies of Jewishness are the elements out of which is constructed again and again a new word for the world." [132] This "religious creativity" of the Jews, Buber feels, has manifested itself in many historical shapes and forms, but perhaps most profoundly and significantly in prophetism, Essenism, early Christianity, Hasidism, and the Zionist halutziut.

Hasidism has been an enduring influence in Buber's life and thought. Originally, Buber regarded Hasidism as "the most powerful and unique phenomenon which the Diaspora has produced," and contrasted it with rabbinic Judaism, much to the latter's disadvantage. Later, however, he came to feel that Hasidism was "merely a concentrated movement, the concentration of all those elements which are to be found in a less condensed form everywhere in Judaism, even in 'rabbinic' Judaism." [133] From Hasidism, Buber drew, perhaps without fully realizing it, what he needed for the formation of his thought at the particular stage of his thinking in which he found himself: at first, he drew largely on the mystical element, and then, increasingly, on the existential element in Hasidic teaching.[134] Primarily, however, Hasidism has meant to Buber the most impressive effort made at the realization of true community from the days of the prophets to the time of the beginnings of halutziut in Palestine in recent years. "Hasidism was the one great attempt in the history of the Diaspora to make a reality of the original choice and to found a true and just community based on religious principles. . . .[135] This structure found its perfection about two centuries ago in Hasidism, which was built on little communities bound together by brotherly love. . . .[136] This attempt failed for a number of reasons, among others because it did not aim for the independence, for the self-determination of the people; or to state it differently, because its connections with Palestine were only sporadic and not influenced by the desire for national liberation." [137] Because it lacked this Zionist spirit, Hasidism degenerated into corruption and futility.

In this understanding of Hasidism, Buber's "philosophy" of Zionism is already implied. Zionism was for him in earlier days primarily a movement of the spiritual and cultural "renewal" of Jewry; the Zionism he has stood for in the past two decades, however, represents an original religio-social synthesis. His Zionism today is essentially a call to take up the task which Hasidism attempted and at which it failed, under conditions appropriate to the task. This task is the "unperformed task" that has hung over Jewry from the days of the prophets, the task of building true community. "At that time [in the days of the prophets], we did not carry out that which was imposed upon us; we went into exile with our task unperformed; but the command remained with us, and it has become more urgent than ever. We need our own soil in order to fulfill it; we need the freedom to order our own life, no attempt can be made on foreign soil and under foreign statute . . . Our one desire is that at last we may be able to obey." [138] This conception of Zionism stands poles apart from the political nationalism dominant in the Zionist movement, which Buber has always resisted, although vestiges of a romantic "folk nationalism" are not absent even from his latest formulations. The really serious problem which this conception raises, apart from the rather utopian notion that true community can be realized in history if only it is attempted in Palestine under conditions of Jewish "national" independence, is that it essentially denies any specifically Jewish task or vocation for the Jews in the Diaspora, that is, for the great majority of Jews in the world since the days of the Second Commonwealth.

Buber has generally not attempted to disclaim this rather extraordinary consequence of his Zionist position, but he has on occasion tried to mitigate it by pointing to the transcendence of justice in love. "In the Diaspora, it is true, a comprehensive realization of the principle of justice could not be aspired to, since that would have required an autonomous national entity, autonomous national institutions, which could only be hoped for with the return to the Holy Land; but the higher, the decisive principle which alone can knit together the relationship to God and the relationship to man—the principle of love—requires neither organization nor institutions, but can be given effect at any time, at any place." [139] Whether this dubious separation of love from justice, as though one could be fulfilled without invoking the other, meets the dilemma involved in the "denial of the Galut" is another question.

Like prophetism, Hasidism, and religio-social Zionism, Christianity has always appeared to Buber as an authentically Jewish movement soon corrupted by alien influences. His inability to free himself entirely from the "liberal" understanding of Christianity so characteristic of the nineteenth and early twentieth century has made it difficult for Buber to share Franz Rosenzweig's profound vision of the unity and difference of these two "views of reality" in the divine economy of salvation.[140] But he has a strong sense of the vocation of Jewry by its very existence to "give the world no rest so long as the world has not God" [141] and to testify to the unredeemedness of this "already redeemed" world. The Jew "feels this lack of redemption against his own skin, he tastes it on his tongue, the burden of the unredeemed world lies on him." [142] And in the final analysis, as in the last paragraph of his magnificent address in 1930 to a conference on Christian missions to the Jews ("The Two Foci of the Jewish Soul"), he achieves the Rosenzweigian vision:

What have you and we in common? [he asks] If we take the question literally, a book and an expectation. To you, the book is a forecourt; to us it is the sanctuary. But in this place we can dwell together, and together listen to the voice that speaks there . . . Your expectation is directed toward a second coming, ours to a coming which has not been anticipated by a first . . . But we can wait for the advent of the One together, and there are moments when we may prepare the way before him together.

Pre-messianically, our destinies are divided . . . This is a gulf which no human power can bridge. But it does not prevent the common watch for a unity to come to us from God, which, soaring above all of your imagination and all of ours, affirms and denies, denies and affirms what you hold and what we hold, and replaces all the creedal truths of earth by the ontological truth of heaven, which is one.

It behooves both you and us to hold inviolably fast to our own true faith, that is, to our own deepest relationship to truth . . . Our task is not to tolerate each other's waywardness, but to acknowledge the real relationship in which both stand to the truth.[143]

Buber's earlier writings reveal a distant, often hostile, attitude to traditional rabbinism, and although the sharpness has been much mitigated with the years, Buber's position in regard to the rabbinic halakah remains fundamentally negative. It is a position that is complex and defies simple definition. In part, it stems from his kind of Zionism, which sees the present "restoration" to Palestine as the resumption of a pre-exilic task, and therefore tends to devaluate Jewish productivity in the Diaspora; of this productivity the Talmud, and the main halakic tradition it embodies, are of course the chief expression.[144] In Buber's negative attitude to the halakah, there is also a kind of "pre-nomianism," a Judaism that, as it were, antecedes the law. "My point of view," he explains, "diverges from the traditional one; it is not a-nomistic, but neither is it entirely nomistic . . . The teaching of Judaism comes from Sinai; it is Moses' teaching. But the soul of Judaism is pre-Sinaitic; it is the soul which approached Sinai, and there received what it did . . . The law put on the soul, and the soul can never again be understood outside of the law; yet the soul itself is not the law." [145]

But fundamentally, it would seem, Buber's inability to accept the halakah is his fear that through becoming codified in the law, the demand of God is "objectified" and robbed of its inner power; he is afraid of the illusion of premature fulfillment. Law, of course, is necessary, for "without law, that is, without some clearcut and transmissible line of demarcation between that which is pleasing to God and that which is displeasing to him, there can be no historical continuity of divine rule upon earth"; [146] but the Torah of God, which is "God's instruction in his way," may not without peril be made into a "separate objectivum." [147] "The will to the covenant with God through the perfected reality of life in true community can only emerge in power where one does not believe that the covenant with God is already fulfilled in essence through the observance of prescribed forms."[148] Concern over the danger of a self-righteous evasion of total responsibility through the meticulous observance of prescribed forms is certainly a very real one, and was shared by Franz Rosenzweig, yet Rosenzweig did not find it necessary to take Buber's attitude to the halakah. The controversy between the two, if controversy it can be called, which resulted in a masterly essay by Franz Rosenzweig and a number of striking letters from Martin Buber,[149] will remain of perennial interest to all those concerned with the structure of Jewish faith.

Recent years have seen a remarkable deepening of Buber's

influence upon important sections of world Jewry, and Buber's teaching on the nature and destiny of Israel is receiving a more responsive hearing. On his part, Buber has become more concerned with the responsibility of Jewry to say its word to the world. One of his American addresses, "The Silent Question," is devoted to this concern. What can Judaism tell the world? "This is its message: *You yourself must begin.* Existence will remain meaningless for you if you yourself do not penetrate into it with active love and if you do not in this way discover its meaning for yourself . . . Meet the world with the fullness of your being, and you shall meet God . . . If you wish to believe, love." [150]

But can present-day Jewry speak this word to the world? "Will Jewry itself perceive that its very existence depends upon the revival of its religious existence? . . . Judaism will live only if it brings to life the primeval Jewish relationship to God, the world, and mankind." [151]

VI.   It is easy to hear in Buber echoes of many voices in the contemporary world of thought since he has influenced so much of it, and his own thinking has throughout developed in fruitful dialogue with the men of his age. He was early influenced by the giants of German idealism and romanticism, and by the German mystics, Meister Eckhart and Jacob Boehme. Hasidism, in both its mystical and existential strains, has permeated his thinking from his youth. But of all nineteenth century figures, it was Kierkegaard, Dostoevsky, and Nietzsche who, by his own account, have meant most to him, and with them too his intellectual relations have been complex and many-sided. He has always closely followed the thought of his day, and his comments on Scheler, Heidegger, Sartre, Jung, Bergson, and Simone Weil, to mention but a few of the names that occur in his more recent writing, are among the most illuminating in contemporary criticism. But fundamentally, Buber's thinking has been his own in a way that can be said of few other men; everything that comes from him bears the mark of his unique personality and life experience. In him the word and the deed have indeed been fused in the authentic unity of the lived life.

PART I: *Of Human Existence*

I AND THOU

To man the world is twofold, in accordance with his twofold attitude.

The attitude of man is twofold, in accordance with the twofold nature of the primary words which he speaks.

The primary words are not isolated words, but combined words.

The one primary word is the combination *I-Thou*.

The other primary word is the combination *I-It*; wherein, without a change in the primary word, one of the words *He* or *She* can replace *It*.

Hence the *I* of man is also twofold.

For the *I* of the primary word *I-Thou* is a different *I* from that of the primary word *I-It*.

Primary words do not signify things, but they intimate relations.

Primary words do not describe something that might exist independently of them, but being spoken they bring about existence.

Primary words are spoken from the being.

If *Thou* is said, the *I* of the combination *I-Thou* is said along with it.

If *It* is said, the *I* of the combination *I-It* is said along with it.

The primary word *I-Thou* can only be spoken with the whole being.

The primary word *I-It* can never be spoken with the whole being.

There is no *I* taken in itself, but only the *I* of the primary word *I-Thou* and the *I* of the primary word *I-It*.

When a man says *I* he refers to one or other of these. The *I* to which he refers is present when he says *I*. Further, when he says *Thou* or *It*, the *I* of one of the two primary words is present.

The existence of *I* and the speaking of *I* are one and the same thing.

When a primary word is spoken the speaker enters the word and takes his stand in it.

The life of human beings is not passed in the sphere of transitive verbs alone. It does not exist in virtue of activities alone which have some *thing* for their object.

I perceive something. I am sensible of something. I imagine something. I will something. I feel something. I think something. The life of human beings does not consist of all this and the like alone.

This and the like together establish the realm of *It*.

But the realm of *Thou* has a different basis.

When *Thou* is spoken, the speaker has no thing for his object For where there is a thing, there is another thing. Every *It* is bounded by others; *It* exists only through being bounded by others. But when *Thou* is spoken, there is no thing. *Thou* has no bounds.

When *Thou* is spoken, the speaker has no *thing;* he has indeed nothing. But he takes his stand in relation.

It is said that man experiences his world. What does that mean?

Man travels over the surface of things and experiences them. He extracts knowledge about their constitution from them: he wins an experience from them. He experiences what belongs to the things.

But the world is not presented to man by experiences alone. These present him only with a world composed of *It* and *He* and *She* and *It* again.

I experience something. If we add "inner" to "outer" experiences, nothing in the situation is changed. We are merely following the uneternal division that springs from the lust of the human race to whittle away the secret of death. Inner things or outer things, what are they but things and things!

I experience something. If we add "secret" to "open" experiences, nothing in the situation is changed. How self-confident is that wisdom which perceives a closed compartment in things, reserved for the initiate and manipulated only with the key. O secrecy without a secret! O accumulation of information! It, always It!

The man who experiences has no part in the world. For it is 'in him," and not between him and the world, that the experience arises.

The world has no part in the experience. It permits itself to be experienced, but has no concern in the matter. For it does nothing to the experience, and the experience does nothing to it.

As experience, the world belongs to the primary word *I-It*.
The primary word *I-Thou* establishes the world of relation.

The spheres in which the world of relation arises are three.
First, our life with nature. There the relation sways in gloom, beneath the level of speech. Creatures live and move over against us, but cannot come to us, and when we address them as *Thou,* our words cling to the threshold of speech.

Second, our life with men. There the relation is open and in the form of speech. We can give and accept the *Thou*.

Third, our life with intelligible forms. There the relation is clouded, yet it discloses itself; it does not use speech, yet begets it. We perceive no *Thou,* but nonetheless we feel we are addressed and we answer—forming, thinking, acting. We speak the primary word with our being, though we cannot utter *Thou* with our lips.

But with what right do we draw what lies outside speech into relation with the world of the primary word?

In every sphere in its own way, through each process of becoming that is present to us, we look out toward the fringe of the eternal *Thou;* in each we are aware of a breath from the eternal *Thou;* in each *Thou* we address the eternal *Thou*.

The *Thou* meets me through grace—it is not found by seeking. But my speaking of the primary word to it is an act of my being, is indeed *the* act of my being.

The *Thou* meets me. But I step into direct relation with it. Hence the relation means being chosen and choosing, suffering and action in one; just as any action of the whole being, which means the suspension of all partial actions and consequently of all sensations of actions grounded only in their particular limit-ation, is bound to resemble suffering.

The primary word *I-Thou* can be spoken only with the whole being. Concentration and fusion into the whole being can never take place through my agency, nor can it ever take place with-out me. I become through my relation to the *Thou;* as I be-come *I,* I say *Thou.*

All real living is meeting.

The relation to the *Thou* is direct. No system of ideas, no foreknowledge, and no fancy intervene between *I* and *Thou.* The memory itself is transformed, as it plunges out of its isola-tion into the unity of the whole. No aim, no lust, and no an-ticipation intervene between *I* and *Thou.* Desire itself is trans-formed as it plunges out of its dream into the appearance. Every means is an obstacle. Only when every means has col-lapsed does the meeting come about.

In face of the directness of the relation, everything indirect becomes irrelevant. It is also irrelevant if my *Thou* is already the *It* for other *I's* ("an object of general experience"), or can become so through the very accomplishment of this act of my being. For the real, though certainly swaying and swinging, boundary runs neither between experience and non-experience, nor between what is given and what is not given, nor yet be-tween the world of being and the world of value; but cutting indifferently across all these provinces, it lies between *Thou* and *It,* between the present and the object.

The present, and by that is meant not the point which indi-cates from time to time in our thought merely the conclusion of "finished" time, the mere appearance of a termination which is fixed and held, but the real, filled present, exists only in so far as actual presentness, meeting, and relation exist. The present arises only in virtue of the fact that the *Thou* becomes present.

The *I* of the primary word *I-It,* that is, the *I* faced by no *Thou,* but surrounded by a multitude of "contents," has no present, only the past. Put in another way, in so far as man rests satisfied with the things that he experiences and uses, he lives in the past, and his moment has no present content. He has nothing but objects. But objects subsist in time that has been.

The present is not fugitive and transient, but continually present and enduring. The object is not duration, but cessation, suspension, a breaking off and cutting clear and hardening, absence of relation and of present being.

True beings are lived in the present; the life of objects is in the past.

Appeal to a "world of ideas" as a third factor above this opposition will not do away with its essential twofold nature. For I speak of nothing else but the real man, of you and of me, of our life and of our world—not of an *I*, or a state of being, in itself alone. The real boundary for the actual man cuts right across the world of ideas as well.

To be sure, many a man who is satisfied with the experience and use of the world of things has raised over or about himself a structure of ideas, in which he finds refuge and repose from the oncome of nothingness. On the threshold he lays aside his inauspicious everyday dress, wraps himself in pure linen, and regales himself with the spectacle of primal being, or of necessary being; but his life has no part in it. To proclaim his ways may even fill him with well-being.

But the mankind of mere *It* that is imagined, postulated, and propagated by such a man has nothing in common with a living mankind where *Thou* may truly be spoken. The noblest fiction is a fetish, the loftiest fictitious sentiment is depraved. Ideas are no more enthroned above our heads than resident in them; they wander amongst us and accost us. The man who leaves the primary word unspoken is to be pitied; but the man who addresses instead these ideas with an abstraction or a password, as if it were their name, is contemptible.

In one of the three examples it is obvious that the direct relation includes an effect on what confronts me. In art, the act of the being determines the situation in which the form becomes the work. Through the meeting that which confronts me is fulfilled, and enters the world of things, there to be endlessly active, endlessly to become *It*, but also endlessly to become *Thou* again, inspiring and blessing. It is "embodied"; its body emerges from the flow of the spaceless, timeless present on the shore of existence.

The significance of the effect is not so obvious in the relation with the *Thou* spoken to men. The act of the being which provides directness in this case is usually understood wrongly as being one of feeling. Feelings accompany the metaphysical and metapsychical fact of love, but they do not constitute it. The accompanying feelings can be of greatly differing kinds. The feeling of Jesus for the demoniac differs from his feeling for the beloved disciple; but the love is the one love. Feelings are "entertained": love comes to pass. Feelings dwell in man; but man dwells in his love. That is no metaphor, but the actual truth. Love does not cling to the *I* in such a way as to have the *Thou* only for its "content," its object; but love is *between I and Thou*. The man who does not know this, with his very being know this, does not know love; even though he ascribes to it the feelings he lives through, experiences, enjoys, and expresses. Love ranges in its effect through the whole world. In the eyes of him who takes his stand in love, and gazes out of it, men are cut free from their entanglement in bustling activity. Good people and evil, wise and foolish, beautiful and ugly, become successively real to him; that is, set free they step forth in their singleness, and confront him as *Thou*. In a wonderful way, from time to time, exclusiveness arises—and so he can be effective, helping, healing, educating, raising up, saving. Love is responsibility of an *I* for a *Thou*. In this lies the likeness—impossible in any feeling whatsoever—of all who love, from the smallest to the greatest and from the blessedly protected man, whose life is rounded in that of a loved being, to him who is all his life nailed to the cross of the world, and who ventures to bring himself to the dreadful point—to love *all men*.

Let the significance of the effect in the third example, that of the creature and our contemplation of it, remain sunk in mystery. Believe in the simple magic of life, in service in the universe, and the meaning of that waiting, that alertness, that "craning of the neck" in creatures will dawn upon you. Every word would falsify; but look! round about you beings live their life, and to whatever point you turn you come upon being.

Relation is mutual. My *Thou* affects me, as I affect it. We are moulded by our pupils and built up by our works. The "bad" man, lightly touched by the holy primary word, becomes one who reveals. How we are educated by children and by animals! We live our lives inscrutably included within the streaming mutual life of the universe.

You speak of love as though it were the only relation between men. But properly speaking, can you take it even only as an example, since there is such a thing as hate?

So long as love is "blind," that is, so long as it does not see a *whole* being, it is not truly under the sway of the primary word of relation. Hate is by nature blind. Only a part of a being can be hated. He who sees a whole being and is compelled to reject it is no longer in the kingdom of hate, but is in that of human restriction of the power to say *Thou*. He finds himself unable to say the primary word to the other human being confronting him. This word consistently involves an affirmation of the being addressed. He is therefore compelled to reject either the other or himself. At this barrier, the entering on a relation recognizes its relativity, and only simultaneously with this will the barrier be raised.

Yet the man who straightforwardly hates is nearer to relation than the man without hate and love.

But this is the exalted melancholy of our fate, that every *Thou* in our world must become an *It*. It does not matter how exclusively present the *Thou* was in the direct relation. As soon as the relation has been worked out, or has been permeated with a means, the *Thou* becomes an object among objects—perhaps the chief, but still one of them, fixed in its size and its limits. In the work of art, realization in one sense means loss of reality in another. Genuine contemplation is over in a short time; now the life in nature, that first unlocked itself to me in the mystery of mutual action, can again be described, taken to pieces, and classified—the meeting-point of manifold systems of laws. And love itself cannot persist in direct relation. It endures, but in interchange of actual and potential being. The human being who was even now single and unconditioned, not something lying to hand, only present, not able to be experienced, only able to be fulfilled, has now become again a *He* or a *She*, a sum of qualities, a given quantity with a certain shape. Now I may take out from him again the color of his hair or of his speech or of his goodness. But so long as I can do this, he is no more my *Thou* and cannot yet be my *Thou* again.

Every *Thou* in the world is by its nature fated to become a thing, or continually to re-enter into the condition of things. In objective speech, it would be said that every thing in the world, either before or after becoming a thing, is able to appear to an

I as its *Thou.* But objective speech snatches only at a fringe of real life.

The *It* is the eternal chrysalis, the *Thou* the eternal butterfly—except that situations do not always follow one another in clear succession, but often there is a happening profoundly twofold, confusedly entangled.

The fundamental difference between the two primary words comes to light in the spiritual history of primitive man. Already in the original relational event he speaks the primary word *I-Thou* in a natural way that precedes what may be termed visualization of forms—that is, before he has recognized himself as *I*. The primary word *I-It*, on the other hand, is made possible at all only by means of this recognition—by means, that is, of the separation of the *I*.

The first primary word can be resolved, certainly, into *I* and *Thou*, but it did not arise from their being set together; by its nature it precedes *I*. The second word arose from the setting together of *I* and *It*; by nature it comes after *I*.

In the primitive relational event, in virtue of its exclusiveness, the *I* is included. While, that is to say, there are in it, in accordance with its being, only the two partners, the man and that which confronts him, in their full actuality, and while the world becomes in it a dual system, the man, without yet perceiving the *I* itself, is already aware of that cosmic pathos of the *I*.

On the other hand, the *I* is not yet included in the natural, actual event which is to pass over into the primary word *I-It*, into the experience with its relation to *I*. This actual event is the separation of the human body, as the bearer of its perceptions, from the world round about it. The body comes to know and to differentiate itself in its peculiarities; the differentiation, however, remains one of pure juxtaposition, and hence cannot have the character of the state in which *I* is implied.

But when the *I* of the relation has stepped forth and taken on separate existence, it also moves, strangely tenuous and reduced to merely functional activity, into the natural, actual event of the separation of the body from the world round about it, and awakens there the state in which *I* is properly active. Only now can the conscious act of the *I* take place. This act is the first form of the primary word *I-It*, of the experience in its relation to *I*. The *I* which stepped forth declares itself to be the bearer, and the world round about to be the object, of the perceptions. Of course, this happens in a "primitive" form and not in the form of a "theory of knowledge." But whenever the sentence "I see the tree" is so uttered that it no longer tells of a relation between the man—*I*—and the tree—*Thou*—but establishes the perception of the tree as object by the human consciousness, the barrier between subject and object has been set up. The primary word *I-It*, the word of separation, has been spoken.

Through the *Thou* a man becomes *I*. That which confronts him comes and disappears, relational events condense, then are scattered, and in the change consciousness of the unchanging partner, of the *I*, grows clear, and each time stronger. To be sure, it is still seen caught in the web of the relation with the *Thou*, as the increasingly distinguishable feature of that which reaches out to and yet is not the *Thou*. But it continually breaks through with more power, till a time comes when it bursts its bonds, and the *I* confronts itself for a moment, separated as though it were a *Thou;* as quickly to take possession of itself, and from then on to enter into relations in consciousness of itself.

Only now can the other primary word be assembled. Hitherto the *Thou* of relation was continually fading away, but it did not thereby become an *It* for some *I*, an object of perception and experience without real connection—as it will henceforth become. It became rather an *It*, so to speak, for itself, an *It* disregarded at first, yet waiting to rise up in a new relational event. Further, the body maturing into a person was hitherto distinguished, as bearer of its perceptions and executor of its impulses, from the world round about. But this distinction was simply a juxtaposition brought about by its seeing its way in the situation, and not an absolute severance of *I* and its object. But now the separated *I* emerges, transformed. Shrunk from substance and fulness to a functional point, to a subject which experiences and uses, *I* approaches and takes possession of all *It* existing "in and for itself," and forms in conjunction with it the other primary word. The man who has become conscious of *I*, that is, the man who says *I-It*, stands before things, but not over against them in the flow of mutual action. Now with the magnifying glass of peering observation he bends over particulars and objectifies them, or with the field-glass of remote inspection he objectifies them and arranges them as scenery, he isolates them in observation without any feeling of their exclusiveness, or he knits them into a scheme of observation without any feeling of universality. The feeling of exclusiveness he would be able to find only in relation; the feeling of universality only through it. Now for the first time he experiences things as sums of qualities. From each relational experience qualities belonging to the remembered *Thou* had certainly remained sunk in his memory; but now for the first time, things are for him actually composed of their qualities. From the simple memory of the relation, the man, dreaming or fashioning or thinking, according to his nature, enlarges the nucleus, the substance that showed itself in the *Thou* with power and gathered up in itself all qualities. But now also for the first time he sets things in space and time, in causal connection, each with its own place and appointed course, its measurability and conditioned nature.

The *Thou* appears, to be sure, in space, but in the exclusive situation of what is over against it, where everything else can be only the background out of which it emerges, not its boundary and measured limit. It appears, too, in time, but in that of the event which is fulfilled in itself: it is not lived as part of a continuous and organized sequence, but is lived in a "duration" whose purely intensive dimension is definable only in terms of itself. It appears, lastly, simultaneously as acting and as being acted upon—not, however, linked to a chain of causes, but, in its relation of mutual action with the *I*, as the beginning and the end of the event. This is part of the basic truth of the human world, that only *It* can be arranged in order. Only when things, from being our *Thou*, become our *It*, can they be co-ordinated. The *Thou* knows no system of co-ordination.

But now that we have come so far, it is necessary to set down the other part of the basic truth, without which this would be a useless fragment—namely, a world that is ordered is not the world-order. There are moments of silent depth in which you look on the world-order fully present. Then, in its very flight, the note will be heard; but the ordered world is its indistinguishable score. These moments are immortal, and most transitory of all; no content may be secured from them, but their power invades creation and the knowledge of man, beams of their power stream into the ordered world and dissolve it again and again. This happens in the history both of the individual and of the race.

To man the world is twofold, in accordance with his twofold attitude.

He perceives what exists round about him—simply things, and beings as things; and what happens round about him— simply events, and actions as events; things consisting of qualities, events of moments; things entered in the graph of place, events in that of time; things and events bounded by other things and events, measured by them, comparable with them: he perceives an ordered and detached world. It is to some extent a reliable world, having density and duration. Its organization can be surveyed and brought out again and again; gone over with closed eyes, and verified with open eyes. It is always there, next to your skin, if you look on it that way, cowering in your soul, if you prefer it so. It is your object, remains your object as long as you wish, and remains a total stranger, within you and without. You perceive it, take it to yourself as the "truth," and it lets itself be taken; but it does not give itself to you. Only concerning it may you make yourself "understood" with others; it is ready, though attached to everyone in a different way, to be an object common to you all. But you cannot meet others in it. You cannot hold on to life without it, its reliability sustains you; but should you die in it, your grave would be in nothingness.

Or, on the other hand, man meets what exists and becomes as what is over against him, always simply a *single* being and each thing simply as being. What exists is opened to him in happenings, and what happens affects him as what is. Nothing is present for him except this one being, but it implicates the whole world. Measure and comparison have disappeared; it lies with yourself how much of the immeasurable becomes reality for you. These meetings are not organized to make the world, but each is a sign of the world-order. They are not linked up with one another, but each assures you of your solidarity with the world. The world which appears to you in this way is unreliable, for it takes on a continually new appearance; you cannot hold it to its word. It has no density, for everything in it penetrates everything else; no duration, for it comes even when it is not summoned, and vanishes even when it is tightly held. It cannot be surveyed, and if you wish to make it capable of survey, you lose it. It comes, and comes to bring *you* out; if it does not reach you, meet you, then it vanishes; but it comes back in another form. It is not outside you, it stirs in the depth of you; if you say "soul of my soul" you have not said too

much. But guard against wishing to remove it into your soul
—for then you annihilate it. It is your present; only while you
have it do you have the present. You can make it into an object for yourself, to experience and to use; you must continually do this—and as you do it, you have no more present. Between you and it there is mutual giving: you say *Thou* to it
and give yourself to it, it says *Thou* to you and gives itself to
you. You cannot make yourself understood with others concerning it, you are alone with it. But it teaches you to meet
others, and to hold your ground when you meet them. Through
the graciousness of its comings, and the solemn sadness of its
goings, it leads you away to the *Thou* in which the parallel
lines of relations meet. It does not help to sustain you in life, it
only helps you to glimpse eternity.

The world of *It* is set in the context of space and time.

The world of *Thou* is not set in the context of either of these.

The particular *Thou*, after the relational event has run its
course, is *bound* to become an *It*.

The particular *It*, by entering the relational event, *may* become a *Thou*.

These are the two basic privileges of the world of *It*. They
move man to look on the world of *It* as the world in which he
has to live, and in which it is comfortable to live, as the world,
indeed, which offers him all manner of incitements and excite-
ments, activity and knowledge. In this chronicle of solid benefits, the moments of the *Thou* appear as strange lyric and dramatic episodes, seductive and magical, but tearing us away to
dangerous extremes, loosening the well-tried context, leaving
more questions than satisfaction behind them, shattering security—in short, uncanny moments we can well dispense with. For
since we are bound to leave them and go back into the "world,"
why not remain in it? Why not call to order what is over
against us, and send it packing into the realm of objects? Why,
if we find ourselves on occasion with no choice but to say
Thou to father, wife, or comrade, not say *Thou* and mean *It*?
To utter the sound *Thou* with the vocal organs is by no means
the same as saying the uncanny primary word; more, it is
harmless to whisper with the soul an amorous *Thou*, so long
as nothing else in a serious way is meant but *experience* and
make use of.

It is not possible to live in the bare present. Life would be
quite consumed if precautions were not taken to subdue the

present speedily and thoroughly. But it is possible to live in the bare past, indeed only in it may a life be organized. We only need to fill each moment with experiencing and using, and it ceases to burn.

And in all the seriousness of truth, hear this: without *It* man cannot live; but he who lives with *It* alone is not a man.

The extended lines of relations meet in the eternal *Thou*.

Every particular *Thou* is a glimpse through to the eternal *Thou*; by means of every particular *Thou*, the primary word addresses the eternal *Thou*. Through this mediation of the *Thou* of all beings, fulfilment and non-fulfilment of relations comes to them: the inborn *Thou* is realized in each relation and consummated in none. It is consummated only in the direct relation with the *Thou* that by its nature cannot become *It*.

Men have addressed their eternal *Thou* with many names. In singing of him who was thus named, they always had the *Thou* in mind: the first myths were hymns of praise. Then the names took refuge in the language of *It*; men were more and more strongly moved to think of and to address their eternal *Thou* as an *It*. But all God's names are hallowed, for in them he is not merely spoken about, but also spoken to.

Many men wish to reject the word God as a legitimate usage, because it is so misused. It is indeed the most heavily laden of all the words used by men. For that very reason, it is the most imperishable and most indispensable. What does all mistaken talk about God's being and works (though there has been, and can be, no other talk about these) matter in comparison with the one truth that all men who have addressed God had God himself in mind? For he who speaks the word God and really has *Thou* in mind (whatever the illusion by which he is held), addresses the true *Thou* of his life, which cannot be limited by another *Thou*, and to which he stands in a relation that gathers up and includes all others.

But when he, too, who abhors the name, and believes himself to be godless, gives his whole being to addressing the *Thou* of his life, as a *Thou* that cannot be limited by another, he addresses God.

If we go on our way and meet a man who has advanced towards us and has also gone on *his* way, we know only our part of the way, not his—his we experience only in the meeting.

Of the complete relational event we know, with the knowledge of life lived, our going out to the relation, our part of the way. The other part only comes upon us, we do not know it; it comes upon us in the meeting. But we strain ourselves on it if we speak of it as though it were some thing beyond the meeting.

We have to be concerned, to be troubled, not about the other side but about our own side, not about grace but about will. Grace concerns us in so far as we go out to it and persist in its presence; but it is not our object.

The *Thou* confronts me. But I step into direct relation with it. Hence the relation means being chosen and choosing, suffering and action in one; just as any action of the whole being which means the suspension of all partial actions, and consequently of all sensations of actions grounded only in their particular limitation, is bound to resemble suffering.

This is the activity of the man who has become a whole being, an activity that has been termed doing nothing: nothing separate or partial stirs in the man any more, thus he makes no intervention in the world; it is the whole man, enclosed and at rest in his wholeness, that is effective—he has become an effective whole. To have won stability in this state is to be able to go out to the supreme meeting.

To this end the world of sense does not need to be laid aside as though it were illusory. There is no illusory world, there is only the world—which appears to us as twofold in accordance with our twofold attitude. Only the barrier of separation has to be destroyed. Further, no "going beyond sense-experience" is necessary; for every experience, even the most spiritual, could yield us only an *It*. Nor is any recourse necessary to a world of ideas and values; for they cannot become presentness for us. None of these things is necessary. Can it be said what really is necessary? Not in the sense of a precept. For everything that has ever been devised and contrived in the time of the human spirit as precept, alleged preparation, practice, or meditation, has nothing to do with the primal, simple fact of the meeting. Whatever the advantages in knowledge or the wielding of power for which we have to thank this or that practice, none of this affects the meeting of which we are speaking; it all has its place in the world of *It* and does not lead one step, does not take *the* step, out of it. Going out to the relation cannot be taught in the sense of precepts being given. It can only be in-

dicated by the drawing of a circle which excludes everything
that is not this going out. Then the one thing that matters is
visible, full acceptance of the present.

To be sure, this acceptance presupposes that the further a
man has wandered in separated being the more difficult is the
venture and the more elemental the reversal. This does not
mean a giving up of, say, the *I*, as mystical writings usually
suppose: the *I* is as indispensable to this, the supreme, as to
every relation, since relation is only possible between *I* and
Thou. It is not the *I*, then, that is given up, but that false self-
asserting instinct that makes a man flee to the possessing of
things before the unreliable, perilous world of relation which
has neither density nor duration and cannot be surveyed.

Every real relation with a being or life in the world is exclusive. Its *Thou* is freed, steps forth, is single, and confronts
you. It fills the heavens. This does not mean that nothing else
exists; but all else lives in *its* light. As long as the presence of
the relation continues, this its cosmic range is inviolable. But as
soon as a *Thou* becomes *It*, the cosmic range of the relation
appears as an offence to the world, its exclusiveness as an exclusion of the universe.

In the relation with God, unconditional exclusiveness and
unconditional inclusiveness are one. He who enters on the
absolute relation is concerned with nothing isolated any more,
neither things nor beings, neither earth nor heaven; but everything is gathered up in the relation. For to step into pure
relation is not to disregard everything but to see everything in
the *Thou*, not to renounce the world but to establish it on
its true basis. To look away from the world, or to stare at it,
does not help a man to reach God; but he who sees the world
in him stands in his presence. "Here world, there God" is the
language of *It;* "God in the world" is another language of *It;*
but to eliminate or leave behind nothing at all, to include the
whole world in the *Thou*, to give the world its due and its truth,
to include nothing beside God but everything in him—this
is full and complete relation.

Men do not find God if they stay in the world. They do not
find him if they leave the world. He who goes out with his
whole being to meet his *Thou*, and carries to it all being that
is in the world, finds him who cannot be sought.

Of course God is the "wholly Other"; but he is also the
wholly Same, the wholly Present. Of course he is the *Mys-*

terium Tremendum that appears and overthrows; but he is also the mystery of the self-evident, nearer to me than my *I*.

If you explore the life of things and of conditioned being, you come to the unfathomable; if you deny the life of things and of conditioned being, you stand before nothingness; if you hallow this life, you meet the living God.

Man's sense of *Thou*, which experiences in the relations with every particular *Thou* the disappointment of the change to *It*, strives out but not away from them all to its eternal *Thou;* but not as something is sought: actually there is no such thing as seeking God, for there is nothing in which he could not be found. How foolish and hopeless would be the man who turned aside from the course of his life in order to seek God; even though he won all the wisdom of solitude and all the power of concentrated being, he would miss God. Rather is it as when a man goes his way and simply wishes that it might be the way: in the strength of his wish his striving is expressed. Every relational event is a stage that affords him a glimpse into the consummating event. So in each event he does not partake, but also (for he is waiting) does partake, of the one event. Waiting, not seeking, he goes his way; hence he is composed before all things, and makes contact with them which helps them. But when he has *found,* his heart is not turned from them, though everything now meets him in the one event. He blesses every cell that sheltered him, and every cell into which he will yet turn. For this finding is not the end, but only the eternal middle, of the way.

It is a finding without seeking, a discovering of the primal, of origin. His sense of *Thou,* which cannot be satiated till he finds the endless *Thou,* had the *Thou* present to it from the beginning; the presence had only to become wholly real to him in the reality of the hallowed life of the world.

God cannot be inferred in anything—in nature, say, as its author, or in history as its master, or in the subject as the self that is thought in it. Something else is not "given" and God then elicited from it; but God is the Being that is directly, most nearly, and lastingly, over against us, that may properly only be addressed, not expressed.

The spheres in which the world of relation is built are three.
First, our life with nature, in which the relation clings to the threshold of speech.

Second, our life with men, in which the relation takes on the form of speech.

Third, our life with intelligible forms, where the relation, being without speech, yet begets it.

In every sphere in its own way, through each process of becoming that is present to us, we look out toward the fringe of the eternal *Thou;* in each we are aware of a breath from the eternal *Thou;* in each *Thou* we address the eternal *Thou.*

All spheres are compassed in the eternal *Thou,* but it is not compassed in them.

A modern philosopher supposes that every man necessarily believes either in God or in "idols," that is, in some sort of finite good—his nation, his art, power, knowledge, the amassing of money, "the ever new subjugation of woman"—which has become for him an absolute value and has set itself up between him and God; it is only necessary to demonstrate to him the conditioned nature of this good, in order to "shatter" the idol, and the diverted religious act will automatically return to the fitting object.

This conception presupposes that man's relation to the finite goods he has "idolized" is of the same nature as his relation to God, and differs only in its object; for only with this presupposition could the mere substitution of the true for the false object save the erring man. But a man's relation to the "special something" that usurps the throne of the supreme value of his life, and supplants eternity, rests always on experiencing and using an *It,* a thing, an object of enjoyment. For this relation alone is able to obstruct the prospect which opens toward God—it is the impenetrable world of *It;* but the relation which involves the saying of the *Thou* opens up this prospect ever anew. He who is dominated by the idol that he wishes to win, to hold, and to keep—possessed by a desire for possession—has no way to God but that of reversal, which is a change not only of goal but also of the nature of his movement. The man who is possessed is saved by being wakened and educated to solidarity of relation, not by being led in his state of possession toward God. If a man remains in this state, what does it mean when he calls no longer on the name of a demon or of a being demonically distorted for him, but on the name of God? It means that from now on he blasphemes. It is blasphemy when a man wishes, after the idol has crashed behind

the altar, to pile up an unholy sacrifice to God on the desecrated place.

He who loves a woman, and brings her life to present realization in his, is able to see in the *Thou* of her eyes a beam of
the eternal *Thou*. But he who eagerly desires "ever new subjugation"—do you wish to hold out to his desire a phantom of
the Eternal? He who serves his people in the boundlessness of
destiny, and is willing to give himself to them, is really thinking of God. But do you suppose that the man to whom the nation is a god, in whose service he would like to enlist everything (for in the nation's he exalts his own image), need only
be given a feeling of disgust—and he would see the truth? And
what does it mean that a man is said to treat money, embodied
non-being, "as if it were God"? What has the lust of grabbing
and of laying up treasure in common with the joy in the presence of the Present One? Can the servant of Mammon say
Thou to his money? And how is he to behave toward God
when he does not understand how to say *Thou?* He cannot
serve two masters—not even one after the other: he must first
learn to serve *in a different way*.

He who has been converted by this substitution of object
now "holds" a phantom that he calls God. But God, the eternal
Presence, does not permit himself to be held. Woe to the man
so possessed that he thinks he possesses God!

What is the eternal, primal phenomenon, present here and
now, of that which we term revelation? It is the phenomenon
out of which a man does not emerge, from the moment of the
supreme meeting, the same being as he entered into it. The
moment of meeting is not an "experience" that stirs in the receptive soul and grows to perfect blessedness; rather, in that
moment, something happens to the man. At times, it is like a
light breath; at times, like a wrestling-bout, but always—it *happens.* The man who emerges from the act of pure relation that
so involves his being has now in his being something more that
has grown in him, of which he did not know before and whose
origin he is not rightly able to indicate. However the source of
this new thing is classified in scientific orientation of the world,
with its authorized efforts to establish an unbroken causality,
we, whose concern is real consideration of the real, cannot have
our purpose served with subconsciousness or any other apparatus of the soul. The reality is that we receive what we did not
hitherto have, and receive it in such a way that we know it

has been given to us. In the language of the Bible, "those who wait upon the Lord shall renew their strength." In the language of Nietzsche, who in his account remains loyal to reality, "we take and do not ask who it is there that gives."

Man receives, and he receives not a specific "content," but a Presence, a Presence as power. This Presence and this power include three things, undivided, yet in such a way that we may consider them separately. First, there is the whole fulness of real mutual action, of the being raised and bound up in relation: the man can give no account at all of how the binding in relation is brought about, nor does it in any way lighten his life—it makes life heavier, but heavy with meaning. Secondly, there is the inexpressible confirmation of meaning. Meaning is assured. Nothing can any longer be meaningless. The question about the meaning of life is no longer there. But were it there, it would not have to be answered. You do not know how to exhibit and define the meaning of life, you have no formula or picture for it, and yet it has more certitude for you than the perceptions of your senses. What does the revealed and concealed meaning purpose with us, desire from us? It does not wish to be explained (nor are we able to do that), but only to be done by us. Thirdly, this meaning is not that of "another life," but that of this life of ours, not one of a world "yonder," but that of this world of ours, and it desires its confirmation in this life and in relation with this world. This meaning can be received, but not experienced; it cannot be experienced but it can be done, and this is its purpose with us. The assurance I have of it does not wish to be sealed within me, but it wishes to be born by me into the world. But just as the meaning itself does not permit itself to be transmitted and made into knowledge generally current and admissible, so confirmation of it cannot be transmitted as a valid Ought; it is not prescribed, it is not specified on any tablet, to be raised above all men's heads. The meaning that has been received can be proved true by each man only in the singleness of his being and the singleness of his life. As no prescription can lead us to the meeting, so none leads from it. As only acceptance of the Presence is necessary for the approach to the meeting, so in a new sense is it so when we emerge from it. As we reach the meeting with the simple *Thou* on our lips, so with the *Thou* on our lips we leave it and return to the world.

That before which, in which, out of which, and into which we live, even the mystery, has remained what it was. It has become present to us and in its presentness has proclaimed itself to us as salvation; we have "known" it, but we acquire no knowledge from it which might lessen or moderate its mysteriousness. We have come near to God, but not nearer to unveiling being or solving its riddle. We have felt release, but not discovered a "solution." We cannot approach others with what we have received, and say: "You must know this, you must do this." We can only go, and confirm its truth. And this, too, is no "ought," but we can, we *must*.

This is the eternal revelation that is present here and now. I know of no revelation and believe in none whose primal phenomenon is not precisely this. I do not believe in a self-naming of God, a self-definition of God before men. The Word of revelation is *I am that I am*. That which reveals is that which reveals. That which is *is,* and nothing more. The eternal source of strength streams, the eternal contact persists, the eternal voice sounds forth, and nothing more.

2

THE QUESTION TO THE SINGLE ONE[1]

The Unique One and the Single One

Only by coming up against the category of the "Single One," and by making it a concept of the utmost clarity, did Søren Kierkegaard become the one who presented Christianity as a paradoxical problem for the single "Christian." He was only able to do this owing to the radical nature of his solitariness. His Single One cannot be understood without his solitariness, which differed in kind from the solitariness of the earlier Christian thinkers, such as Augustine or Pascal, whose name one would like to link with his. It is not irrelevant that beside Augustine stood a mother, and beside Pascal a sister, who maintained the organic connection with the world as only a woman as the envoy of elemental life can; whereas the central event of Kierkegaard's life, and the core of the crystallization of his thought, was the renunciation of Regina Olsen as representing woman and the world. Nor may this solitariness be compared with that of a monk or a hermit; for the monk or hermit, renunciation stands essentially only at the beginning, and even if it must be achieved and practiced ever anew, it is not that which constitutes the life theme, the basic problem, the stuff out of which all teaching is woven. But for Kierkegaard, this is just what renunciation is. It is embodied in the category of the Single One, "the category through which, from the religious standpoint, time and history and the race must pass" (Kierkegaard, 1847).

By means of an opposition, we can first of all be precisely

aware what the Single One, in a special and specially important sense, is not. A few years before Kierkegaard outlined his "Report to History" under the title *The Point of View for My Work as an Author*, in whose "Two Notes" the category of the Single One found its adequate formulation, Max Stirner published his book about "The Unique One." [2] This, too, is a border concept like the Single One, but from the other end. Stirner, a pathetic nominalist and unmasker of ideas, wanted to dissolve the alleged remains of German idealism (so he regarded Ludwig Feuerbach) by raising not the thinking subject nor man, but the concrete present individual, as "the exclusive I" to be the bearer of the world, that is, of "his" world.

Here this Unique One "consuming himself" in "self-enjoyment" is the only one who has primary existence; only the man who comes to such a possession and consciousness of himself has primary existence—on account of the "unity and omnipotence of our I that is sufficient to itself, for it lets nothing be but itself." Thus, the question of an essential relation between him and the other is eliminated as well. He has no essential relation except to himself (Stirner's alleged "living participation" "in the person of the other" is without essence, since the other has in his eyes no primary existence). That is, he has only that remarkable relation with the self which does not lack certain magical possibilities (since all other existence becomes the haunting of ghosts that are half in bonds, half free), but is so empty of any genuine power to enter into relation that it is better to describe as a relation only that in which not only *I* but also *Thou* can be said. This border product of a German Protagoras is usually underrated; the loss of reality which responsibility and truth have suffered in our time has here if not its spiritual origin, certainly its exact conceptual proclamation. "The man who belongs to himself alone . . . is by origin free, for he acknowledges nothing but himself," and "true is what is Mine," are formulas which forecast a congealing of the soul unsuspected by Stirner in all his rhetorical assurance. But also many a rigid collective *We*, which rejects a superior authority, is easily understood as a translation from the speech of the Unique One into that of the *Group-I*, which acknowledges nothing but itself—a translation carried out against Stirner's intention, for Stirner hotly opposes any plural version.

Kierkegaard's Single One has this in common with its counterpoint, Stirner's Unique One, that both are border categories; it has no more in common than this, but also it has no less.

The category of the Single One, too, means not the subject or "man," but concrete singularity; yet not the individual who discovers his existence, but rather the person who is finding himself. But this finding oneself, however primordially remote from Stirner's "utilize thyself," is not akin either to that "know thyself" which apparently troubled Kierkegaard very much. For it means a becoming, a becoming, moreover, under a weight of seriousness that, for the West at least, emerged only with Christianity. It is, therefore, a becoming which (though Kierkegaard says that his category was used by Socrates "for the dissolution of heathendom") is decisively different from that effected by the Socratic "maieutic." "No one is excluded from being a Single One except he who excludes himself by wishing to be 'crowd.' " Here not only is "Single One" opposed to "crowd," but also becoming is opposed to a particular mode of being which evades becoming. That may still be in tune with Socratic thought. But what does it mean, to become a Single One? Kierkegaard's account shows clearly that the nature of his category is no longer Socratic. It runs, "to fulfil the first condition of all religiosity" is "to be a single man." It is for this reason that the Single One is "the category through which, from the religious standpoint, time and history and the race must pass."

Since the concept of religiosity has since lost its definiteness, what Kierkegaard means must be more precisely defined. He cannot mean that to become a Single One is the presupposition of a condition of the soul, called religiosity. It is not a matter of a condition of the soul, but a matter of existence in that strict sense in which—precisely by fulfilling the personal life—it passes, in its essence, beyond the boundary of the person. Then being, familiar being, becomes unfamiliar, and no longer signifies my being, but my participation in the Present Being. That this is what Kierkegaard means is expressed in the fundamental word that the Single One "corresponds" to God. In Kierkegaard's account, then, the concept "of all religiosity" has to be more precisely defined by "of all religious reality." But since this also is exposed to the epidemic sickening of the word in our time, by which every word is at once covered with the leprosy of routine and changed into a slogan, we must go further, as far as possible, and, giving up the vexatious word "religion," take a risk, but a necessary risk, and explain the phrase as meaning "of all real human dealings with God." That Kierkegaard means this is shown by his reference to a "speaking with

God." And indeed a man can have dealings with God only as a Single One, as a man who has become a Single One. This the Old Testament—though there a people too meets the Godhead as a people—expresses by permitting only a person bearing a name, Enoch, Noah, to "have dealings with Elohim." Not before a man, in perfect reality—that is, in finding himself—can say *I*, can he, in perfect reality—that is, to God—say *Thou*. And even if he does it in a community, he can only do it "alone." "As the 'Single One,' he [every man] is alone, alone in the whole world, alone before God." That is—what Kierkegaard, strangely, does not think of—thoroughly unsocratic: in the words "the divine gives me a sign," Socrates' "religiosity" is represented in a way significant for all ages; but the words "I am alone before God" are unthinkable as coming from him. Kierkegaard's "alone" is no longer of Socrates; it is of Abraham—Genesis 12:1 and 22:2 alike demand, in the same words "Go before thee," the power to free oneself of all bonds, the bonds to the world of fathers and to the world of sons—and it is of Christ.

Clarity demands a further twofold distinction. First, with respect to mysticism. Mysticism too lets man be alone before God, but not as the Single One. The relation to God which it thinks of is the absorption of the *I;* the Single One ceases to exist if he cannot, even in devoting himself, say *I*. As mysticism will not permit God to assume the servant's form of the speaking and acting person, of a creator, of a revealer, and to tread the way of the Passion through time as the partner of history, suffering along with it all destiny, so it prohibits man, as the Single One persisting as such, from really praying and serving and loving, such as can be done only by an *I* to a *Thou*. Mysticism only tolerates the Single One in order that he may ultimately dissolve. But Kierkegaard knows, at any rate in relation to God, what love is, and thus he knows that there is no self-love that is not self-deceit (since he who loves—and it is he who matters—loves only the other and essentially not himself), but that without being and remaining oneself, there is no love.

The second necessary distinction is with respect to Stirner's Unique One. (For the sake of conceptual precision, this expression is to be preferred to the more humanistic ones, such as Stendhal's *égotiste*.)

A preliminary distinction must be made with respect to so-called individualism, which has also produced a "religious" variety. The Single One, the person ready and able to "stand alone before God," is the counterpart of what, in the not distant past, was still called—using a term which is treason to the spirit of Goethe—personality; and man's becoming a Single One is the counterpart of "personal development." All individualism, whether it is called aesthetic or ethical or religious, finds a cheap and easy pleasure in man provided only he is "developing." In other words, "ethical" and "religious" individualism are only inflections of the "aesthetic"—which is as little genuine *aesthesis* as the former are genuine *ethos* and genuine *religio*.

Morality and piety, where they have in this way become an autonomous aim, must also be reckoned among the shows and show pieces of a spirit that no longer knows about being, but only about its reflections.

Where individualism ceases to be wanton, Stirner begins. He is also, it is true, concerned with the "shaping of free personality," but in the sense of a severance of the "self" from the world: he is concerned with tearing apart his existential ties and bonds, with breaking free from all ontic otherness of things and lives, which now may only serve as "nourishment" of his selfhood. The contrapuntal position of Stirner's Unique One to Kierkegaard's Single One becomes clearest when the questions of responsibility and truth are raised.

For Stirner, both are bound to be false questions. But it is important to see that though intending to destroy both basic ideas, he has destroyed only their routine forms, and thus, contrary to his whole intention, has prepared for their purification and renewal. Historically minded contemporaries have spoken disparagingly of him as a modern sophist; since then, the function of the sophists, and consequently of their like in later times, has been recognized as the function of dissolving and preparing. Stirner may have understood Hegel just as little as Protagoras did Heraclitus; but even as it is meaningless to reproach Protagoras with laying waste the gardens of the great cosmologist, so Stirner remains untouched when he is ridiculed as the unwitting and profane interloper in the fields of post-Kantian philosophy. Stirner is not, any more than the sophists were, a curious interlude in the history of human thought. Like them, he is an *epeisodion* in the original sense. In his monologue, the action secretly changes; what follows is a new thing: as Protagoras leads towards his contemporary Socrates, Stirner leads towards his contemporary Kierkegaard.

Responsibility presupposes one who addresses me primarily, that is, from a realm independent of myself, and to whom I am answerable. He addresses me about something that he has entrusted to me and that I am bound to take care of loyally. He addresses me from his trust, and I respond in my loyalty or refuse to respond in my disloyalty; or, having fallen into disloyalty, I wrestle free of it by the loyalty of the response. To be so answerable to a trusting person about an entrusted matter that loyalty and disloyalty step into the light of day—but both are not of the same right, for now loyalty, born again, is permitted to conquer disloyalty—this is the reality of responsibility. Where no primary address and claim can touch me, where everything is "my property," responsibility has become a phantom. At the same time, life's character of mutuality is dissipated. He who ceases to make a response ceases to hear the Word.

But this reality of responsibility is not what is questioned by Stirner; it is unknown to him. He simply does not know what of elemental reality happens between life and life, he does not know the mysteries of address and answer, claim and disclaim, word and response. He has not experienced this because it can only be experienced when one is not closed to the otherness, the ontic and primal otherness of the other—to the primal otherness of the other, which, of course, even when the other is God, must not be confined to a "total otherness." What Stirner with his destructive power successfully attacks is the surrogate for a reality that is no longer believed; he attacks the fictitious responsibility before reason, an idea, a nature, an institution, all manner of illustrious ghosts, all that in essence is not a person, and hence cannot really, like father and mother, prince and master, husband and friend, like God, make you answerable. He wishes to show the nothingness of the word which has decayed into a phrase; he has never known the living word, he unveils what he knows. Ignorant of the reality whose appearance is appearance, he proves its nature to be appearance. Stirner dissolves the dissolution. "What you call responsibility is a lie!", he cries, and he is right: it is a lie. But there is a truth. And the way to it lies freer after the lie has been seen through.

Kierkegaard means true responsibility when, rushing in a parabola past Stirner, he speaks thus of the crowd and the Single One: "Being in a crowd either completely releases the Single One from repentance and responsibility, or else weakens his sense of responsibility. since the crowd leaves only a fraction of responsibility to him." These words, to which I intend to return, no longer imply any illusion of a responsibility without a receiver; they imply genuine responsibility, now recognized once more, in which the demander demands of me the entrusted good, and I must open my hands or they petrify.

Stirner has unmasked as unreal the responsibility which is only ethical by exposing the non-existence of the alleged receivers as such. Kierkegaard has proclaimed anew the responsibility which is in faith.

And as with responsibility so with truth itself: here the parabolic meeting becomes even more uncanny.

"Truth . . . exists only—in your head." "The truth is a—creature." "For Me there is no truth, for nothing passes beyond Me." "So long as you believe in the truth, you do not believe in yourself. . . . You alone are the truth." What Stirner undertakes here is the dissolution of *possessed* truth, of "truth" as a general good that can be taken into possession and possessed, that is at once independent of, and accessible to, the person. He does not undertake this like the sophists or other sceptics by means of epistemology. He does not seem to have been acquainted with the epistemological method; he is as audaciously naive in his behavior as though Hume and Kant had never lived. But neither would epistemology have achieved for him what he needed; for it, and the solipsist theory as well, lead only to the knowing subject, and not to the concrete human person at which Stirner aims with undeviating fanaticism. The means by which he undertakes the dissolution of possessed truth is the demonstration that it is conditioned by the person. "True is what is Mine." Here already lies hidden the fundamental principle of our day: "What I take as true is defined by what I am." To this, two statements may be taken as alternatives or as a combination—to Stirner's horror, certainly, but in logical consistency as an inescapable interpretation. There is first the statement, "And what I am is conditioned by my complexes," and second, the statement, "And what I am is conditioned by the class I belong to," with all their variants. Stirner is the involuntary father of modern psychological and sociological relativism, which for its part (to anticipate) is at once true and false.

But again Stirner is right, again he dissolves the dissolution. *Possessed* truth is not even a creature; it is a ghost, a succubus with which a man may succeed in effectively imagining he is living, but with which he cannot live. You cannot devour the truth; it is not served up anywhere in the world; you cannot even gape at it, for it is not an object. And yet, there does exist a participation in the being of inaccessible truth—for the man who stands its test and "makes it true." There exists a real relation of the whole human person to the unpossessed, unpossessable truth, and it is completed only in standing the test and "making it true." This real relation, whatever it is called, is the relation to the Present Being.

The rediscovery of truth, disenthroned in the human world by the semblance of truth, but in truth eternally irremovable—a truth which cannot be possessed but which can be served, and for which service can be given by perceiving *and* standing test—is accomplished by Kierkegaard in a paradoxical series of statements. It begins with the words, "He who communicates it [the truth] is only the Single One. Its communication is again only for the Single One; for this view of life, 'the Single One,' is the very truth." You must listen carefully. Not that the Single One exists, and not that he should exist, is described as the truth, but "this view of life," which consists in the Single One's existing, and which is therefore simply identified with him: to be the Single One is the communication of the truth, that is, the human truth. "The crowd," says Kierkegaard, "produces positions of advantage in human life," which "overlook in time and the world the eternal truth—the Single One." "You alone are the truth" is what Stirner says. "The Single One is the truth," is what is said here. That is the uncanny parabolic phenomenon of words to which I have referred. In a "time of dissolution" (Kierkegaard), there is the blank point at which the No and the Yes move up to and pass one another with all their power, but purely objectively and without consciousness. Now Kierkegaard continues: "The truth cannot be communicated and received except as it were before God's eyes, by God's help; so that God is there, is the medium as he is the truth. . . . For God is the truth and its medium." Thus "the Single One is the truth," and "God is the truth." That is so because the Single One "corresponds" to God. Hence Kierkegaard can say that the category of the Single One is and remains "the fixed point which can resist pantheist confusion." The Single One corresponds to God. For "man is akin to the Godhead." In Old Testament language, the Single One realizes the "image" of God precisely through having become a Single One. In the language in which alone a generation, wrestling with the problem of truth, succumbing to it, turning from it, but also exploring it ever anew, can understand, the Single One existentially stands the test of the appearing truth by "the personal existence expressing what is said" (rather, "what is unsaid"). There is this human side of truth—in human existence. God is the truth because he is; the Single One is the truth because he reaches toward his existence.

Stirner has dissolved the truth which is only noetic, and against all his knowledge and desire, cleared a space into which Kierkegaard's believed and tested truth has entered, the truth which can no longer be obtained and possessed by the *noesis* alone, but which must be existentially realized in order to be inwardly known and communicated.

But there is still a third and last point of contact and repulsion. For Stirner, every man is the Unique One if only he discards all ideological ballast (to which for him what is religious belongs), and settles down as owner of his world property. For Kierkegaard, "every, absolutely every man" "can and ought" to be "the Single One"—only he must . . . what, indeed, must he? He must become a Single One. For "the matter is thus: this category cannot be taught by precept; it is something that you can *do,* it is an *art,* . . . and moreover an art whose practice could cost the artist, in time, his life." But when we investigate closely to see if there is a more exact definition anywhere, even if not precisely one that can be taught by precept, one will be found—no more than one, no more than a single word, but it will be found: it is "obey." This is what is under all circumstances prohibited to Stirner's Unique One by his author. It is easy to discover that behind all Stirner's prohibitions to his Unique One this stands as the real, comprehensive, and decisive prohibition. With this one verb, with this word of "doing," Kierkegaard finally thrusts off the spirit which, without either of them knowing it, had approached so near, too near, in the time of dissolution.

And yet—the illumination of our time makes it visible—the two, primally different, primally strange to one another, concerning one another in nothing, but with one another concerning us, work together, not a hundred years ago but today, the one announcing decay as decay, the other proving the eternal structure to be inviolable. To renounce obedience to any usurping lord is Stirner's demand; Kierkegaard has none of his own —he repeats the ancient, misused, desecrated, outworn, inviolable "Obey the Lord." If a man becomes a Single One, "then obedience is all right," even in the time of dissolution, where otherwise obedience is not all right.

Stirner leads men out of all kinds of alleys into the open country where each is the Unique One and the world is his property. There they bustle in futile and noncommittal life, and nothing comes of it but bustle, till one after the other begins to notice what this country is called. Kierkegaard leads to a "narrow pass"; his task is "where possible to induce the many, to invite them, to stir them to press through this narrow pass, the 'Single One,' through which, note well, none passes unless he becomes the 'Single One,' since in the concept itself the opposite is excluded." I think, however, that in actual history the way to this narrow pass is through that open country that first is called individual egoism, and then collective egoism, and, finally, by its true name, despair.

But is there really a way through the narrow pass? Can one really become the Single One?

"I myself do not assert of myself," says Kierkegaard, "that I am that one. For I have indeed struggled for it, but have not yet grasped it, in the continued fight never forgetting that it is beyond human strength to be 'the Single One' in the highest sense."

"In the highest sense": that is spoken with a Christian and a christological reference; it manifests the paradox of the Christian task. But it is also convincing to the non-Christian. It has in it the assertion that no man can say of himself that he has become the Single One, since a higher sense of the category always remains unfulfilled beyond him; but it also has in it the assertion that every man can nevertheless become a Single One. Both are true.

"The eternal, the decisive, can be worked for only where one man is; and to become this one man, which all men can, means to let oneself be helped by God." This is the way.

And yet it is not the way, for reasons of which I have not spoken in this section and of which I now have to speak.

The Single One and His Thou

Kierkegaard's "to become a Single One" is, as we have seen, not meant Socratically. The goal of this becoming is not the "right" life, but entry into a relation. "To become" here means to become *for* something—"for" in the strict sense in which the circle of the person himself is transcended. It means to be made ready for the one relation which can be entered into only as the Single One, the one, the relation for whose sake man exists.

This relation is an exclusive one, the exclusive one, and this, according to Kierkegaard, means that it is the excluding relation, excluding all others; more precisely, that it is the relation which in virtue of its unique, essential life drives all other relations into the realm of the unessential.

"Everyone should be chary about having to do with 'the others,' and should essentially speak only with God and with himself," Kierkegaard says in his exposition of the category. Everyone, so it is to be understood, because everyone can be the one.

This joining of the "with God" with the "with himself" is a serious incompatibility that nothing can mitigate. All the enthusiasm of the philosophers for monologue, from Plato to Nietzsche, hardly touches the simple experience of faith that speaking with God is something *toto genere* different from "speaking with oneself," whereas, remarkably enough, it is not something *toto genere* different from speaking with another human being. For in the latter case, there is in common the fact of being approached, grasped, addressed, which cannot be anticipated in any depth of the soul; but in the former, there is no such common fact in spite of all the soul's adventures in doubling roles—games, intoxications, dreams, visions, surprises, overwhelmings, overpowerings—in spite of all tensions and divisions, and in spite of all the noble and powerful images for traffic with oneself. "Then one became two": that can never be *ontically* true, just as the reverse "one and one in one" of mysticism can never be ontically true. Only when I have to do with another essentially—that is, in such a way that he is no longer a phenomenon of my *I*, but instead is my *Thou*—do I experience the reality of speech with another, in the irrefragable genuineness of mutuality. *Abyssus abyssum clamat:* what that means the soul first experiences when it reaches its frontier and finds itself faced by one that is simply not the soul itself and yet is a self.

But on this point Kierkegaard seems to correct himself. In the passage in his Journals where he asks the question, "And how does one become a Single One?", the answer begins with the formulation, obviously more valid for the problem there under discussion, that one should be, "regarding the highest concerns, related solely to God."

If, in this statement, the word "highest" is understood as limiting in its content, then this is self-evident: the highest concerns can be put only to the highest. But it cannot be meant this way; that is clear from the other statement, "Everyone should. . . ." If both are taken together, then Kierkegaard's meaning is evident: the Single One has to do *essentially*—is not to be "chary"—only with God.

But thereby the category of the Single One, scarcely properly discovered, is already fatefully misunderstood.

Kierkegaard, the Christian concerned with "contemporaneity" with Jesus, here contradicts his master.

To the question—which was not merely directed at "tempting" him, but was rather a current and significant controversial question of the time—as to which was the all-inclusive and fundamental commandment, the "great" commandment, Jesus replied by connecting the two Old Testament commandments between which the choice lay: "Love God with all your might" and "Love your neighbor as one like yourself." [3] Both are to be "loved," God and the "neighbor" (that is, not man in general, but the man who meets me time and again in the context of life), but in different ways. The neighbor is to be loved "as one like myself" (not "as I love myself"; in the final reality, one does not love oneself, but one should rather learn to love oneself through love of one's neighbor); to him I should show love as I wish it shown to me. But God is to be loved with all my soul and all my might. By connecting the two, Jesus brings to light the Old Testament truth that God and man are not rivals. Exclusive love of God ("with *all* your heart") is, *because he is God,* inclusive love, ready to accept and include all love. It is not himself that God creates, not himself he redeems; even when he "reveals himself," it is not himself he reveals: his revelation does not have himself as object. He limits himself in all his limitlessness; he makes room for creatures, and so, in the love of him, he makes room for love to creatures.

"In order to come to love," says Kierkegaard about his renunciation of Regina Olsen, "I had to remove the object." That is sublimely to misunderstand God. Creation is not a hurdle on the road to God; it is the road itself. We are created along with one another and directed to a life with one another. Creatures are placed in my way so that I, their fellow creature, by means of them and with them, may find the way to God. A God reached by excluding them would not be the God of all beings in whom all being is fulfilled. A God in whom only the parallel lines of single approaches intersect is more akin to the "God of the philosophers" than to the "God of Abraham, Isaac, and Jacob." God wants us to come to him by means of the Reginas he has created, and not by renunciation of them. If we remove the object, then—we remove the object altogether. Without an object, artificially producing the object from the abundance of the human spirit and calling it God, this kind of love has its being in the void.

"The matter must be brought back to the monastery from which Luther broke out." So Kierkegaard defines the task of the time. "Monastery" can here mean only the institutional safeguarding of man from an essential relation—inclusive of his whole being—to any others but God. And certainly, to one so safeguarded, the orientation toward the point called God is made possible with a precision not to be attained otherwise. But what "God" means in this case is, in fact, only the end point of a human line of orientation. The real God is hardly to be reached by a line shorter than each man's longest, which is the line embracing the world that is accessible to him. For the real God is the Creator, and all beings stand before him in relation to one another in his creation, becoming useful for his creative purpose in living with one another. To teach an acosmic relation to God is not to know the Creator. Acosmic worship of a God of whom one knows, as does Kierkegaard, that it is of his grace "that he wills to be a person in relation to you," is Marcionism, and not even consistent Marcionism; for this worship does not separate the creator and the redeemer, as it would have to do were it consistent.

But one must not overlook the fact that Kierkegaard is not at all concerned to put Luther breaking out of the monastery in the wrong. On one occasion, he treats Luther's marriage as something removed from all natural personal life, from all directness between man and wife, as a symbolic action, a deed representing and expressing the turning point of the spiritual history of the West. "The most important thing," he makes Luther say, "is that it becomes notorious that I am married." But behind Luther's marrying Katharina, there emerges, unnamed but clear, Kierkegaard's not marrying Regina. "Put the other way round, one could say . . . in defiance of the whole nineteenth century, I cannot marry." Here there is added as a new perspective the qualitative difference between historical epochs. Certainly, on Kierkegaard's view, it is true for both ages that the Single One should not have to do essentially with any others but God; according to him, then, Luther speaks not essentially but only symbolically with Katharina: though bound to the world, he remains essentially worldless and "alone before God." But the symbolic actions are opposed: by the one, the word of a new bond with the world—even if, perhaps, in the end, a bond that is not binding—is spoken to the one century; by the other, the word of a new, and in any event binding, renunciation is spoken to the other century. What is the reason? Because the nineteenth century has given itself up to the "crowd," and "the crowd is untruth."

But now two things are possible. Either the bond with the world preached with his life by Luther is in Kierkegaard's view neither binding, nor "essential," nor necessary for the leading of Luther's age to God. But that would make Luther one who permits what is not binding to be effective as something that is binding; it would make him one who has a different thing to say for men than he has for God, who treats the sacrament as though it were fulfilled outside God; it would make Luther one whose symbolic action possessed no authority. Or else, on the other hand, the bond with the world preached with his life by Luther is in Kierkegaard's view binding, and essential, and necessary for leading to God. Then the difference between the two epochs, which is indubitably a qualitative one, would enter in what is basically independent of history, more so than birth and death—the relation of the Single One to God. For the essential quality of this relation cannot be of one kind in the former century and of another in the latter; it cannot in the one go right through the world, and in the other go over and beyond the world. Human representations of the relation change, the truth of the relation is unchangeable because it stands in eternal mutuality; it is not man who defines his approach to it, but the Creator who, in the unambiguity of his creation of man, has instituted the approach.

It is certainly not possible to speak of God other than dialectically, for he does not come under the principle of contradiction. Yet there is a limit to dialectic where assertion ceases, but where there is knowledge. Who is there who confesses the God whom Kierkegaard and I confess who could suppose in decisive insight that God wants Thou to be truly said only to him, but to all others merely an unessential and fundamentally invalid word—that God demands of us to choose between him and his creation? The objection is raised that the world as a fallen world is not to be identified with the creation. But what fall of the world could be so mighty that it could *for him* break it away from being his creation? That would be to make the action of the world into something more powerful than God's action, into something compelling him.

The essential is not that we should see things as standing out from God, nor as being absorbed in him, but that we should "see things in God," the things themselves. To apply this to our relations with creatures: only when all relations, uncurtailed, are taken into the one relation, do we set the circle of our life's world round the sun of our being.

Certainly that is the most difficult thing, and in order to be able to do it, man must let himself be helped from time to time by an inner-worldly "monastery." Our relations to creatures are always threatening to become incapsulated. As the world itself is sustained in its independence as the world through striving to be closed against God, though as creation it is open to him, so every great bond of man—though in it he perceives his connection with the infinite—protects itself vigorously against continually debouching into the infinite. Here the monastic forms of life in the world, the loneliness in the midst of life into which we turn as into hostelries, help us prevent the connection between the conditioned bonds and the one unconditioned bond from slackening. This, too, if we do not wish to see our participation in the Present Being die off, is an indispensable interchange, the systole of the soul to its diastole. The loneliness must know the quality of strictness, of a monastery's strictness, in order to do its work. But it must never wish to tear us away from creatures, never refuse to send us off to them. If it failed to do that, it would act contrary to its own law and would close us up, instead of enabling us, as is its function, to keep open the gates of finitude.

Kierkegaard does not conceal from us for a moment that his resistance to a bond with the world, his religious doctrine of loneliness, is based on personal nature and personal destiny. He confesses that he "ceased to have common speech" with men. He notes that the finest moment in his life is in the bath house, before he dives into the water: "I have nothing more to do with the world." He exposes before our eyes some of the roots of his "melancholy." He knows precisely what has brought him to the point of being chary about having to do with others, and of essentially speaking only with God and with himself. And yet, as soon as he begins with the "direct" language, he expresses it as an imperative: let *everyone* do so. Continually he points to his own shadow—and wants to leap across it. He is a being excepted and exposed, and certainly so are we all, for so is man as man. But Kierkegaard has moved to the fringe of being excepted and exposed, and maintains equilibrium only

by means of the extraordinary balance of his "author's" ret-
icently communicative existence with all the complicated safe-
guards of the "pseudonyms"; whereas we are not on the fringe,
and that is no "not yet" nor any sort of compromising, no
shirking of melancholy; it is organic continuance and grace of
preservation, and it is significant for the future of the spirit.
Kierkegaard behaves in our sight like a schizophrenic, who
tries to win over the beloved individual into "his" world as if it
were the true one. But it is not the true one. We, ourselves
wandering on the narrow ridge, must not shrink from the sight
of the jutting rock on which he stands over the abyss; nor may
we step on it. We have much to learn from him, but not the
final lesson.

Our rejection can be supported by Kierkegaard's own teaching. He describes "the ethical" as "the only means by which
God communicates with 'man'" (1853). The context of the
teaching naturally prevents us from understanding this in the
sense of an absolutizing of the ethical. But it must be understood in such a way that not merely an autarcic ethic, but also
an autarcic religion, is inadmissible, so that as the ethical cannot be freed from the religious neither can the religious be
freed from the ethical without ceasing to do justice to the
present truth. The ethical no longer appears here, as in Kierkegaard's earlier thought, as a "stage" from which a "leap" leads
to the religious, a leap by which a level is reached that is quite
different and has a different meaning; here it dwells in the
religious, in faith and service. This ethical can no longer mean
a morality belonging to a realm of relativity, time and again
overtaken and invalidated by the religious; it means *essential*
acting and suffering in relation to men, coordinated with the
essential relation to God. But only he who has to do with men
essentially can essentially act and suffer in relation to them. If
the ethical is the only means by which God communicates with
man, then I am forbidden to speak essentially only with God
and myself. And so indeed it is. I do not say that it is forbidden
to Kierkegaard on his rock, alone with the mercy of the Merci-
ful. I say only that it is forbidden to you and to me.

Kierkegaard is deeply conscious of the dubiousness which
arises from the negativizing extension of the category of the
Single One. "The frightful thing," he writes in his Journal, and
we read it, as he wrote it, with fear and trembling, "is that
precisely the highest form of piety, to let everything earthly go,
can be the highest egoism." Here obviously a distinction is

made according to motive, and the idea of egoism used here is an idea of motivation. If we put in its place an objective idea, an idea of a state of affairs, the statement is changed to a still more frightful one: "Precisely what appears to us as the highest form of piety—to let everything earthly go—is the highest egoism."

Is it true that the Single One "corresponds" to God? Does he realize the "image" of God solely by having become a Single One? One thing is lacking for that—and it is the decisive thing.

"Certainly," says Kierkegaard, "God is no egoist, but he is the infinite Ego." Yet thereby too little is said of the God whom we confess—if one dares to say anything at all. He hovers over his creation not as over a chaos; he embraces it. He is the infinite *I* that makes every *It* into his *Thou*.

The Single One corresponds to God when he, in his human way, embraces the bit of the world offered to him as God embraces his creation in his divine way. He realizes the image when, as much as he can in a personal way, he says *Thou* with his being to the beings living round about him.

No one can refute Kierkegaard as well as Kierkegaard himself. Reasoning with and judging himself, he corrects his own spirit from its depths, often before it has uttered its word. In 1843, Kierkegaard enters this unforgettable confession in his Journal: "Had I had faith, I would have remained with Regina." By this he means: "Had I really believed that 'with God all things are possible,' hence also the resolution of this—my melancholy, my powerlessness, my fear, my fateful alienation from woman and from the world—then I would have remained with Regina." But while he means this, he says something else too, namely, that the Single One, if he really believes, and that means if he is really a Single One (which, as we saw, he has become for the one relation of faith), can and may have to do essentially with another. And behind this there lurks the extreme that he who can and may also *ought* to do this. "The only means by which God communicates with man is the ethical." But the ethical in its plain truth means to help God by loving his creation in his creatures, by loving it towards him. For this, to be sure, one must let oneself be helped by him.

"The Single One is the category through which, from the religious standpoint, time and history and the race must pass." What is this "religious standpoint"? One beside others? The standpoint toward God, gained by standing aside from all others? God one object beside other objects, the chosen one beside the rejected ones? God as Regina's successful rival? Is that still God? Is that not merely an object adapted to the religious genius? (Note that I am not speaking of true holiness, for which, as it hallows *everything*, there is no "religious standpoint.") Religious genius? Can there be religious geniuses? Is that not a *contradictio in adjecto?* Can the religious be a specification? "Religious geniuses" are theological geniuses. Their God is the God of the theologians. Admittedly, that is not the God of the philosophers, but neither is it the God of Abraham, Isaac, and Jacob. The God of the theologians, too, is a logicized God, and so is the God even of a theology which will speak only dialectically and makes light of the principle of contradiction. So long as they practise theology, they do not get away from religion as a specification. When Pascal, in a volcanic hour, made that stammering distinction between God and God, he was no genius but a man experiencing the primal glow of faith; at other times, however, he was a theological genius, and dwelt in a specifying religion, out of which the happening of that hour had lifted him.

Religion as a specification misses its mark. God is not an object beside objects, and hence cannot be reached by renunciation of objects. God is, indeed, not the cosmos, but even less is he being *minus* cosmos. He is not to be found by subtraction, and not to be loved by reduction.

The Single One and the Body Politic

Kierkegaard's thought circles round the fact that he essentially renounced an essential relation to a definite person. He did not resign this casually, or in the relativity of the many experiences and decisions of life, or with the soul alone, but essentially. The essential nature of his renunciation, its downright positive essentiality, is what he wants to express by saying: "In defiance of the whole nineteenth century, I cannot marry." The renunciation becomes essential through its representing in concrete biography the renunciation of an essential relation to the world as that which hinders being alone before God. Moreover, as I have already said, this does not happen just once, as when a man enters a monastery and thereby cuts himself off from the world and lives outside it; it is peculiarly enduring: the renunciation becomes the center of a spiritual coordinate system whose every point is determined in relation to this point. It is in this way that the system receives its true existential character, by means of which it has given the impulse to a new philosophy and a new theology. And certainly, there belongs to this secularly significant concreteness of biography the curiously manifold motivation—which is undoubtedly legitimate, and is to be found piecemeal in the soundings of inwardness— of the renunciation which Kierkegaard expresses directly and indirectly, by suggestion and by concealment. But beyond that, on a closer consideration, it is to be noted that there arises, between the renunciation and an increasingly strong point of view an attitude which is finally expressed with penetrating clarity in the "Two Notes" to the "Report to History," a secret and unexpressed connection important for Kierkegaard and for us.

"The crowd is untruth." "This consideration of life, the Single One, is the truth." "No one is excluded from becoming a Single One except he who excludes himself by wanting to be crowd." And again: " 'The Single One' is the category of the spirit, of spiritual awakening and revival, and is as sharply as possible opposed to politics." The Single One and the crowd, the "spirit" and "politics": this opposition is not to be separated from that in which Kierkegaard enters the world, expressing it symbolically by means of his renunciation.

Kierkegaard does not marry "in defiance of the whole nineteenth century." What he describes as the nineteenth century is the "age of dissolution," the age of which he says that a single man "cannot help it or save it"; he can "only express that it is going under"—going under, if it cannot reach God through the "narrow pass." And Kierkegaard does not marry, in a symbolic action of negation, in defiance of this age, because it is the age of the "crowd" and the age of "politics." Luther married in symbolic action, because he wanted to lead the believing man of his age out of a rigid religious separation—which finally separated him from grace itself—to a life with God in the world. Kierkegaard does not marry (this, of course, is not part of the manifold subjective motivation, but is the objective meaning of the symbol) because he wants to lead the unbelieving man of his age, who is entangled in the crowd, to become single, to the solitary life of faith, to be alone before God. Certainly, "to marry or not to marry" is the representative question when the monastery is in view. If the Single One really must be, as Kierkegaard thinks, a man who does not have to do essentially with others, then marriage hinders him if he takes it seriously —and if he does not take it seriously, then, in spite of Kierke-

gaard's remark about Luther, it cannot be understood how he,
as an existing person, can be "the truth." For man, with whom
alone Kierkegaard is fundamentally concerned, there is the additional factor that in his view woman stands "quite differently
from man in a dangerous rapport to finitude." But there is
still something special to be made clear at this point.

If one makes a fairly comprehensive survey of the whole
labyrinthine structure of Kierkegaard's thought about renunciation, it will be recognized that he is speaking not solely of
a hard, hard-won renunciation of life with a person; but in
addition, he is speaking of the positively valued renunciation of
life with an impersonal being, conditioned by life with a person
—an impersonal being, which in the foreground of the happening is called "people," and in the background, "the crowd."
This being, however, in its essence—of which Kierkegaard
knows or wants to know nothing—rejects these descriptions as
caricatures and acknowledges as its true name only that of *res
publica,* in English the "body politic." When Kierkegaard says
the category of the "Single One" is "as sharply as possible opposed to politics," he obviously means an activity that has essentially lost touch with its origin, the *polis.* But this activity,
however degenerate, is one of the decisive manifestations of the
body politic. Every degeneration indicates its genus, and in
such a way that the degeneration is never related to the genus
simply as present to past, but as in a distorted face, the distor-
tion is related to the form persisting beneath it. The body
politic, which is sometimes also called the "world," that is, the
human world, seeks, knowingly or unknowingly, to realize in
its genuine formations the togetherness of men according to
creation. The false formations distort, but they cannot eliminate, the eternal origin. Kierkegaard, in his horror of malformation, turns away; but the man who has not ceased to
love the human world in all its abasement sees genuine form
even today. Supposing that the crowd is untruth, it is only a
state of affairs in the body politic; how truth is here related to
untruth must be part and parcel of the true question to the
Single One, and the warning against the crowd can be only its
preface.

From this standpoint, that special matter can be made clear
of which I said that it is an additional reason for Kierkegaard's
considering marriage to be an impediment. Marriage, essentially
understood, brings one into an essential relation to the "world";
more precisely, to the body politic, to its malformation and its

genuine form, to its sickness and its health. Marriage, as the decisive union of one with another, confronts one with the body politic and its destiny—man can no longer shirk that confrontation in marriage; he can only prove himself in it or fail. The isolated person, who is unmarried or whose marriage is merely a fiction, can maintain himself in isolation; the "community" of marriage is part of the great community, contributing its own problems to the general problems, bound up with its hope of salvation to the hope of the great being that in its most miserable state is called the crowd. He who "has entered on marriage," who has entered into marriage, has taken in earnest, in the intention of the sacrament, the fact that the other *is*, the fact that I cannot legitimately share in the Present Being without sharing in the being of the other, the fact that I cannot answer the lifelong address of God to me without answering at the same time for the other, the fact that I cannot be answerable without being at the same time answerable for the other as one who is entrusted to me. But in this way, he has decisively entered into relation with otherness; and the basic structure of otherness, in many ways uncanny, but never quite unholy or incapable of being hallowed, in which I and the others who meet me in my life are inwoven, is the body politic. It is to this, into this, that marriage intends to lead us. Kierkegaard himself makes one of his pseudonyms, the "married man" of the *Stages*, express this, though in the style of a lower point of view which is meant to be overcome by a higher. But it is a lower point of view only when trivialized; there is no higher, because to be raised above the situation in which we are set never yields in truth a higher point of view. Marriage is the exemplary bond; it carries us as does no other into the greater bondage, and only as those who are bound can we reach the freedom of the children of God. Expressed with reference to the man: woman certainly stands "in a dangerous rapport to finitude," and finitude is certainly the danger, for nothing threatens us so sharply as the danger that we remain clinging to it. But our hope of salvation is forged on this very danger, for our human way to the infinite leads only through fulfilled finitude.

The Single One is not the man who has to do with God essentially, and only unessentially with others, who is unconditionally concerned with God, and conditionally with the body politic. The Single One is the man for whom the reality of relation with God as an exclusive relation includes and encompasses the possibility of relation with all otherness, and for whom the whole body politic, the reservoir of otherness, offers just enough otherness for him to pass his life with it.

The Single One in Responsibility

I say, therefore, that the Single One, that is, the man living in responsibility, can make even his political decisions properly only from that ground of his being where he is aware of the event as divine speech to him; if he lets the awareness of this ground be choked off by his group, he is refusing to give God an actual reply.

What I am speaking of has nothing to do with "individualism." I do not consider the individual to be either the starting point or the goal of the human world. But I consider the human person to be the irremovable central place of the struggle between the world's movement away from God and its movement toward God. This struggle takes place today to a very great extent in the realm of public life, not between group and group, but within each group. Yet the decisive battles in this realm as well are fought in the depth, in the ground or the groundlessness, of the person.

Our age is intent on escaping from the demanding "ever anew" of such an obligation of responsibility by a flight into a protective "once for all." The last generation's intoxication with freedom has been followed by the present generation's passion for bondage; the untruth of intoxication has been followed by the untruth of hysteria. He alone is true to the one Present Being who knows he is bound to his place—and precisely there free for his proper responsibility. Only those who are bound and free in this way can still produce what can be truly called community. Yet even today, the believing man, if he adheres to something that is presented in a group, may do right to join it. But belonging to it, he must remain submissive with his whole life, therefore with his group life as well, to the One who is his Lord. His responsible decision will thus at times be opposed to, say, a tactical decision of his group. At times, he will be moved to carry the fight for the truth, the human, uncertain-certain truth which is brought forward by the depth of his conscience, into the group itself, and thereby establish or strengthen an inner front within it. This can prove more important for the future of our world than all fronts that are drawn today between groups or between associations of groups; for this front, if it is everywhere upright and strong, may run as a secret unity across all groups.

What the right is none of the groups of today can come to know except through men who belong to them staking their own souls to discover and then reveal it, however bitter, to their companions—charitably if possible, cruelly if must be. Into this fiery furnace, the group plunges time and again, or it dies an inward death.

And if one still asks if one may be certain of finding what is right on this steep path, once again the answer is *no;* there is no certainty. There is only a chance; but there is no other chance but this. The risk does not ensure the truth for us; but it, and it alone, leads us to where the breath of truth is to be felt.

The Question

In the human crisis which we are experiencing today, these two have become questionable—the person and the truth.

We know from the act of responsibility how they are linked together. For the responsible response to exist, the reality of the person is necessary, whom the word meets and claims in the event; and the reality of the truth is necessary to which the person goes out with united being and which he is, therefore, able to receive only in the word, as the truth which concerns himself, in his particular situation, and not in any general way.

The question in which the person and the truth have today been placed is the question to the Single One.

The person has become questionable through being collectivized.

This collectivizing of the person is associated in history with a basically different undertaking in which I too participated and to which I must therefore confess now. It is that struggle of recent decades against the idealistic concepts of the sovereign, world-embracing, world-sustaining, world-creating *I*. The struggle was conducted (among other ways) by reference to the neglected creaturely bonds of the concrete human person. It was shown how fundamentally important it is to know at every moment of thought this as well—that the one who thinks is bound, in different degrees of substantiality, but never purely functionally, to a spatial realm, to an historical hour, to the human race, to a people, to a family, to a society, to a vocational group, to a community holding like convictions. This entanglement in the manifold *We*, when factually known, wards off the temptation of ideas of sovereignty: man is placed in a narrow creaturely position. But he is enabled to recognize that this is his true extent, for being bound means being bound up in relation.

But it happened that a tendency of a quite different origin and nature prevailed over the new insights, which exaggerated and perverted the perception of bonds into a doctrine of serfdom. Primacy is ascribed here to a collectivity. The collectivity receives the right to hold the person who is bound to it bound in such a way that he ceases to have complete responsibility. The collectivity becomes what really exists, the person becomes derivative. In every realm which joins him to the whole, he is to be deprived a personal response.

Thereby the immeasurable value which constitutes man is imperilled. The collectivity cannot enter instead of the person into the dialogue of the ages which the Godhead conducts with mankind. Human perception ceases, the human response is dumb, if the person is no longer there to hear and to speak. It is not possible to reduce the matter to private life; only in the uncurtailed measure of lived life, that is, only with the inclusion of participation in the body politic, can the claim be heard and the reply spoken.

The truth, on the other hand, has become questionable through being politicized.

The sociological doctrine of the age has exercised a relativizing effect, laden with consequences, on the concept of truth, by proving the dependence of thought on social processes, and thus the connection of thought with existence. This relativization was justified in that it bound the "truth" of a man to his conditioning reality. But its justification was perverted into the opposite when its proponents omitted to draw the basic boundary line between what can and what cannot be understood as conditioned in this way. That is, they failed to comprehend the person in his *total* reality, wooing the truth and wrestling for it. If we begin with the Single One as a total being, who wishes to know with the totality of his being, we find that the force of his desire for the truth can, at decisive points, burst the "ideological" bonds of his social being. The man who thinks "existentially"—that is, the man who stakes his life on his thinking—brings into his real relation to the truth not merely his conditioned qualities, but also the unconditioned nature, transcending them, of his quest, of his grasp, of his indomitable will for the truth, which also carries along with it the whole personal power of standing his test and "making his truth true." We shall certainly be able to make no distinction, in what he has, time and again, discovered as the truth, between what can and what cannot be derived from the social factor. But it is an ineluctable duty to affirm what cannot be so derived as a border concept, and thus to point out, as the unattainable horizon of the distinction made by the sociology of knowledge, what takes place between the underivable in the knowing person and the underivable in the object of his knowledge. This duty has been neglected. Consequently, the political theory of modern collectivisms was easily able to take over the principle which lay at hand, and to proclaim what corresponded to the (real or supposed) life interests of a group as its legitimate and unappealable truth. Over against this, the Single One could no longer appeal to a truth which could be known and tested by him.

This marks the beginning of a disintegration of human faith in the truth which can never be possessed, and yet may be comprehended in an existentially real relation; it marks the beginning of the paralysis of the human search for the truth.

"What I speak of," says Kierkegaard, "is something simple and straightforward—that the truth for the Single One only exists in his producing it himself in action." More precisely, man finds the truth to be true only when he stands its test and "makes it true." Human truth is here bound up with the responsibility of the person.

"True is what is Mine," says Stirner. Human truth is here bound up with the human person's lack of responsibility. Collectivisms translate this into the language of the group: "True is what is Ours."

But in order that man may not be lost, there is need of persons who are not collectivized, and of truth which is not politicized.

There is need of persons, not merely of "representatives" in some sense or other, chosen or appointed, who relieve those represented of responsibility, but also of "represented" who on no account let themselves be represented with regard to responsibility. There is need of the person as the unrelinquishable ground from which alone the entry of the finite into conversation with the infinite becomes possible.

There is need of man's faith in the truth as that which is

independent of him, which he cannot acquire for himself, but with which he can enter into a real life relationship; the faith of human persons in the truth as that which sustains them all together, in itself inaccessible but disclosing itself to him who really woos it in the fact of responsibility which awaits test.

That man may not be lost there is need of the person's responsibility to truth in his historical situation. There is need of the Single One who stands over against all being which is present to him, and thus also over against the body politic, and guarantees all being which is present to him, and thus also the body politic.

True community and true commonwealth will be realized only to the extent to which the Single Ones out of whose responsible life the body politic is renewed become real.

3

GOOD AND EVIL

The First Stage

Human life as a specific entity which has stepped forth from nature begins with the experience of chaos as a condition perceived in the soul.

Only through this experience and as its materialization could the concept of chaos, which is to be derived from no other empirical finding, arise and enter into the mythic cosmogonies.

In a period of evolution, which generally coincides with puberty without being tied to it, the human person inevitably becomes aware of the category of possibility, which of all living creatures is represented just in man, manifestly the only one for whom the real is continually fringed by the possible.

The evolving human person I am speaking of is disconcerted by possibility as an infinitude. The plenitude of possibility floods over his small reality and overwhelms it. Phantasy, the imagery of possibilities which, in the Old Testament, God pronounces evil because it distracts from his divinely given reality and plays with potentialities, imposes the form of its indefiniteness upon the definiteness of the moment. The substantial threatens to be submerged in the potential. Swirling chaos, "confusion and desolation" (Gen. 1:2), has forced its way in.

But as, in the stage I am speaking of, everything which appears or happens to man is transformed into motor energy, into the capacity and desire for action, so too the chaos of possibilities of being, having forced an entry, becomes a chaos of possibilities of action. It is not things which revolve in the vortex, but the possible ways of joining and overcoming them.

This impelling universal passion is not to be confounded with the so-called libido, without whose vital energy it naturally could not endure, but to reduce it to which signifies a simplification and animalization of human reality. Urges in the psychological sense are abstractions; but we are speaking of a total concrete occurrence at a given hour of a person's life. Moreover, these urges are, *per definitionem*, "directed toward something"; but lack of direction is characteristic of the vortex revolving within itself.

The soul driven round in the dizzy whirl cannot remain fixed within it; it strives to escape. If the ebb that leads back to familiar normality does not make its appearance, there exist for it two issues. One is repeatedly offered it: it can clutch at any object, past which the vortex happens to carry it, and cast its passion upon it; or else, in response to a prompting that is still incomprehensible to itself, it can set about the audacious work of self-unification. In the former case, it exchanges an undirected possibility for an undirected reality, in which it does what it wills not to do, what is preposterous to it, the alien, the "evil"; in the latter, if the work meets with success, the soul has given up undirected plenitude in favor of the one taut string, the one stretched beam of direction. If the work is not successful, which is no wonder with such an unfathomable undertaking, the soul has nevertheless gained an inkling of what direction, or rather *the* direction, is—for in the strict sense, there is only one. To the extent to which the soul achieves unification, it becomes aware of direction, becomes aware of itself as sent in quest of it. It comes into the service of good or into service for good.

Finality does not rule here. Again and again, with the surge of its enticements, universal temptation emerges and overcomes the power of the human soul; again and again, innate grace arises from out of its depths and promises the utterly incredible: you can become whole and one. But always there are, not left and right, but the vortex of chaos and the spirit hovering above it. Of the two paths, one is a setting out upon no path, pseudo-decision which is indecision, flight into delusion and ultimately into mania; the other is the path, for there is only one.

The same basic structure of the occurrence, however, only become briefer and harder, we reencounter in innumerable situations in our later lives. They are the situations in which we feel it incumbent upon us to make the decision which, from our person, and from our person as we feel it "purposed" for us, answers the situation confronting us. Such a decision can only be taken by the whole soul that has become one; the whole soul, in whatever direction it was turned or inclined when the situation came upon us, must enter into it; otherwise we shall bring forth nothing but a stammer, a pseudo-answer, a substitute for an answer. The situations, whether more biographical or more historical in character, are always—even though often behind veils—cruelly harsh, because the unrecoverable passage of time and of our lives is so, and only with the harshness of unified decision can we prove ourselves equal to them. It is a cruelly hazardous enterprise, this becoming a whole, becoming a form, this crystallization of the soul. Everything in the nature of inclination, of indolence, of habits, of fondness for possibilities, which has been blustering and swaggering within us, must be overcome, and overcome, not by elimination, by suppression, for genuine wholeness can never be achieved like that, never a wholeness where downtrodden appetites lurk in the corners. Rather must all these mobile or static forces, seized by the soul's rapture, plunge of their own accord, as it were, into the mightiness of decision and dissolve within it. Until the soul as form has such great power over the soul as matter, until chaos is subdued and shaped into cosmos, what an immense resistance! It is thus understandable enough that the occurrence—which at times, as we know to be the case with dreams encompassing a whole drama, lasts no longer than a moment—so frequently terminates in a persistent state of indecision. The anthropological retrospective view of the person (which indeed is incorrectly termed "view," for if our memory proves strong enough we experience such past occurrences with all our senses, with the excitation of our nerves and the tension or flaccidity of our muscles) announces to us as evil all these and all other indecisions, all the moments in which we did no more than leave undone that which we knew to be good. But is evil then not, by its nature, an action? Not at all; action is only the type of evil happening which makes evil manifest. But does not evil action stem precisely from a decision to evil? The ultimate meaning of our exposition is that it too stems primarily from indecision, providing that by decision we understand, not a partial, a pseudo decision, but that of the whole soul. For a partial decision, one which leaves the forces opposing it untouched, and certainly which the soul's highest forces, being the true constructional substance of the person purposed for me, watch, pressed back and powerless, but shining in the protest of the spirit, cannot be termed decision in our sense. Evil cannot be done with the whole soul; good can only be done with the whole soul. It is done when the soul's rapture, proceeding from its highest forces, seizes upon all the forces and plunges them into the purging and transmuting fire, as into the mightiness of decision. Evil is lack of direction, and that which is done in it and out of it is the grasping, seizing, devouring, compelling, seducing, exploiting, humiliating, torturing, and destroying of what offers itself. Good is direction, and what is done in it; that which is done in it is done with the whole soul, so that in fact all the vigor and passion with which evil might have been done is included in it. In this connection is to be recalled that Talmudic interpretation of the biblical pronouncement of God concerning imagination, or the "evil urge," whose whole vigor must be drawn into the love of God in order truly to serve him.

The foregoing is intended and able to give no more than an anthropological definition of good and evil as, in the last instance, it is revealed to the human person's retrospection, his cognizance of himself in the course of the life he has lived. We learn to comprehend this anthropological definition as similar in nature to the biblical tales of good and evil, whose narrator must have experienced Adam as well as Cain in the abyss of his own heart. But it is neither intended nor able to provide any criterion over and above that, neither for the use of theoretical meditation concerning the entities "good" and "evil," nor, certainly, for the use of the questioning man, who is not spared inquiry and investigation into what, in the sense of design, is good and what evil, groping and feeling his way in the obscurity of the problematics, and even doubt, as to the validity of the concepts themselves. The former and the latter will have to find their criterion, or their criteria, elsewhere, will have to achieve it otherwise: he who meditates seeks to learn something else than what happens, he who inquires cannot make his choice according to whether it will lead to his soul becoming whole. Between their requirements and our anthropological insight, there is only one link, which is, of course, an important one. It is the presentiment implanted in each of us, but unduly neglected in each, the presentiment of what is meant and purposed for him and for him alone—no matter whether by creation, or by "individuation"—and to fulfil which, to become which, is demanded of and entrusted to him, and the resulting possibility of comparison time and again. Here, too, there is a criterion, and it is an anthropological one; of course, by its nature, it can never extend beyond the sphere of the individual. It can assume as many shapes as there are individuals, and nonetheless is never relativised.

The Second Stage

It is far more difficult to ascertain the human reality corresponding to the myths of Ahriman's choice and Lucifer's downfall. It is in the nature of the matter that here the assistance of retrospection is only very rarely open to us; those who have once surrendered themselves to evil with their innermost being will hardly ever, not even after a complete conversion, be capable of that deliberate, reliably recollecting and interpreting retrospection which can alone advance our insight. In the literature of those able to recount their fate, we shall almost never encounter such a report; everything confronting us in this domain is, apparently of necessity, highly colored or sentimentalized, and so thoroughly that we are unable to distil out of it the occurrences themselves, inner and outer likewise. What psychological research on phenomena of a similar nature has brought to light are naturally purely neurotic borderline cases, and, with very few exceptions, not capable of illuminating our problem. Here our own observations, whose methods are adapted to that which is essential to our purpose, must set in. To supplement them, by far the richest contribution is offered by historical and, in particular, biographical literature. It is a question of concentrating our attention on those personal crises whose specific effect on the person's psychic dynamic is to render it obdurate and secretive. We then find that these crises are of two clearly distinguishable kinds: negative experiences with our environment, which denies us the confirmation of our being that we desire, underlie the one; negative experiences with oneself, in that the human person cannot say yes to himself, underlie the other—the only one that concerns us here. We will leave aside mixed forms.

We have seen how man repeatedly experiences the dimension of evil as indecision. The occurrences in which he experiences it, however, do not remain in his self-knowledge a series of isolated moments of non-decision, of becoming possessed by the play of the phantasy with potentialities, of plunging in this possession upon that which offers itself; in self-knowledge, these moments merge into a course of indecision, as it were into a fixation in it. This negativation of self-knowledge is, of course, again and again "repressed," as long as the will to simple self-preservation dominates the will to being-able-to-affirm-oneself. To the extent, on the other hand, to which the latter asserts itself, the condition will change into one of acute auto-problematics: man calls himself in question, because his self-knowledge no longer enables him to affirm and confirm himself. This condition now either assumes a pathological form, that is, the relationship of the person to himself becomes fragile and intricate; or the person finds the way out where he hardly expected it, namely through an extreme effort of unification, which astonishes him in its power and effectiveness, a decisive act of decision, precisely that, therefore, which in the amazingly apposite language of religion is called "conversion"; or a third process takes place, something entitled to a special status amongst the singularities of man, and to the consideration of which we must now turn.

Because man is the sole living creature known to us in whom the category of possibility is so to speak embodied, and whose reality is incessantly enveloped by possibilities, he alone amongst them all needs confirmation. Every animal is fixed in its this-being, its modifications are preordained, and when it changes into a caterpillar and into a chrysalis its very metamorphosis is a boundary; in everything together it remains exactly what it is, therefore it can need no confirmation; it would, indeed, be an absurdity for someone to say to it, or for it to say to itself: You may be what you are. Man as man is an audacity of life, undetermined and unfixed; he therefore requires confirmation, and he can naturally only receive this as individual man, in that others and he himself confirm him in his being-this-man. Again and again, the yes must be spoken to him, from the look of the confidant and from the stirrings of his own heart, to liberate him from the dread of abandonment, which is a foretaste of death. At a pinch, one can do without confirmation from others if one's own reaches such a pitch that it no longer needs to be supplemented by the confirmation of others. But not vice versa: the encouragement of his fellow-men does not suffice if self-knowledge demands inner rejection, for self-knowledge is incontestably the more reliable. Then man, if he cannot readjust his self-knowledge by his own conversion, must withdraw from it the power over the yes and no; he must render affirmation independent of all findings and base it, instead of on "judgment-of-oneself," on a sovereign willing-oneself; he must choose himself, and that not "as he is intended"—this image must, rather, be totally extinguished—but just as he is, as he has himself resolved to intend himself. They are recognizable, those who dominate their own self-knowledge, by the spastic pressure of the lips, the spastic tension of the muscles of the hand, and the spastic tread of the foot. This attitude corresponds to what I have called the third process, which leads out of auto-problematics "into the open": one need no longer look for being, it is here, one is what one wants and one wants what one is. It is of this that the myth is speaking when it recounts that Yima proclaimed himself his own creator. Just this too Prudentius reports of Satan, and the great legendary motif of the pact with him is clearly derived from the view that he who has achieved self-creation will be ready to assist men to it.

From this point, the meaning of that paradoxical myth of the two spirits, one of whom chose evil, not without knowing it to be evil, but as evil, is also revealed to us. The "wicked" spirit—in whom, therefore, evil is already present, if only *in statu nascendi*—has to choose between the two affirmations: affirmation of himself and affirmation of the order which has established and eternally establishes good and evil, the first as the affirmed and the second as the denied. If he affirms the order, he must himself become "good," and that means he must deny and overcome his present state of being. If he affirms himself, he must deny and reverse the order; to the yes position, which "good" had occupied, he must bring the principle of his own self-affirmation, nothing else must remain worthy of affirmation than just that which is affirmed by him; his yes to himself determines the reason and right of affirmation. If he still concedes any significance to the concept "good," it is this: precisely that which I am. He has chosen himself, and nothing, no quality and no destiny, can any longer be signed with a no if it is his.

This too explains why Yima's defection is called a lie. By glorifying and blessing himself as his own creator, he commits the lie against being, yea, he wants to raise it, the lie, to rule over being—for truth shall no longer be what he experiences as such, but what he ordains as such. The narrative of Yima's life after his defection says with super-clarity all that remains to be said here.

4

THE LOVE OF GOD AND THE IDEA OF DEITY: ON HERMANN COHEN

I. In those scribbled lines affecting us as cries of the very soul, which Pascal wrote after two ecstatic hours, and which he carried about with him until his death, sewn into the lining of his doublet, we find under the heading *Fire* the note: "God of Abraham, God of Isaac, God of Jacob—not of the philosophers and scholars."

These words represent Pascal's change of heart. He turned, not from a state of being where there is no God to one where there is a God, but from the God of the philosophers to the God of Abraham. Overwhelmed by faith, he no longer knew what to do with the God of the philosophers, that is, with the God who occupies a definite position in a definite system of thought. The God of Abraham, the God in whom Abraham had believed and whom Abraham had loved ("The entire religion of the Jews," remarks Pascal, "consisted only of the love of God"), is not susceptible of introduction into a system of thought precisely because he is God. He is beyond each and every one of those systems, absolutely and by virtue of his nature. What the philosophers describe by the name of God cannot be more than an idea. But God, "the God of Abraham," is not an idea; all ideas are absorbed in him. Nor is that all. If I think even of a state of being in which all ideas are absorbed, and think some philosophic thought about it as an idea—then I am no longer referring to the God of Abraham. The "passion" peculiar to philosophers is, according to a hint dropped by Pascal, pride. They offer humanity their own system in place of God.

"What!" cries Pascal, "the philosophers recognized God and desired not merely that men should love him, but that they should reach their level and then stop!" It is precisely because the philosophers replace him by the image of images, the idea, that they remove themselves and remove the rest of us furthest from him. There is no alternative. One must choose. Pascal chose, during one of those all-overthrowing moments, when he felt his sick-bed prayer was answered: "To be apart from the world, divested of all things, lonely in your Presence, in order to respond to your justice with all the motions of my heart."

Pascal himself, to be sure, was not a philosopher but a mathematician, and it is easier for a mathematician to turn his back on the God of the philosophers than for a philosopher. For the philosopher, if he were really to wish to turn his back on that God, would be compelled to renounce the attempt to include God in his system in any conceptual form. Instead of including God as one theme among others, that is, as the highest theme of all, his philosophy both wholly and in part would be compelled to point toward God, without actually dealing with him. This means that the philosopher would be compelled to recognize and admit the fact that his idea of the Absolute was dissolving at the point where the Absolute *lives;* that it was dissolving at the point where the Absolute is loved; because at that point the Absolute is no longer the "Absolute" about which one may philosophize, but God.

II.   Those who wish clearly to grasp the nature of the endless and hopeless struggle which lay in wait for the philosopher of the critical period should read the very long notes in Kant's unfinished posthumous work, written over a period of seven years during his old age. They reveal a scene of incomparable existential tragedy. Kant calls the principle constituting the transition to the completion of the transcendental philosophy by the name of the "Principle of Transcendental Theology"; here his concern is with the questions, "What is God?" and "Is there a God?"

Kant explains: "The function of transcendental philosophy is still unresolved: Is there a God?" As long as there was no reply to that question, the task of his philosophy was still unfulfilled; at the end of his days, when his spiritual powers were waning, it was "still unresolved." He toiled on at this problem, constantly increasing his efforts, from time to time weaving the answer, yet time and again unraveling the woof. He reached an extreme formulation: "To think him and to believe in him is an identical act." Furthermore, "the thought of him is at one and the same time the belief in him and his personality." But this faith does not result in God's becoming existent for the philosophy of the philosopher. "God is not an entity outside of me, but merely a thought within me." Or, as Kant says on another occasion, "merely a moral relation within me."

Nevertheless, he possesses a certain kind of "reality." "God is only an idea of reason, but one possessing the greatest practical internal and external reality." Yet it is obvious that this kind of reality is not adequate to make the thought about God identical with the "belief in him and his personality." Transcendental philosophy, whose task was to ascertain whether there is a God, finally found itself compelled to state: "It is preposterous to ask whether there is a God."

The contradiction goes even deeper when Kant treats belief from this point of view. He incidentally outlines a fundamental distinction between "to believe God" and "to believe in God." "To believe God" obviously means God's being the ideational content of one's faith. This is a deduction from the fact that "to believe in God" means in the terminology of Kant, as he himself expressly states, to believe in a living God. To believe in God means, therefore, to stand in a personal relationship to that God, a relationship in which it is possible to stand only toward a living entity.

This distinction becomes still clearer through Kant's addendum: to believe "not in an entity which is only an idol and is not a personality." It follows that a God who is not a living personality is an idol. Kant comes that close at this point to the *reality* of faith. But he does not permit its validity to stand. His system compels him decisively to restrict what he has said. The same page of manuscript contains the following passage: "The idea of God as a living God is nothing but the inescapable fate of man." But if the idea of God is only that, then it is totally impossible to "believe in God" legitimately; that is, it is impossible to stand in a personal relationship with him. Man, declares the philosopher, is compelled to believe in him the moment he thinks God. But the philosopher is compelled to withdraw the character of truth from this faith, and together with it the character of reality (any reality, that is, which is more than merely psychological). Here, apparently of necessity, that which was decisive for Pascal, as it was for Abraham, is missing—namely, the love of God.

III. But a philosopher who has been overwhelmed by faith *must* speak of love.

Hermann Cohen, the last in the series of great disciples of Kant, is a shining example of a philosopher who has been overwhelmed by faith.

Belief in God was an important point in Cohen's system of thought as early as in his youth, when it interested him as a psychological phenomenon. His explanations of "the origin of the mythology of gods" and of the "poetic act" involved in "god-creating fantasy," contained in his study on "Mythological Conceptions Concerning God and Soul" which appeared in 1868 in Steinthal's periodical, *Zeitschrift fuer Voelkerpsychologie,* was an expression of this interest. Faith was there treated as relative to psychological distinction; but in the course of the development of Cohen's philosophical system faith's status as an independent concept, distinct from knowledge, was to become questionable.

In his "Ethics of Pure Will" (1904), Cohen writes: "God must not become the content of belief, if that belief is to mean something distinct from knowledge." Of the two kinds of belief which Kant distinguishes in his posthumous work, namely, "to believe God" (that is, to introduce the idea of God into a system of knowledge), and "to believe in a living God" (that is, to have a vital relationship to him as a living entity), Cohen rejects the second even more strongly than Kant. In this way, he means to overcome the "great equivocality" of the word "belief." Whereas Kant saw in the idea of God only the "fate" of the human species, Cohen wishes to "separate the concept of life from the concept of God." He finds support for his argument in Maimonides (though he limited the extent of that support three years later, saying that Maimonides had been careful to distinguish between the concept of life when applied to God and the same concept when applied to man, a distinction on the part of Maimonides which entirely differs from Cohen's distinction).

God is an idea for Cohen, as he was for Kant. "We call God an idea," says Cohen, "meaning the center of all ideas, the idea of truth." God is not a personality; as such he only appears "within the confines of myth." And he is no existence at all, neither a natural existence nor a spiritual, "just as in general the idea cannot be linked with the concept of existence." The concept of God is introduced into the structure of ethical thought, because, as the idea of truth, it is instrumental in establishing the unity of nature and morality. This view of God as an idea Cohen regards as "the true religiosity," which can evolve only when every relation involving belief in a living God is shown to be problematical, and nullified. God's only place is within a system of thought. The system defends itself with stupendous vigor against the living God who is bound to make questionable its perfection, and even its absolute authority. Cohen, the thinker, defends himself against the belief which, rising out of an ancient heritage, threatens to overwhelm him. He defends himself with success, the success of the system-creator. Cohen has constructed the last home for the God of the philosophers.

And yet Cohen was overwhelmed by faith in more exemplary fashion than any other of the contemporary philosophers, although his labors to incorporate God into a system were in no way hindered. On the contrary: from that moment, his labors turned into an admirable wrestling with his own experience.

Cohen objectified the results of his succumbing to faith by merging it in his system of concepts. Nowhere in his writings does he directly state it, but the evidence is striking. When was it that the decisive change occurred?

IV. The answer lies in the change that crept into Cohen's way of thinking about the love of God. It was only at a late period that Cohen, who concurrently with the development of his system was dealing in a series of essays with the heritage of the Jewish faith, gave an adequate place to the cornerstone of that faith, the love of God, the essential means by which the Jewish faith realized its full and unique value. Only three years after the "Ethics," in his important research into "Religion and Morality," whose formulations, even keener than those of the "Ethics," interdict "interest in the so-called person of God and the so-called living God," declaring that the prophets of Israel "combated" the direct relation between man and God, do we find a new note about the love of God. "The more that the knowledge of God is simultaneously felt to be love of God, the more passionate becomes the battle for faith, the struggle for the knowledge of God and for the love of God." It is evident that at this point Cohen is beginning to approach the *vital* character of faith. Yet the love of God still remains something abstract and not given to investigation.

Once again, three years later, Cohen's short essay on "The Love of Religion" begins with the curious sentence, "The love of God is the love of religion," and its first section ends with the no less curious sentence, "The love of God is therefore the knowledge of morality." If we carefully consider the two uses of the word "is," we are able to distinguish a purpose: which is to classify something as yet unclassified but nevertheless obtruding as central; to classify it by a process of identification with something else already comprehended, and thus put it in its place. But that identification does not prove successful. All that is necessary to see this clearly is to compare the above-cited sentences with any one of the biblical verses which enjoin or praise the love of God, which are the origin of that concept. What Cohen is enjoining and praising at this point is something essentially and qualitatively different from the love of religion and the knowledge of morality, although it includes both. Yet in Cohen's revision of his Berlin lectures of 1913-14, published in 1915 under the title, "The Concept of Religion in the System of Philosophy," he gives expression to a love which does away once and for all with that curious "is."

"If I love God," says Cohen (and this use of his of "I" touches the heart of the reader, like every genuine "I" in the work of every genuine philosopher), "then I no longer think him . . ." (and that "no longer" is almost direct testimony) ". . . only the sponsor of earthly morals. . . ." But what? But the avenger of the poor in world history! "It is that avenger of the poor whom I love." And later, to the same effect: "I love in God the father of man." At this point, "father" means the "shield and aid of the poor," for "Man is revealed to me in the poor man."

How long a way have we come from the "love of religion"! Yet the new element in Cohen is expressed with even greater clarity and energy: "Therefore shall the love of God exceed all knowledge. . . . A man's consciousness is completely filled when he loves God. Therefore, this knowledge, which absorbs all others, is no longer merely knowledge, but love." And it is extremely logical that the biblical commandment to love God is cited and interpreted at this point in the same connection: "I cannot love God without devoting my whole heart as living for the sake of my fellow-men, without devoting my entire soul as responsive to all the spiritual trends in the world around me, without devoting all my force to this God in his correlation with man."

At this point I wish to introduce an objection related, admittedly, not to these statements of Cohen's, but to another that has a connection with them. Cohen speaks of the paradox "that I have to love man." "Worm that I am," he continues, "consumed by passions, cast as bait for egoism, I must nevertheless love man. If I am able to do so, and so far as I am able to do so, I shall be able to love God." Strong words these, yet the lives of many important persons controvert the last sentence. The teaching of the Bible overcomes the paradox in a precisely contrary fashion. The Bible knows that it is impossible to command the love of man. I am incapable of feeling love toward every man, though God himself command me. The Bible does not directly enjoin the love of man, but by using the dative puts it rather in the form of an *act* of love (Lev. 19:18, 34). I must act lovingly toward my *rea*, my "companion" (usually translated "my neighbor"), that is toward every man with whom I deal in the course of my life, including the *ger*, the "stranger" or "sojourner"; I must bestow the favors of love on him, I must treat him with love as one who is "like unto me." (I must love "to him"; a construction found only in these two verses in the Bible.) Of course I must love him not merely with superficial gestures but with an essential relationship. It lies within my power to will it, and so I can accept the commandment. It is not my will which gives me the emotion of love toward my "neighbor" aroused within me by my behavior.

On the other hand, the Torah commands one to love God (Deut. 6:5; 10:12; 11:1); only in that connection does it enjoin heartfelt love of the sojourner who is one's "neighbor" (Deut. 10:19)—because God loves the sojourner. If I love God, in the course of loving him, I come to love the one whom God loves, too. I can love God as God from the moment I know him; and Israel, to whom the commandment is addressed, does know him. Thus I can accept the injunction to love my fellowman.

Cohen is, to be sure, actually referring to something else. For now he raises the question whether he should take offense at God's being "only an idea." "Why should I not be able," he replies, "to love ideas? What is man after all but a social idea, and yet I can love him as an individual only through and by virtue of that fact. Therefore, strictly considered, I can only love the social idea of man."

To me, it seems otherwise. Only if and because I love this or that specific man can I elevate my relation to the social idea of man into that emotional relationship involving my whole being which I am entitled to call by the name of love. And what of God? Franz Rosenzweig warned us that Cohen's idea of God should not be taken to mean that God is "only an idea" in Cohen's eyes. The warning is pertinent; Rosenzweig is right to emphasize that an idea for Cohen is not "only an idea." Yet, at the same time, we must not ignore that other "only," whose meaning is quite different indeed in Cohen's phrase, "a God who is only an idea." Let us, if we will, describe our relation to the idea of the beautiful and the idea of the good by the name of love—though in my opinion all this has content and value for the soul only in being rendered concrete and made real. But to love God differs from that relationship in essential quality. He who loves God loves him precisely insofar as he is not "only an idea," and can love him *because* he is not "only an idea." And I permit myself to say that though Cohen indeed thought of God as an idea, Cohen too loved him as— God.

V. In the great work prepared after "The Concept of Religion," and posthumously published under the title of "Religion of Reason from the Sources of Judaism," Cohen returns with even greater prominence to this problem: "How can one love an idea?"—and replies: "How can one love anything save an idea?" He substantiates his reply by saying: "For even in the love of the senses one loves only the idealized person, only the idea of the person." Yet even if it were correct that in the love of "the senses" (or more correctly, in the love which comprehends sensuality), one loves only the idealized person, that does not at all mean that nothing more than the idea of the person is loved; even the idealized person remains a person, and has not been transformed into an idea. It is only because the person whom I idealize actually exists that I can love the idealized one. Even though for Dante it was *la gloriosa donna della mia mente*, yet the decisive fact is that first he saw the real Beatrice, who set the "spirit of life" trembling in him. But does not the motive force which enables and empowers us to idealize a beloved person arise from the deepest substance of that beloved person? Is not the true idealization in the deepest sense a *discovery* of the essential self meant by God in creating the person whom I love?

"The love of men for God," says Cohen, "is the love of the moral ideal. I can love only the ideal, and I can comprehend the ideal in no other way save by loving it." Even on this level, the very highest for the philosopher who is overwhelmed by faith, he declares what the love of God is, and not what it includes. But man's love for God is *not* love of the moral ideal; it only includes that love. He who loves God only as the moral ideal is bound soon to reach the point of despair at the conduct of the world where, hour after hour, all the principles of his moral idealism are apparently contradicted. Job despairs because God and the moral ideal seem diverse to him. But he who answered Job out of the tempest is more exalted even than the ideal sphere. He is not the archetype of the ideal, but he contains the archetype. He issues forth the ideal, but does not exhaust himself in the issuing. The unity of God is not the Good; it is the Supergood. God desires that men should follow his revelation, yet at the same time he wishes to be accepted and loved in his deepest concealment. He who loves God loves the ideal and loves God more than the ideal. He knows himself to be loved by God, not by the ideal, not by an idea, but even by him whom ideality cannot grasp, namely, by that *absolute personality* we call God. Can this be taken to mean that God "is" a personality? The absolute character of his personality, that paradox of paradoxes, prohibits any such statement. It only means that God loves as a personality and that he wishes to be loved like a personality. And if he was not a person in himself, he, so to speak, became one in creating man, in order to love man and be loved by him—in order to love me and be loved by me. For, even supposing that ideas can also be loved, the fact remains that persons are the only ones who love. Even the philosopher who has been overwhelmed by faith, though he afterward continue to hug his system even more closely than before, and to interpret the love between God and man as the love between an idea and a person—even he, nevertheless, testifies to the existence of a love between God and man that is basically reciprocal. That philosophy too, which, in order to preserve the Being (*esse, Sein*) of God, deprives him of existence (*existentia, Dasein*), indicates however unintentionally the bridge standing indestructibly on the two pillars, one imperishable and the other ever crumbling, God and man.

VI. Cohen once said of Kant: "What is characteristic of his theology is the non-personal *in the usual sense,* the truly spiritual principle—the sublimation of God into an idea." And he adds: "And nothing less than this is the deepest basis of the Jewish idea of God." As far as Kant is concerned, Cohen was correct in this judgment. But throughout Kant's posthumous work we can see emerging every now and then resistance to this sublimation of God into an idea, a sublimation which later even more prominently prevents in Cohen the linking of the idea with the concept of existence.

"Under the concept of God," writes Kant, "Transcendental Philosophy refers to a substance possessing the greatest existence"; but he also qualifies God as "the ideal of a substance which we create ourselves." What we have in these notes, which sometimes appear chaotic, are the records of a suit at law, the last phase which the thought of the idea of God assumes for its thinker, of a suit between the two elements, "idea" and "God," which are contained in the idea of God—a suit which time and again reverts to the same point, until death cuts it short. Cohen set out to put the idea into a sequence so logical as to make it impossible for any impulse to opposition to develop. Even when overwhelmed by faith, Cohen continued the struggle to preserve this sequence. In so doing, he was of the opinion that "the deepest basis of the Jewish idea of God" was on his side. But even the deepest basis of the Jewish idea of God can be achieved only by plunging into that word by which God revealed himself to Moses, "I shall be there" (Ex. 3:14; part of the phrase commonly translated "I am that I am"). It gives exact expression to the personal "existence" of God (not to his abstract "being"), and expression even to his living presence, which most directly of all his attributes touches the man to whom he manifests himself. The speaker's self-designation as the God of Abraham, God of Isaac, and God of Jacob (Exod. 3:15) is indissolubly united with that manifestation of "I shall be there," and he cannot be reduced to a God of the philosophers.

But the man who says, "I love in God the father of man," has essentially already renounced the God of the philosophers in his innermost heart, even though he may not confess it to himself. Cohen did not consciously choose between the God of the philosophers and the God of Abraham, rather believing to the last that he could succeed in identifying the two. Yet his inmost heart, that force from which thought too derives its vitality, had chosen and decided for him. The identification had failed, and of necessity had to fail. For the idea of God, that masterpiece of man's construction, is only the image of images, the most lofty of all the images by which man imagines the imageless God. It is essentially repugnant to man to recognize this fact, and remain satisfied. For when man learns to love God, he senses an actuality which rises above the idea. Even if he makes the philosopher's great effort to sustain the object of his love as an object of his philosophic thought, the love itself bears witness to the existence of the Beloved.

5

GOD AND THE SPIRIT OF MAN

This book discusses the relations between religion and philosophy in the history of the spirit, and deals with the part that philosophy has played in its late period in making God and all absoluteness appear unreal.

If philosophy is here set in contrast to religion, what is meant by religion is not the massive fulness of statements, concepts, and activities that one customarily describes by this name and that men sometimes long for more than for God. Religion is essentially the act of holding fast to God. And that does not mean holding fast to an image that one has made of God, nor even holding fast to the faith in God that one has conceived. It means holding fast to the existing God. The earth would not hold fast to its conception of the sun (if it had one), nor to its connection with it, but to the sun itself.

In contrast to religion so understood, philosophy is here regarded as the process, reaching from the time when reflection first became independent to its more contemporary crisis, the last stage of which is the intellectual letting go of God.

This process begins with man's no longer contenting himself, as did the pre-philosophical man, with picturing the living God, to whom one formerly only called—with a call of despair or rapture which occasionally became his first name—as a Something, a thing among things, a being among beings, an It.

The beginning of philosophizing means that this Something changes from an object of imagination, wishes, and feelings to one that is conceptually comprehensible, to an object of

108

thought. It does not matter whether this object of thought is called "Speech" (*Logos*), because in all and each one hears it speak, answer, and directly address one; or "the Unlimited" (*Apeiron*), because it has already leapt over every limit that one may try to set for it; or simply "Being," or whatever. If the living quality of the conception of God refuses to enter into this conceptual image, it is tolerated alongside of it, usually in an unprecise form, as in the end identical with it or at least essentially dependent on it. Or it is depreciated as an unsatisfactory surrogate, helpful to men incapable of thought.

In the progress of its philosophizing, the human spirit is ever more inclined to fuse characteristically this conception, of the Absolute as object of an adequate thought, with itself, the human spirit. In the course of this process, the idea which was at first noetically contemplated finally becomes the potentiality of the spirit itself that thinks it, and it attains on the way of the spirit its actuality. The subject, which appeared to be attached to being in order to perform for it the service of contemplation, asserts that it itself produced and produces being. Until, finally, all that is over against us, everything that accosts us and takes possession of us, all partnership of existence, is dissolved in free-floating subjectivity.

The next step already takes us to the stage familiar to us, the stage that understands itself as the final one and plays with its finality: the human spirit, which adjudges to itself mastery over its work, annihilates conceptually the absoluteness of the absolute. It may yet imagine that it, the spirit, still remains there as bearer of all things and coiner of all values; in truth, it has also destroyed its own absoluteness along with absoluteness in general. The spirit can now no longer exist as an independent essence. There now exists only a product of human individuals called spirit, a product which they contain and secrete like mucus and urine.

In this stage, there first takes place the conceptual letting go of God because only now philosophy cuts off its own hands, the hands with which it was able to grasp and hold him.

But an analogous process takes place on the other side, in the development of religion itself (in the usual broad sense of the word).

From the earliest times, the reality of the relation of faith, man's standing before the face of God, world-happening as dialogue, has been threatened by the impulse to control the power yonder. Instead of understanding events as calls which make demands on one, one wishes oneself to demand without having to hearken. "I have," says man, "power over the powers I conjure." And that continues, with sundry modifications, wherever one celebrates rites without being turned to the Thou and without really meaning its Presence.

The other pseudo-religious counterpart of the relation of faith, not so elementally active as conjuration but acting with the mature power of the intellect, is unveiling. Here one takes the position of raising the veil of the manifest, which divides the revealed from the hidden, and leading forth the divine mysteries. "I am," says man, "acquainted with the unknown, and I make it known." The supposedly divine It that the magician manipulates as the technician his dynamo, the gnostic lays bare —the whole divine apparatus. His heirs are not "theosophies" and their neighbors alone; in many theologies also, unveiling gestures are to be discovered behind the interpreting ones.

We find this replacement of I-Thou by an I-It in manifold forms in that new philosophy of religion which seeks to "save" religion. In it, the "I" of this relation steps ever more into the foreground as "subject" of "religious feeling," as profiter from a pragmatist decision to believe, and the like.

Much more important than all this, however, is an event penetrating to the innermost depth of the religious life, an event which may be described as the subjectivizing of the act of faith itself. Its essence can be grasped most clearly through the example of prayer.

We call prayer in the pregnant sense of the term that speech of man to God which, whatever else is asked, ultimately asks for the manifestation of the divine Presence, for this Presence becoming dialogically perceivable. The single presupposition of a genuine state of prayer is thus the readiness of the whole man for this Presence, simple-turned-towardness, unreserved spontaneity. This spontaneity, ascending from the roots, succeeds time and again in overcoming all that disturbs and diverts. But in this our stage of subjectivized reflection not only the concentration of the one who prays, but also his spontaneity, is assailed. The assailant is consciousness, the overconsciousness of this man here that he is praying, that he is *praying*, that *he* is praying. And the assailant appears to be invincible. The subjective knowledge of the one turning-toward about his turning-toward, this holding back of an I which does not enter into the action with the rest of the person, an I to which the action is an object —all this de-possesses the moment, takes away its spontaneity.

The specifically modern man who has not yet let go of God knows what that means: he who is not present perceives no Presence.

One must understand this correctly: this is not a question of a special case of the known sickness of modern man, who must attend his own actions as spectator. It is the confession of the Absolute into which he brings his unfaithfulness to the Absolute, and it is the relation between the Absolute and him upon which this unfaithfulness works, in the midst of the statement of trust. And now he too who is seemingly holding fast to God becomes aware of the eclipsed Transcendence.

What is it that we mean when we speak of an eclipse of God which is even now taking place? Through this metaphor we make the tremendous assumption that we can glance up to God with our "mind's eye," or rather being's eye, as with our bodily eye to the sun, and that something can step between our existence and his as between the earth and the sun. That this glance of the being exists, wholly unillusory, yielding no images yet first making possible all images, no other court in the world attests than that of faith. It is not to be proved; it is only to be experienced; man has experienced it. And that other, that which steps in between, one also experiences, today. I have spoken of it since I have recognized it, and as exactly as my perception has allowed me.

The double nature of man, as the being that is both brought forth from "below" and sent from "above," results in the duality of his basic characteristics. These cannot be understood through the categories of the individual man existing-for-himself, but only through the categories of his existing as man-with-man. As a being who is sent, man exists over against the existing being before which he is placed. As a being who is brought forth, he finds himself beside all existing beings in the world, beside which he is set. The first of these categories has its living reality in the relation I-Thou, the second has its reality in the relation I-It. The second always brings us only to the aspects of an existing being, not to that being itself. Even the most intimate contact with another remains covered over by an aspect if the other has not become Thou for me. Only the first relation, that which establishes essential immediacy between me and an existing being, brings me precisely thereby not to an aspect of it, but to that being itself. To be sure, it brings me only to the existential meeting with it; it does not somehow put me in a position to view it objectively in its being. As soon as an objective viewing is established, we are given only an aspect and ever again only an aspect. But it is also only the relation I-Thou in which we can meet God at all, because of him, in absolute contrast to all other existing beings, no objective aspect can be attained. Even a vision yields no objective viewing, and he who strains to hold fast an afterimage after the cessation of the full I-Thou relation has already lost the vision.

It is not the case, however, that the I in both relations, I-Thou and I-It, is the same. Rather where and when the beings around one are seen and treated as objects of observation, reflection, use, perhaps also of solicitude or help, there and then another I is spoken, another I manifested, another I exists than where and when one stands with the whole of one's being over against another being and steps into an essential relation with him. Everyone who knows both in himself—and that is the life of man, that one comes to know both in himself and ever again both—knows whereof I speak. Both together build up human existence; it is only a question of which of the two is at any particular time the architect and which is his assistant. Rather, it is a question of whether the I-Thou relation remains the architect, for it is self-evident that it cannot be employed as assistant. If it does not command, then it is already disappearing.

In our age, the I-It relation, gigantically swollen, has usurped, practically uncontested, the mastery and the rule. The I of this relation, an I that possesses all, makes all, succeeds with all, this I that is unable to say Thou, unable to meet a being essentially, is the lord of the hour. This selfhood that has become omnipotent, with all the It around it, can naturally acknowledge neither God nor any genuine absolute which manifests itself to men as of non-human origin. It steps in between and shuts off from us the light of heaven.

Such is the nature of this hour. But what of the next? It is a modern superstition that the character of an age acts as fate for the next. One lets it prescribe what is possible to do and hence what is permitted. One surely cannot swim against the stream, one says. But perhaps one can swim with a new stream whose source is still hidden? In another image, the I-Thou relation has gone into the catacombs—who can say with how much greater power it will step forth! Who can say when the I-It relation will be directed anew to its assisting place and activity!

The most important events in the history of that embodied possibility called man are the occasionally occurring beginnings of new epochs, determined by forces previously invisible or unregarded. Each age is, of course, a continuation of the preceding one, but a continuation can be confirmation and it can be refutation.

Something is taking place in the depths that as yet needs no name. Tomorrow even it may happen that it will be beckoned to from the heights, across the heads of the earthly archons. The eclipse of the light of God is no extinction; even tomorrow that which has stepped in between may give way.

PART II: *Of Social Life*

1

THE IDEA

Among the sections of the Communist Manifesto which have exerted the most powerful influence on the generations up to our own day is the one entitled "Der kritisch-utopistische Sozialismus und Kommunismus" (Critical-Utopian Socialism and Communism).

Marx and Engels were entrusted by the League of the Just with the formulation of a communist credo—an important preliminary to the convocation of a universal communist congress, the Union of all the Oppressed, planned for 1848. The League directorate decided that in this credo fundamental expression also be given to the "position as regards the socialist and communist parties," that is, a line of demarcation be laid down distinguishing the League from the affiliated movements, by which were meant primarily the Fourierists, "those shallow folk," as they are called in the draft of the credo which the central authority presented to the London congress of the League. In the draft written by Engels, there is as yet no mention of "utopian" socialists or communists; we hear only of people who put forward "superlative systems of reform," "who, on the pretext of reorganizing society, want to bolster up the foundation of existing society, and consequently of the society itself," and who are therefore described as "bourgeois socialists" to be attacked—a description which, in the final version, applies in particular to Proudhon. The distance between the Engels draft and the final version drawn up substantially by Marx is immense.

The "systems," those of Saint-Simon, Fourier, and Owen being mentioned (in Marx's original version Cabet, Weitling, and even Babeuf are also named as authors of such systems), are all described as the fruit of an epoch in which industry was not yet developed, and hence the "proletariat" problem was not yet grasped; instead, there appeared those same systems which could not be other than fictitious, fantastic, and utopian, having as their aim to abolish that very class conflict which was only just beginning to take shape, and from which the "universal transformation of society" was ultimately to proceed. Marx was here formulating afresh what he had said shortly before in his polemic against Proudhon: "These theoreticians are utopians; they are driven to seek science in their own heads, because things are not yet so far advanced that they need only give an account of what is happening before their eyes and make themselves its instruments." The criticism of existing conditions on which the systems are built is recognized as valuable explanatory material; on the other hand, all their positive recommendations are condemned as bound to lose all practical value and theoretical justification in the course of historical development.

We can only assess the political character of this declaration in the framework of the socialist-communist movement of the time if we realize that it was directed against the views which had prevailed in the League of the Just itself, and were supplanted by Marx's ideas. Marx characterized these views twelve years after the appearance of the Communist Manifesto as a "secret doctrine" consisting of a "hodge-podge of Anglo-French socialism or communism and German philosophy"; and to this he opposed his "scientific insight into the economic structure of bourgeois society as the only tenable theoretical basis." The point now, he says, was to show that it "was not a matter of bringing some utopian system or other into being, but of consciously participating in the historical revolutionary process of society that was taking place before our eyes." The polemical or anti-utopian section of the Manifesto thus signifies an internal political action in the strictest sense: the victorious conclusion of the struggle which Marx, with Engels at his side, had waged against the other so-called—or self-styled—communist movements, primarily in the League of the Just itself (which was now called the League of Communists). The concept "utopian" was the last and most pointed shaft which he shot in this fray.

I have just said: "with Engels at his side." Nevertheless, reference should not be omitted to a number of passages from the introduction with which Engels, some two years before the Manifesto was drafted, had prefaced his translation of a fragment from the posthumous writings of Fourier. Here, too, he speaks of those same doctrines which are dismissed as utopian in the Manifesto; here, too, Fourier, Saint-Simon, and Owen are quoted; here, too, a distinction is made in their works between the valuable criticism of existing society and the far less relevant "schematization" of a future one. But earlier he says: "What the French and the English were saying ten, twenty, even forty years ago—and saying very well, very clearly, in very fine language—is at long last, and in fragmentary fashion, becoming known to the Germans, who have been 'hegelizing' it for the past year or at best rediscovering it after the event, and bringing it out in a much worse and more abstract form as a wholly new discovery." And Engels adds word for word: "I make no exception even of my own works." The struggle thus touched his own past. Still more important, though, is the following pronouncement: "Fourier constructs the future for himself after having correctly recognized the past and present." This must be weighed against the charges which the Manifesto lays at the door of utopianism. Nor should we forget that the Manifesto was written only ten years after Fourier's death.

What Engels says thirty years after the Manifesto in his book against Dühring about these "three great utopians," and what passed with a few additions into the influential publication, *The Evolution of Socialism from Utopia to Science,* a little later, is merely an elaboration of the points already made in the Manifesto. It is immediately striking that again only the same three men, "the founders of socialism," are discussed, those very people who were "utopians" "because they could not be anything else at a time when capitalist production was so little developed," men who were compelled "to construct the elements of a new society out of their heads because these elements had not yet become generally visible in the old society." In the thirty years between the Manifesto and the anti-Dühring book, is it true that no socialists had emerged who, in Engels' opinion, deserved the epithet "utopian" as well as his notice, but who could not be conceded those extenuating circumstances, since in their day economic conditions were already developed and the "social tasks" no longer "hidden"? To name only one, and of course the greatest, Proudhon—one of whose earlier books, *The Economic Contradictions or the Philosophy of Poverty*, Marx had attacked in his famous polemic written before the Manifesto—from Proudhon a series of important works had meanwhile appeared which no scientific theory about the social situation and the social tasks could afford to overlook; did Proudhon also (from whose book, albeit attacked by Marx, the Communist Manifesto had borrowed the concept of the "socialist utopia") belong to the utopians, but to those who could not be justified? True, in the Manifesto he had been named as an example of the "conservative or bourgeois socialists," and in the polemic against him, Marx had declared that Proudhon was far inferior to the socialists "because he has neither sufficient courage nor sufficient insight to raise himself, if only speculatively, above the bourgeois horizon"; and after Proudhon's death, he asserted in a public obituary that even then he would have to reaffirm every word of this judgment; a year later, he explained in a letter that Proudhon had done "immense harm," and by his "sham criticism and sham opposition to the utopians," had corrupted the younger generation and the workers. But still another year later, nine years before writing the anti-Dühring book, Engels stated in one of the seven reviews which he published anonymously on the first volume of Marx's *Capital*, that Marx wanted to "provide socialist strivings with the scientific foundation which neither Fourier, nor Proudhon, nor even Lassalle, had been able to give" —from which there clearly emerges the rank he awarded to Proudhon despite everything.

In 1844, Marx and Engels, in their book *The Holy Family*, had discovered in Proudhon's work on property a scientific advance which "revolutionizes political economy and makes a science of political economy possible for the first time"; they had further declared that not only did he write in the interests of the proletariat, but that he was a proletarian himself and his work was "a scientific manifesto of the French proletariat" of historic significance. And as late as May 1846, in an anonymous essay, Marx had called him a "communist," in a context, moreover, which makes it obvious that Proudhon was still a representative communist in his eyes at the time, some six months before the polemic was written. What had happened in the meantime to move Marx to so radical an alteration of his judgment? Certainly, Proudhon's *Contradictions* had appeared, but this book in no way represented a decisive modification of Proudhon's views; the violent diatribe against communist (by

which Proudhon meant what we would call "collectivist") uto-
pias is only a more detailed elaboration of his criticism of the
"communauté," which can be read in his first discussion on
property (1840), so highly praised by Marx. However, Proudhon's rejection of Marx's invitation to collaboration had preceded the *Contradictions.* The situation becomes clearer when
we read what Marx wrote to. Engels in July 1870, after the
outbreak of war: "The French need a thrashing. If the Prus-
sians win, the centralization of state power will subserve the
centralization of the German working class. German domination would furthermore shift the focus of the West European
workers' movement from France to Germany, and you have
merely to compare the movement in the two countries from
1866 up to now to see that the German working class is superior both in theory and in organization to the French. Its
supremacy over that of the French on the world stage would at
once mean the supremacy of *our* theory over Proudhon's, etc."
It is thus eminently a matter of *political* attitude. Hence it
must be regarded as consistent that Engels should describe
Proudhon soon afterwards in a polemic against him (*On the
Housing Question*) as a pure dilettante, confronting economics
helplessly and without knowledge, one who preaches and la-
ments "where we offer proofs." At the same time, Proudhon
is clearly labelled a utopian: the "best world" he constructs is
already "crushed in the bud by the foot of onward-marching
industrial development."

I have dwelt on this topic at some length because something
of importance can best be brought to light this way. Originally,
Marx and Engels called those people utopians whose thinking
had preceded the critical development of industry, the proletariat, and the class war, and who therefore could not have taken
this development into account; subsequently, the term was lev-
elled indiscriminately at all those who, in the estimation of
Marx and Engels, did not in fact take account of it, and of
these the late-comers either did not understand how to do so,
or were unwilling, or both. The epithet "utopian" thereafter
became the most potent weapon in the struggle of Marxism
against non-Marxian socialism. It was no longer a question of
demonstrating the correctness of one's own opinion in the face
of a contrary opinion; in general, one found science and truth
absolutely and exclusively in his own position, and utopianism
and delusion in the rival camp. To be a "utopian" in our age
means to be out of step with modern economic development,

and what modern economic development is we, of course, learn from Marxism. Of those "prehistoric" utopians, Saint-Simon, Fourier, and Owen, Engels had declared in 1850 in his *German Peasant War* that German socialist theory would never forget that it stood on the shoulders of these men, "who, despite all their fantasticalness and all their utopianism, must be counted among the most significant minds of all time, men who anticipated with genius countless truths whose validity we can now prove scientifically." But here again—and this is consistent from the political point of view—it is no longer considered possible that there might be living at the time men, known and unknown, who anticipated truths the validity of which would be scientifically proved in the future, truths which contemporary "science"—that is, the trend of knowledge which not infrequently identifies itself with science in general—was determined to regard as invalid, exactly as had been the case with those "founders of socialism" in their day. They were utopians as forerunners; these are utopians as obscurantists. They blazed the trail for science; these obstruct it. Fortunately, however, it is sufficient to brand them utopians to render them innocuous.

Perhaps, I may be allowed to cite a small personal experience as an instance of this method of "annihilation by labels." In Whitsun, 1928, there took place in my former home town of Heppenheim a discussion,[1] attended mainly by delegates from religious socialist circles, dealing with the question of how to foster anew those spiritual forces of mankind on which the belief in a renewal of society rests. In my speech, in which I laid particular emphasis on the generally neglected and highly concrete questions of decentralization and the status of the worker, I said: "It is of no avail to call 'utopian' what we have not yet tested with our powers." That did not save me from a critical remark on the part of the chairman, who simply relegated me to the ranks of utopian socialists and left it at that.

But if socialism is to emerge from the blind alley into which it has strayed, among other things the catchword "utopian" must be taken apart and examined for its true content.

2

IN THE MIDST OF CRISIS

For the past three decades, we have felt that we were living in the initial phases of the greatest crisis humanity has ever known. It grows increasingly clear to us that the tremendous happenings of recent years, too, can be understood only as symptoms of this crisis. It is not merely a crisis brought about by one economic and social system being superseded by another, more or less ready to take its place; rather are all systems, old and new, equally involved in the crisis. What is in question, therefore, is nothing less than man's whole existence in the world.

Ages ago, far beyond our calculation, this creature "man" set out on his journey—from the point of view of nature, a well-nigh incomprehensible anomaly; from the point of view of the spirit, an incarnation hardly less incomprehensible, perhaps unique; from the point of view of both, a being whose very essence it was to be threatened with disaster every instant, both from within and without, a being exposed to deeper and deeper crises. During the ages of his earthly journey, man has multiplied what he likes to call his "power over nature" at an increasingly rapid tempo, and he has borne what he likes to call the "creations of his spirit" from triumph to triumph. But at the same time, he has felt more and more profoundly, as one crisis succeeded another, how fragile were all his glories; and in moments of clairvoyance, he has come to realize that in spite of everything he likes to call "progress," he is not travelling along the high road at all, but is rather picking his precarious way along a narrow ridge between two abysses. The graver the crisis becomes, the more earnest and consciously responsible is the knowledge demanded of us, for although what is demanded is a deed, only that deed which is born of knowledge will help to overcome the crisis. In a time of great crisis, it is not enough to look back to the immediate past in order to bring the enigma of the present nearer to solution; we have to bring the stage of the journey we have now reached face to face with its beginnings, so far as we can picture them.

The essential thing among all those things which once helped man to emerge from nature, and notwithstanding his feebleness as a natural being, to assert himself—more essential even than the making of a "technical" world out of things expressly formed for the purpose—was this: that he banded together with his own kind for protection and for hunting, food gathering, and work, and did so in such a way that from the very beginning, and thereafter to an increasing degree, he faced the others as more or less independent entities, and communicated with them as such, addressing and being addressed by them in that manner. This creation of a "social" world out of persons at once mutually dependent and independent differed in kind from all similar undertakings on the part of animals, just as the technical work of man differed in kind from all animal works. Apes, too, make use of some stick they happen to find as a lever, a digging tool, or a weapon, but that is a matter of chance only; apes cannot conceive and produce a tool as an object constituted so and not otherwise, having an existence of its own. And again, many of the insects live in societies built up on a strict division of labor, but it is precisely this division of labor that governs absolutely their relations with one another; they are all as it were tools—their own society is the thing that makes use of them for its "instinctive" purposes; there is no improvisation, no degree, however modest, of mutual independence, no possibility of "free" regard for one another, and thus no person-to-person relationship. Just as the specific technical creations of man mean the conferring of independence on things, so his specific social creation means the conferring of independence on beings of his own kind. It is in the light of this specifically human idiosyncrasy that we have to interpret man's journey with all its ups and downs, as well as the point we have reached on this journey, our great and particular crisis.

In the evolution of mankind hitherto, this, then, is the line that predominates: the forming and reforming of communities on the basis of growing personal independence, their mutual recognition and collaboration on that basis. The two most important steps that the man of early times took on the road to human society can be established with some certainty. The first was that inside the individual clan, each individual, through an extremely primitive form of the division of labor, was recognized and utilized in his special capacity, so that the clan increasingly took on the character of an ever-renewed association of persons, each the vehicle of a different function. The second was that different clans would, under certain conditions, band together in quest of food and to conduct campaigns, consolidating their mutual help as custom and law that took firmer and firmer root, so that as once between individuals, so now between communities, people discerned and acknowledged differences of nature and function. Wherever genuine human society has since developed, it has always been on this same basis of functional autonomy, mutual recognition, and mutual responsibility, whether individual or collective. Power centers of various kinds split off, organizing and guaranteeing the common order and the security of all; but to the political sphere in the stricter sense, the state with its police system and its bureaucracy, there was always opposed the organic, functionally organized society as such, a great society built up of various societies, the great society in which men lived and worked, competed with one another and helped one another; and in each of the big and little societies composing it, in each of these communes and communities, the individual human being, despite all the difficulties and conflicts, felt himself at home as once he had felt in the clan, felt himself approved and affirmed in his functional independence and responsibility.

All this underwent increasing change as the centralistic political principle subordinated the decentralistic social principle to itself. The crucial thing here was not that the state, particularly in its more or less totalitarian forms, weakened and gradually displaced the free associations, but that the political principle with all its centralistic features percolated into the associations themselves, modifying their structure and their whole inner life, and thus politicized society more and more. The assimilation of society into the state was accelerated by the fact that, as a result of modern industrial development and its ordered chaos, involving the struggle of all against all for access to raw materials and for a larger share of the world market, there grew up, in place of the older conflicts between states, conflicts between whole societies. The individual society, feeling itself threatened not only by its neighbors' lust for aggression, but also by things in general, knew no way of salvation save in complete submission to the principle of centralized power; and in the democratic forms of society no less than in its totalitarian forms, it made this its guiding principle. Everywhere, the only thing of importance was the minute organization of power, the unquestioning observance of slogans, the saturation of the whole of society with the real or supposed interests of the state. Concurrently with this, there has taken place an internal development. In the monstrous confusion of modern life, only thinly disguised by the reliable functioning of the economic and state apparatus, the individual clings desperately to the collectivity. The little society in which he was embedded cannot help him; only the great collectivities, so he thinks, can do that, and he is all too willing to let himself be deprived of personal responsibility: he only wants to obey. And the most valuable of all goods—life between man and man—gets lost in the process: autonomous relationships become meaningless, personal relationships wither, and the very spirit of man hires itself out as a functionary. The personal human being ceases to be the living member of a social body, and becomes a cog in the "collective" machine. Just as his degenerate technology is causing man to lose the feel of good work and proportion, so the degrading social life he leads is causing him to lose the feel of community—precisely when he is so full of the illusion of living in perfect devotion to his community.

A crisis of this kind cannot be overcome by struggling to get back to an earlier stage of the journey, but only by trying to master the problems as they are, without minimizing them. There is no going back for us, we have to go through with it. But we shall only get through if we know *where* we want to go.

We must begin, obviously, with the establishment of a vital peace which will deprive the political principle of its supremacy over the social principle. And this primary objective cannot in its turn be reached by any devices of political organization, but only by the resolute will of all peoples to cultivate the territories and raw materials of our planet and govern its inhabitants *together*. At this point, however, we are threatened by a danger greater than all previous ones: the danger of a gigantic centralization of power covering the whole planet and devouring all free community. Everything depends on not handing the work of planetary management over to the political principle.

Common management is only possible as socialistic management. But if the fatal question for contemporary man is: can he or can he not decide in favor of, and educate himself up to, a common socialistic economy?, then the propriety of the question lies in an inquiry into socialism itself: what sort of socialism is it to be, under whose aegis is the common economy of man to come about, if at all?

The ambiguity of the terms we are employing is greater here than anywhere else. People say, for instance, that socialism is the passing of the control of the means of production out of the hands of the entrepreneurs into the hands of the collectivity; but again, it all depends on what you mean by "collectivity." If it is what we generally call the state—that is to say, an institution in which a virtually unorganized mass allows its affairs to be conducted by "representation," as they call it—then the chief change in a socialistic society will be this, that the workers will feel themselves represented by the holders of power. But what is representation? Does not the worst defect of modern society lie precisely in everybody letting himself be represented *ad libitum?* And in a "socialistic" society, will there not, on top of this passive political representation, be added a passive economic representation, so that, with everybody letting himself be represented by everybody else, we reach a state of practically unlimited representation, and hence, ultimately, the reign of practically unlimited centralist accumulation of power? But the more a human group lets itself be represented in the management of its common affairs, and the more it lets itself be represented from the outside, the less communal life there is in it, and the more impoverished it becomes as a community. For community—not the primitive sort, but the sort possible and appropriate to modern man— declares itself primarily in the common and active management of what it has in common, and without this it cannot exist.

The primary aspiration of all history is a genuine community of human beings—genuine because it is *community all through.* A community that failed to base itself on the actual and communal life of big and little groups living and working together, and on their mutual relationships, would be fictitious and counterfeit. Hence everything depends on whether the collectivity into whose hands the control of the means of production passes will facilitate and promote, in its very structure and in all its institutions, the genuine common life of the various groups composing it—on whether, in fact, these groups themselves become proper foci of the productive process; therefore, on whether the masses are so organized in their separate organizations (the various "communities") as to be as powerful as the common economy of man permits; therefore, on whether centralist representation goes only so far as the new order of things absolutely demands. The fateful question does not take the form of a fundamental either-or; it is only a question of the right line of demarcation that has to be drawn ever anew—the thousandfold system of demarcation between the spheres which must of necessity be centralized and those which can operate in freedom, between the degree of government and the degree of autonomy, between the law of unity and the claims of community. Unwearying scrutiny of conditions in terms of the claims of community, as something continually exposed to the depredations of centralist power; custody of the true boundaries, ever changing in accordance with changing historical conditions: such would be the task of humanity's spiritual conscience, a Supreme Court unexampled in kind, the right true representation of a living idea. A new incarnation is waiting here for Plato's "guardians."

Representation of an idea, I say, not of a rigid principle, but of a living form that wants to be shaped in the daily stuff of this earth. Community should not be made into a principle; it, too, should always satisfy a situation rather than an abstraction. The realization of community, like the realization of any idea, cannot occur once and for all time; always it must be the moment's answer to the moment's question, and nothing more.

In the interests of its vital meaning, therefore, the idea of community must be guarded against all contamination by sentimentality and emotionalism. Community is never a mere attitude of mind, and if it is feeling, it is an inner disposition that is felt. Community is the inner disposition or constitution of a life in common, which knows and embraces in itself hard "calculation," adverse "chance," the sudden access of "anxiety." It is community of tribulation, and only because of that is it community of spirit; it is community of toil, and only because of that is it community of salvation. Even those communities which call the spirit their master and salvation their promised land, the "religious" communities, are community only if they serve their lord and master in the midst of simple, unexalted, unselected reality, a reality not so much chosen by them as sent to them just as it is; they are community only if they prepare the way to the promised land through the thickets of this pathless hour. True, it is not "works" that count, but the work of faith does. A community of faith truly exists only when it is a community of work.

The real essence of community is to be found in the fact, manifest or otherwise, that it has a center. The real beginning of a community is when its members have a common relation to the center overriding all other relations: the circle is described by the radii, not by the points along its circumference. And the originality of the center cannot be discerned unless it is discerned as being transpicuous to the light of something divine. All this is true, but the more earthly, the more creaturely, the more attached the center is, the truer and more transpicuous it will be. This is where the "social" element comes in, not as something separate, but as the all-pervading realm where man stands the test; and it is here that the truth of the center is proved. The early Christians were not content with the community that existed alongside of, or even above, the world and they went into the desert so as to have no more community save with God, and no more disturbing world. But it was shown them that God does not wish man to be alone with him, and above the holy impotence of the hermit, there rose the brotherhood. Finally, going beyond St. Benedict, St. Francis entered into alliance with all creatures.

Yet a community had no need to be "founded." Wherever historical destiny had brought a group of men together in a common fold, there was room for the growth of a genuine community; there was no need of an altar to the city deity in their midst when the citizens knew they were united round— and by—the Nameless. A living togetherness, constantly renewing itself, was already there, and all that needed strengthening was the immediacy of relationships. In the happiest instances, common affairs were deliberated and decided not through representatives, but in gatherings in the market place, and the unity that was felt in public permeated all personal contacts. The danger of seclusion might hang over the community, but the communal spirit banished it, for here this spirit flourished as nowhere else, and broke windows for itself in the narrow walls, with a large view of people, mankind, and the world.

All this, I may be told, has gone irrevocably and for ever. The modern city has no agora, and modern man has no time for negotiations of which his elected representatives can very well relieve him. The pressure of numbers and the forms of organization have destroyed any real togetherness. Work forges other personal links than does leisure, sport again others than politics; the day is neatly divided, and the soul too. These links are material ones; though we follow our common interests and tendencies together, we have no use for "immediacy." The collectivity is not a warm, friendly gathering, but a great link-up of economic and political forces inimical to the play of romantic fancies, understandable only in terms of quantity, expressing itself in actions and effects—a thing to which the individual has to belong with no intimacies of any kind, but all the time conscious of his energetic contribution. Any "unions" that resist the inevitable trend of events must disappear. There is still the family, of course, which, as a domestic community, seems to demand and guarantee a modicum of communal life; but it too will either emerge from the crisis in which it is involved as an association for a common purpose, or else it will perish.

Faced with this medley of correct premises and absurd conclusions, I declare in favor of a rebirth of the commune. A rebirth—not a bringing back. It cannot, in fact, be brought back, although I sometimes think that every touch of helpful neighborliness in the apartment house, every wave of warmer comradeship in the lulls and "knock-offs" that occur even in the most perfectly "rationalized" factory, means an addition to the world's community content; and although a rightly constituted village commune sometimes strikes me as being more real than a parliament, still it cannot be brought back. Yet, whether a rebirth of the commune will ensue from the "water and spirit" of the social transformation that is imminent, on this, it seems to me, hangs the whole fate of the human race. An organic commonwealth—and only such commonwealths can join together to constitute a well formed and articulated race of men —will never build itself up out of individuals, but only out of small and ever smaller communities: a nation is a community to the degree that it is a community of communities. If from the crisis which today has all the appearance of disintegration, the family does not emerge purified and renewed, then the state will be nothing more than a machine stoked with the bodies of generations of men. The community that would be capable of such a renewal exists only as a residue. If I speak of its rebirth, I am not thinking of a permanent world situation, but an altered one. By the new communes—they might equally well be called the new cooperatives—I mean the subjects of a changed economy: the collectives into whose hands the control of the means of production is to pass. Once again, everything depends on whether they will be ready.

Just how much economic and political autonomy—for they will of necessity be economic and political units at once—will have to be granted to them is a technical question that must be asked and answered over and over again, but asked and answered beyond the technical level, in the knowledge that the internal authority of a community hangs together with its external authority. The relationship between centralism and decentralization is a problem which, as we have seen, cannot be approached in principle, but like everything that has to do with the relationship between idea and reality, only with great spiritual tact, with the constant and tireless weighing and measuring of the right proportion between them. Centralization—but only so much as is indispensable in the given conditions of time and place. And if the authorities responsible for the drawing and redrawing of lines of demarcation keep an alert conscience, the relations between the base and the apex of the power pyramid will be very different from what they are now, even in states that call themselves communist, that is, claim they are struggling for community. There will have to be a system of representation, too, in the sort of social pattern I have in mind, but it will not, as now, be composed of the pseudo-representatives of amorphous masses of electors, but of representatives well tested in the life and work of the communes. The represented will not, as they are today, be bound to their representatives by some windy abstraction, by the mere phraseology of a party program, but concretely, through common action and common experience.

The essential thing, however, is that the process of community building run all through the relations of the communes with one another. Only a community of communities merits the title of commonwealth.

The picture I have hastily sketched will doubtless be put away among the documents of "utopian socialism" until the storm turns them up again. Just as I do not believe in Marx's "gestation" of the new form, so neither do I believe in Bakunin's virgin birth from the womb of revolution. But I do believe in the meeting of idea and fate in the creative hour.

3

AN EXPERIMENT THAT DID NOT FAIL

The era of advanced capitalism has broken down the structure of society. The society which preceded it was composed of various societies; it was complex and pluralistic in structure. This is what gave it its peculiar social vitality, and enabled it to resist the totalitarian tendencies inherent in the prerevolutionary centralistic state, though many elements were very much weakened in their autonomous life. This resistance was broken by the policy of the French Revolution, which was directed against the special rights of all free associations. Thereafter, centralism in its new, capitalistic form succeeded where the old had failed, that is, in atomizing society. Exercising control both over the machine and, with its help, over the whole of society, capitalism wants to deal only with individuals, and the modern state aids and abets it by progressively dispossessing groups of their autonomy. The militant organizations which the proletariat erects against capitalism—trades unions in the economic sphere and the [labor] party in the political—are unable, in the nature of things, to counteract this process of dissolution, since they have no access to the life of society itself or to its foundations in production and consumption. Even the transfer of capital to the state could not modify the social structure, even were the state to establish a network of compulsory associations, since these latter, having no autonomous life, are unfitted to become the cells of a new socialist society.

From this point of view, the heart and soul of the cooperative movement is to be found in the trend in society toward structural renewal, toward the reacquisition, in new tectonic forms, of internal social relationships, toward the establishment of a new *consociatio consociationum*. It is, as I have shown, a fundamental error to view this trend as romantic or utopian merely because in its early stages it had romantic reminiscences and utopian fantasies. At bottom, it is thoroughly "topical" and constructive—that is to say, it aims at changes which, in the given circumstances and with the means at its disposal, are quite feasible. And psychologically speaking, it is based on a human need that is eternal, even though it has often been forcibly suppressed or rendered insensible: the need of man to feel that his own house is a part of some greater, all-embracing structure in which he is at home, the need to feel that the others with whom he lives and works all acknowledge and confirm his individual existence. An association based on community of views and aspirations alone cannot satisfy this need; the only thing that can do so is an association which makes for communal living. But here the cooperative organization of production or consumption proves, each in its own way, inadequate, because both touch the individual only at a certain point and do not mold his actual life. On account of their merely partial or functional character, all such organizations are alike unfitted to act as cells of a new society. Both of these partial forms have undergone vigorous development, but the consumer cooperatives only in highly bureaucratic forms, and the producer cooperatives in highly specialized forms, so that they are today less able than ever to embrace the whole life of society. The consciousness of this fact is leading to a synthetic form, the full cooperative. By far the most powerful effort in this direction is the village commune, where communal living is based on the amalgamation of production and consumption—production being understood not as agriculture alone, but as the organic union of agriculture and industry, with the handicrafts as well.

The repeated attempts that have been made during the last one hundred and fifty years, both in Europe and America, to found village settlements of this kind, whether communistic or cooperative in the narrower sense, have mostly met with failure.[2] I would apply the word "failure" not merely to those settlements, or attempts at settlements, which after a more or less brief existence either disintegrated completely or took on a capitalist complexion; I would also apply it to those that maintained themselves in isolation. For the real, the truly structural task of the new village communes begins with their *federation,* that is, their union under the same principle that operates in their internal structure. Hardly anywhere has this come about. Even where, as with the Dukhobors in Canada, a sort of federative union exists, the federation itself continues to be isolated and exerts no attractive or educative influence on society as a whole, with the result that the task never gets beyond its beginnings, and consequently there can be no talk of success in the socialist sense. It is remarkable that Kropotkin saw in these two elements—isolation of the settlements from one another and isolation from the rest of society—the efficient causes of their failure even as ordinarily understood.

The socialistic task can only be accomplished to the degree that the new village commune, combining the various forms of production, and uniting production and consumption, exerts a structural influence on the amorphous urban society. This influence will only make itself felt to the full if, and to the extent that, further technological developments facilitate and actually require the decentralization of industry; but even now a pervasive force is latent in the modern communal village, and it may spread to the towns. It must be emphasized again that the tendency we are dealing with is constructive and "topical": it would be romantic and utopian to want to destroy the town, as once it was romantic and utopian to want to destroy the machine, but it is constructive and "topical" to try to transform the town organically in closest possible alliance with technological developments, and to try to turn it into an aggregate composed of smaller units. Indeed, many countries today show significant beginnings in this respect.

As I see history and the present, there is only one all-out effort to create a full cooperative which justifies our speaking of success in the socialistic sense, and that is the Jewish village commune in its various forms, as found in Palestine. No doubt, it, too, is up against grave problems in the sphere of internal relationships, federation, and influence on society at large, but it alone has proved its vitality in all three spheres. Nowhere else in the history of communal settlements is there this tireless groping for the form of community life best suited to this particular human group, nowhere else this continual trying and trying again, this going at it and keeping at it, this critical awareness, this sprouting of new branches from the same stem and out of the same formative impulse. And nowhere else is there this alertness to one's own problems, this constant facing up to them, this tough will to come to terms with them, and this indefatigable struggle—albeit seldom expressed in words—to overcome them. Here, and here alone, do we find in the emergent community organs of self-knowledge whose very sensitiveness has constantly reduced its members to despair—but this is a despair that destroys wishful thinking only to raise up in its stead a greater hope which is no longer emotionalism but sheer work. Thus on the soberest survey and on the soberest reflection, one can say that in this one spot in a world of partial failures, we can recognize a non-failure— and, such as it is, a signal non-failure.

What are the reasons for this? There is no better way of getting to know the peculiar character of this cooperative colonization than by following up these reasons.

One element has been repeatedly pointed out—that the Jewish village commune in Palestine owes its existence not to a doctrine but to a situation, to the needs, the stress, the demands of the situation. In establishing the "kvutza," or village commune, the primary thing was not ideology, but work. This is certainly correct, but with one limitation. True, the point was to solve by collaborating certain problems of work and construction which Palestinian reality forced on the settlers; what a loose conglomeration of individuals could not, in the nature of things, hope to overcome, or even try to overcome, things being what they were, the collective could attempt to do and actually succeeded in doing. But what is called the "ideology"—I personally prefer the old but untarnished word "ideal" —was not just something to be added afterwards, that would justify the accomplished fact. In the spirit of the members of the first Palestinian communes, ideal motives joined hands with the dictates of the hour; and among the motives there was a curious mixture of memories of the Russian artel, impressions left over from reading the so-called "utopian" socialists, and the half-unconscious after-effects of the Bible's teachings about social justice. The important thing is that this ideal motive remained loose and pliable in almost every respect. There were various dreams about the future: people saw before them a new, more comprehensive form of the family; they saw themselves as the advance guard of the workers' movement, as the direct instrument for the realization of socialism, as the prototype of the new society; they had as their goal the creation of a new man and a new world. But nothing of this ever hardened into a cut-and-dried program. These men did not, as everywhere else in the history of cooperative settlements, bring a plan with them, a plan which the concrete situation could only fill out, but not modify. The ideal gave an impetus, but no dogma; it stimulated, but did not dictate.

More important, however, is that behind the Palestinian situation that set the tasks of work and reconstruction, there was the historical situation of a people visited by a great external crisis and responding to it with a great inner change. Further, this historical situation threw up an élite—the halutzim, or pioneers—drawn from all classes of the people, and thus beyond class. The form of life appropriate to this élite was the village commune, by which I mean not a single note, but the whole scale, ranging from the social structure of "mutual aid" to the commune itself. This form was the best fitted to fulfil the tasks of the nuclear halutzim, and at the same time the one in which the social ideal could materially influence the national idea. As the historical conditions have shown, it was impossible for this élite, and the form of life it favored, to become static or isolated; all its tasks, everything it did, its whole pioneering spirit made it the center of attraction and a central influence. The pioneer spirit (halutziut) is, in all its parts, related to the growth of a new and transformed national community; had it become self-sufficient, it would have lost its soul. The village commune, as the nucleus of the evolving society, had to exert a powerful pull on the people dedicated to this evolution, and it had not merely to educate its friends and associates for genuine communal living, but also to exercise a formative structural effect on the social periphery. The dynamics of history determined the dynamic character of the relations between village commune and society.

This suffered a considerable setback when the tempo of the crisis in the outer world became so rapid, and its symptoms so drastic, that the inner change could not keep pace with them. To the extent that Palestine was turned from the one and only land of the aliyah ("ascent") into a country of immigrants, a quasi-halutziut came into being alongside the genuine halutziut. The pull exerted by the commune did not abate, but its educative powers were not adapted to the influx of very different human material, and this material sometimes succeeded in influencing the tone of the community. At the same time, the commune's relations with society at large underwent a change. As the structure of the society altered, it withdrew more and more from the transforming influence of the focal cells; indeed, it began, in its turn, to exert an influence on them—not always noticeable at first, but unmistakable today—by seizing on certain essential elements in them and assimilating them to itself.

In the life of peoples, and particularly peoples who find themselves in the midst of some historical crisis, it is of crucial importance whether genuine élites (which means élites that do not usurp, but are called to their central function) arise, whether these élites remain loyal to their duty to society, establishing a relationship to it rather than to themselves, and finally, whether they have the power to replenish and renew themselves in a manner conformable with their task. The historical destiny of the Jewish settlements in Palestine brought the élite of the halutzim to birth, and it found its social nuclear form in the village commune. Another wave of this same destiny has thrown up, together with the quasi-halutzim, a problem for the real halutzim élite. It has caused a problem that was always latent to come to the surface. They have not yet succeeded in mastering it, and yet must master it before they can reach the next stage of their task. The inner tension between those who take the *whole* responsibility for the community on their shoulders and those who somehow evade it can be resolved only at a very deep level.

The point where the problem emerges is neither the individual's relationship to the idea, nor his relationship to the community, nor yet his relationship to work; on all these points, even the quasi-halutzim gird up their loins, and do by and large what is expected of them. The point where the problem emerges, where people are apt to slip, is in their relationship to their fellows. By this I do not mean the question, much discussed in its day, of the intimacy that exists in the small kvutza and the loss of this intimacy in the large kvutza; I mean something that has nothing whatever to do with the size of the commune. It is not a matter of intimacy at all; intimacy appears when it must, and if it is lacking, that's all there is to it. The question is rather one of openness. A real community need not consist of people who are perpetually together, but it must consist of people who, precisely because they are comrades, have mutual access to one another and are ready for one another. A real community is one which in every point of its being possesses, potentially at least, the whole character of community. The internal questions of a community are thus in reality questions relating to its own genuineness, hence to its inner strength and stability. The men who created the Jewish communes in Palestine instinctively knew this, but the instinct no longer seems to be as common or as alert as it was. Yet it is in this most important field that we find the remorselessly clear-sighted collective self-observation and self-criticism to which I have already drawn attention. But to understand and value it aright, we must see it together with the amazingly positive relationship—amounting to a regular faith—which these men have to the inmost being of their commune. The two things are two sides of the same spiritual world, and neither can be understood without the other.

In order to make the causes of the non-failure of these Jewish communal settlements in Palestine sufficiently vivid, I began with the non-doctrinaire character of their origins. This character also determined their development in all essentials. New forms and new intermediate forms were constantly branching off—in complete freedom. Each grew out of the particular social and spiritual needs as these came to light—in complete freedom; and each acquired, even in the initial stages, its own ideology—in complete freedom; each struggled to propagate itself, and to spread and establish its proper sphere—all in complete freedom. The champions of the various forms each had his say; the pros and cons of each individual form were frankly and fiercely debated—always, however, on the plane which everybody accepted as obvious, the common cause and the common task, where each form recognized the relative justice of all the other forms in their special functions. All this is unique in the history of cooperative settlements. What is more, nowhere, as far as I can see, in the history of the socialist movement were men so deeply involved in the process of differentiation, and yet so intent on preserving the principle of integration.

The various forms and intermediate forms that arose in this way at different times and in different situations represented different kinds of social structure. The people who built them were generally aware of this, as also of the particular social and spiritual needs that actuated them. They were not aware to the same extent that the different forms corresponded to different human types, and that just as new forms branched off from the original kvutza, so new types branched off from the original halutz, each with its special mode of being and each demanding its particular sort of realization. More often than not, it was economic and similar external factors that led certain people to break away from one form and attach themselves to another. But in the main, each type looked for the social realization of its peculiarities in this particular form, and on the whole, found it there. And not only was each form based on a definite type; it molded, and keeps on molding, that type. It was and is intent on developing it; the constitution, organization, and educational system of each form are—no matter how consciously or unconsciously—dedicated to this end. Thus, something has been produced which is essentially different from all the social experiments that have ever been made—not a laboratory where everybody works for himself, alone with his problems and plans, but an experimental station where, on common soil, different colonies or "cultures" are tested out according to different methods for a common purpose.

Yet here, too, a problem emerged, no longer within the individual group, but in the relation of the groups to one another; nor did it come from without. It came from within—in fact, from the very heart of the principle of freedom.

Even in its first undifferentiated form, a tendency towards federation was innate in the kvutza, to merge the kvutzot into some higher social unit; and a very important tendency it was, since it showed that the kvutza implicitly understood that it was the cell of a newly structured society. With the splitting off and proliferation of the various forms—from the semi-individualistic form which jealously guarded personal independence in its domestic economy, way of life, children's education, etc., to the pure communistic form—the single unit was supplanted by a series of units in each of which a definite form of colony, and a more or less definite human type, constituted itself on a federal basis. The fundamental assumption was that the local groups would combine on the same principle of solidarity and mutual help as prevailed within the individual group. But the trend toward a larger unit is far from having atrophied in the process. On the contrary, at least in the kibbutz, or collectivist, movement, it asserts itself with great force and clarity. It recognizes the federative kibbutzim—units where the local groups have pooled their various aspirations—as a provisional structure; indeed, a thoughtful leader of the movement calls them a substitute for a commune of communes. Apart from the fact, however, that individual forms—especially, for instance, the moshavim, or semi-individualistic labor settlements, though these do not fall short of any of the other forms in the matter of communal economic control and mutual help—are already too far removed from the basic form

to be included in a unitary plan, in the kibbutz movement itself subsidiary organizations stand in the way of the trend toward unification which strives to embrace and absorb them.
Each has developed its own special character and consolidated
it in the unit, and it is natural that each should incline to view
unification as an extension of its own influence. But something
else has been added that has led to an enormous intensification
of this attitude on the part of the single units, and that is political development. Twenty years ago, a leader of one of the
large units could say emphatically: "We are a community, not
a party." This has radically changed in the meantime, and the
conditions for unification have been aggravated accordingly.
The lamentable fact has emerged that the all-important attitude
of neighborly relationship has not been adequately developed,
although not a few cases are on record of a rich and flourish-
ing village giving generous help to a young and poor neighbor
which belonged to another unit. In these circumstances, the
great struggle that has broken out on the question of unification, particularly in the last decade, is the more remarkable.
Nobody who is a socialist at heart can read the great document
of this struggle, the Hebrew compilation entitled *The Kibbutz
and the Kvutza,* edited by the late labor leader, Berl Katznel-
son, without losing himself in admiration of the high-minded
passion with which these two camps fought with one another
for genuine unity. The union will probably not be attained save
as the outcome of a situation that makes it absolutely necessary.
But that the men of the Jewish communes have labored so
strenuously with one another, and against one another, for the
emergence of a *communitas communitatum,* that is to say, for
a structurally new society: this will not be forgotten in the
history of mankind's struggle for self-renewal.

I have said that I see in this bold Jewish undertaking a
"signal non-failure." I cannot say a signal success. To become
that, much has still to be done. Yet it is in this way, in this
kind of tempo, with such setbacks, disappointments, and new
ventures, that real changes are accomplished in this our mortal
world.

But can one speak of this non-failure as "signal"? I have
pointed out the peculiar nature of the premises and conditions
that led to it. And what one of its own representatives has said
of the kvutza, that it is a typically Palestinian product, is true
of all these forms.

Still, if an experiment conducted under certain conditions

has proved successful up to a point, we can set about varying it under other, less favourable conditions.

There can hardly be any doubt that we must regard the last war as the end of the prelude to a world crisis. This crisis will probably break out—after a somber "interlude" that cannot last very long—first among some of the nations of the West, who will be able to restore their shattered economy in appearance only. They will see themselves faced with the immediate need for radical socialization, above all, the expropriation of the land. It will then be of absolutely decisive importance who is the real subject of an economy so transformed, and who is the owner of the social means of production. Is it to be the central authority in a highly centralized state, or the social units of urban and rural workers, living and producing on a communal basis, and their representative bodies? In the latter case, the remodelled organs of the state will discharge the functions of adjustment and administration only. On these issues will largely depend the growth of a new society and a new civilization. The essential point is to decide on the fundamentals: a restructuring of society as a league of leagues, and a reduction of the state to its proper function, which is to maintain unity, or a devouring of an amorphous society by the omnipotent state—socialist pluralism or so-called socialist unitarianism—the right proportion, tested anew every day according to changing conditions, between group freedom and collective order, or absolute order imposed indefinitely for the sake of an era of freedom alleged to follow "of its own accord." So long as Russia has not undergone an essential inner change—and today we have no means of knowing when and how that will come to pass—we must designate one of the two poles of socialism between which our choice lies by the formidable name of "Moscow." The other, I would make bold to call "Jerusalem."

4

"AND IF NOT NOW, WHEN?"

We are living in an age of the depreciation of words. The intellect with its gift for language has been all too willing to put itself at the disposal of whatever trends prevail at the time. Instead of letting the word grow out of the thought in responsible silence, the intellect has manufactured words for every demand with almost mechanical skill. It is not only the intellectuals who are now finding a suspicious reception for their disquisitions, who must suffer for this "treason." [3] What is worse is that their audience, above all the entire younger generation of our time, is deprived of the noblest happiness of youth, the happiness of believing in the spirit. It is easily understood that many of them now see nothing but "ideologies" in intellectual patterns, nothing but pompous robes for very obvious group interests, that they are no longer willing to believe there is a truth over and above parties, over and above those who wield power and are greedy for it. They tell us, tell one another, and tell themselves, that they are tired of being fed on lofty illusions, that they want to go back to a "natural" foundation, to unconcealed instincts, that the life of the individual, as well as that of every people, must be built up on simple self-assertion.

No matter what others may do, we, my friends, should not choose this way. If we really are Jews, meaning the bearers of a tradition and a task, we know what has been transmitted to us. We know that there is a truth which is the seal of God, and we know that the task we have been entrusted with is to let this one truth set its stamp on all the various facets of our

life. We are not the owners of this truth, for it belongs to
God. We ourselves cannot use the seal, but we can be the wax
that takes the seal. Every individual is wax of a different form
and color, but all are potentially receptive to the stamp of truth,
for all of us, created "in the image of God," are potentially
able to become images of the divine. We are not the owners of
the truth, but this does not mean that we must depend either
on vain ideologies or on mere instincts, for every one of us has
the possibility of entering into a real relationship to truth. Such
a relationship, however, cannot grow out of thinking alone,
for the ability to think is only one part of us; but neither is
feeling enough. We can attain to such a relationship only
through the undivided whole of our life as we live it. The intellect can be redeemed from its last lapse into sin, from the
desecration of the word, only if the word is backed and
vouched for with the whole of one's life. The betrayal of the
intellectuals cannot be atoned for by the intellect retreating
into itself, but only by its proffering to reality true service in
place of false. It must not serve the powers of the moment and
what they call reality—not the short-lived semblance of truth.
The intellect should serve the true great reality, whose function it is to embody the truth of God; it must serve. No matter
how brilliant it may be, the human intellect which wishes to
keep to a plane above the events of the day is not really alive.
It can become fruitful, beget life and live, only when it enters
into the events of the day without denying, but rather proving,
its superior origin. Be true to the spirit, my friends, but be
true to it on the plane of reality. Our first question must be:
what is the truth? what has God commanded us to do? But
our next must be: how can we accomplish it from where we
are?

We shall accomplish nothing at all if we divide our world
and our life into two domains: one in which God's command
is paramount, the other governed exclusively by the laws of
economics, politics, and the "simple self-assertion" of the group.
Such dualism is far more ominous than the naturalism I spoke
of before. Stopping one's ears so as not to hear the voice from
above is breaking the connection between existence and the
meaning of existence. But he who hears the voice and sets a
limit to the area beyond which its rule shall not extend is not
merely moving away from God, like the person who refuses to
listen; he is standing up directly against him. The atheist does
not know God, but the adherent of a form of ethics which

ends where politics begin has the temerity to prescribe to God, whom he professes to know, how far his power may extend. The polytheists distribute life and the world among many powers. As far as they are concerned, Germany has one god and France another; there is a god of business, and a god of the state. Each of these domains has its own particular code of laws, and is subject to no superior court. Western civilization professes one God and lives in polytheism. We Jews are connected to this civilization with thousands of strands, but if we share in its dualism of life and profession of faith, we shall forfeit our justification for living. If we were only one nation among others, we should long ago have perished from the earth. Paradoxically, we exist only because we dared to be serious about the unity of God and his undivided, absolute sovereignty. If we give up God, he will give us up. And we do give him up when we profess him in synagogue and deny him when we come together for discussion, when we do his commands in our personal life, and set up other norms for the life of the group we belong to. What is wrong for the individual cannot be right for the community, for if it were, then God, the God of Sinai, would no longer be the Lord of peoples, but only of individuals. If we really are Jews, we believe that God gives his commands to men to observe throughout their whole life, and that whether or not life has a meaning depends on the fulfilment of those commands. And if we consult our deep inner knowledge about God's command to mankind, we shall not hesitate an instant to say that it is peace. There are many among us who think this command is intended for some more propitious future; for the present, we must participate in the universal war, in order to escape destruction. But it is only if we do participate in this war that we shall be destroyed; for as far as we are concerned, there is only one possible kind of destruction: God letting us slip out of his hand.

I frequently hear some among us saying: "We too want the spirit of Judaism to be fulfilled; we too want the Torah to issue forth from Zion, and we know that to realize this purpose the Torah must not be mere words, but actual life; we want God's word on Zion to become a reality. But this cannot happen until the world again has a Zion, and so first of all we want to build up Zion, and to build it—with every possible means." It may, however, be characteristic of Zion that it *cannot* be built with "every possible means," but only *bemishpat* (Is. 1:27), only "with justice." It may be that God will refuse to receive his sanctuary from the hands of the devil. Suppose a man decided to steal and rob for six years, and in the seventh, to build a temple with the fortune thus amassed; suppose he succeeded—would he really be rearing temple walls? Would he not rather be setting up a den of robbers (Jer. 7:11), or a robber's palace, on whose portals he dares to engrave the name of God? It is true that God does not build his own house. He wants us to build it with our human hands and our human strength, for "house" in this connection can mean only that at long last we may begin to live God's word on earth! But after we have laid the foundations of this house by his means, *bemishpat*, do you really imagine that God is not strong enough to let it be finished by those same means? If you do imagine that, stop talking about Judaism, Jewish spirit, and Jewish teachings! For Judaism is the teaching that there is really only One Power which, while at times it may permit the sham powers of the world to accomplish something in opposition to it, never permits such accomplishment to stand. But whatever is done in the service of that power, and done in such a way that not only the goal but the means to that goal are in accord with the spirit of justice, will survive, even though it may have to struggle for a time, and may seem in great peril, and weak compared to the effective sham powers.

I should like to bring a concept of the utmost importance home even to those who cannot or will not understand the language of religion, and therefore believe that I am discussing theology. I am speaking of the *reality of history*. In historical reality, we do not set ourselves a righteous goal, choose whatever way to it an auspicious hour offers, and, following that way, reach the set goal. If the goal to be reached is like the goal which was set, then the nature of the way must be like the goal. A wrong way, that is, a way in contradiction to the goal, must lead to a wrong goal. What is accomplished through lies can assume the mask of truth; what is accomplished through violence, can go in the guise of justice, and for a while the hoax may be successful. But soon people will realize that lies are lies at bottom, that in the final analysis, violence is violence, and both lies and violence will suffer the destiny history has in store for all that is false. I sometimes hear it said that a generation must sacrifice itself, "take the sin upon itself," so that coming generations may be free to live righteously. But it is self-delusion and folly to think that one can lead a dissolute life and raise one's children to be good and

happy; they will usually turn out to be hypocrites or tor-
mented.

History has much to teach us, but we must know how to
receive her teaching. These temporary triumphs which are apt
to catch our attention are nothing but the stage setting for
universal history. If we keep our eyes fixed on the foreground,
the true victories, won in secret, sometimes look like defeats.
True victories happen slowly and imperceptibly, but they have
far-reaching effects. In the limelight, our faith that God is the
Lord of history may sometimes appear ludicrous; but there is
something secret in history which confirms our faith.

He who makes peace, our sages taught, is God's fellow
worker. But addressing conciliatory words to others and oc-
cupying oneself with humane projects is not the way to make
peace. We make peace, we help bring about world peace, if we
make peace wherever we are destined and summoned to do so:
in the active life of our own community and in that aspect of
it which can actively help determine its relationship to another
community. The prophecy of peace addressed to Israel is not
valid only for the days of the coming of the Messiah. It holds
for the day when the people will again be summoned to take
part in shaping the destiny of its earliest home; it holds for
today. "And if not now, when?" (Mishnah, Sayings of the
Fathers, 1:14). Fulfilment in a Then is inextricably bound up
with fulfilment in the Now.

PART III: *Of Biblical Faith*

1

SAGA AND HISTORY

In order to learn at first hand who Moses was and the kind of life that was his, it is obviously necessary to study the biblical narrative. There are no other sources worthy of serious consideration; comparison of reports, normally the chief means of ascertaining historical truth, is not possible here. Whatever has been preserved of Israel's traditions since ancient times is to be found in this one book. Not so much as the vestige of a chronicle dating from that period, or deriving from the nations with whom the Children of Israel established contact on their journey from Egypt to Canaan, has been preserved; and not the vaguest indication of the event in question is to be found in ancient Egyptian literature.

The biblical narrative itself is basically different in character from all that we usually classify as serviceable historical sources. The happenings recorded there can never have come about, in the historical world as we know it, after the fashion in which they are described. The literary category within which our historical mode of thinking must classify this narrative is the saga; and a saga is generally assumed to be incapable of producing within us any conception of a factual sequence.

Further, it is customary to accept as a fundamental tenet of the non-dogmatic biblical scholarship of our day the view that the tales in question belong to a far later epoch than the events related, and that it is the spirit of that later epoch which finds expression in them; or, even more, the spirit of the sundry and various later periods to which are ascribed the "sources," the different constituent parts of which the story is composed or compiled according to the prevalent view. Thus Homer, for example, to take an analogous case, provides us with a picture of the epoch in which he himself lived rather than of the one in which his heroes did their deeds.

Assuming that to be the case, just as little could be ascertained regarding Moses' character and works as is to be ascertained of Odysseus'; and we would perforce have to rest content with the possession of a rare testimony to the art with which court writers commissioned by the kings of Israel, or the more popular (in the original sense of the word) prophets of the nation, wrought the image of its founder out of material entirely inaccessible to us.

The scholarship of our own epoch, however, has prepared the way for another and deeper insight into the relation between saga or legend and history. For example, the philologist Hermann Usener indicated (in 1897) [1] that what finds expression in the saga is not a post-factum transfiguration of an historical recollection, but a process which follows on the events, "in their footsteps, so to say." At a more recent date (in 1933)[2], the Iranologist Ernst Herzfeld observed that "saga and the writing of history start out from the identical point, the event," and that it is the saga which in particular preserves historical memories, "not of what the consequences show to be 'historical event,' but of that which roused the emotions of the men undergoing the experience." It is possible to formulate even more precisely the nature of the issue involved. The man of early times met the unplanned, unexpected events which transformed the historical situation of his community at a single stroke with a fundamental stirring of all the elements in his being; a state of affairs properly described by the great Germanist Jacob Grimm (1813)[3] as "objective enthusiasm." It is a primeval state of amazement which sets all the creative forces of the soul to work. What happens is therefore not a mere recasting of the event perceived by imagination become paramount; the experience itself is creative. "Periods of a more sensuous religious emotion," says Usener, "see vast, bright, superhuman figures passing before the victorious troops and bringing death and defeat to the ranks of the foe." Here the emphasis should be put on the word "see." The historical wonder is no mere interpretation; it is something actually seen. Even the subsequent comprehension of the flashing lightning-like visions within the consecutive report of the saga is not

arbitrary in character. An organic and organically creative
memory is here at work.

That this early saga, close as it is to the time of the event,
tends to assume rhythmical form, can well be understood. It
is not due solely to the fact that enthusiasm naturally expresses
itself in rhythm. Of greater importance is the basic idea characterizing this stage of human existence that historical wonder
can be grasped by no other form of speech save that which is
rhythmically articulated, of course in oral expression (a basic
concept which is closely associated with the time-old relation
between rhythm and magic). This is sustained by the wish to
retain unchanged for all time the memory of the awe-inspiring
things that had come about; to which end a transmission in
rhythmical form is the most favorable condition. Occasionally,
the saga assumes specifically lyrical form; as in the Song of
Deborah, where the bard mocks and curses as from the very
battle.

Hence, alongside the more registrative forms of historical
record, conditioned by the court and its requirements, which
constitute a stage preliminary to the scientific writing of history, and which develop from the royal lists of the Sumerians
to the well-constructed chronicles of the biblical books of
Kings, the historical song and the historical saga exist as spontaneous forms of popular preservation by word of mouth of
"historical" events, such events, that is, as are vital in the life
of the tribe. It is of importance to investigate the sociological
character of these types.

The saga is the predominant method of preserving the memory of what happens, as long as tribal life is stronger than state
organization. As soon as the latter becomes more powerful, on
the other hand, the unofficial popular forms are overshadowed
through the development of an annalistic keeping of records by
order of the governing authority.

If a saga assumes poetic form in its early stage, it remains
virtually unchanged for a long time, even when it is transmitted by word of mouth alone, save that passages may be introduced which describe the course of events subsequent to the
initial incident giving rise to the saga. Reminiscences not included in the poem may under certain circumstances condense
into a parallel account, so that, as in the case of the story of
Deborah, prose is found side by side with poetry; or, more correctly speaking, a loosely cadenced version accompanies the
more strictly versified form. If the saga, however, does not as

sume this strict form at about the time of the event, but remains in its "mobile" state, it will be variously treated by different narrators, without any need to assume a conscious wish to introduce changes. Differing religious, political, and family tendencies, simultaneous and parallel to one another as well as consecutive, find expression in the treatment, with the result that a product already current in the tradition is "rectified," that is, supplemented or actually transformed in one or another detail. This continuous process of crystallization is something entirely different in character from compilation and welding of elements from various sources.

Such a state of affairs invests research with the duty of establishing a critique of tradition. The student must attempt to penetrate to that original nucleus of saga which was almost contemporary with the initial event. The attempt is rendered difficult, *inter alia,* by the fact that the literature of the ages saw fit to round off the saga material by supplementary data; as, for instance, where it was felt that the unknown or only superficially known birth and childhood story of the hero must not be left untold.

Here the procedure of investigation must necessarily be reductive. It must remove layer after layer from the images as set before it, in order to arrive at the earliest of all.

There can be no certainty of arriving by this method at "what really happened." However, even if it is impossible to reconstitute the course of events themselves, it is nevertheless possible to recover much of the manner in which the participating people experienced those events. We become acquainted with the meeting between this people and a vast historical happening that overwhelmed it; we become conscious of the saga-creating ardor with which the people received the tremendous event and transmitted it to a molding memory. This, however, should certainly not be understood to mean that the only results we can expect to obtain lie in the field of group psychology. The meeting of a people with events so enormous that it cannot ascribe them to its own plans and their realization, but must perceive in them deeds performed by heavenly powers, is of the genuine substance of history. In so far as the saga begins near the event, it is the outcome and record of this meeting.

The critique of tradition involved in the interpretation of the saga approximates us to the original meeting. At the sight of it, we have to stand without being able to educe an "objective state of affairs." We shall not regain an historical nucleus of the saga by eliminating the function of enthusiasm from it. This function is an inseparable element of the fragment of history entrusted to our study. Yet, in every case, we can and should test whether and how the narrative can be connected with and incorporated in the historical circumstances. Here history cannot be dissevered from the historical wonder; but the experience which has been transmitted to us, the experience of event as wonder, is itself great history and must be understood out of the element of history; it has to be fitted within the frame of the historical. Whether Sinai was a volcano cannot be determined historically, nor is it historically relevant. But that the tribes gathered at the "burning mountain" comprehended the words of their leader Moses as a message from their God, a message that simultaneously established a covenant between them and a covenant between him and their community, is essentially an historical process, historical in the deepest sense; it is historical because it derives from historical connections and sets off fresh historical connections. When faced by such tales, it is wrong to talk of an "historization of myth"; it might be preferable to describe them as a mythization of history, remembering that here, unlike the concept familiar in the science of religion, myth means nothing other than the report by ardent enthusiasts of that which has befallen them. And it may very well be doubted whether, in the last resort, the report of an unenthusiastic chronicler could have come closer to the truth. There is no other way of understanding history than the rational one, but it must start off with the overcoming of the restricted and restrictive *ratio*, substituting for it a higher, more comprehensive one.

However, two factors should be emphasized as having contributed greatly to the strength of the historical content of the Moses saga.

To begin with, the central figures of the Bible saga are not, as in so many hero-tales, merged in or amalgamated with persons belonging to mere mythology; the data regarding their lives have not been interwoven with stories of the gods. Here all the glorification is dedicated solely to the God who brings about the events. The human being acting under the God's orders is portrayed in all his untransfigured humanity. The wonder-working staff in his hand does not transform him into a possessor of superhuman powers; when once he uses that staff unbidden, he is subject to judgment. And when he descends from Sinai with radiant face, the radiance is not a shining forth from his own being, but only the reflection of some higher light. This withdrawing of the human being from the mythical element steeps the tale in an atmosphere of august sobriety, a dry atmosphere, one might almost say, which frequently permits a glimpse of an historical nucleus.

Besides, precise inspection goes to show that the early narrator of the deeds of Moses aimed not at beautiful or instructive individual sagas, but at a continuity of events. It is true that in the report of the journey through the wilderness, for example, we meet repeatedly with episodes, but they are introduced in a connection which obviously derives not from later harmonizing literary tendencies (like the Book of Joshua, for instance), but from a powerful primitive emotion which is the passionate recollection of a sequence of unheard-of events. Nor yet does the relation found here appear to show anything of the poetic composition of the epos; it is the practically related sequence of the itinerary. The latter may possibly have been worked up from an inexact or mutilated tradition to a state of questionable completeness; maybe the associated temporal sequence has been transformed by didactic aims and number symbolism; but the origin, the memory of a journey in the course of which the nation came into being, and the zealous purpose of preserving on record the stations of that journey, has remained unobliterated. In the literature of the world, the specifically historical can undoubtedly be found only where the principle of original connection is to be met with; here it cannot be denied.

All this leads to a threefold critical task which, difficult as it may be, nevertheless seems in some degree to be capable of accomplishment. It is necessary to draw a distinction between saga produced near the historical occurrences, the character of which is enthusiastic report, and saga which is further away from the historical event, and which derives from the tendency to complete and round off what is already given. Therefore, it is necessary to establish a further distinction, within the former, between the original components and their subsequent treatment. Finally, it is also necessary to penetrate to the historical nucleus of the saga as far as possible. Naturally, it is impossible to produce a coherent historical picture in this way, which is the only one scientifically permissible; yet we are entitled to hope genuine historical outlines may be ascertained. The distinction drawn should not be understood in the sense of elim-

ination; as we have seen, the saga element too, in so far as it
is characterized by closeness to history, is historically important,
being a document of the reception of what befell in the minds
of those whom it befell. Yet we may go further; what was
added later is also of importance for us. Even the men who
round off and supplement do what they do not arbitrarily but
under the sustained urge of the primeval impulse. Tradition is
by its nature an uninterrupted change in form; change and
preservation function in the identical current. Even while the
hand makes its alterations, the ear hearkens to the deeps of
the past; not only for the reader but also for the writer himself
does the old serve to legitimize the new. The Moses who had
his being long ago is properly expanded by the one who has
come into being in the course of long ages. It is our aim to
come nearer to the former by our testing and selective work on
the text; the latter is given to us directly. We must hold both
in view without confusing them; we must comprehend the
brightness of the foreground and gaze into the dark deeps of
history.

At the same time, we must bear in mind that the forces
which formed the saga are in essence identical with those which
reigned supreme in history; they are the forces of a faith. For
this faith, which is in character a history faith, a faith relating
largely to historical time as such, did not merely treat a transmitted material after the fact; it cannot be imagined as absent
from this material. The transmitted events are steeped in it;
the persons who furthered the events believed in it, did in it
what had to be done, and experienced in it what had to be
experienced. The research of our day has reached the point, in
the course of its radical doubts and queries, of providing fresh
ground for an old certainty: that the biblical tales of the early
Israelitic days report an early Israelitic faith. Whatever the mixture of fact and legend may be in the events related, the indwelling story of faith which inheres in them is authentic in
all its main lines. What we learn of the faith determining the
active and the receptive life of those persons is not, as scholarship supposed for some time, a "projection" of a later religious
development against the surface of the earlier epoch, but is, in
essence, the religious content of the latter. And it is this faith
which shaped the saga that was near to history and at subsequent stages also shaped the more distant saga.

In its character, this saga is "sacred legend," since the rela tion to God of the men of whom it tells is a fundamental constituent. But this history, too, is in its character "sacred history," because the people who work and suffer in it work and suffer as they do in virtue of their relationship to their God.

2

HOLY EVENT

We know nothing of Israel's religious situation in the Egyptian age, and we can only conjecture on the basis of scattered disconnected phrases (e.g., Ezek. 20:7f.) that it was out of a state of religious decay that Moses stirred them up. We can proceed only by putting the period of the Exodus alongside that of the fathers.

When we pass from the atmosphere of the patriarchal tradition, as we have tried to picture it hypothetically, and enter the atmosphere of the Exodus tradition, we are confronted at the first glance with something new. But it is quickly manifest that this does not mean a change in the deity, but a change in men. We have already seen that the deity is in essence no other than the primitive deity. Against this the human partner is essentially changed; therefore, the situation common to the two is entirely different; and with this the sphere in which the deity acts is so different that one may easily think the very character of this activity to be changed, and one does not recognize the identity of the agent. The new thing from the human side is that here we have "people," not "a people" in the strictest sense, but at all events the element "people." That is to say, this collection of men is no more a company assembled around the recipients of revelation and their kinsmen as in the patriarchal age, but a something that is called "Israel" and which the deity can acknowledge to be "his people"—again it is not of decisive importance whether this people comprises all the tribes of Israel, or only some of them, the rest having been left in Canaan or having returned thither before this. We do not know whether "Israel" originally was the name of a people or the name of a "holy confederacy," to which the tribes were gathered together by the leadership of Moses,[4] and gave themselves, after their sacred call, the name "Israel," the meaning of which probably is not "God strives," but "God rules." [5]

But if this is the original explanation of "Israel," then this community has already, in consequence of the special historical conditions, reached, at the moment of the exodus—that is, at the moment when we are able to perceive them historically —that stage of self-evident unitedness, so that we are justified in applying to them the name "people," even though they do not yet possess all the marks reckoned as belonging to this concept. And if "Israel" was already in origin the name of a people, then it is only at this point, at the exodus from Egypt, not in Egypt itself, that the people comes into actual existence, and only at this point is the name "Israel" perfectly manifest as "the visible program of God's sovereignty." [6] And the deity now acts historically upon this people seen by him as an absolute unity, the same deity whom the fathers discovered as the guardian God accompanying them. The change which we think we perceive in him as we now advance in time is nothing but the transformation of the situation into an historical one, and the greatness of Moses consists in the fact that he accepts the situation and exhausts its possibilities. No external influence is to be found here. Indeed, it is vain to attempt to find here a Kenite ingredient; YHVH has taken over nothing from the Egyptian god Aton, who is brought into the picture as "monotheistic," and other things which may have approached him have not touched his nature. This God has become manifest as a God of history, because he became the God of Israel, this Israel that only now came into being, that only now he was able to "find" (Hos. 9:10), and because this Israel only now has entered the realm of history. He reveals himself to it: what was hidden in prehistoric time is made historically manifest. Our path in the history of faith is not a path from one kind of deity to another, but in fact a path from the "God who hides himself" (Is. 45:15) to the One who reveals himself.

If we look at the first of the writing prophets, Amos, and examine the traditions which he handles concerning this activity of YHVH, and ask what are the reminiscences that he knows to be common to all his hearers, these two appear before us: the leading from Egypt through the desert (Am.

2:10; 3:1; 9:7); and the appropriation which the deity expresses in a word reminiscent of the marriage union (Gen. 4:1), but later uses to indicate the primal mission of the prophet (Jer. 1:5), "You have I known" (Am. 3:2). The first of these two, talked over by everyone and thought to be understood by all—"I have brought you up" (2:10)—Amos shows (9:7) to be something that is in no way peculiar to Israel, but the fundamental fact of the historic contact of this leader God with the peoples. It is with set purpose that record is here kept of the names of the two neighboring peoples who fought most mightily with all Israel or Judah, the one in early times, the other in the immediate past. In these instances, very painful as they are to you—this is the force of the prophet's words—you see that this God of yours, of whose historic dealing with you you boast, deals historically with other peoples as with you, leading each of them on its wanderings and singling out its lot. The second thing, not familiar to the people as to its expression and sense, but corresponding in the people's memory to the events of revelation and covenant-making, he lays bare as the *supra-historical election* to be binding absolutely, peculiar "only" to Israel among all the peoples: "Therefore"—and now comes the iron word from the Decalogue—"will I visit upon you all your iniquities." YHVH has not revealed himself to any other family of the "families of the earth" save only to this Israel, and to them he has revealed himself really as the "zealous God." And in the mouth of Amos' contemporary, Hosea, who presupposes no general thought or teaching, but expresses directly the things of the heart, YHVH illustrates his zealousness by his experience with Israel in the desert: I loved them (11:1) and they betrayed me (9:10; 11:2; 13:6).

Those Semitic peoples who call their tribal deities by the name *malk*, meaning originally counsellor, arbitrator, leader, and only afterwards receiving the meaning of king, appear to have expressed by this name not the oracle power of the settlement but the leadership in primitive wanderings and conquest. These are nomad gods, leader gods of the tribe, which, through the political change of meaning of the word, become afterwards "kings"; the type of this tribal god, although not the name, we find in the message of Jephthah to the king of the "Ammonites" (or more correctly the king of Moab), where he tells him that Chemosh his god "disinherited" other peoples even as YHVH had done, in order to give a land to the people led by him (Judg. 11:23f.). Amos' saying about the bringing up of the Aramaeans disposes of such a notion: the peoples do not know who is their liberator, they each call him by a different name, each one thinks it has one of its own, whereas we know the One, because he "has known" us. This is the *national* universalism of the prophetic faith.

The Mosaic age does not possess this religious view of the history of peoples, but it does have the fundamental religious experience which opens the door to this view. What is preserved for us here is to be regarded not as the "historization" of a myth or of a cult drama, nor is it to be explained as the transposition of something originally beyond time into historical time:[7] a great history-faith does not come into the world through interpretation of the extra-historical as historical, but by receiving an occurrence experienced as a "wonder," that is, as an event which cannot be grasped except as an act of God. Something happens to us, the cause of which we cannot ascribe to our world; the event has taken place just now, we cannot understand it, we can only believe it (Ex. 14:31). It is a holy event. We acknowledge the performer (15:1, 21): "I will sing unto YHVH, for he has verily risen, the horse and its rider he has cast into the sea." [8]

In this undeniably contemporary song, the deliverance is asserted as a holy event. A later song, which nevertheless is very ancient in form, vocabulary, and sentence construction, the song framing "the Blessing of Moses," praises in its first half (the second half tells of the conquest of the land) a series of divine appearances in the wilderness,[9] beginning with the appearance at Mount Sinai. From the difficult text, it can be understood that the "holy ones" of the people collect round YHVH, when they camp "at his feet" (cf. Ex. 24:10); that later the people receive from the divine words the "instruction" (*torah*) which Moses "commands"; that so "the congregation of Jacob" becomes YHVH's "inheritance"; and that finally the heads of the tribes gather together and proclaim YHVH to be king over them. What is recorded here of the holy event can only be reconstructed incompletely out of the exodus story. The fact that the proclamation is lacking here is probably to be explained by the fear which they felt of the influence—so combated by the prophets—of the *melek* cult of the neighboring peoples, that is to say, of the penetration of child sacrifice into Israel. Isaiah is the first (6:5) directly to give YHVH the title *melek*, king, after forcibly demonstrating the uncleanness of the people over against him. But we still have preserved for us another echo of the proclamation, namely the last verse of the Song of the Sea (Ex. 15:18), which although it is not so near in time to the event as the opening of the Song, yet clearly is "not long after the event about which it tells." [10] Here proclamation is made triumphantly that the divine kingdom will stand forever. This is to be understood not in the light of the state concept of kingship, nor on the basis of the later idea of a cosmic-cultic kingdom of the God, but only as the recognition by wandering tribes of their divine Leader: the sovereignty of this Leader over his people is proclaimed.

Thus, over against the two sayings of Amos, we have before us two series of events. The first comprises the deliverance from Egypt and the leading through the wilderness to Canaan; the second comprises the revelation, the making of the cove-nant, and the setting up of an order of the people by the leadership of the divine *melek*. That is to say, the first series exists for the sake of the second. So we are to understand the words "unto me" in the first Sinai message (Ex. 19:4), which still precedes the revelation in the thunderstorm.[11] YHVH bears the people, as the eagle from time to time bears one of its young on its wing (a late form of the picture is found in Deut. 32:11), to the place of revelation: if the people hearken to the voice that now speaks to them, they will become for YHVH, whose is all the earth, a "peculiar treasure" among all the peoples that are his; they will become for him, the King, a "king's realm" (cf. II Sam. 3:28), surrounding him near at hand and serving him directly, a circle of *kohanim*, that is, "foremost ones at the king's hand" (so I Chron. 18:17 calls the office, while II Sam. 8:18 gives it the name *kohanim*, meaning those who minister to the king), a "holy" (hallowed, set apart for him) *goy* (body of people). The saying dates apparently from the time before the division of the Israelite kingdom,[12] and it is already influenced by the political changes of meaning in the concept *melek;* but it is clear that a traditional basic view of the meaning of the events, the exodus and the making of the covenant, became crystallized in it. YHVH acts as *melek* in the sense of sovereign. So through a holy event there comes into existence this category decisive from the point of view of the history of faith, of the "holy people," the hallowed body of people, as image and claim; at a later time, after the people had broken the covenant again and again, this category changed and was replaced by the messianic promise and hope.

Both series of events are blended together in a most noteworthy way in the great holy object, indeed the greatest of all holy objects created by the "nomadic faith," the faith of a people seeking a land and believing in the divine Leader who brings them to it—namely, the ark.[13] It clearly cannot be dated any later; for there is to be found in it all the incentive and motive force of the holy adventure, all its symbol-begetting power. And in spite of the many parallels in the history of religion to one or other aspect of the ark,[14] it can hardly be maintained that the ark is borrowed from anywhere, for its nature lies precisely in the unity of these different aspects. It carries the cherub throne of the Lord who, seated thereon, guides the wandering and the battle (here both are still absolutely interconnected the one with the other); and together with this is the ark proper containing the tablets. These are called "the testimony," because it is by them that the covenant is always attested anew, and so the ark is also called "the ark of the covenant." Neither of the two could be wanting. This holy object is a visible unity of the two divine activities: the activity of the Leader, who now, in the historic situation, has become also "a man of war" (Ex. 15:3); and the activity of the Revealer, whose revelation, once it had taken place, is never more to be concealed and hidden, but must remain carved on stone or written on a scroll. At the same time, even this is characteristically not attached to a place: the tablets are fixed in the ark, but the ark is by nature mobile, moving in the tent and outside it, for it is forbidden to remove the staves (25:15). Even after the ark stands firm in the temple in Jerusalem, they are not removed (I Kings 8:8); but this means only reverence for tradition and symbolism, and not any longer a direct notion of the leader deity. The double call, originating in the wilderness (Num. 10:35f.), to the Lord of the ark, who travels and halts with the camp, "Rise up YHVH" and "Return YHVH," and the "melek shout" because Israel's God is "with him" (23:21), is no more heard. His special name "YHVH of hosts" (that is, the host of the people and the host of heaven, concerning both of which the Song of Deborah speaks) is still in the mouth of the people, but its real meaning is no longer really known—until Amos comes and expounds it again.

The paradox on which the sanctity of the ark is based (every "holy" thing is founded on a paradox) is this, that an invisible deity becomes perceptible as one who comes and goes. According to tradition, as far as we can still recognize it, the ark must be brought into the "tent of meeting"—not the tent which is described in all its parts in Scripture, and which really cannot be conceived in the wilderness, but the tent of the Leader ("the tent" of Ex. 33:7ff.)—after atonement for sin had been made. The image of the steer, which has no other design than to be a likeness of that very God "who brought you up from the land of Egypt," (32:4), was put up to make the leadership permanently perceptible. In the hour of forgiveness, God grants (33:14, 17) that his "face" will go with the people. The meaning of this is that a visibleness is conceded which in fact is none; that is to say, not the visibleness of an "image" or a "shape" (20:4), but as in a vision of the ancients (24:10), the visibleness of a *place*. This is the hour in which the holy object is born. Later, men attempted to render the principle that could no longer be reconstructed in its reality more conceivable by means of a concept of the *kabod*, that is, the fiery "weight" or "majesty" of the God radiating from the invisible, which now "fills" again and again the "dwelling" of the tent (40:34), just as it had "taken dwelling" upon the mount (24:16). In truth, this idea of a filling of the tent, so that Moses "cannot come into the tent of meeting" (40:35), contradicts its character and purpose. The true tent—formerly Moses' leader tent, and now that of the leader deity—is characterized by just this that Moses enters it for the sake of "meeting" the deity, and that "everyone who seeks YHVH" (33:7) can hand over his petition to Moses who will talk it over with the deity. It is of the essence of the leadership that there is the divine word in dialogue: informative and initiative speaking. The informative function passes afterwards from the divine speech to the oracle vessels called Urim and Thummim, and from the *nabi*—for as such the former writing prophets know Moses from tradition (Hos. 12:13)—to the priest; whereas the initiative speech, the genuine speech of the Leader which is no answer but a commission and a command, is henceforth also spoken only to the *nabi*, whom "the hand" seizes and sends. Kings rule, priests minister in their office, while the man of the Spirit, without power or office, hears the word of his Leader.

Besides the moveable divine abode, yet another feature of the nomadic period has entered into the life of the settled community and so deeply that it persisted long after the age of the settlement and shared the subsequent wanderings of the people in all ages and generations, becoming almost a perpetual renewal of the first event: the feast of the Passover.[15] A nomadic feast, as it certainly was in primitive times, it was transformed by the holy event into a feast of history; but that which recurs in the festival is the act of going forth, the beginning of the journeyings; the nomadic feast, without any historical character, becomes the historical feast. With loins girt, with feet shod, and with staff in hand, in the haste of departure they eat the sacrifice (Ex. 12:11). The Israelites do what was done formerly, not only performing the action, but in the performance doing it. Through the length and breadth of history, in every new home in a strange land, on this night the stimulus of the God-guided wanderings is active again, and history happens. The Israelites recount the story of the feast, this story which "cannot be the literary product of a later source," but which "contains facts," "solid tradition, springing from the ground of historic events." [16] But it is not the purpose to recount only what happened there and then. In the night of the Passover, "the assembled company is fused together in every year and in all the world with the first cult confederates and attains that unity, which existed formerly at the first occasion in Egypt." [17] As they who keep the covenant in life know it to be the covenant which "YHVH our God made with us in Horeb," "not with our fathers," but "with us our very selves here this day, all of us being alive" (Deut. 5:2f.), so telling the story of God's leading, they experience his historic deed as occurring to themselves. In his footsteps, they are wakeful through the night, which was a night of watching for YHVH and is now a night of watching for all the children of Israel in their generations (Ex. 12:42).

Berith, covenant, between YHVH and Israel denotes an expansion of the leadership and the following so as to cover every department of the people's life. The fundamental relationship represented perceptibly, that the deity—and it is the same in whatever form (pillar of fire, etc.) or even in no form (ark, "face")—goes before the company of wanderers and they follow after him, and know in their heart that his way is the right way, this relationship is now taken as an all-embracing relationship founded as an everlasting bond in the making of the covenant. Here the mutual character of this relationship is announced, but the people feel already that a covenant with such a deity as this means no legal agreement, but a surrender to the divine power and grace. The most sublime expression of this is given in two sayings of YHVH (3:14 and 33:19), which by their sentence structure are shown to belong to each other (two similar verbal forms linked by the word *asher,* meaning "whoever," "whomever"). The first says that indeed the deity is always present but in every given hour in the appearance that pleases him, that is to say, he does not allow himself to be limited to any form of revelation, and he does not limit himself to any of them; and the second says that he bestows his grace and mercy on whom he will, and lets no one order a criterion for him nor himself orders any. But connected with this is that element called YHVH's "demonism," [18] the dread of which overcomes us whenever we read about YHVH meeting Moses, his chosen and sent one, and "seeking to kill him" (4:24). This is no survival, no "primitive fiend" which has entered, as it were, by mistake from earlier polydemonism into this purer sphere, but it is of the essential stuff of early biblical piety, and without it the later form cannot be understood. The deity claims the chosen one or his dearest possession, falls upon him in order to set him free afterwards as a "blood bridegroom," as a man betrothed and set apart for him by his blood. This is the most ancient revelation of grace: the true grace is the grace of death, a gracing; man owes himself to the deity from the beginning. And here too, as with Jacob (Gen. 32), the event is sicnificantly linked with a journey ordered earlier: the wanderer has to go through the dangerous meeting in order to attain the final grace of the Leader-God.

The idea of following the deity raises itself—no longer in the Mosaic, but still in an early biblical age—to the idea of imitating the deity, notably in the interpretation of the greatest institution set up by Moses, the Sabbath. It appears that the Sabbath too was not created *ex nihilo,* although its origin is not yet clear.[19] It is certain that the material used for this institution was adopted by a mighty force of faith, recast and molded into an indestructible creation of the life of the faithful. It is impossible to think of an age later than that of Moses in which this could have happened. Many think the "ethical Decalogue" (Ex. 20) to be later than the "cultic" (34), but the latter, with its harvest and pilgrimage feasts, presupposes an agricultural usage, whereas the former is yet "timeless," not yet stamped with any particular organized form of human society;[20] the "cultic" is seen, after detailed examination, to be a "secondary mixture," whereas the "ethical" in its fundamental core is known to have a primary, "apodictic" character.[21] The Sabbath ordinance contained in it, in the original shorter version—beginning apparently with the word "remember" and continuing as far as "thy God"—is the ordinance of setting apart the seventh day for YHVH (that is to say, a day not ordered for cultic reasons, but freed of all authority of command except that of the one Lord). On this day, men do not do, as on other days, "any work"; the meaning of this for the nomad shepherd, for the shepherd who cannot neglect his flock, is that he puts off all "jobs which he can do today or leave to tomorrow," that he interrupts the cultivation of land in the oasis, that he does not journey to new places of pasture, and so on.[22] It is only in the age of the settlement that the Sabbath becomes a strict day of rest. Among the established and illustrative sayings that come up for consideration (we find in the Pentateuch seven variants of the ordinance), two are of special importance, Ex. 23:12 and Ex. 31:12ff. It is customary to connect them with different "sources" from different periods, but a very rare verb (which is only found elsewhere in the Bible once, in the apparently contemporaneous story of Absalom, II Sam. 16:14), meaning "to draw one's breath," links the two, the "social" and the "religious" motives, in the true biblical repetitive style, referring to one another and explaining one another. The one says that the purpose of the Sabbath ordinance was that the beast might rest and that men whose work is obligatory, that is to say, the slave and the hireling sojourner, who *must needs* work all the week, might draw breath. The other passage, which sets out the Sabbath ordinance in the most solemn form and imposes the death penalty upon those who transgress it, belongs in the original core of its first part (vv. 13-15 in a shorter version) to the species of ordinances in the "apodictical style" of which Alt writes.[23] Having examined them fundamentally in their typical difference from all the rest of the later Canaanite-influenced "casuistical" forms, he rightly says "that the rise of this species was possible when the bond-relationship to YHVH and the resulting institution of making and renewing the covenant with him came into being." But to this part of the ordinance is added a second, obviously a later expansion, in which the Sabbath is designated as an "everlasting covenant" and a "sign for ever," "for in six days YHVH made the heaven and the earth, and on the seventh day he rested and drew breath." The crass anthropomorphism binds together the deity and the tired, exhausted slave, and with words arousing the soul calls the attention of the free man's indolent heart to the slave; but at the same time, it sets

up before the community the loftiest sense of following the
Leader. Everyone that belongs to the essence of Israel—and the
servants, the sojourners included, belong to it—shall be able to
imitate YHVH without hindrance.

"The sayings in the apodictic form," says Alt,[24] "mostly have
to do with things with which casuistic law did not deal at all,
and by its secular nature could not deal. For the question is
here, on the one hand, the sacred sphere of contact with the
divine world, . . . and, on the other hand, the holy realms in
men's life together . . . religion, morals, and law are here still
unseparated." And again,[25] "in Israel's apodictic law an aggres-
sive, as yet quite unbroken force operates, a force which subjects every realm of life to the claim of absolute authority of
YHVH's will over his people; it therefore cannot recognize any
secular or neutral zone." These words fit our view that YHVH
as "God of Israel" does not become the lord of a cultic order
of faith, shut up within itself, but the lord of an order of people, covering all spheres of life—that is to say, a *melek,* and a
melek taking his authority seriously, unlike the gods of other
tribes. I do not mean to go too far beyond Alt's carefully
weighed thesis, and to connect with Sinai the whole series of
these sayings, rhythmically constructed so as to engrave them
upon the memory of the people, sayings among which there
recurs again and again the "I" of the speaking God and the
"thou" of the hearing Israel; but even in those that bear the
scent of the field about them, we feel that the fiery breath of
Sinai has blown upon them. They are fragments of a people's
order subject to the divine sovereignty.

Just as the term "divine sovereignty" means not a specialized
religious authority but a sovereignty operating on all of the
reality of community life, so the term "people's order" means
not the order of an indefinite society but of a completely definite people. To what is called, in the Song of Deborah and in
other ancient passages of Scripture, "people of YHVH," a secular concept can approximate, namely, that of "a true people,"
that is, a people that realizes in its life the basic meaning of
the concept *am* ("people"), of living one *im* ("with") another;
it approximates to it, though, to be sure, it does not actually
reach it. The "social" element in the apodictic laws is to be
understood not as the task of bettering the living conditions of
society, but as that of establishing a true people, the covenant
partner of the *melek;* the tribes are as yet a people only by
God's act and not by their own. If while, for example, in the

passages where it is ordered (Ex. 22:21 EV 22) not to afflict the widow and orphan, or (22:20 EV 21; 23:9) to oppress the sojourner, the reference is to individuals dependent on others, lacking security, subject to the might of the mighty, the object of such commands is not the single person, but the "people of YHVH," this people which shall rise, but cannot rise so long as social distance loosens the connections of the members of the people and decomposes their direct contact with one another. The *melek* YHVH does not want to rule a crowd, but a community. There is already recognizable here the prophetic demand for social righteousness, which reached its highest peak in the promise of the union of the peoples into a confederacy of mankind through the mediation of the "servant" coming forth from Israel (Is. 42:6).

Hence we see that the agricultural statute, with its ordinances for the periodical interruption of the family's privilege of eating the fruits of its allotted ground, the remission of debts in the Sabbatical year, and the leveling of all possessions in the year of Jubilee, is only late with regard to its literary setting (Lev. 25); but with regard to its contents it presents "a transposition of the patriarchal conditions of the wilderness age to the agricultural conditions of Palestine," and is designed so that "the absolute coherence of the people" will live on in the consciousness of the common possession of land.[26] This common ownership is by its nature God's property, as we know from ancient Arabic parallels,[27] and the undeniably early saying, "Mine is the land, for you are sojourners and settlers with me" (v. 23), expresses the ancient claim of the divine Leader, his claim to all the land of settlement.[28] We have already seen how in the patriarchal story the places occupied in Canaan were called by their divine names as signifying their owner, just as great estates are called by the names of their owners. (Ps. 49:12 EV 11). The divine ownership of the ground and the whole people's possession of it originate in a unity meant to last forever, whereas the rights of the individual are only conditional and temporary.

Within the ancient people's order, as we can deduce it from the apodictic laws, we find the sacred sphere of contact with the divine world substantially "only in the sense of keeping away all practices directed to gods or spirits other than YHVH, or implying a misuse of things belonging to him and therefore holy, as for example his name or the Sabbath." [29] Only a single short sacrificial statute (Ex. 20:24ff.) can be cited here in its original form, purified of additions.[30] The words, "in every place, where I cause my name to be remembered, I will come unto thee and bless thee," derive from the true character of the ancient nomad deity who does not allow himself to be kept to any mountain or temple. Sacrifices were apparently not customary in the wilderness apart from the nomadic offering of the firstborn of the flock (13:12; 34:19), except in extraordinary situations (the joining of Kenites, the ratification of the Sinai covenant). And there appears to have been no fixed sacrificial cult with special sacrificial rules; Amos was probably following a reliable tradition in this connection (5:25), although he gave it an extreme interpretation.

But there is one more feature belonging to this *melek* covenant between God and people, this leading and following, and that is the person of the mediator. The revelation, the making of the covenant, the giving of the statutes, was carried out by the "translating" utterance of a mortal man; the questions and requests of the people are presented by the words of this person; the kind of man who bears the word from above downwards and from below upwards is called *nabi*, announcer. So Hosea (12:14 EV 13) calls Moses. In the earlier parts of the Pentateuch, Moses is not so designated directly; in a remarkable story (Num. 12), an ancient verse inserted in it (vv. 6b-8a) sets Moses apparently above the *nebiim:* for they only know the deity by visions, whereas to Moses, "his servant," he speaks "mouth to mouth" (not mouth to ear, but really mouth to mouth "inspiring"; cf. also Ex. 33:11, "face to face, as when a man speaks to his neighbor"), and moreover not in riddles, which a man must still explain, but so that the hearing of the utterance is itself a "sight" of the intention. And this just fits the concept of the *nabi*, known also in a later verse of the Pentateuch (Ex. 7:1; cf. 4:16), where the "god" who speaks into a person is, so to say, dependent on the *nabi* who speaks out. It is relatively unimportant when this term came into existence, but it is important that the thing is as old as Israel. In the story, composed out of the saga material in a strictly consistent form, we are told in a manifold repetition of the roots *ra'ah, hazah* (to see) (Gen. 12:1, 7; 13:14, 15; 15:1; 17:1; 18:1, 2a, 2b), of the series of visions Abraham saw, until he became the mediator between below and above, an undismayed mediator, pleading with God (18:25), who now declares him to be a *nabi* (20:7); in this story, the prevailing view in prophetic circles of the antiquity of prophecy is obviously expressed. The temporary order of seer-prophet recalls an ancient note on word changes, which tells us more than mere word history (I Sam. 9:9). At all events, no age in the history of early Israelite faith can be understood historically without considering as active therein this type of man with his mission and function, his declaration and mediation. Whatever else Moses is or does, his prophecy, his ministry of the word, is the center of his nature and work. It is true, he does not "prophesy," the prophetic mission in the strict sense belonging to a later and different situation between God and people; but he does everything a prophet should in this early situation: he represents the Lord, he enunciates the message, and he commands in his name.

Here we meet a problem, which historically, both in the spiritual and the political sense, is singularly important.[31] The divine *melek* leads the *kahal*, the assembly of men,[32] by means of the one favored and called by him, the bearer of the "charismatic" power, the power of grace. This power, however, is not based, as with oriental kings, upon the myth of divine birth or adoption, but upon the utterly unmythical secret of the personal election and vocation, and is not hereditary. After the man's death, it is necessary to wait until the *ruah*, the stormy breath ("spirit") of the deity, rushes into another man. (Of the transmission of the visible charisma, the "splendor," or part of it, to a man "in whom there is spirit," Scripture speaks only once, the transmission by Moses to "his servant" Joshua, Num. 27:15ff. The doubtfulness of this passage was later increased considerably with the insertion of the Urim as a determining power of leadership, vv. 21f.). Because of this, the commission, and therefore the actual leadership, is discontinuous, which in the time of the conquest served the semi-nomads ill, for even without this they were given to unlimited family and tribal particularism, loosening the YHVH confederation and weakening "Israel's" power of action. Joshua's attempt to secure the continued unity of the people by getting rid of the family idols and by founding a tribal amphictyony[33] around a cult-directed center only, succeeded but partially, as can be seen from the Song of Deborah. The divine *melek*, who wishes to determine the whole life of the community, is not content to be replaced by a cult deity, to whom it is sufficient to offer sacrifice at the yearly pilgrimages. The Sinai enthusiasm for the absolute God rises again and expresses itself in the activity and song of the Deborah circle. But the increasing difficulties of completing the as yet incomplete conquest, and of strengthening a position against hostile neighbors, result in arousing against this theopolitical ardor a "realist-political" movement, which aims at establishing the hereditary charisma known to Israel from the great powers, and thus achieving a dynastic security of continuity. The opposition of those faithful to the *melek* arises with special strength in the days of Gideon, whose refusal to accept the royal crown may be regarded as historically true.[34] But already his son Abimelech stands in the opposite camp. And a national catastrophe, which the people may be inclined to see as a defeat of the Leader God himself, occurs; on the battlefield of Ebenezer, the victorious Philistines capture the ark of the covenant, which went at the head of the Israelite host. This hour represents the turning point in the history of Israelite faith.

3

"UPON EAGLES' WINGS"

The hour has come. The sign promised to Moses by the voice which spoke from the burning bush is now about to be fulfilled. "At this mountain," Israel is to enter the service of the God. What had come into being yonder only as word must now take on flesh. It is the hour: not of revelation, which had begun with that call "Moses!"; it is the hour of the "covenant." The man aflame with the urgent truth of his mission has fulfilled the first charge laid upon him: he has brought the people to the Mountain of God. "In the third month after the departure of the Children of Israel from Egypt, to the very day, they came to the wilderness of Sinai. . . . And Israel camped there, facing the mountain." And now, as Moses, unsummoned, like a messenger who is come to report to his lord the execution of a mission, ascends the mountain "to the God," which assuredly means to the place of that earlier revelation, the voice comes, as it were, to meet him; and YHVH entrusts him with the mission unto the house of Jacob.

This message is a rhythmic utterance, in which once again almost every word stands in the place fixed for it by sound and sense. Only one sentence, "when ye hearken, hearken unto my voice and keep my covenant," does not appear to be in place within the firm rhythm here, but would seem to indicate either a reworking or an interpolation. Enigmatically singular and independent, the passage as a whole has sometimes been attributed to later literary strata, with which it actually has certain concepts and turns of phrase in common. In our days, however, the view is increasingly being held[35] that here we have an old, genuinely traditional fragment which goes back to Moses himself; if not verbally, then at all events in basic content. Indeed, I know no other text which expresses so clearly and effectively as this what I would like to call the theopolitical idea of Moses; namely, his conception of the relation between YHVH and Israel, which could not be other than political in its realistic character, yet which starts from the God and not from the nation in the political indication of goal and way. In order to see this clearly, we must certainly treat the speech as early; that is, we must understand the weightiest words in it not in the sacral meaning with which they have been vested in the course of time, but in their aboriginal sense.

"You have seen what I did in Egypt. I bore you upon eagles' wings and brought you unto me" (Ex. 19:4). The first part of this verse summarizes the negative aspect of a decisive point of view. In order that Israel might come here to the God, it was necessary for that to befall the Egyptians which had befallen them; and it also had to befall them in such a fashion that Israel itself should see that which befell. Only as those who saw, and seeing "confided," could they be brought to YHVH, to the meeting with him. And so they were brought to him "upon eagles' wings." Those who consider such an image as this to be no more than a happy metaphor miss the intent of the whole passage. The basis of comparison here is not the speed of the eagles or their strength, which would be an introduction scarcely suited to a first divine manifesto to the assembled people; at that moment, something fundamentally important regarding the historical relationship between YHVH and Israel has to find its expression through the figure of speech used. This is achieved in an image which is admittedly too meager to be fully comprehended by us: but the early listener or reader certainly grasped the sense. Later, it may nevertheless have proved desirable to elucidate it by means of expansion, and a poetic commentary which we have reason to assume reflects the traditional view has been preserved in the late "Song of Moses" (Deut. 32:1).

Here YHVH is likened in his historical relationship with Israel to the eagle, who stirs up his nest and hovers above it in order to teach his young how to fly. That the latter are taken to mean the peoples cannot be doubted, as in the Song, shortly before (*ibid.*, 8), the Highest had allotted their territories to the nations and had fixed their boundaries. The great eagle spreads out his wings over the nestlings; he takes up one of them, a shy or weary one, and bears it upon his pinions until it can at length dare the flight itself and follow the father in his mounting gyrations. Here we have election, deliverance, and education all in one.

The verse following likewise certainly dealt in its original form with the *berith*, the "covenant," which called for mention at this spot. Yet it must be assumed that no demand, after the fashion of a prerequisite condition for everything that was to follow, was made in it for a docile observance of the sections of the covenant by Israel, but that the verse contained the hitherto unconveyed notification that YHVH wished to make a *berith* with Israel. The original meaning of *berith* is not "contract" or "agreement"; that is, no conditions were originally stipulated therein, nor did any require to be stipulated.

In order to gain an idea of what is really comprehended in this concept, we can best start with the story of David, which consists of chroniclers' tales that were certainly recorded for the most part soon after the events with which they deal. Here we find two kinds of *berith,* which are not conceptually differentiated from each other. One is the alliance between two people who stand to some degree on the same level, like that concluded by David and Jonathan (I Sam. 18:3, 23:18). This we may describe on the basis of Arab and other analogies as a covenant of brotherhood. That this leads to a mutual undertaking of unconditional support, a faithfulness even unto death, is not stated, and does not have to be stated, for it stands to reason. The two covenanters have just become brethren, which is quite enough in a social form where the clan is still the central reality of communal life. Any detailed agreement is superfluous.

The other kind of *berith* is found most clearly in the covenant which David, now king of Judah, concludes with the elders of the northern tribes (II Sam. 5:3). Here there is no common level; the person at the higher level of power concludes a covenant, not "with" the submitting ones, but "for them." Here, too, no special agreement is necessary, and indeed there is no room for any such thing. The relation of overlordship and service, into which the two partners enter, is the decisive factor. Engagements, concessions, constitutional limitations of power may be added, yet the covenant is founded not on them but on the basic fact of rule and service. According to its principal form, I classify this kind of *berith* as the royal covenant.[36] It is this kind which YHVH makes with Israel.

The argument cannot be offered against this view that in the Genesis narrative there is another kind of covenant, which the God makes either with living creatures in general (Gen. 9:9ff.), or with a chosen family (Gen. 6:18, 17:2ff.). This, too, is not a contract, but an assumption into a life-relationship, a relationship comprehending the entire life of the men involved—according to the situation, however, not into a relationship which has a political, theopolitical character. Only here, only in the Sinai covenant and its later renewals, is it a *berith* between YHVH and the people, between him and Israel, no longer Israel as the "seed of Abraham," out of which a people has to grow, but as the people which has grown out of that seed. And in accordance with this, the concept of royal dominion is also expressly introduced here (Gen. 17:6). This life relationship between the King and his people is the important thing. In the narrative of the conclusion of the covenant itself, a "Book of the Covenant" is certainly read out by Moses (Ex. 24:7f.), and the covenant is considered to be concluded "upon all these words." This book, however, has the character not of an agreement but of a royal proclamation. The laws contained therein are registered accordingly in the record of the making of the covenant as those proclaimed in that hour (Ex. 34:27). But these laws cannot claim any priority over those which may be proclaimed later on, and when the people declare after the reading that they wish "to do and to hear," they clearly signify that they bind themselves not in respect of specific ordinances as such, but in respect of the will of their Lord, who issues his commands in the present and will issue them in the future, in the respect of the life relationship of service to him.

Those who maintain the Kenite hypothesis argue:[37] "If YHVH had been the God of Israel even before Moses, a covenant would have been superfluous; for it would have stood to reason that YHVH was the God of Israel and Israel the people of YHVH. Contracts are only made where the demands of the contracting parties differ and may under certain circumstances become opposed to one another. For this reason it follows of necessity from the idea of covenant that Israel and YHVH had hitherto been strangers to one another." But *berith* is not the same as agreement or contract. YHVH and Israel enter into a new relation to one another by making the covenant, a relation which had not previously been in existence, and further could not have been in existence because Israel as a nation, as a nation which was able to elect itself a king and submit to his service, had been constituted only in that hour. YHVH, speaking from the flame, had anticipated this hour with that *ammi* of his. He now proclaims that the hour has come, and utters the words about his kingdom. In its present form, the narrative has the people begin with the proclamation of the king in the final verse of the Song of the Sea. The older tradition, however, was obviously that according to which the first and decisive word was uttered from above.

The proclamation of the covenant is immediately followed by YHVH's assurance that Israel will be for him "a peculiar treasure among all the nations." *Segulah*, the Hebrew word translated in the Authorized Version as "peculiar treasure," means a possession which is withdrawn from the general family property because one individual has a special relation to it and a special claim upon it. The meaning of the word as employed in connection with the relation between YHVH and Israel is immediately explained here by the words "for the whole earth is mine." It is impossible to express more clearly and unequivocally that the liberation from Egypt does not secure the people of Israel any monopoly over their God. From this phrase there is a direct line leading to the warning of the prophet (Amos 9:7), which also refers to the Exodus, the warning which glorifies this God as the one who has also guided other nations in their wanderings, even the neighboring nations which are foes of Israel, and which glorifies this God as the liberator of the nations. The expression "peculiar treasure" is directly imperilled by an atmosphere of restriction and self-assurance, unless it is accompanied by such an explanation. This we can see in three cases (Deut. 7:16, 14:21, 26:18), where the word is used in the book of Deuteronomy (a work which may well have developed from a collection of traditional sayings of Moses in a number of variant forms, rather like the Hadith of Mohammed in Islamic tradition). All these three passages are associated with the concept of the "holy people," which is also derived from the Eagle Speech. The danger of particularist misunderstanding is so obvious that in the first passage a warning is issued against ascribing the choice made by God to their own importance. The Eagle Speech itself opposes the haughty stressing of the choice by the subsequent message that the choice means a charge imposed on them and nothing more; and that therefore the choice, so to say, exists only negatively unless the charge is also fulfilled.

This message became obscured for later generations by the

fact that, as already mentioned, its great concepts no longer retained their original concreteness, but were understood in accordance with a technical waning of meaning. When one reads "you shall become unto me a kingdom of priests and a holy people," it at first strikes us almost irresistibly as though it is not the theopolitical idea of a factual divine domination which finds expression here, but a cult conception which aims at being all-embracing. But that is not so. The period whose loftiest thought was given shape by the Eagle Speech was concerned not with "religion," but with God and people; that is, with God's people on a basis of political and social realism, with what might almost be called a pre-state divine state. The word *mamlakah*, which is translated "kingdom," means king's rule, and likewise area of the king's rule; and the word *kohanim*, which usually means priests, is synonymous, where it describes a secular court office, with "the first at the hand of the king" (Cf. I Sam. 8:18 with I Chron. 18:17), or with companion, adjutant (I Kings 4:5; cf. II Sam. 20:26 and I Chron. 27:33). The *mamlakah* comprises those particular servants of the king who attend immediately upon him. *Mamleketh kohanim* therefore means the direct sphere of rule of the lord, composed of those of his companions who are at his immediate disposal, his immediate retinue. All of them, all the Children of Israel, stand in the identical direct and immediate relationship of retainers to him.

To this corresponds the second member of the sentence, "a holy people." And this balancing phrase, as is so frequent in parallelisms of the kind, is simultaneously a completion, and indeed a clarifying completion, of the sense. As the elemental meaning of the biblical concept of holiness we have to assume a power drawn and concentrated within itself, which, however, radiates forth and is capable of exerting both a destructive and a "hallowing" effect. In relation to YHVH, holiness is regarded as his direct power, dispensing both good and ill, and thence as the derived quality of those things and beings which are separated from out of the unspecified common realm, the "profane," and are dedicated or dedicate themselves to YHVH, and which, since they are dedicate to him, and as long as they are so dedicate to him, are hallowed by his only force.

Therefore *goy kadosh*, as complement of that *memleketh kohanim* which means the charging and appointment by God, thus requires and implies a spontaneous and ever renewed act on the part of the people. They have to dedicate themselves to

YHVH and remain dedicate to him, and further they must do this as *goy*, that is, with their corporeal national existence. Hence, the intention is not the behavior of the members of the people, as it is later (Ex. 22:30), of all members of the people as individuals, as for example, that they shall refrain from unclean, polluting foods; the point at issue is the behavior of the national body as such. Only when the nation with all its substance and all its functions, with legal forms and institutions, with the whole organization of its internal and external relationships, dedicates itself to YHVH as its Lord, as its *melek,* does it become his holy people; only then is it a holy people.

And specifically as that, and as that alone, can it render its divine Leader the services for which he has selected it: as "the first to his hand" of the "whole earth," which is "his"; in order to transmit his will, which it fulfils by means of its own life. It is laid upon Israel to factualize, by way of this office and this dedication, YHVH's choice of them as a "peculiar treasure" among all peoples; this is the *berith* he wishes to conclude with them.

The biblical narrative makes Moses "offer" his theopolitical message to the elders, and "the whole people" answer through the latter that they will do what YHVH has said, that is, that they will enter the *melek* covenant which he wishes to conclude with them. That what took place at Sinai was understood even in early tradition as such a covenant, as a royal pronouncement from above and as an acclamation of royalty from below, is indicated by the hymn which is placed as the frame of the so-called "Blessing of Moses" (Deut. 33:1-7, 26-29). Even radical critics[38] conclude from the resemblance between this psalm and the Song of Deborah "that in itself it may be old and indeed very old." But since Israel is twice referred to in it under the name "Yeshurun," which is otherwise found only in two late passages, it is assumed that the language of the text before us is not so much archaic as archaicizing. In both those other passages, however, this name which would appear to derive from the old folk-singers (compare the title of an old collection of songs, *Sepher Hayashar* or Book of the Upright), has been taken over with a conscious purpose. Following a few difficult, and in part incomprehensible verses, the hymn reads with absolute clarity (*ibid.,* 5): "And there came about in Yeshurun a king, when the heads of the people foregathered, the tribes of Israel together." No interpretation other than a reference to what happened at Sinai, which is mentioned at the commencement of the hymn, serves to do justice to this important passage. The great *melek* message appears to be the one which is lauded in the preceding verse as "the teaching which Moses commanded us." [39]

Historically considered, the idea finding expression in the Eagle Speech and associated texts is the challenge offered to Pharaonism by the Hebrew tribes, departing from Egypt into freedom. The freedom is understood by their leader as God's freedom, and that means as God's rule. Historically considered, this means the rule of the Spirit through the persons charismatically induced and authorized as the situation warrants, its rule on the basis of the just laws issued in the name of the Spirit. The entire conception of this royal covenant, which aims at being all-embracing, is only possible when and because the God who enters into the covenant is just and wishes to introduce a just order into the human world. Justice as an attribute is in some degree implicit in the old Semitic conception of the tribal gods as judges of the tribes.[40] It achieved completion in the God-conception of Israel. The just law of the just *melek* is there in order to banish the danger of "Bedouin" anarchy, which threatens all freedom under God. The unrestrained instinct of independence of the Semitic nomads, who do not wish to permit anybody to rise above them and to impose his will upon them,[41] finds its satisfaction in the thought that all the Children of Israel are required to stand in the same direct relation to YHVH, but it achieves restraint through the fact that YHVH himself is the promulgator and guardian of the law. Both together, the kingship of God as the power of his law over human beings and as the joy of the free in his rule, achieve expression in the ideal image of Israel which is found in an old lyric utterance[42] attributed to the heathen prophet Balaam (Num. 23:21): "One beholds no trouble in Jacob and one sees no toilsomeness in Israel, YHVH his God is with him and *melek* jubilation is in him." YHVH the "Present One" is really present among his people, who therefore proclaim him as their *melek*.

During the period following the conquest of Palestine, the *melek* title was rarely employed for YHVH, obviously in order to differentiate him from the "religious and political Canaanite world with its divine kings and its monarchistic state forms," [43] and particularly because these *melek* or *"moloch"* gods demanded children as sacrifices.[44] But the idea of divine rule remained in existence, as can be seen from the narratives of Gideon and Samuel.[45] During the early period of David's rule, it once again, as I would suppose, received magnificent poetic formulation in the four verses now placed at the end of Psalm 24, praising YHVH the "hero of war" and "the king of glory," who enters Jerusalem invisibly enthroned on the Ark of the Covenant. But the factual meaning had already begun to undergo its transformation into the symbolic. Under the influence of the dynasty, which consistently opposed all attempts of the Spirit to influence public life, the conception of divine rule soon became quite pallid. Only Isaiah, in the notes of his annunciatory vision (Is. 6:5), dared to contrast YHVH as "the," that is, as the true, *melek* with King Uzziah, whom he had smitten with leprosy. In all later Psalms which sing of YHVH's ascent to the throne, he is only the Cosmocrator, which means far more in appearance but far less in reality. For the true kingship does not exist without a people who recognize the king. When the whole world appears in those Psalms as such a people, the action is thereby shifted to an eschatological level, to a future becoming-perfect of the creation. Unlimited recognition of the factual and contemporary kingship of God over the whole national existence, however, is what was required of Israel, in the midst of the historical reality, by the message which found its form in the Eagle Speech.

4

THE WORDS ON THE TABLETS

Certain excerpts from a "Theosophia," presumably written by an Alexandrian of the fifth century C.E.,[46] have come down to us. In these, we are told, among many other memorabilia, that Moses had actually written two decalogues. The first and hence older of them reads, "For their altars ye shall smash, their pillars ye shall break, their sacred poles ye shall cut down," and so on. This refers, of course, to Exodus 34:13-26, out of which it would be possible to construct ten commandments, though with a certain amount of difficulty. The second is the decalogue of tradition, Exodus 20:2-17. To give this view expression in modern scientific terminology, it means that Moses preceded his "ethical" decalogue with an earlier "cultic" one, which starts polemically and then goes on to various prescriptions. That the commencement proposed by the author, which begins with "his" and refers to the peoples already mentioned, cannot be any real commencement, was apparently not noticed by him.

In a dissertation on the Tablets of Moses, prepared with "indescribable toil," which the University of Strasbourg rejected, Goethe undertook to prove "that the Ten Commandments were not actually the covenantal laws of the Israelites." A year and a half later, he returned to this thesis in a little paper entitled "Two important and hitherto unclarified Biblical Questions thoroughly dealt with for the first time by a country priest in Swabia." In this paper, he has his country priest offer a view largely identical with that finding expression in the "Theosophia," which was unknown to Goethe. He begins, however, with the sentence "Thou shalt worship no other God," which might indeed be the starting-point for a decalogue. Goethe sets out to overcome the "troublesome old error" that the covenant "by which God pledged himself to Israel" could "be based on universal obligations." What is regarded by us as the decalogue is only "the introduction to the legislation" which, in the view of the Swabian village pastor, contains doctrines "that God presupposed in his people as human beings and Israelites." Behind this, however, lies Goethe's actual idea, though not without some contradiction of what has been said: that the history and doctrine of the People Israel had a particularist and not a universal character until the time when Christianity was grafted on to its stem. Some decades later, in his notes and studies to the "West-Oestlicher Divan," Goethe declared that he had endeavored to separate "what would be fitting to all lands, to all moral people" from that "which especially concerns and is binding on the People Israel." He did not specify this separation in any greater detail; in any case, however, his views as they find expression in his early work remain a pace behind those of his masters Hamann and Herder, who recognized in that particularism the earthly vehicle without which nothing universal can achieve earthly life.

A century after the "Two Questions," Wellhausen, who was long followed and in wide circles still is followed without restriction by critical Bible study, undertook to prove the priority of the "Goethean Law of the Two Tablets" by means of a comprehensive critical analysis of sources. Exodus 20 and Exodus 34, he held, are diametrically opposed. "There the commandments are almost entirely moral; here they are exclusively ritual." [47] And obviously, in accordance with a view still prevalent in our own days, the ritual decalogue must be older and in fact original. The decalogue of Exodus 20 accordingly appears to be influenced by the prophetic protest against ritualism, whereas that of Exodus 34 would mirror the primitive pansacralism of the Moses epoch, though after a fashion conditioned by the setting actually found in Canaan.

If we consider this so-called "cultic" decalogue without prejudice, we find that it is not a complete whole in itself like the "ethical" one, but consists of a compilation of appendices and complements—chiefly, furthermore, such as would comprehensibly derive from a transition to regular agriculture and the civilization associated therewith. Most of them, supplements almost exclusively, are also to be found in the same or an analogous form in the so-called "Book of the Covenant" (Ex. 20:22 to 23:19). The complements, on the other hand, in no case refer to the laws of this book, but only to those which are found either in the "ethical decalogue" itself or else in prescriptions to be found earlier in the text. Thus, the provisions for the sacrifice or redemption of the animal first-born (Ex. 13:11 ff.) are extended to horned cattle (cf. Ex. 22:29). Two characteristic complements to Exodus 20 are provided: the prohibition of images, which in that context has as its subject only such as are hewn and carved (this still remains to be shown), is extended there to graven images (cf. Ex. 20:23), while the commandment of Sabbath rest is rendered more stringent by being made applicable even to the seasons of ploughing and harvesting, the times of most pressing work in the fields. From all this, it may reasonably be concluded that this compilation was younger than the decalogue in its original form. It has therefore been justly described more recently as a "secondary mixed form," [48] save that it may certainly be considered as older than the redaction of the Book of the Covenant in our possession, since it assuredly did not borrow the doublets from the latter. Still, the selection was clearly made in accordance with a specific attitude, so that we may well assume to have before us the "house-book of a Palestinian sanctuary," [49] prepared from old material.

Critical research of the Wellhausen school has for the greater part not, or only inadequately, recognized the real character of this composition. In general, it has not ceased to stress its "great age" and the "influence of the foundation of the religion of Moses" [50] that finds expression in it; as against which the date of the decalogue was shifted into ever later times, until the assumption was made that it could belong only to the exilic or post-exilic age,[51] and must in fact constitute the catechism of the religious and moral duties of Israel in exile,[52] and as such must be "a product of the religious needs of Israel in exile." [53] Supporters of a more moderate point of view still found it necessary to explain that the Ten Commandments were "both impossible and superfluous for archaic Israel." [54]

As against this negative self-certainty, the past three decades have seen the emergence of the feeling that it is necessary to examine the situation once again, irrespective of all preconceptions and theories.

For the greater part, the argument had been conducted on the basis of single commandments, which were held to be incompatible with the social and cultural, moral and literary conditions of the early period; to which the protagonists of the Mosaic origin of the decalogue had replied by characterizing the passages which were questionable in respect of content and language as later supplements, and in turn laid bare an incontestably original decalogue. Now, however, the stress is being increasingly shifted from the parts to the whole.

The thesis of the impossibility of such high ethical standards in those days lost its force when the publication and translation of Egyptian and Babylonian texts led to the dissemination of information regarding, and to appreciation of, a reality in the history of the human mind which has received the name of the "ancient Oriental moral code," but which might rather be regarded as the ancient Oriental tendency to commingle cultic prohibitions and postulates with those of a moral kind. In those texts which have become best known and are also most characteristic—a confession of the dead before the judges of the dead found in the Egyptian Book of the Dead (deriving from the period in which the Exodus from Egypt took place), and a "catalogue of sins" from the Babylonian conjuration tablets—the moral part is the greater by far;[55] and this fact is quite sufficient in itself to break down the general assumption that cult necessarily preceded ethics. But even if we turn our attention to the so-called primitive races and read, say, the tribal lore of an East African tribe,[56] which the elders pass on to adolescents about to be admitted into the community, we observe that their real concern is with the correct relations between the members of a family, the members of a clan; there is, furthermore, the important fact of the repeated stressing that this is the will of the god, of the "Heaven Man." The most thoroughgoing opponents of a Mosaic origin for the decalogue therefore no longer reject the possibility that Moses may have proclaimed moral commandments such as those to be found in the decalogue. "The moral commandments of the decalogue," says one of these opponents,[57] "belong to those basic laws with which even the most primitive of societies cannot dispense."

So the question at issue is now held to be whether Moses could have regarded the moral commandments "as the totality of the basic prescriptions of religion," and whether he really presented "the *collection* of these commandments as the religious and moral norm par excellence"—which, however, "would appear improbable and unthinkable in the highest degree, according to the evidence of the sources." "The question," says another critic,[58] "is not whether Moses could have established certain individual religious and moral demands with this content, but whether Moses, taking into consideration all that we otherwise know of his religious attitude, can be believed to have been capable of compressing the basic demands of religiousness and morality into this decalogue, while excluding from it all the other motives which at the time were of importance in religious and moral life; whether he can be supposed to have done this with a genius which would find its parallel only in Jesus, and which, indeed, would needs have been far greater in the case of Moses, who stands at the beginning of religious development, than in that of Jesus."

What is meant by the words "all that we otherwise know of his religious attitude" in this context is explained as follows: from the material of the most ancient sagas, we received quite a different picture of the personality of Moses than that which we must assume in order to comprehend the decalogue as having been his work. "Moses the sorcerer, the healer, the dispenser of oracles, the Faustian magician is a different figure from the man who summarized the essence of piety and morality in the few lapidary sentences of the decalogue." But quite irrespective of the basic problem, regarding which it is possible to hold very different views—the problem as to which are the oldest sagas, and even assuming that in these Moses appears as a thaumaturgist and the like, what conclusions could be drawn from this? On the same page of a book to which the scholar just quoted refers, we first read:[59] "Moses the Faustian magician is an entirely believable figure of the steppes," and then: "the deeds of the ancient heroes were already felt by their contemporary world as wonders and enchantments, and those heroes themselves may likewise easily have regarded them in the same way." That Moses himself experienced and understood many of his own deeds, particularly the decisive ones, as "wonders," or more correctly, as deeds of his God performed through him, is obvious—which, however, does not transform him into a "Faustian magician," but if anything into the contrary; yet the idea that he himself regarded anything he did as "sorcery" seems to me to lie beyond all proof. In legend, to be sure, and to some degree even in the legend which blossomed in the minds and memories of those who were present, something of the kind may have taken place—clearly under the influence of Egyptian conceptions;[60] those people, thirsting for miracle, whose remolding memory allowed them to remember events as they did not occur and could not have occurred, were prepared to transform God himself into a sorcerer, and with him his messenger. The same process was doubtless at work, and very early at that, in the legend of Jesus. It was not enough to glorify his healings; the legend set him also walking on the sea, giving his commands to the winds and turning water into wine. Great is the work of the saga, and as ever it still thrills our heart;[61] that, however, should not prevent us from penetrating wherever possible beyond the veil of legend and, as far as we can, viewing the pure form which it conceals.

In this, nothing helps us so much, with Moses as with Jesus and others, as those utterances which, by use of criteria other than a general judgment derived from the saga material about the "religious attitude" of a person, may properly be attributed to the specific man with whom we deal. There is certainly no doubt that Moses took over archaic rites that were charged with magical meaning. Yet, as we have seen in the case of the Passover, the Sabbath, and the Blood Covenant, he brought about a fundamental transformation of meaning in them without thereby depriving them of any of their vitality, rather rejuvenating this very vitality by transmuting it from a nature to an historical vitality. The change in meaning which he introduced was drawn by him from the same ground of faith, the same kind and power of faith, which was given imperishable form in the first three of the Ten Commandments. It is not hard to understand, when one has at length touched this ground of faith, that Moses should have worded these, and specifically these, basic demands—no less but likewise no more —and fashioned them into a unity.

An attempt must be made, however, to render the situation even clearer in its details.

What the critics have more recently been using as arguments against the Mosaic origin of the decalogue refers, as has been said, not to the content of the individual commandments, but to their elevation to the level of fundamentals of religion, or, I would prefer to say, to fundamentals of community life under the rule of God. This has been demonstrated with particular impressiveness in connection with the prohibition of statues and images; nor can we choose any better example in order to elucidate the actual facts.

One of the most radical of critics has admitted[62] that the iconoclastic movement in later Israel may with some justification have referred itself to Moses. As among the ancient Arabs and in the early days of the Semitic cultures in general, art does not appear to have been put to use in the cult practices. We know that the pre-Islamic Arabs[63] were beginning to convert stones into images of gods by bringing out a natural resemblance—say, to a human head—with the aid of art. Between this primitive cultural situation and the later tendencies directed against images of the god, there lay the essential difference that the primitive Semites regarded their imageless cult as a natural usage, whereas it constituted a program of reform for the later ones. What is natural would not require to be fixed by any separate or special commandment. The cult in which absence of images is a principle could therefore, it is claimed, not derive from the days of Moses.

Edvard Lehmann has justly pointed out[64] that it is often difficult to decide whether a cult is imageless because it does not yet require images or because it no longer requires them. But there are historically important constellations in which the appearance of a great personality during the pre-image period anticipates the highest teachings of the post-image period in a simple form that cannot be improved upon.

We must first realize that matters are by no means simple as regards the pre-image stage in Mosaic Israel, if we assume that Israel was then under Egyptian influence, not in the matter of belief in some gods or other, but in respect of the custom of making images of the gods believed in. If this was indeed the case, a conflict must necessarily have come about between those who could not or did not wish to break down this influence, and those who wished to eradicate it. If, however, we assume that the unabbreviated wording of the "prohibition of images" is of early date (I mean that, although only Ex. 20:4a belongs to the original text, the rest of the verse was added very early), the prospects continue to expand before us, seeing that in that case we have more than a prohibition of images. For that prohibition is followed by a prohibition of the worship of any of the figures that could be perceived in the heavens, on the earth, or in the water ("And every figure that . . . and that . . . and that . . . , bow not down before them and serve them not"). In Egypt, the great national gods appeared in the forms of beasts and other natural beings. Hence, once the "other gods" have been excluded in verse 3, there is an implicit prohibition of worshipping YHVH himself in an image or in one of the natural forms.

We penetrate even deeper when we base our viewpoint on what we know of the God of Israel.

Originally, he was what has been called a "god of way," [65] but he differed in character from all the other gods of way. The function of a god of way, who accompanies and protects the wandering nomads and the caravans through the wilderness, was exercised in Mesopotamia by the moon, the god "who opens the way," and his assistants. In Syria, it was the evening star who served this purpose. (Characteristically enough, such a god of way of the Nabataeans, whose name meant roughly "he who accompanies the tribe," was apparently considered by Epiphanius to be the deified Moses.[66]) It is assuredly something more than a mere coincidence that the name of the city of Haran, which together with Ur was the chief city of the moon cult and in which Abraham separated from his clan, meant way or caravan, and would appear to have designated the spot "where the caravans met and from which they started out." [67] The God by whom Abraham, after "straying away" from Haran, is led in his wanderings, differs from all solar, lunar, and stellar divinities, apart from the fact that he guides only Abraham and his own group,[68] by the further fact that he is not regularly visible in the heavens, but only occasionally permits himself to be seen by his chosen, whenever and wherever it is his will to do so. This necessarily implies that various natural objects and processes are on occasion regarded as manifestations of the God, and that it is impossible to know for certain where or wherein he will next appear.

It may be supposed, and is readily understandable, that among the Hebrew tribes resident in Egypt the guiding function of the ancient clan God had been forgotten. But this clearly is what revives within the spirit of Moses in Midian when he meditates upon the possibility of bringing forth the tribes. The God who meets him wishes to resume his guiding function, but for "his people" now. With his words, "I shall be present howsoever I shall be present," he describes himself as the one who is not restricted to any specific manner of manifestation, but permits himself to be seen from time to time by those he leads and, in order to lead them, to be seen by them after the fashion which he prefers at the given moment.[69]

Thus it can be understood that clouds, and smoke, and fire,

and all kinds of visual phenomena are interpreted by Moses as manifestations from which he has to decide as to the further course through the wilderness, as to the whither and the how. But always, and that is the fundamental characteristic, YHVH remains the invisible one, who only permits himself to be seen in the flame, in "the very heavens," in the flash of the lightning. Admittedly anthropomorphic manifestations also alternate with these, but none of them shows an unequivocally clear-cut figure with which YHVH might be identified.

For this reason, he should not be imaged, that is, limited to any one definite form; nor should he be equated with one or another of the "figures" in nature, that is, restricted to any one definite manifestation. He is the history God that he is only when he is not localized in nature, and precisely because he makes use of everything potentially visible in nature, of every kind of natural existence, for his manifestation. The prohibition of "images" and "figures" was absolutely necessary for the establishment of his rule, for the investiture of his absoluteness before all current "other gods."

No later hour in history required this with such force; every later period which fought images could do nothing more than renew the ancient demand. Just what was immediately opposed to the founder-will of Moses makes no difference: whether the memories of the great Egyptian sculptures or the clumsy attempts of the people themselves to create, by means of some slight working of wood or stone, a reliable form in which the divinity could be taken with them. Moses certainly saw himself as facing a conflicting tendency, namely, that natural and powerful tendency which can be found in all religions, from the most crude to the most sublime, to reduce the divinity to a form available for and identifiable by the senses. The fight against this is not a fight against art, which would certainly be in contrast with the report of Moses' initiative in carving the images of the cherubim; it is a fight to subdue the revolt of fantasy against faith. This conflict is to be found again, in more or less clear-cut fashion, at the decisive early hours, the plastic hours, of every "founded" religion, that is, of every religion born from the meeting of a human person and the mystery. Moses more than anybody who followed him in Israel must have established the principle of the "imageless cult," or more correctly of the imageless presence of the invisible, who permits himself to be seen.[70]

Thus, in the case of the sentence whose antiquity has been

the most strongly disputed, we have shown that the roots of these commandments and prohibitions derive from a specific time and situation. However, this leaves open the decisive question as to whether the whole decalogue as such, as collection and composition, can be explained in terms of this specific time and situation, whether it can be assumed that Moses separated and unified precisely these phrases as an absolute norm, out of the wealth of existent or nascent statements regarding the right and the unright, regarding what should be and what should not be, while excluding all cultic elements.

First, we once again meet the argument of "primitivity," although in attenuated form. It is claimed [71] that at the Mosaic epoch the religion of Israel could not have possessed tendencies such as would have permitted the appearance of a "catechism," in which the cult is consciously thrust into the background and the main content of the religion is reduced to purely ethical statements. An assumption that this could have occurred is said to be based on "a lack of understanding of both the mentality and the civilization of the Mosaic epoch." [72] The "prelogical" thinking of those times is supposed to have included the primacy of the "sacral system," for "in his religion and the practice of his cult, primitive man has the means of producing everything that he urgently needs." [73] And in this sense, even "the loftiest efflorescence of Egyptian culture" is regarded as primitive.

The use of such a concept of primitiveness leads to a questionable simplification of religious history. Religions as complexes of popular practices and traditions are more or less "primitive" at all times and among all peoples. The inner struggle for faith, for the personally experienced reality, is nonprimitive in all religions. A religious change, an interior transformation which also alters the structure, never takes place, however, without an internal conflict. Particularly in the case of the religion of Israel, we cannot comprehend its ways and changes at all unless we pay attention to the inner dialectic, to the struggle, ever recurrent at various stages and in various forms, for the truth of belief, for revelation.

That this conflict began at the time of Moses, and indeed that he waged the primal fight from which everything subsequent, including the great protests of the prophets against a cult emptied of intention, can find its starting point, is proved, even though generally in legendary form, by the great and the small stories which tell of the "murmuring," the rebellion, the insurrection, in most of which we recognize or sense the presence of a religious problem in the background. The people wish for a tangible security, they wish to "have" the God, they wish to have him at their disposal through a sacral system; but it is this security which Moses cannot and must not grant them.

This, however, should not in any way be taken to mean that Moses had "founded a clear and conscious anti-cultic religion," [74] that is, a religion directed against the cult. Nothing is so likely to interfere with an historical cognition that is one not of categories but of facts as the introduction of alternatives formulated in so extreme a fashion. There can be no talk here of a simple rejection of the cult. It is quite enough to bear in mind, to begin with, that a semi-nomadic life does not encourage a high degree of cult practices and institutions; here in particular there is clearly a very ancient tendency "to place morality above the cult." [75] Further, it should also be remembered that all those elements which were likely to militate against the exclusive service of YHVH have been eliminated. For what remained there was need of a change not of form, but only of sense and content, in order to satisfy the purpose of Moses. The sacral principle remained; but the sacral assurance, the sacral power of utilizing the God, was uprooted, as was demanded by his character and essence. This sacral power was replaced by the consecration of men and things, of times and places, to the One who vouchsafes his presence amid his chosen people, if only the latter persevere in the royal covenant.

And why are there no cultic ordinances in the decalogue? Why is it that in the domain of cult nothing more is done than the prohibition of the false, not the prescription of the correct deeds? Why is the prescription of circumcision not to be found? Why is Sabbath observance required, but not that of the New Moon festival? Why the Sabbath, but not the Passover? Does not this, for instance, indicate a late origin, seeing that in exile, far from the Temple, the Sabbath came to be the center of religious life?

All these and similar questions taken together mean: why does the decalogue contain these precise commandments, these and none other, no more and no less? Why have these been joined together as the norm, and where in those early days could the principle have been found in accordance with which the association took place? Naturally, this question also includes the analogous questions which arise within the ethical field, such as: is it possible to suppose that in the time of Moses there could have been a prohibition of "coveting," which, in contrast to all the other prohibitions, was aimed not at action but at a state of mind? Or, on the other hand, why is there no prohibition of lying? [76]

It is desirable to offer a single and comprehensive answer to all these questions, and necessarily that answer will have to deal with both selection and composition. Hence the literary category as such must be a subject of interest. Why should there be a decalogue or anything resembling a decalogue? Why these ten commandments and no others? Why, which in turn means: to what end? To what end, and that in turn means: when?

In order to find an answer, we must first disabuse ourselves of the widely held view that the decalogue is a "catechism" which supplies the essence of the Israelite religion in summary fashion, in articles of faith that can be counted on the ten fingers, specially "prepared for learning by heart." [77] If we have to think of ten fingers, then rather those of the law-giver himself, who was first a law-finder, and who, so to say, sees in his two hands an image of the completeness requisite ere he raises those two hands towards the multitude. We miss the essential point if we understand the decalogue to be "the catechism of the Hebrews in the Mosaic period." [78] A catechism means an instruction for the person who has to be in a position to demonstrate his full membership in a religious community on the basis of general statements which he recites either in complete or in abbreviated form. Such a catechism is therefore prepared partly in the third person as a series of statements, and partly in the first as a series of articles of personal faith.

The soul of the decalogue, however, is to be found in the word "Thou." Here nothing is either stated or confessed, but orders are given to the one addressed, to the listener. In distinction to all catechisms and compositions resembling catechisms, everything here has reference to that specific hour in which the words were spoken and heard. It is possible that only the man who wrote down the words had once had the experience of feeling himself addressed; possibly he transmitted that which he heard to his people not orally, taking the "I" of the God in his own mouth as though it were his own, but only in written form, preserving the necessary distance. At all times, in any case, only those persons really grasped the decalogue who literally felt it as having been addressed to themselves, only those, that is, who experienced that first one's state of being addressed as though they themselves were being addressed. Thanks to its "thou," the decalogue means the preservation of the divine voice.

And if we now no longer formulate the question from the point of view of literary criticism, but in accordance with strictly historical categories, the decalogue again shows its difference in kind, its antithesis in fact to all catechisms. It is both legislation and promulgation, in the precise historical sense. What this means is that the intention to be recognized in it refers neither to articles of faith nor to rules of behavior, but to the constituting of a community by means of common regulation. This has been obscured through the fact that the contents of the single commandments are partly "religious" and partly "ethical," and that if the single commandments are considered on their own, they seem, even in their totality, to be directed towards the religious and ethical life of the individual, and appear to be capable of realization there. Only when the Ten Commandments are considered as a whole can it be recognized that no matter how repeatedly the individual alone is addressed, it is nevertheless not the isolated individual who is meant. If the "religious" commandments are taken by themselves, and the "ethical" by themselves, it is almost possible to gain the impression that they derived from a culture in which religion and morality have already become separate spheres, each with a special system and a special form of speech. If they are regarded in their connection, however, it will be observed that there are no such separate fields at all here, but only one as yet undifferentiated common life, which requires a constitution containing both "religious" and "ethical" elements in order to achieve a uniform growth.

Here the unifying force has to start from the conception of a divine lord. The disparate material out of which the people develop shapes itself into a closed national form as a result of their common relation to him. Only as the people of YHVH can Israel come into being and remain in being. The constitution appears not as something objective, to be taken at its own intrinsic value, but as an allocution by him, something which can be actualized only in and through a living relationship with him. It therefore begins by his designation of himself as the One who brought forth and liberated the Israel addressed, including each and every person addressed in Israel. God does not wish to speak as the Lord of the world that he is (Ex. 19:5b), but as the One who has led them forth from Egypt. He wishes to find recognition in the concrete reality of that historic hour; it is from that starting point that the people have to accept his rule.

This calls for and conditions a threefold commandment through a threefold prohibition. First: a commandment of an exclusive relationship of worship by means of the prohibition of other gods "in my face." Secondly: a commandment of self-dedication to his invisible but nevertheless manifesting presence, by means of a prohibition of all sensory representations. Thirdly: a commandment of faith to his name as the truly Present One, through the prohibition of carrying that name over to any kind of "illusion," [79] and thus of admitting that any kind of illusive thing whatsoever can participate in the presence of the Present One. This, to be sure, prohibits idol-worship, image-worship, and magic-worship. But the essential reason for which they have been prohibited is the exclusive recognition of the exclusive rule of the divine Lord, the exclusive leadership of the divine Leader; to this end it is necessary to recognize him as he is, and not in the shape with which people would like to endow him.

This first part of the decalogue, which bases the life of the community on the rule of the Lord, is built up in five phrases, all beginning "Thou shalt not" (the two phrases, beginning with "for," appear to be later supplements). If the final verse of the third section is restored to an original shorter version, it can be seen to consist likewise of five phrases beginning "Thou shalt not." (Therefore, to be precise, we have a group of twelve commandments before us.) Between these two groups comes a central section containing the commandment of the Sabbath and the commandment to honor parents (in shorter versions), both commencing with a positive injunction. The first, a "religious" one, refers back to what went before; the second as "ethical" refers ahead to those that follow.

Between the two of them, however, there is a connection other than the purely formal one. The two of them, and only these two among all of the Ten Commandments, deal with *time,* articulated time; the first with the closed succession of weeks in the year, the second with the open succession of generations in national duration. Time itself is introduced into the constitutional foundation of national life by being partly articulated in the lesser rhythm of the weeks, and partly realized in its given articulation through the greater rhythm of the generations. The former requirement is provided for by the repeated "remembering" of the Sabbath day as that which has been consecrated to YHVH; the latter, by the "honoring" of the parents. Both together ensure the continuity of national time; the never-to-be-interrupted consecution of consecration, the never-to-be-broken consecution of tradition.

There is no room here for the mention of special individual festivals alongside the Sabbath. The Sabbath represents the equal measure, the regular articulation of the year, and further, one which is not simply taken over from nature, which is not strictly lunar, but is based on the concept of the regular consecration of every seventh day. It is not the exceptional, not that which has to be done only at certain times and on certain occasions, but that which is of all time, that which is valid at all times, for which alone place must be found in the basic constitution. The cult is not in any way excluded, but only its general prerequisite postulates, as they are expressed in the first part of the decalogue, and not its details, have found acceptance here in accordance with the main purpose.

If the first part deals with the *God* of the community, and the second with the *time,* the one-after-the-other of the community, the third is devoted to the *space,* the one-with-the-other of the community in so far as it establishes a norm for the mutual relations between its members. There are four things above all which have to be protected in order that the community may stand firm in itself. They are life, marriage, property, and social honor. And so the damaging of these four basic goods and basic rights of personal existence is forbidden in the most simple and pregnant of formulas. In the case of the first three, the verb does not even possess any object; as a result of which the impression is given of a comprehensive and absolute prescription.

But these four commandments in themselves are not enough to protect the community from disorganization through the many kinds of inner conflicts that might break out. They apply only to actions, to the active outcome of passions or feelings of ill-will directed against the personal sphere of other people; they do not involve attitudes which have not passed into action.

There is one attitude, however, which destroys the inner connection of the community even when it does not transform itself into action, and which indeed, precisely on account of its passive or semi-passive persistence, may become a consuming disease of a special kind in the body politic. This is the attitude of envy. The prohibition of "covetousness," no matter whether it was without any object in its original form,[80] or read, "Do not covet the house [i.e., the content of the personal life in general, household, property, and prestige (cf. Ex. 1:21)] of your fellow-man," is to be understood as a prohibition of envy. The point here is not merely a feeling of the heart, but an attitude of one man to another which leads to a decomposition of the very tissues of society. The third part of the decalogue can be summarized in its basic tendency as: Do not spoil the communal life of Israel at the point at which you are placed.

Since, as we have seen, it is the will towards inner stability of the community which determined the selection of commandments and prohibitions, we must, if the decalogue is ascribed to a later period, necessarily note the absence of some phrase reading more or less as follows: Do not oppress thy fellow-man. In a community which was being broken up from within—as we know was the case during the period of the kings in Israel—by a vast increase of social inequality, by the misuse of the power of property to gain possession of smaller properties, by the exploitation of the economically weaker and dependent; in a community wherein, generation after generation, rang the great protest of the prophets, no central and authoritative collection of the laws indispensable for the inner strengthening of the community could have been thinkable which did not expressly combat social injustice. It is appropriate to a period in which, to be sure, inequality of property is already to be found, but in which, taking the whole situation into account, that inequality does not yet lead to any fateful abuses, so that the immediately obvious danger deriving from it is envy and not oppression.

But we can fix the period in question even more precisely. Within the individual clan, and even within the individual tribe, there had always been, as we are also aware from other Semitic peoples, a solidarity which interdicted and directly punished every transgression of a member against the personal sphere of life of another. What was lacking in wandering Israel, fused together of related and unrelated elements, joined on its wanderings by other elements, was a sense of solidarity as between the tribes. What Israel needed was the extension of its tribal solidarity to the nation. The members of each separate tribe knew "Thou shalt not kill," "Thou shalt not commit adultery," "Thou shalt not steal"; they had these deeply engraved in their consciousness in respect of other members of their own tribe. An analogous "Israelite" consciousness, however, had hardly begun to come into being. The constituting of a people out of clans and tribes, which Moses undertook, made the expansion of the specific tribal prohibitions to the relations between the components of the people as a whole an unconditional necessity. At no later period was the need so urgent as at this plastic and fateful hour, in which it was necessary to build the "House of Israel" out of unequally suited, unequally cut stones. A wandering into the unknown had begun under the most difficult external circumstances. Before that wandering could be given a destination, it was necessary to shape, no matter in how raw and clumsy a fashion, a folk character which would enable the folk, as a homogeneous being, to follow a road to a destination. This, in turn, indispensably required the proclamation of a basic constitution founded on the principles of the unlimited rule of the one God, the continuance of Israel through the changes of years and generations, and the inner cohesion of those members of Israel living as contemporaries at any one period.

The situation of Moses has been compared, not unjustly,[81] with that of Hammurabi, who made his code in order to establish a strong unity among all the city communities of his kingdom, despite their many and varied customs and laws. But Hammurabi was the victorious ruler of a firmly established kingdom; Moses was the leader of an inchoate, stubborn horde during its transition from a lack of freedom to a problematic freedom.

Admittedly, we must not imagine Moses as a planning, selecting, and composing legislator directed by certain motives of "biological social necessity"; for his consciousness, as for that of his successors in the work of codification, "only the demand of the law was decisive, in order to manifest divine commands that are of absolute authority." [82] But here we are not justified in attempting to discriminate too precisely between conscious and unconscious processes. Moses can only be understood as deriving from the soil of an elemental unity between religion and society. He undertook the paradoxical task of leading forth the Hebrew tribes only because he had been possessed, in his direct experience, by the certainty that this was the will of the God who called those tribes his people. He aims at nothing else than to prepare the community for this God, who has declared that he is ready to be their convenantal Lord; but, and for that very reason, he must provide Israel with a basic constitution, in order to make Israel united and firm in itself. For him God's dominion over the people, and the inner cohesion of the people, are only two aspects of the same reality. From out of those words, "I, YHVH, am thy God who brought thee out of the land of Egypt," which flow into his expectant spirit, come forth all the remaining ones in a stream that is not to be stayed; and as they come forth, they gain their strict order and form. To be sure, he is not concerned with the soul of man, he is concerned with Israel; but he is concerned with Israel for the sake of YHVH. For this reason, all those who came after him in Israel, and were concerned with the soul of man, had to start from his law.

Thus, in so far as any historical conclusions are at all permissible from texts such as those before us, we have to recognize in the decalogue "the constitution by which the host of Moses became united with their God and likewise among themselves," [83] save that this host should not as it sometimes is, be understood to be a "religious" union, a "Yahveh League," [84] a cult association,[85] a "congregation";[86] for, despite their deliquescent state, reminiscent as it is of a saturated solution before crystallization, they are a complete society, a people that is coming into being. It is a "unique event in human history" [87] that the decisive process of crystallization in the development of a people should have come about on a religious basis. Irrespective of the importance of the typological view of phenomena in the history of the spirit, the latter, just because it is history, also contains the atypical, the unique in the most precise sense. This is true particularly of the religious document of that crystalloid unification: of the decalogue.

It has been supposed [88] that, in spite of the fact that the original short form to be laid bare within it "contains nothing which speaks against its composition at the time of Moses," nevertheless "it is impossible to trace it back to Moses himself, because in its literary style every decalogue is impersonal." But do we really know so much of decalogues in general that we have to subject this one to a typological view in order to discover what is possible and what is impossible in respect of it? All other sections of the Pentateuch and of other books of the Bible which it has been the practice to describe as decalogues are either loose and, as it were, accidental, or else are of indubitably literary origin; this one alone is fully self-consistent in its nucleus, and aims at the mark like a perfect instrument, each word charged with the dynamism of an historical situation. We cannot under any condition regard something of this

kind as an "impersonal" piece of writing, but, if at all, only
as the work of that particular man upon whom it was incumbent to master the situation. This may be an hypothesis,
but it is undoubtedly the only one which affords what is requisite: namely, the insertion of a combination of words found
in literature into a sequence of events such as would be possible
within history.

A demand is voiced, and quite properly, to ascertain what
"situation in life" such a text may have had, which means,
more or less, at which celebration it was likely to have been
regularly read aloud. Even more important, however, than
the question of that which is regularly recurrent, namely, of
the reality of the calendar, is that of the first time, that of the
reality of innovation. This too can be answered only by hypothesis and assumption, but it can be answered.

If we attempt to gain the view of a sequence of events from
the texts which we have sifted, it is first necessary, despite
everything which may appear to speak in its favor, to reject
the theory that "the decalogue was the document on the basis
of which the covenant was made." [89] The concept of the document in the making of the covenant appears to me to be secondary, and to have derived from the fact that the covenant
was misunderstood at a later period as the conclusion of a contract. In any case, however, the decalogue has the covenant not
as its subject, but as a prerequisite condition.

In a message which must underlie our Eagle Speech, but
which cannot be reconstructed from it, Moses brings to his
rank and file, as he had already brought to the elders, YHVH's
offer to establish the *berith,* which would unite both of them,
the God and the human host, into a living community, in
which YHVH would be *melek* and Israel his *mamlakah,* his
regal retinue; YHVH would be the owner and Israel the special personal property chosen by him; YHVH would be the
hallowing Leader and Israel the *goy* hallowed by him, the national body made holy through him. These are concepts which
I take out of the version before us, but which must already
have been either contained or latent in an undifferentiated
form in the original source if the latter was to fulfil its function.

The host accepts the offer; and in the blood rite which had
already begun earlier, and wherein the two partners share in
the identical living substance, the covenant by which YHVH
becomes *"melek* in Yeshurun" (Deut. 33:5) is concluded. The
process is completed in the contemplation of the heavens and

the holy meal. This might be the proper place for a report of the representative to those represented, in which the word "Israel" was given out and taken up, a report that has not come down to us. What now has to follow sooner or later is the proclamation of the *melek* YHVH. It is this which seems to me to be preserved in the decalogue as restored to its original nucleus. Here YHVH tells the tribes united in "Israel" what has to be done and what left undone by them as Israel, and by each individual person in Israel—an induction into such a new and exclusive relationship will consist, naturally, for the greater part, in a prohibition of that which must henceforward be left undone—in order that a people, the people of YHVH which has to come into being, should come into being. In order that it should really become his people, it must really become a people, and vice versa. The instruction to this is the Ten Commandments.

Whether this proclamation was made immediately after the conclusion of the covenant, or only in the course of the "many days" (Deut. 1:46) of the sojourning at the oasis of Kadesh, is a question that may be left open. It seems to me, on the other hand, as already stated, more likely both from the introduction to the passage commencing "I," as well as from the prose-like structure of the sentences, that the manifestation took place in written form. That it was written down on two tables is a tradition which is worthy of belief. Tables, or stelae, with laws ascribed to the divinity, are known to us both from Babylon and from early Greece, as against which there is not a single historical analogy,[90] to the best of my knowledge, for the frequently assumed imaginary transformation of stone fetishes, thought to have been kept in the ark, into tablets of the law. It may well be conceived that the tablets on which Moses wrote in truly "lapidary" sentences the basic constitution given by YHVH to his people "in order to instruct them" [91] were erected and again and again inspected and read out, until the departure from that spot made it necessary to place them in the ark.

The story of the tables as told in the book of Exodus consists of a series of tremendous scenes, which have always aroused fervent emotions in believing hearts. Moses summoned to the summit of the mountain in order to receive the tables which YHVH himself has written for the instruction of the Children of Israel (Ex. 24:12); Moses ascending into God's cloud and remaining there for forty days and forty nights (*ibid.*, 18); Moses receiving from God the "Tables of the Testimony" written by his finger (Ex. 31:18); Moses on the way down from the mountain becoming aware of the "unbridled" people, and in flaming fury, flinging the tables from his hands, so that they smash on the mountainside (Ex. 32:19); Moses, at the command of YHVH, hewing two fresh tables from the stone "like the first," in order that God may write upon them again, and again ascending the mountain with them (Ex. 34:1, 4); Moses with the tables in his hand receiving from the mouth of the God who "passes by him," the revelation of God's qualities (*ibid.*, 5-7); Moses again standing forty days and forty nights on the mountain without food or drink and writing on the tables "the words of the covenant, the ten words," he and not YHVH, although YHVH had promised him to do this himself, and hence, from the viewpoint and for the purpose of the redactor, who considered that the two passages were mutually reconcilable, functioning as the writing finger of YHVH (*ibid.*, 28); Moses going down with the new tables, the skin of his face radiant from his contact with God, and he himself unaware of it (*ibid.*, 29).

If we wish to have a sequence of events possible in our human world, we must renounce all such tremendous scenes. Nothing remains for us except the image, capable of being seen only in the barest outline and shading, of the man who withdraws to the loneliness of God's mountain in order, far from the people and overshadowed by God's cloud, to write God's law for the people. To this end, he has hewn stelae out of the stone for himself. It must be stone and not papyrus. For the hard stone is called to testify, to serve as a witness. It sees what there is to see, it hears what there is to hear, and it testifies thereto, making present and contemporary for all coming generations that which it has to see and hear; the stone outlasts the decaying eyes and ears, and goes on speaking. In the same way, Moses, before the covenant was made, had erected twelve memorial stones—such as men making covenants were accustomed to erect (Gen. 31:45ff.)—for the twelve tribes which were to become Israel at that hour.

Now, however, he goes further. After all, there is one means of placing a more comprehensive, clearer, verbally dependable witness upon the stone. That is the wondrous means of writing, which for early Israel was still surrounded by the mystery of its origin, by the breath of God, who makes a gift of it to men. By means of it, one can embody in the stone what has been revealed to one, so that it is no longer simply an event, the making of the covenant; word by word, it continues to serve as evidence of a revelation, of the law of the King. What Moses says may be clumsy, but not what he writes; that is suitable for his time and for the later times in which the stone will testify.

And so he writes on the tables what has been introduced to his senses, in order that Israel may come about; and he writes it fittingly, as a finger of God. And the tables remain as "tables of testimony" or "tables of making present" (Ex. 32: 15),[92] whose function it is to make present unto the generations of Israel forever what had once become word, that is, to set it before them as something spoken to them in this very hour. It may well be assumed, although there is no tradition extant to this effect, that in the days before Samuel the tables were taken out of the ark at extraordinary moments and elevated before the people, as had once been done in the wilderness, in order to restore them to the situation in which they had been at Sinai.[93] Reports about this may have been destroyed after the tables were placed in the Holy of Holies of Solomon's Temple (together with the ark, which was now deprived of its mobile character [I Kings 8:9]), obviously in order that they might become immovable themselves, no longer serving as the occasionally reviving original witnesses, but remaining nothing more than relics of dead stone.

And at an unknown hour they pass out of our ken. The Word alone endures.

5

THE ZEALOUS GOD

For reasons both of style and of content, I have accepted the view that the original decalogue was not as long as that which we now possess, and that it was largely constructed in succinct imperative sentences; which, however, does not in any way mean that an origin in the days of Moses must be denied to all elements which can be separated out after this fashion. This applies in particular to the widely discussed statement about the "jealous God" (Ex. 20:5b-6). With the possible exception of the last two words ("and who keep my command-ments"), which tend to disturb the parallelism of the structure, this has so archaic a stamp that certain of the protagonists of the "original decalogue" [94] have held that it ought to be trans-posed to the commencement of the decalogue in place of the present introductory verse. Yet the introductory verse, the nu-clear passage of the revelation, is so "unmistakably ancient" [95] that it will not do merely to remove it from the place which alone is suitable to it.

The situation is different as regards the verse about the "jealous God." This likewise obviously fits into an early connec-tion, but not necessarily here, in a passage which, in its nature as proclamation of the God as God of the Covenant, with whom the people have just entered into a community of life, does not require any threat of punishment at this particular point. On the other hand, it seems to me that there is an inner association between this and certain other laws, which also point more or less to the period of Moses, but are not included in the decalogue.

"I YHVH thy God am a jealous God, ordaining the iniquity of the fathers upon the sons unto the third and fourth generation of those that hate me, but doing mercy to the thousandth generation of those that love me." Two of the elements of this statement, the characterization of the God as a jealous one and the differentiation between those that hate him and those that love him, are again to be found in similar form in passages which should be regarded as effects and applications of this. A distinction between the foes of YHVH, who are marked for downfall, and those that love him, who ascend in their course like the rising sun, is drawn with the strongest urge of a fighting faith at the close of the Song of Deborah (Judg. 5:31). "Foes" in this song clearly means not merely the foes of Israel, who are for that reason the foes of Israel's divine leader and commander, but also those within the people itself who at the hour of battle refrained from coming to the aid of YHVH, and who are therefore provided with a curse (ibid., 23); "lovers" are those who unconditionally adhere to YHVH and follow him, those devoting themselves to him of their own free will (ibid., 2). It is of great significance that this expression of personal feeling was chosen as the designation of the following of the God; and this applies equally to the decalogue sentence by which, it seems to me, the song had been influenced.[96] The guilty ones have to bear the burden of their guilt as a load extending beyond their own person if they are haters of God; they are faced by the lovers, over whom the flood of mercy pours forth, reaching far beyond them in distant waves.

But what kind of guilt is it that is spoken of here? According to the context of the decalogue, idolatry and the like are meant; and this view seems to be confirmed by the introduction to Goethe's "cultic decalogue" (Ex. 34:14), where the jealousy of YHVH stands in relation to the worship of another god. But the same association is also found in the report of the historic assembly at Shechem, in a verse (Josh. 24:19) which there is no adequate reason for regarding as later than its context. It is clear that in these two passages the thing about which God is jealous is exclusive devotion to him, the rejection of the demands of all other gods. This, however, does not in any way mean of necessity that the statement in the decalogue, considered on its own intrinsic merits, bears an identical meaning. We must therefore now consult it by itself.

Our question must naturally refer to the precise sense of those much discussed words: "ordaining the sins of the fathers upon the children unto the third and fourth generation." The verb *paqad*, which I render by "ordaining" or "coordinating," originally means "to arrange," then "to set in order," "to fix an order," "to restore order." The order between heaven and earth, disturbed by guilt, is restored by the punishment. That this should take place "unto the third and fourth generation" can only mean, since there is no reason to assume any arbitrary introduction of the figures, the precise number of generations or direct lineal successors which a man living to a ripe old age is likely to see gathered round him. This, in turn, can be understood in two different ways: either that the guilty one sees how the consequences of his guilt work themselves out on his grand-children or great-grand-children, or else that his punishment comes to affect those of his descendants who are then alive. The passage in the decalogue itself does not tell us which of the two possible interpretations is correct; and so we must extend our inquiry to other passages, which may stand in some inner connection with it.

When we consider the undoubtedly early laws of the Pentateuch, with the exception of the decalogue, which deal with the punishment of transgression, we find that there are very few, only two to be precise, in which the divine speaker does not rest satisfied with prescribing for the tribunals a punishment fitting the guilt, but offers a prospect of his own vengeful intervention. Both of them (Ex. 22:21-22, 25-26) refer to transgressions of a "social" nature, to an injustice committed against one's fellow-man of such a kind that it is not amenable to human justice. Both divide themselves sharply from their contexts by the force of language and rhythm, which does not recur in any other of the single laws to be found in the so-called Book of the Covenant. Further, none of the collections of ancient Oriental laws with which those of the Bible have been compared offer any kind of analogy to this singularly exalted tone, nor to this kind of divine warning of an expiation of guilt brought about from on high. Most of the modern commentators think of reworking and interpolation when trying to account for this. To me, however, it seems, despite a certain syntactical clumsiness, that the two laws are both cast in the same mold; and it correspondingly seems to me that the small group to which they both belong is part of the oldest stratum of Mosaic legislation, that is, "Words of YHVH," [97] sayings "which appeal to the conscience and the sense of responsibility before the compelling God."

The first of the two laws forbids the oppression of any widow or orphan: "For if he cries, cries unto me, I shall hear, hear his cry, and my wrath will flame, and I shall slay you with the sword, and your wives shall be widows and your children orphans." The unjust community, the community containing both those who behave thus and those who tolerate such behavior, is visited by war, and the offspring living at the time will be affected by the death of the fathers. The second law holds out the prospect of the same divine hearing of the outcry of the oppressed if the right of pledging is subjected to abuse, and behind it as well a judging intervention of the God is to be understood. Both laws have a character which can be described, alike in content and tone, as none other than protoprophetic. The small group of four laws to which they belong leaves me with the impression that they must be the sole remaining vestige of a longer series, in which more succinct commandments, such as verses 20 and 24, may have alternated with expanded ones, such as the two under consideration here. And I could well imagine that the series was introduced by the decalogue statement of the "jealous" God, and that it possibly ended with the phrase which now serves as the close of the small group: "For I am a gracious one."

It may admittedly be argued that the adjective here can mean only "jealous" in the usual sense, as is shown by the usage of the verb deriving from the same root. But the pertinent noun is not infrequently used to characterize the zeal of the fighter, and that is what is meant here. YHVH zealously fights his "haters," and these are not only the people who have other gods "in his face," but also those who break up the society founded and led by him through their injustice to their fellow-men. The "religious" and the "social," the exclusive service of YHVH and the just faith between men, without which Israel cannot become Israel, cannot become the people of YHVH, are closely connected.

I have indicated that social inequality in the midst of the people Israel at the time of Moses had not extended so far that such a commandment as "Thou shalt not oppress thy fellowman" required to be inserted in the basic constitution. At the same time, there certainly must have been already such an amount of oppression in the wandering host that the dangers involved had to be counteracted by single specific laws, which surrounded and completed that central massif. Such single laws were not written on tables, but possibly on a scroll, and presumably not on one single occasion, but in the course of time, in connection with particular happenings, which called for the promulgation of new laws of this kind in order to combat the evil. All this is no more than conjecture, and will probably never become more than conjecture. Yet, in our vision, we see this man Moses at times, following some new and wearing experience with his people, entering the leader's tent, sitting down on the ground, and for a long time weighing in his soul whatever may have befallen, until at length the new comprehension rises to the surface and the new word oppresses his throat, till it finally darts across into the muscles of his hand, permitting a new utterance of the Zealous God to come into being on the scroll.

The effect of the association of this jealousy, or zealousness, with the "social" laws can be seen from the example of a commandment at the beginning of the Book of the Covenant (Ex. 21:2 ff.), the commandment to liberate the "Hebrew" slave in the seventh year. This law, it is known, shows some resemblance to one in the Code of Hammurabi, which specifies liberation as early as the fourth year, though only of those enslaved for debt. The important difference between the two codes lies in the fact that in Israelite law the decision is left to the will of the slave, who, if he refuses to be liberated, has the lobe of his ear pierced as a sign of life-long slavery. (This procedure cannot but remind one of another law in the Hammurabi Code, according to which that particular slave who denies his owner with the words "You are not my lord" has an ear cut off, whereas, in Israel, the slave is marked with the degrading sign because of his having renounced liberty.)

Here the differentiating characteristic is not the practical mildness, but the basic recognition of personal freedom of choice. In Babylonian law, the slave, foreign as well as indigenous, is a "chattel";[98] the Hebrew slave, in Israelite law, is a person. There the relationship is unilateral, while here it is mutual.

The Hittite slave law also shows a noteworthy humaneness. What distinguishes the law of Israel in essence from it is the close relationship between the religious and the social element. Since Israel is the "peculiar property" of YHVH, no person in Israel can be, properly speaking, the slave of any other person in Israel.[99] All belong to the God, and are therefore free to make their own decisions.

This basic feeling, to which "it is impossible to find a parallel within the old Oriental circle," [100] is spirit of Moses' spirit, no matter when the presumably archaic law may have found its actual formulation. And we are also presumably justified in ascribing to the man by whom the Sabbath was inaugurated the initiative for extending the Sabbatical manner of thought into the cycle of the years, in which, as in the days, six units of work and dependence have to be followed by one unit of liberation. Once in history, shortly before the fall of the kingdom (Jer. 34:8 ff.), the king and the princes in Judah understood a military disaster as being due to the non-fulfilment of a particular commandment. It was not a cult law, but that commanding the liberation of the slaves, which they recognized as having been the cause of YHVH's zeal against the beleaguered Jerusalem.

6

THE CONTRADICTION

We read (Num. 16) of another revolt, the one known as the revolt of "Korah and his band." Its nucleus of fact is barely to be identified under the thick layer of tendentious treatment, the purpose of which was clearly to equip the privileged position of the "Aaronid" priests vis-à-vis the "Levites" with all the sanctions of the Mosaic period. The only thing which can be regarded as certain[101] is that in the original report there was no question of any action of the Levites as Levites.

On the other hand, it would be regarding things from far too narrow a perspective if we were to see here nothing more than a protest on the part of the laity against the appointment of the Levites to the cult service, a struggle against the priestly class in general on the ground that priests are held to be superfluous.[102]

Nothing is reported in the early stratum of the Pentateuch with regard to the establishment of an actual priestly class. The existence of priests is referred to in passing on one occasion (Ex. 19:22), but we are told nothing about the functions which were exercised by them. Whatever is found in the so-called Book of the Covenant which implies the exercise of such functions does not offer any adequate grounds for the assumption of an organized priestly class in the days of Moses. Here, in any case, the officiating cult group, if it exists, does not show the quality of *pathos* proper to the sacral power. The obscure hint of an appointment of the Levites—nothing more than such a hint is to be found in the ambiguous phrasing[103]—

following the suppression of the rebellion (Ex. 32:29) can scarcely be regarded, if recourse is had exclusively to the old texts, as more than an indication of services of watch and ward, to be rendered thereafter by the Levites at the tent of the leader, now elevated to the status of tent of God, without any actual priestly activities.

This tent is not a tent of offering. In the old textual stratum, very little information is given about sacrifices; only on very rare and extraordinary occasions are communal and conventional sacrifices made, and then clearly not by any actual priestly caste. With the exception of Moses, nobody engages in the holy action; there is no participation by Levites, and Moses, too, performs his function not as a professional priest, but as the leader of the people, as we afterwards also find, for example, in the case of Samuel. The tent, to be sure, might be described as "an oracle tent," but nobody except Moses has anything to do in the tent with that oracle.

It is true that in a text which probably derives from the time before the period of the kings but is post-Mosaic (Deut. 33:8), reference is made to a divine bestowal of the oracular instruments called Urim and Thummim upon the Levites, or upon one of them. But the narrative texts available to us do not give us any *point d'appui* for relating this to a particular event, and it appears most likely that the instruments, which we hear of in an early story as belonging to the time of Saul, was introduced after the death of Moses and as his legacy, in order to ensure the continuation of the oracular function, which, however, had been conducted by him without any instrument.

Possibly the process of back-dating to the Mosaic period came about by way of the mysterious reference to be found in the Blessing of Moses. In general, it seems to me that the period of the conquest of the land must have been decisive for the development of a regulated and somewhat centralized cult and a permanent (in addition to the fluctuating) priestly class; this can be understood from the entire nexus of circumstances.

Be that as it may, all the reports deriving from early days about the priestly functions of the tribe of Levi are not sufficient, in spite of the penetrating efforts of scholars,[104] to make any common front of "laymen against Levites" seem credible as the historical nucleus of the story of Korah and his band. This nucleus does not appear to have been a protest against any "clerical class," but rather to have been directed against the special status of Moses in person, in which those closest to Moses, though perhaps not Aaron in particular (as in the present text of Num. 16:3), may well have been included.

Here, too, we can best start with a passage which appears to go back to early days, but the wording of which has been so altered in the course of the priestly treatment of the narrative that its antiquity has not been recognized. This passage (Num. 16:3) reads as follows in the form before us: "Enough of you! For all the community, all of them, are holy and YHVH is in their midst, so why do you exalt yourselves over the assembly of YHVH?" The later terms *edah* (community) and *kahal* (assembly, congregation) [105] have been substituted, it seems to me, for the original words *goy* and *am*. This means that the narrative in its present form has been artistically and of set intent constructed round the word *edah*, which is used in a double sense: community (the whole nation) and band (the separate group rising in revolt), while in addition the root *kahal* is used alternatively in the sense of assembling the people and of banding together.[106]

If we restore the original words, two associations which are worthy of remark become clear. The word *goy*, people, associated with the word *kedoshim,* holy, is reminiscent of the expression *goy kadosh,* holy people, found in the Eagle Speech, a form which is found in the Bible at that one place, and at that one place only; and *am YHVH*, people of YHVH, is found in early strata of the Pentateuch (Num. 17:6 belongs to a very late one) only in the words with which Moses replies to Joshua's misgivings in the story of the descent of the Spirit (Num. 11:29): "Would that he grant that the whole people of YHVH were prophets, that YHVH grant his spirit over them!"

The purpose, in suggesting a cross-reference to these two passages, seems to me unmistakable. The protesting party base themselves on the two utterances made by Moses himself, in which he referred to all Israel as holy, as consisting exclusively of direct servants of YHVH, and again to all the individuals in Israel as prophetic carriers of the spirit of God—one, it is true, in the form of a commandment, and the other in that of a wish. "Korah and his band," consisting of Levites and laymen who have confederated, say: "The people do not have to become holy first, the people are holy, for YHVH is in their midst; the whole people is holy, and because it is holy, all the individuals in it are holy."

On this they base their attack against Moses and his kinsfolk: "If all are holy, you have no priority over the others. If all are holy, there is no need for any mediation. If all are holy there is no need for human beings to exercise any power over other human beings. Everybody is given instruction directly by YHVH as to what he is to do."

This contradiction rising out of the midst of the people, which converts the words of Moses into their opposite, changing as it does request and hope into insolent self-assertion, was conditioned and made possible by one of his great works, the establishment of the ark of the covenant. The people as people necessarily understood the occasional descent of YHVH into their midst as a residence of YHVH among them, and such a residence as a guarantee of the holiness of them all, while their common holiness was bound to appear to them as an adequate reason for throwing off the yoke of what should be done and what should not be done, the yoke that this man Moses imposed upon them, the holy people, hour by hour, and day by day, in the name of God, as though God dwelt with him alone, as though he alone had access to God.

Moses had endeavored to preclude this danger by placing the shrine with the tables of the law at the feet of YHVH. But he himself, after all, had made the Invisible more visible to his people than the stone upon which his will was written. For the people as people the Divine Presence meant that they possessed the God, or in other words, that they could transform their own will into the will of God.

The issue here is at bottom something rather different from the question of priestly functions, or indeed the question of cult in general. Though it is directed, to be sure, against Moses, yet no matter how deeply and strongly religious motives are associated with the passions at play here, they are not directed really against Moses as priest. This if only for the reason that though Moses himself, as said, actually carries out or directs the cult acts in which the community as such has to be represented, he does not become a priest as a result; he carries them out and directs them as the man who represents the community where the latter has to act "before God." And equally the fact that he receives and transmits the expressions of God's will does not turn him into a priest, for the manner of this reception does not admit of inclusion in any tradition of divinatory methods: it is unique to him, to Moses; it comes into being from his religious experiences and vanishes with him.

He takes over cult elements and transforms their form and

meaning; he introduces fresh cult elements, but he has no cult office.[107] The priest represents the greatest human specialization that we know. In his mission and his work, Moses is unspecialized; he is conditioned not by an office but by a situation, an historical situation.

Moses' character is eminently historical; that of the priest, even when he delivers an oracle in given historical situations, is eminently non-historical. This, however, does not mean that Moses is "not a priest but a prophet." [108] It is true that the way in which he receives the revelation is largely prophetical, even though the institution of the tent and all that is associated therewith does make a considerable difference; but his activity in history, as leader of the people, as legislator, is what separates him in character from all the bearers of prophecy known to us. For this reason, Moses likewise cannot be understood merely as a combination of priest and prophet; moreover, he is not to be comprehended at all within any exclusively "religious" categories. What constitutes his idea and his task—the realization of the unity of religious and social life in the community of Israel, the substantiation of a divine rule that is not to be cultically restricted but is to comprehend the entire existence of the nation, the theopolitical principle—all this has penetrated to the depths of his personality; it has raised his person above the compartmental system of typology; it has mingled the elements of his soul into a rare unity.

The historical Moses, as far as we are capable of perceiving him, does not differentiate between the spheres of religion and politics, and in him they are not separated. When "Korah and his band" revolt against Moses, it is not to be interpreted as meaning that they rise against his cult privileges as such, for these privileges as such are not stressed and might as well be non-existent.

Rather do they rise at first against the fact that *one* man leads the people in the name of God. But they go beyond this and revolt against the fact that this man decides in the name of God what is right and what is wrong. "The whole people, all of them, are holy," and therefore nobody can give orders or issue prohibitions to anybody else in respect of what the latter's own holiness suggests to him. Since the people are holy, commandments from without are no longer necessary.

It should not be supposed that later stages of development are introduced here into the words of Korah. The attitude which finds expression in these words is known to us from far more primitive stages. In many of those tribes which are labelled as primitive, such motives have contributed vastly to the establishment of secret societies. A chief or shaman, whose authority is supported by a superhuman power, can be combated in two ways. One is to attempt to overthrow him, particularly by shaking faith in the assurance that he will receive that support, and then to take his place, which is precisely what some suppose to have been the nucleus of the story of Korah,[109] that is, a manifestation of the personal struggle for power known to us from all phases of human history, and one which in general leaves the structure of society unchanged. The second method is to cut off the main roots of the leader's power by establishing, within the tribe but external to the official tribal life, a secret society in which the actual, the true, the "holy" communal life is lived, free from the bonds of the "law," a life of "leopards" or "werewolves," in which the wildest instincts are given free rein through mutual support in action that is regarded as holy. Once they have succeeded in abducting the god, all further robbery is no more than taking possession by means of him. This is naturally bound to have vast and varied social and political effects on the life of the tribe, in relation to which the secret society regards itself as the "true" tribe, the backbone and driving force of the tribe, the tribe, so to speak, in so far as it really dares to be its own self.

This phenomenon, which can be observed throughout the world, is regarded much too superficially if it is considered to be nothing more than a masking of the urge of the libido to throw off its fetters. The people who set rebellions of this kind in motion are not merely endeavoring to find a sanction for the satisfaction of repressed lusts, but are in all seriousness desirous of gaining power over the divine might, or more precisely, of actualizing and giving legitimacy to the god-might which a person has in himself, the "free" one as against the one who is "bound" by the chief or shaman. This tendency can, of course, be realized only by placing those who are not members of the secret societies in a state of non-freedom and exposure, in a condition frequently far worse than any previous abuse had ever been, but this is only, one might say, a secondary effect, which is regarded as being unworthy of consideration.

It is easy to adduce analogies at higher levels of development, particularly out of the history of antinomist sects and movements. The issue is always that of "divine freedom" against "divine law," but at these higher levels it becomes even more clear than at the more primitive stages that an isolated divine freedom abolishes itself. Naturally, God rules through men who have been gripped and filled by his spirit, and who on occasion carry out his will not merely by means of instantaneous decisions, but also through lasting justice and law. If their authority as the chosen ones is disputed and extended to all, then the actual dominion is taken away from God, for without law, that is, without any clear-cut and transmissible line of demarcation between that which is pleasing to God and that which is displeasing to him, there can be no historical continuity of divine rule upon earth.

The *true* argument of the rebellion is that in the world of the law what has been inspired always becomes emptied of the spirit, yet continues to maintain its claim of full inspiration; in other words, that the living element always dies off, yet what is left continues to rule over living men. And the *true* conclusion is that the law must again and again immerse itself in the consuming and purifying fire of the spirit, in order to renew itself and again refine the genuine substance out of the dross of what has become false. This lies in the continuation of the line of that Mosaic principle of ever-recurrent renewal.

As against this comes the false argument of the rebels that the law as such displaces the spirit and freedom, and the false conclusion that it ought to be replaced by them. The falsity of this conclusion remains hidden, and even ineffective, so long as the "eschatological" expectation—the expectation of the coming of the direct and complete rule of God over all creatures, or more correctly, of his presence in all creatures, without need of law and representation—is maintained unweakened. As soon as it slackens, it follows historically that God's rule is restricted to the "religious" sphere; everything that is left over is rendered unto Caesar, and the rift which runs through the whole being of the human world receives its sanction.

Indeed, the false would become true as soon as the presence of God comes to be fulfilled in all creatures. It is here that the greatness and the questionability in every genuine eschatology are to be found: its greatness in belief and its questionability in regards to the realities of history. The "Mosaic" attitude is to believe in the future of a "holy people," and to prepare for it within history.

These remarks are essentially relevant to our subject, for they help us to understand the tragedy of Moses. Everything subsequent to the antagonism between Moses and Korah appears to us as having been already present in the seed therein, if only we view Korah in large enough terms. Then we recognize that here the eternal word is opposed by eternal contradiction.

But something peculiar must also be added: the waywardness of Bedouin life, which often survives the nomadic stage.[110] This elementary need of people to be independent of other people may develop in two opposite directions, according to the particular personal temperament with which it is associated. It can grow into an unconditional submission to the will of God and his will alone, but it may also become empty subbornness, which does not wish to bow to any order because order is, after all, nothing but human order. On the one hand, we see here devotion to the kingdom of God carried out by a person's deepest self, such as can and should be inspired in spontaneous fashion; and on the other, resistance offered by the deepest self to the coming of the kingdom, so that a man submits to his own wilfulness and feels, or endeavors to feel, that very wilfulness to be that which is religiously correct, that which brings salvation, that which is holy.

This schizoid development from a common root meets us in Israel as well as in the pre-Islamic and Islamic Arab worlds. When Moses bases Israel's becoming a "king's retinue of *kohanim*," that is, the beginning of the kingdom of God, on spontaneity, on "doing and hearing" without compulsion, he relies upon that Bedouin waywardness, trusting and assuming that they who do not wish to recognize any other master but the Lord of the world alone will truly recognize him. To the present day, Israel has really existed in the precise degree to which Moses has proved right. But by doing what he did, Moses also encouraged the contrary development from the identical root. The fact that Korah is able to make use of Moses' own words against him has a tragic purport.

Moses does not wish to use force; he does not wish to impose himself; he wishes to bring the men of his people so far along that they themselves can become *kohanim* and *nebiim*. He is "humble." But this humility of his, which is one with his fundamental faith in spontaneity and in freedom, is precisely what provokes the "Korahite" reaction among men of the Korah type. Since, however, his whole work, the covenant between God and people, is threatened, he must now doom the rebels to destruction, just as he once ordered Levites to fight against Levites. There is certainly something sinister underlying the legend of the earth which opened its mouth and swallowed up the rebels.

It was the hour of decision. Both Moses and Korah desired the people to be the people of YHVH, the holy people. But for Moses this was the goal. In order to reach it, generation after generation had to choose again and again between the roads, between the way of God and the wrong paths of their own hearts, between "life" and "death" (Deut. 30:15). For this God had introduced good and evil in order that men might find their own way to him.

For Korah, the people, being the people of YHVH, were already holy. They had been chosen by God and he dwelt in their midst, so why should there be further need of ways and choices? The people was holy just as it was, and all within it were holy just as they were; all that needed to be done was to draw the conclusions from this, and everything would be found to be good. It is precisely this which Moses, in a parting speech placed in his mouth, and which appears to be a development of one of his traditional utterances, calls death, meaning the death of the people, as though they were swallowed up while still alive.

Therefore Moses was zealous; he was zealous for his God as the one who sets a goal, and shows a path, and writes a guide to that path on tablets, and orders men to choose again and again, to choose that which is right; and he was zealous against the great and popular mystical Baal which, instead of demanding that the people hallow themselves in order to be holy, treats them as already holy.

Korah calls that Baal by the name of YHVH, but that does not change anything in his essence.

7

BIBLICAL LEADERSHIP

I do not imagine that you will expect me to give you any so-called character sketches of biblical leaders. That would be an impossible undertaking, for the Bible does not concern itself with character, nor with individuality, and one cannot draw from it any description of characters or individualities. The Bible depicts something else, namely, persons in situations. The Bible is not concerned with the difference between these persons; but the difference between the situations in which the person, the creaturely person, the appointed person, stands his test or fails, is all-important to it.

But neither can it be my task to delve beneath the biblical account to a picture more trustworthy historically, to historical data out of which I could piece together an historically useful picture. This too is impossible. It is not that the biblical figures are unhistorical. I believe that we are standing at the beginning of a new era in biblical studies; whereas the past era was concerned with proving that the Bible did not contain history, the coming era will succeed in demonstrating its historicity. By this I do not mean that the Bible depicts men and women and events as they were in actual history; rather do I mean that its descriptions and narratives are the organic, legitimate ways of giving an account of what existed and what happened. I have nothing against calling these narratives myths and sagas, so long as we remember that myths and sagas are essentially memories which are actually conveyed from person to person. But what kind of memory is it which manifests itself in these accounts? I say again: memory, not imagination. It is an organic memory molding its material. We know of it today, because occasionally, though indeed in unlikely and indeed in incredible ways, the existence of great poets with such organic memories still extends into our time. If we want to distinguish between narrators, between a great narrator and one who is simply very talented, the best way is to consider how each of them handles the events of his own life. The great narrator allows the events to drop into him as they happen, careless, trusting, with faith. And memory does its part: what has thus been dropped into it, it molds organically, unarbitrarily, unfancifully into a valid account and narrative—a whole on which admittedly a great deal of conscious work has then to be done, but upon which the distinguishing mark has been put by the unarbitrarily shaping memory. The other narrator registers, he makes an inventory in what he also calls the memory, but which is really something quite different; he preserves the events while they are happening in order to be able to draw them forth unaltered when he needs them. Well, he will certainly draw them forth from the preservative after a fashion unaltered, and fit for use after a fashion, and then he may do with them what he can.

I said that the great poets show us in their way how the nascence of myths and sagas takes place. Each myth, even the myth we usually call the most fantastic of all, is creation around a memory core, around the kernel of the organically shaping memory. It is not that people to whom something like the exodus from Egypt has happened subsequently improvise events, allowing their fancy to add elements which they do not remember and to "embroider" on what happened; what happened continues to function, the event itself is still active and at work in their souls, but these souls, this community soul, is so made that its memory is formative, myth-creating, and the task before the biblical writers is then to work on the product of this memory. Nowhere is there any point where arbitrariness is observable or interference by alien elements; there is in it no juggling.

This being the case, we cannot disentangle the historical from the biblical. The power of the biblical writing, which springs from this shaping memory, is so great, the elemental nature of this memory so mighty, that it is quite impossible to extract any so-called historical matter from the Bible. The historical matter thus obtained would be unreal, amorphous, without significance. But it is also impossible to distill the "historical matter" from the Bible for another reason. In contrast to the sacred historiography of the other nations, there exists in the case of Israel no evidence from profane parallels by which one might correct the sacred documents; there is no historiography of another tendency than that which resides in this shaping memory; and this shaping memory stands under a law. It is this law which I shall try to elucidate by the examples with which I deal today.

In order to bring out still more clearly and exactly what I have in mind, I shall ask you to recall one of the nations with whom Israel came into historical contact and dispute; I do so for the purpose of considering the aspect under which this nation must have regarded one of the biblical leaders. Let us try to imagine how Abraham must have been regarded by one of the nations against whose kings he fought, according to Gen. 14, a chapter whose fundamental historical character seems to me beyond doubt. Undoubtedly Abraham was a historical figure to this nation in the same sense in which we usually speak about history today. But he was no longer Abraham. That which is important for us about Abraham, that which makes him a biblical character, a "Father," that which is the reason why the Bible tells us about Abraham, that is no longer embraced under this aspect; the significance of the figure has vanished. Or, take for instance the Egyptians and Moses, and imagine how an Egyptian historian would have described Moses and his cause. Nothing essential would have been left; it would be a skeleton taking the place of the living person.

All we can do therefore is to refer to the Bible, to that which is characteristic of the biblical leader as the Bible, without arbitrariness, tells of him and thinks of him, under the law of *its* conception of history, *its* living of history, which is unlike anything which we are accustomed to call history. But from this law, from this biblical way of regarding leader and leadership, different from all other ways in which leader and leadership have been regarded, from this have we—from this has Judaism —arisen.

As I now wish to investigate the question of the essence of biblical leadership, I must exclude from the inquiry all those figures who are not *biblical* leaders in the strict sense of the term; and this means, characteristically enough, I must exclude all those figures who appear as continuators, all those who are not called, elected, appointed anew. as the Bible says, directly by God, but who enter upon a task already begun without such personal call—whether it is a disciple to whom the person who is not permitted to finish the task hands over his office, breathing as it were toward his disciple the spirit that breathes upon him; or whether it is a son who succeeds an elected, originally anointed king, without receiving any other anointing than the already customary official one, which is thus no longer the anointing that comes upon a person and turns him into another man.

Thus I do not consider figures like Joshua and Solomon, because the Bible has such figures in common with history—they are figures of universal history. Joshua is a great army leader, a great conqueror, but an historical figure like any other, only with special religious affiliations added, which, however, do not characterize his person. Solomon is an Oriental king, only a very wise one; he does his task, he builds the Temple, but we are not shown that this task colors and determines him. What has happened here is simply that the completion of a task, the completion of a task already intended and already begun, has been taken over by a disciple or a successor. The task of Moses, which he had already begun but was not allowed to complete, was taken over by Joshua; the task of David, which he was not allowed to complete, was taken over by Solomon. In this connection, I recall the words that David and God exchanged in the second book of Samuel on the proposed building of the Temple, and the prohibition against David's carrying it out: "It is not for you," says God, reproving David as he had reproved Moses when he told Moses that it was not for him to bring into their land the people whom he had led out of Egypt. The work is taken away from him, and taken away from him, moreover, in view of his special inner and outer situations; another man has nothing more to do than to bring the work to its conclusion.

Only the elected, only those who begin, are then comprised under the biblical aspect of leadership. A new beginning may also occur within a sequence of generations, as for instance within those which we call the generations of the patriarchs; this is clearly seen in the case of Jacob, with whom something new begins, as the particular way in which revelation comes to him indicates.

I would like first to attempt a negative characterization of the essential features of biblical leadership. It goes beyond both nature and history. To the men who wrote the Bible, nature.

as well as history, is of God, and that in such a way that the biblical cosmogony recounts each separately: in the first chapter, the creation of the world is described as the coming of nature into being; and then in the second chapter, this same creation of the world is described as the rise of history. Both are of God, but then the biblical event goes beyond them, God goes beyond them, not in the sense that they—nature and history—come to be ignored by God, but in the sense that time and again God's hand thrusts through them and interferes with what is happening—it so chooses, so sends, and so commands, as it does not seem to accord with the laws of nature and history to send, to choose, and to command.

I shall here show only by two particularly clear examples what I mean by this. First of all, it is the weak and the humble who are chosen. By nature it is the strong, those who can force their cause through, who are able and therefore chosen to perform the historical deeds. But in the Bible, it is often precisely the younger sons who are chosen—from Abel, through Jacob, Joseph, and Moses, to David; and this choosing is accompanied by a rejection, often a very emphatic rejection, of the older sons; or else those who are chosen were born out of wedlock, or of humble origin. And if it happens that a strong man like Samson appears, a man who has not all these limitations, then his strength is not his own, it is only loaned, not given, and he trifles it away, squanders it, in the manner described, to get it back only in order to die.

A different but no less telling expression of what is meant by this peculiar election against nature is represented by the battle and victory of Gideon. The Bible makes him do the strangest thing any commander ever did. He has an army of ten thousand men, and he reduces its numbers again and again, till only three hundred men remain with him; and with these three hundred he gives battle and conquers.

It is always the same story. The purpose of God is fulfilled, as the Bible itself says in one place, not by might, nor by power, but "by my spirit."

It is "against nature" that in one way or another the leaders are mostly the weak and the humble. The way in which they carry out their leadership is "contrary to history." It is the moment of success which determines the selection of events which seem important to history. "World history" is the history of successes; the heroes who have not succeeded, but who cannot be excluded from it on account of their very conspicuous heroism, serve only as a foil, as it were. True, the conquered have also their place in "world history"; but if we scrutinize how it treats the conquerors and the conquered, what is of importance to history becomes abundantly clear. Granted that one takes Croesus together with Cyrus, that Herodotus has a use for him; nevertheless, in the heart of history, only the conquerors have value. History murmurs a low dirge over the overpowered heroes, but its paean for those who stand firm, who force their cause through, for those who are crowned with success, rings out loud. This is current history, the history which we are accustomed to identify with what happens, with the real happenings in the world, in spite of the fact that this history is based only on the particular principle of picking and choosing, on the selection made by the historian, on the so-called historical consciousness.

The Bible knows nothing of this intrinsic value of success. On the contrary, when it announces a successful deed, it is duty-bound to announce in complete detail the failure involved in the success. When we consider the history of Moses, we see how much failure is mingled in the one great successful action, so much so that when we set the individual events which make up his history side by side, we see that his life consists of one failure after another, through which runs the thread of his success. True, Moses brought the people out of Egypt; but each stage of this leadership is a failure. Whenever he comes to deal with this people, he is defeated by them, let God ever so often interfere and punish them. And the real history of this leadership is not the history of the exodus, but the history of the wandering in the desert. The personal history of Moses' own life, too, does not point back to his youth and to what grew out of it; it points beyond, to death, to the death of the unsuccessful man, whose work, it is true, survives him, but only in new defeats, new disappointments, and continual new failures —and yet his work survives also in a hope which is beyond all these failures.

Or let us consider the life of David. So far as we are told of it, it consists essentially of two great stories of flight. Before his accession to the throne, there are the manifold accounts of his flight from Saul, and then follows an interruption which is not trifling in terms of length and its value for profane history, but which in the account appears paltry enough; and after this there is the flight from Absalom, painted for us in detail. And even where the Bible recounts David's triumph, as for instance with the entry of the ark into Jerusalem, this triumph is clearly described as a disgrace in a worldly sense; this is very unlike the language of "world history." What Michal, his wife, says to David of his triumph, how he ought to have felt ashamed of himself behaving as he did in front of his people—that is the language of profane history, of history *par excellence*. To history such a royal appearance is not permitted, and rightly so, seeing that history is what it is.

And, finally, this glorification of failure culminates in the long line of prophets whose existence is failure through and through. They live in failure; it is for them to fight and not to conquer. It is the fundamental experience of biblical leadership, of the leadership described by one of them, a nameless prophet whose words are preserved in the second part of the Book of Isaiah where he speaks in the first person of himself as "the servant of the Lord," and says of God:

> "He hath made my mouth like a sharp sword,
> In the shadow of his hand hath he hid me;
> And he hath made me a polished shaft—
> In his quiver hath he concealed me!" (Is. 49:2)

This existence in the shadow, in the quiver, is the final word of the leaders in the biblical world—this enclosure in failure, in obscurity, even when one stands in the blaze of public life, in the presence of the whole national life. The truth is hidden in obscurity and yet does its work, though indeed in a way far different from that which is known and lauded as effective by world history.

Biblical leadership falls into five basic types, not according to differences in the personality and character of the leader—I have already said that personality and character do not come into consideration—but according to the difference in the successive situations, the great stages in the history of the people which the Bible describes, the stages in the dialogue between God and the people. For what the Bible understands by history is a dialogue in which man, in which the people, is spoken to and fails to answer, yet where the people in the midst of its failure continually rises up and tries to answer. It is the history of God's disappointments, but this history of disappointments constitutes a way, a way that leads from disappointment to disappointment, and beyond all disappointments; it is the way of the people, the way of man, yes, the way of God through mankind. I said that there are five basic types in accordance with the successive stages of the situations in the dialogue: first, the Patriarch; second, the Leader in the original sense of one who leads the wandering; third, the so-called Judge; fourth, the King, but of course not the king who is a successor, a member of a dynasty, but the founder of the dynasty, called the first anointed; fifth, the Prophet. All these constitute different forms of leadership in accordance with the different situations.

First, the Patriarch. About this there is a current conception which is not quite correct. No rulership is here exercised, and when we understand the conception in its accurate sense, we cannot even speak of any leadership, for there is as yet no people to lead. The conception indicates a way along which the people are to be led beginning with these men. They are fathers. It is for them to beget a people. It is the peculiar point in biblical history where God, as it were, narrows down his original plan for the whole of mankind and causes a people to be begotten that is called to do its appointed work toward the completion of the creation, the coming of the kingdom. The fathers of this people are the men of whom I speak. They are fathers, nothing else. Patriarch expresses too much. They are the real fathers, they are those from whom this tribe, this people, proceeds; and when God speaks to them, when God blesses them, the same thing is always involved: conception and birth, the beginning of a people. And the great story which stands in the middle of the story of the patriarchs—the birth and offering of Isaac—makes exactly this point, in a paradoxical manner. Kierkegaard has presented this paradox very beautifully in the first part of his book *Fear and Trembling*. This paradoxical story of the second in the line of the patriarchs, of his being born and very nearly being killed, shows what is at stake: a begetting, but the begetting of a people standing at the disposal of God—a begetting, but a begetting commanded by God.

We have a people, and the people is in bondage. A man receives the charge to lead it out of bondage. It is he whom I have described as the Leader in the original meaning of the word. It is he who serves in a human way as a tool for the act which God pronounces: "I bore you on eagles' wings, and brought you unto myself" (Ex. 19:4). I have already spoken of his life. But in the middle of his life, the event takes place in which Moses, after the passage through the Red Sea, intones the song in which the people joins, and which is the proclama-

tion of a king. The words with which the song ends proclaim
it: "King shall the Lord be for ever and ever" (Ex. 15:18). The
people has here chosen God himself for its king, and that
means that it has made a vital and experienced truth out of the
tradition of a divine kingdom which was common to all Semitic peoples, but which never had been taken quite seriously.
The Hebrew leaders are so much in earnest about it that after
the land has been conquered they undertake to do what is
"contrary to history": they try to build up a society without a
ruling power save only God. It is that experiment in primitive
theocracy of which the Book of Judges tells, and which degen-
erates into anarchy, as is shown by the examples given in the
last part of it.

The so-called Judge constitutes the third type of leadership.
This type is to be understood as relating to the attempt made
by a leading group among the people who are dominated by
the desire to make actual the proclamation of God as king,
and try to induce the people to follow them. This attempt miscarries time and again. Time and again, the people, to use the
biblical phrase, falls away from God. But we can also express
this in the language of history: time and again the people fall
apart; it is one and the same thing whichever language we use.
The attempt to establish a society under no other domination
than God's, this too can be expressed in the language of history,
or if one likes, in the language of sociology: the attempt to
establish a society on pure voluntarism, which fails over and
over again. The people falls away. This is always succeeded by
an invasion on the part of one of the neighboring peoples, and
Israel, from an historical point of view fallen apart and dis-
united, does not stand firm. But in its conquered state, it
again makes itself subject to the will of God, resolves anew to
accept God's rule, and again a divine mission occurs: there is
always a leader whom the spirit lays hold of as it laid hold of
Moses. This leader, whose mission it is to free the people, is the
Judge, or more correctly, "he who makes right"; he makes
this right exist in the actual world for the people—which after
its return to God now again has right on its side—by defeating
the enemy. This is the rhythm of the Book of Judges; it might
almost be called a tragic rhythm, were it not that the word
tragic is so foreign to the spirit of biblical language.

But in this Book of Judges, there is also something being
prepared. The experience of failure, of the inability to bring
about this intended naïve, primitive theocracy becomes ever

deeper; ever stronger grows the demand for a human kingdom. Judges itself is in its greater part written from an anti-monarchical standpoint. The kings of the nations file before one in a way determined by this point of view, which reaches its height in that ironic fable of Jotham's (Judg. 9). But in its final chapters, the Book of Judges has to acknowledge the disappointment of the theocratic hope, because the people is as it is, because men are as they are. And so kingship is demanded under Samuel. And it is granted by God. I said before, the way leads through the disappointments. Thus, the demand of the people is, as it were, laid hold of and consecrated from above, for by the anointing of the King a man is transformed into the bearer of a charge laid upon him. But this is no longer —as was the case with the Judge—a single charge the completion of which brings his leadership to an end; it is a governor's charge which goes beyond individual acts, indeed beyond the life of individual men. Anointing may also imply the beginning of a dynasty, if the king is not rejected by God, as Saul was.

The kingdom is a new stage in the dialogue, a new stage of attempt and failure; only in this stage the account lays the burden of the failure on the king and not any longer, as in the Book of Judges, on the whole people. It is no longer those who are led but the leader himself who fails, who cannot stand the test of the charge, who does not make the anointing come true in his own person—a crucial problem in religious history. The history of the great religions, and in general all great history, is bound up with the problem: how do human beings stand the test of what is here called anointing?

The history of the kings is the history of the failure of him who has been anointed to realize the promise of his anointing. The rise of messianism, the belief in the anointed king who realizes the promise of his anointing, is to be understood only in this context.

But now, in the situation of the failure of kings, the new and last type of leader in biblical history arises, the leader who above all other types is "contrary to history," the Prophet, he who is appointed to oppose the king, and even more, to oppose history. When God says to Jeremiah, "I have made thee . . . a brazen wall against the whole land" (Jer. 1:18), it is really so; the prophet stands not only against the ruler but against the people itself. The prophet is the man who has been set up against his own natural instincts that bind him to the community, and who likewise sets himself up against the will of the people to live on as they have always lived, which, naturally, for the people is identical with the will to live. It goes without saying that not only the rulers but also the people treat the prophet as their enemy in the way in which, as a matter of history, it falls to the lot of such men to be treated. These experiences of suffering which thus come upon the prophet join together to form that image of the servant of the Lord, of his suffering and dying for the sake of God's purpose.

When the Bible then tries to look beyond these manifestations of leadership to one which no longer stands amidst disintegration and failure, when the idea of the messianic leader is conceived, it means nothing else by it than that at last the answer shall be given: from out of mankind itself the word shall come, the word that is spoken with the whole being of man, the word that answers God's word. It is an earthly consummation which is awaited, a consummation in and with mankind. But this precisely is the consummation toward which God's hand pushes through that which he has created, through nature and through history. This is what the messianic belief means, the belief in the real leader, in the setting right of the dialogue, in God's disappointment coming to an end. And when a fragment of an apocryphal gospel has God say to Jesus: "In all the prophets have I awaited thee, that thou wouldst come and I rest in thee, for thou art my rest," this is the late elaboration of a truly Jewish conception.

The biblical question of leadership is concerned with something greater than moral perfection. The biblical leaders are the foreshadowings of the dialogical man, of the man who commits his whole being to God's dialogue with the world, and who stands firm throughout this dialogue. The life of those people to whom I have referred is absorbed in this dialogue, whether the dialogue comes about through an intervention, as in Abraham's talk with God about Sodom, or Moses' after the sin of the golden calf; or whether it comes about through a resistance they offer against that which comes upon them and tries to overpower them (but their resistance ends in submission, which we find documented from Moses to Jeremiah); or whether the dialogue comes about through the struggle for a purpose and a task, as we know from that dialogue which took place between David and God. Whatever the way, man enters into the dialogue again and again; imperfect entry, but yet one which is not refused, an entry which is determined to persevere in the diological world. All that happens is here experienced as dialogue; what befalls man is taken as a sign; what man tries to do and what miscarries is taken as an attempt and a failure to answer, as a stammering attempt to respond as well as one can.

Because this is so, biblical leadership always means a process of being led. These men are leaders insofar as they allow themselves to be led, that is, insofar as they accept that which is offered them, insofar as they take upon themselves the responsibility for that which is entrusted to them, insofar as they make real that which has been laid upon them from outside of themselves, make it real with the free will of their own being, in the "autonomy" of their person.

So long as we remember this, we can make the lives of these leaders clear. Almost always what we see is the taking of a man out of the community. God lifts the man out of the community, cuts him off from his natural ties; from Abraham to Jeremiah he must go forth out of the land in which he has taken root, away to the place where he has to proclaim the name of God—it is the same story, whether it is a wandering over the earth like Abraham's, or a becoming utterly alone in the midst of the people as in the case of the prophets. They are drawn out of their natural community; they fight with it, they experience in this community the inner contradiction of human existence. All this is intensified to the utmost precisely in the prophets. The great suffering of the prophets, preserved for us by Jeremiah himself in a small number of (in the highest sense of the word) autobiographical sayings, is the ultimate expression of this condition.

But this ever widening gulf between leader and community, the ever greater failure of the leader, the leader's ever greater incompatibility with "history"—this means, from the biblical standpoint, the gradual overcoming of history. What we are accustomed to call history is from the biblical standpoint only the façade of reality. It is the great failure, the refusal to enter into the dialogue, not the failure in the dialogue, as exemplified by biblical man. This great refusal is sanctioned with the imposing sanction provided by so-called history. The biblical point of view repudiates with ever increasing strength this two-dimensional reality, most strongly in the prophets; it proclaims that the way, the real way, from the creation to the kingdom is trod not on the surface of success, but in the depths of failure. The real work, from the biblical point of view, is the late recorded, the unrecorded, the anonymous work. The real work is done in the shadow, in the quiver. Official leadership fails more and more, leadership devolves more and more upon the secret. The way leads through the work which history does not write down, and which history cannot write down, work which is not ascribed to him who did it, but which possibly at some time in a distant generation will emerge as having been done, without the name of the doer—the secret working of the secret leadership. And when the biblical writer turns his eyes toward the final, messianic overcoming of history, he sees how the outer history becomes engulfed, or rather how both the outer history and the inner history fuse, how the secret which the leadership had become rises up out of the darkness and illumines the surface of history, how the meaning of biblical history is consummated in the whole reality.

8

PLATO AND ISAIAH

Plato was about seventy-five years old when the assassination of the prince Dion, master of Syracuse, his friend and disciple, put an end to the enterprise of founding a republic in accordance with the concepts of the philosopher. It was at this time that Plato wrote his famous letter to his friends in Sicily, in which he rendered an account of his lifelong ambition to change the structure of the state (which for him included the structure of society), of his attempts to translate this purpose into reality, and of how he failed in these attempts. He wrote to them that, having observed that all states were poorly governed, he had formed the opinion that man would not be free from this evil until one of two things happened: either true philosophers were charged with the function of government, or the potentates who ruled states lived and acted in harmony with the precepts of philosophy. Plato had formulated this thesis—though somewhat differently—about twenty years earlier as the central passage of his *Republic*. The central position which he gave this passage indicates that in the final analysis he believed that individuals, above all, leaders, were of prime importance rather than any particular institutions—such institutions as the book deals with. According to Plato, there are two ways of obtaining the right persons as leaders: either the philosopher himself must come to power, or he must educate those who rule to conduct their lives as philosophers.

In his memorable tractate *Zum ewigen Frieden*, Kant opposed this thesis of Plato's without mentioning him by name. The rebuttal is part of a passage which appeared only in the second edition, and which Kant designated as a "secret article" of his outline on international law. He wrote: "Because the wielding of power inevitably destroys the free judgment of reason, it is not to be expected that kings should philosophize or philosophers be kings, nor even to be desired. But one thing is indispensable to both philosophers and kings, because the possession of sovereign power inevitably corrupts the free judgment of reason, and that is that kings or kingly nations—that is, nations which govern themselves on the basis of laws of equality—should not dispense with or silence the class of philosophers, but let them express themselves in public." Previously, Kant had emphasized that this was not meant to suggest that the state should prefer its power to be represented by the principles of the philosopher rather than the dicta of the jurist, but merely that the philosopher should be heard. This line of thought is a clear indication not only of resignation, but also of disappointment in the spirit itself, for Kant had been forced to relinquish faith in the spirit's ability to rise to power and, at the same time, remain pure. We may safely assume that Kant's disillusionment is motivated by his knowledge of the course of church history, which, in the more than two thousand years intervening between Plato and himself, came to be the spirit's actual history of power.

Plato believed both in the spirit and in power, and he also believed in the spirit's call to the assumption of power. The power he saw was decadent, but he thought it could be regenerated and purified by the spirit. The young Plato's own grave and epochal encounter with "history" took place when the city-state of Athens condemned and executed his teacher Socrates because he had disobeyed the authority of power, and obeyed the Voice. And yet, among all those who concerned themselves with the state, Socrates alone knew how to educate the young for a true life dedicated to the community; like the seer Tiresias in Hades, he was the only one spiritually alive amid a swarm of hovering shades. Plato regarded himself as Socrates' heir and deputy. He knew himself to be called to renew the sacred law and to found the just state based on law. And he knew that for this reason he had a right to power. But while the spirit is ready to accept power at the hands of God or man, it is not willing to seize it. In *The Republic,* Socrates is asked whether the philosophic man would, if he is as Socrates describes him, be at all apt to concern himself with affairs of state. To this question Socrates replies that the philosophic man, in his own state, would certainly concern himself with such matters, but the state which he conceives and which is suitable to him would have to be one other than his native land, "unless there is some divine intervention." But even prior to this passage, he speaks of the man who is blessed with spirit and yet confronts a furious mob, confronts them without confederates who could help maintain justice, and feels like one who suddenly finds himself surrounded by wild beasts. Such a man, he goes on to say, will henceforth keep silent, attend to his own work, become a spectator, and live out his life without doing any wrong to the end of his days. But when Socrates' listeners interpose that such a man will thus have accomplished a great work by the time he dies, he contradicts them, saying: "But not the greatest, since he has not founded the state which befits him." That is the gist of Plato's resignation. He was called to Syracuse and went there time after time, even though there too he suffered one disappointment after another. He went because he was called and because there is always the possibility that the divine voice may be speaking in the voice of man. According to Dion's words, there was a possibility that then, if ever, the hope to link the philosophers and the rulers of great states to each other could be fulfilled. Plato decided to "try." He reports that he was ashamed not to go to Syracuse, lest he should seem to himself to be nothing but "words." "Manifest," is the word he once used to Dion; we must manifest ourselves by truly being what we profess in words. He had used the word "must," not "should." He went and failed, returned home, went once more, and still another time, and failed again. When he came home after the third failure, he was almost seventy. Not until then did the man whom Plato had educated come into power. But before he was able to master the confusion of the people, he was murdered by one who had been his fellow student at Plato's Academy.

Plato held that mankind could recover from its ills only if either the philosophers—"whom we termed useless"—became kings, or the kings became philosophers. He himself hoped first for the one and then for the other of these alternatives to occur as the result of "divine intervention." But he was not elevated to a *basileus* in Greece, and the prince whom he had educated to be a philosopher did not master the chaos in Sicily. One might possibly say that the peace which Timoleon of Corinth established in Sicily after the death of this prince was achieved under the touch of Plato's spirit, and that Alexander, who later united all of Greece under his rule, had certainly not studied philosophy with Plato's most renowned disciple without benefit to himself; but neither in the one case nor the other was Plato's ideal of the state actually realized. Plato did not regenerate the decadent Athenian democracy, and he did not found the republic he had projected in theory.

But does this glorious failure prove that the spirit is always helpless in the face of history?

Plato is the most sublime instance of that spirit which proceeds in its intercourse with reality from its own possession of truth. According to Plato, the perfect soul is one which remembers its vision of perfection. Before its life on earth, the soul had beheld the idea of the good. In the world of ideas, it had beheld the shape of pure justice, and now, with the spirit's growth, the soul recollects what it had beheld in the past. The soul is not content to know this idea and to teach others to know it. The soul wishes to infuse the idea of justice with the breath of life and establish it in the human world in the living form of a just state. The spirit is in possession of truth; it offers truth to reality; truth becomes reality through the spirit. That is the fundamental basis of Plato's doctrine. But this doctrine was not carried out. The spirit did not succeed in giving reality the truth it wished to give. Was reality alone responsible? Was not the spirit itself responsible as well? Was not its very relationship to the truth responsible? These are questions which necessarily occur to us in connection with Plato's failure.

But the spirit can fail in another and very different way.

"In the year that King Uzziah died" (Is. 6:1), Isaiah had a vision of the heavenly sanctuary in which the Lord chose him as his prophet. The entire incident points to the fact that King Uzziah was still alive. The king had been suffering from leprosy for a long time. It is well known that in biblical times leprosy was not regarded merely as one ailment among others, but as the physical symptom of a disturbance in man's relationship to God. Rumor had it that the king had been afflicted because he had presumed to perform sacral functions in the sanctuary of Jerusalem which exceeded his rights as a merely political lieutenant of God. Moreover, Isaiah feels that Uzziah's leprosy was more than a personal affliction, that it symbolized the uncleanness of the entire people, and Isaiah's own uncleanness as well. They all have "unclean lips" (Is. 6:5). Like lepers, they must all cover "their upper lip" (Lev. 13:45), lest by breath or word their uncleanness go forth and pollute the world. All of them have been disobedient and faithless to the true king, to the king whose glory Isaiah's eyes now behold in his heavenly sanctuary. Here God is called *ha-melek*, and this is the first time in the Scriptures that he is designated so nakedly, so plainly, as the King of Israel. *He* is the king. The leper whom the people call "king" is only his faithless lieutenant. And now the true king sends Isaiah with a message to the entire people, at the same time telling the prophet that his message will fail; he will fail, for the message will be misunderstood, misinterpreted, and misused, and thus confirm the people—save for a small "remnant"—in their faithlessness, and harden their hearts. At the very outset of his way, Isaiah, the carrier of the spirit, is told that he must fail. He will not suffer disappointment like Plato, for in his case failure is an integral part of the way he must take.

Isaiah does not share Plato's belief that the spirit is a possession of man. The man of spirit—such is the tradition from time immemorial—is one whom the spirit invades and seizes, whom the spirit uses as its garment, not one who houses the spirit. Spirit is an event, it is something which happens to man. The storm of the spirit sweeps man where it will, and then storms on into the world.

Neither does Isaiah share Plato's belief that power is man's possession. Power is vouchsafed man to enable him to discharge his duties as God's lieutenant. If he abuses this power, it destroys him, and in place of the spirit which came to prepare him for the use of power, an "evil spirit" comes upon him (I Sam. 16:14). The man in power is responsible to one who interrogates him in silence, and to whom he is answerable, or all is over with him.

Isaiah does not believe that spiritual man has the vocation to power. He knows himself to be a man of spirit and without power. Being a prophet means being powerless, and powerless confronting the powerful and reminding them of their responsibility, as Isaiah reminded Ahaz "in the highway of the fuller's field" (Is. 7:3). To stand powerless before the power he calls to account is part of the prophet's destiny. He himself is not out for power, and the special sociological significance of his office is based on that very fact.

Plato believed that his soul was perfect. Isaiah did not. Isaiah regarded and acknowledged himself as unclean. He felt how the uncleanness which tainted his breath and his words was burned from his lips so that those lips might speak the message of God.

Isaiah beheld the throne and the majesty of him who entrusted him with the message. He did not see the just state which Plato beheld in his mind's eye as something recollected. Isaiah knew and said that men are commanded to be just to one another. He knew and said that the unjust are destroyed by their own injustice. And he knew and said that the rule of justice was coming, and that a just man would rule as the faithful lieutenant of God. But he knew nothing and said nothing about the inner structure of that rule. He had no idea; he had only a message. He had no institution to establish; he had only to proclaim. His proclamation was in the nature of criticism and demand.

His criticism and demands are directed toward making the people and their prince recognize the reality of the invisible sovereignty. When Isaiah uses the word *ha-melek*, it is not in the sense of a theological metaphor, but in that of a political constitutional concept. But this sovereignty of God which he propounded is the opposite of the sovereignty of priests, which is commonly termed theocracy and which has very properly been described as "*the* most unfree form of society," for it is "unfree through the abuse of the highest knowable to man." [111] None but the powerless can speak the true king's will with regard to the state, and remind both the people and the government of their *common* responsibility toward this will. The powerless man can do so because he breaks through the illusions of current history and recognizes potential crises.

That is why his criticism and demands are directed toward society, toward the life men live together. A people which seriously calls God himself its king must become a true people, a community all the members of which are governed by honesty without compulsion, kindness without hypocrisy, and the brotherliness of those who are passionately devoted to their divine Leader. When social inequality, when distinction between the free and the unfree splits the community and creates chasms between its members, there can be no true people, there can be no longer "God's people." So the criticism and demands are directed toward every individual on whom other individuals depend, everyone who has a hand in shaping the destinies of others, and that means they are directed toward everyone of us. When Isaiah speaks of justice, he is not thinking of institutions, but of you and me, because without you and me, the most glorious institution becomes a lie.

Finally, the criticism and demands apply to Israel's relationship to other nations. They warn Israel not to consent to the making of treaties, not to rely on this or that so-called world power, but to "keep calm" (Is. 7:4; 30:15), to make our own people a true people, faithful to its divine King; and then we will have nothing to be afraid of. "The head of Damascus," Isaiah said to Ahaz in the highway of the fuller's field, "is Rezin, and the head of Samaria, Pekah," meaning "but you know who is the head of Jerusalem—if you want to know." But "if ye will not have faith, surely ye shall not endure" (cf. Is. 7:9). There has been much talk in this connection of "utopian" politics which would relate Isaiah's failure to that of Plato, who wrote the utopian *Republic*. What Isaiah said to Ahaz is accepted as a sublimely "religious" but politically valueless utterance, meaning one which lends itself to solemn quotation but is not applicable to reality. Yet the only political chance for a small people hemmed in between world powers is the metapolitical chance to which Isaiah pointed. He proclaimed a truth which could not, indeed, be tested in history up to that time, but only because no one had ever thought of testing it. Nations can be led to peace only by a people which has made peace a reality within itself. The realization of the spirit has a magnetic effect on mankind which despairs of the spirit. That is the meaning which Isaiah's teachings have for us. When the mountain of the Lord's house is "established" on the reality of true community life, then, and only then, will the nations "flow" toward it (Is. 2:2), there to learn peace in place of war.

Isaiah too failed, as was predicted when he was called to give God's message. The people and the king opposed him, and even the king's successor, who attached himself to Isaiah, was found wanting in the decisive hour, when he flirted with the idea of joining the Babylonian rebel against Assyria. But this failure is quite different from Plato's. Our very existence as Jews testifies to this difference. We live by that encounter in the highway of the fuller's field, we live by virtue of the fact that there were people who were deadly serious about this *ha-melek* in relation to all of their social and political reality. They are the cause of our survival until this new opportunity to translate the spirit into the reality we have a presentiment of. We may yet experience an era of history which refutes "history." The prophet fails in one hour in history, but not so far as the future of his people is concerned. For his people preserve his message as something which will be realized at another hour, under other conditions, and in other forms.

The prophet's spirit does not, like Plato's, believe that he possesses an abstract and general, a timeless concept of truth. He always receives only one message for one situation. That is exactly why after thousands of years, his words still address the changing situations in history. He does not confront man with a generally valid image of perfection, with a Pantopia or a Utopia. Neither has he the choice between his native land and some other country which might be "more suitable to him." In his work of realization, he is bound to the *topos*, to this place, to this people, because it is the people who must make the *beginning*. But when the prophet feels like one who finds himself surrounded by wild beasts, he cannot withdraw to the role of the silent spectator, as Plato did. He must speak his message. The message will be misunderstood, misinterpreted, misused; it will even confirm and harden the people in their faithlessness. But its sting will rankle within them for all time.

9

THE MAN OF TODAY
AND THE JEWISH BIBLE

Biblia, books, is the name of a book, of a Book composed of many books. It is really one book, for one basic theme unites all the stories and songs, sayings and prophecies contained within it. The theme of the Bible is the encounter between a group of people and the Lord of the world in the course of history, the sequence of events occurring on earth. Either explicitly or by implication, the stories are reports of encounters. The songs lament the denial of the grace of encounter, plead that it may be repeated, or give thanks because it has been vouchsafed. The prophecies summon man who has gone astray to turn, to return to where the encounter took place, promising him that the torn bond shall once more be made whole. If this book transmits cries of doubt, it is the doubt which is the destiny of man, who after having tasted nearness must experience distance and learn from distance what it alone can teach. When we find love songs in the Bible, we must understand that the love of God for his world is revealed through the depths of love human beings can feel for one another.

Since this book came into being, it has confronted generation after generation. Each generation must struggle with the Bible in its turn, and come to terms with it. The generations are by no means always ready to listen to what the book has to say, and to obey it; they are often vexed and defiant; nevertheless, the preoccupation with this book is part of their life, and they face it in the realm of reality. Even when generations negated the book, the very negation confirmed the book's claim upon them; they bore witness to the book in the very act of denying it.

The picture changes when we shift to the man of today, and by this, I mean the "intellectual" man of our time, the man who holds it important for intellectual values to exist, and admits—yes, even himself declares—that their reality is bound up with our own power to realize them. But if we were to question him and probe down to truth—and we do not usually probe that far down—he would have to own that this feeling of his about the obligations of the spirit is in itself only intellectual. It is the signature of our time that the spirit imposes no obligations. We proclaim the rights of the spirit, we formulate its laws, but they enter only into books and discussions, not into our lives. They float in mid-air above our heads, rather than walk the earth in our midst. Everything except everyday life belongs to the realm of the spirit. Instead of union, a false relationship obtains between the spirit and everyday life. This relationship may shape up as spurious idealism, toward which we may lift our gaze without incurring any obligation to recover from the exigencies of earth; or it may present itself as spurious realism, which regards the spirit as only a function of life and transforms its unconditionality into a number of conditional characters: psychological, sociological, and others. It is true that some contemporaries realize all the corroding consequences of this separation of two interdependent entities, a corrosion which is bound to penetrate into deeper and deeper strata, until the spirit is debased into a willing and complacent servant of whatever powers happen to rule the world. The men of whom I am speaking have pondered how this corrosion can be halted, and have appealed to religion as the only power which is still capable of bringing about a new union between spirit and world. But what goes by the name of religion nowadays will never bring about such a union. For nowadays, "religion" itself is part of the detached spirit. It is one of the subdivisions—one which is in high favor, to be sure—of the structure erected over and above life, one of the rooms on the top floor, with a very special atmosphere of its own. But this sort of religion is not an entity which includes all of life, and in this its present status, can never become one. It has lost its unity, and so it cannot lead man to inner unity. It has adapted itself to this twofold character of human existence. To exert an influence on contemporary man, religion itself would have to return to reality. And religion was always real only when it was free of fear, when it shouldered the load of concreteness instead of rejecting it as something belonging to another realm, when it made the spirit incarnate, and sanctified everyday life.

The so-called Old Testament constitutes the greatest document of such reality. Two traits—which are, however, interrelated—set it apart from the other great books of the world religions. One trait is that in the "Old Testament," both events and words are placed in the midst of the people, of history, of the world. What happens does not happen in a vacuum existing between God and the individual. The Word travels by way of the individual to the people, so that they may hear and translate it into reality. What happens is not superior to the history of the people, it is nothing but the secret of the people's history made manifest. But that very fact places the people acted upon in opposition to the nations which represent—in their own eyes—an end in themselves, to groups concerned only with their own welfare, to the "breath of world history." This people is called upon to weld its members into a community that may serve as a model for the so many and so different peoples. The historical continuity of "seed" and "earth" is bound up with the "blessing" (Gen. 12ff.), and the blessing with the mission. The Holy permeates history without divesting it of its rights.

The second trait is that in the Bible the law is designed to cover the natural course of man's life. Eating meat is connected with animal sacrifice; matrimonial purity is sanctified month after month; man is accepted as he is with all his urges and passions and included in holiness, lest his passions grow into a mania. The desire to own land is not condemned, and renunciation is not demanded, but the true lord of the land is God, and man is nothing but a "sojourner" in his midst. The Landlord makes a harmonious balance of property ownership, lest inequality arise, grow, and break the bond between the members of the community. Holiness penetrates nature without violating it. The living spirit wishes to spiritualize and quicken life; it wishes spirit and life to find the way to one another; it wishes spirit to take shape as life, and life to be clarified through spirit. The spirit wishes creation to attain perfection through itself. The function of this book is to bear witness to the spirit's will to perfection and to command service to the spirit in its search for union with life. If we accept the Old Testament as merely "religious writing," as a subdivision of the detached spirit, it will fail us, and we must needs fail it. If we seize upon it as the expression of a reality which comprises all of life, we really grasp it, and it grasps us. But contemporary man is scarcely capable of this grasp any longer. If he "takes any interest" at all in the Scriptures, it is an abstract, purely "religious" interest, and more often not even that, but an interest connected with the history of religion or civilization, or an aesthetic interest, or the like—at any rate it is an interest that springs from the detached spirit with its numerous autonomous domains. Man of today is not like the generations of old, who stood before the biblical word in order to hearken to or to take offense at it. He no longer confronts his life with the Word; he locks life away in one of many unholy compartments, and then he feels relieved. Thus he paralyzes the power which, of all powers, is best able to save him.

Before demonstrating in greater detail and by way of examples what power the Jewish Bible has to guide the life of the man of today, I must broach the basic question which the thoughtful reader is asking himself at this point. Even if this man of today, even if we were able to approach this whole book with our whole selves, would we not still lack the indispensable prerequisite to its true reception? Would we be able to believe it? Could we believe it? Can we do more than believe that people once did believe as this book reports and claims?

The man of today has no access to a sure and solid faith, nor can it be made accessible to him. If he examines himself seriously, he knows this and may not delude himself further. But he is not denied the possibility of holding himself open to faith. If he is really serious, he too can open himself up to this book, and let its rays strike him where they will. He can give himself up and submit to the test without preconceived notions and without reservations. He can absorb the Bible with all his strength, and wait to see what will happen to him, whether he will not discover within himself a new and unbiased approach to this or that element in the book. But to this end, he must read the Jewish Bible as though it were something entirely unfamiliar, as though it had not been set before him ready-made, at school and after in the light of "religious" and "scientific" certainties; as though he had not been confronted all his life with sham concepts and sham statements which cited the Bible as their authority. He must face the book with a new attitude as something new. He must yield to it, withhold nothing of his being, and let whatever will occur between himself and it. He does not know which of its sayings and images will overwhelm him and mold him, from where the spirit will ferment and enter into him, to incorporate itself anew in his body. But he holds himself open. He does not believe anything a priori; he does not disbelieve anything a priori. He reads aloud the words written in the book in front of him; he hears the word he utters, and it reaches him. Nothing is prejudged. The current of time flows on, and the contemporary character of this man becomes itself a receiving vessel.

In order to understand the situation fully, we must picture to ourselves the complete chasm between the Scriptures and the man of today.

The Jewish Bible has always approached and still does every generation with the claim that it must be recognized as a document of the true history of the world, that is to say, of the history according to which the world has an origin and a goal. The Jewish Bible demands that the individual fit his own life into this true history, so that "I" may find my own origin in the origin of the world, and my own goal in the goal of the world. But the Jewish Bible does not set a past event as a midpoint between origin and goal. It interposes a movable, circling midpoint which cannot be pinned to any set time, for it is the moment when I, the reader, the hearer, the man, catch through the words of the Bible the voice which from earliest beginnings has been speaking in the direction of the goal. The midpoint is this mortal and yet immortal moment of mine. Creation is the origin, redemption the goal. But revelation is not a fixed, dated point poised between the two. The revelation at Sinai is not this midpoint itself, but the perceiving of it, and such perception is possible at any time. That is why a psalm or a prophecy is no less "Torah," that is, instruction, than the story of the exodus from Egypt. The history of this people—accepting and refusing at once—points to the history of all mankind, but the secret dialogue expressed in the psalms and prophecies points to my own secret.

The Jewish Bible is the historical document of a world swinging between creation and redemption, which, in the course of its history, experiences revelation, a revelation which

I experience *if I am there*. Thus, we can understand that the resistance of the man of today is that of his innermost being.

The man of today has two approaches to history. He may contemplate it as a "freethinker," and participate in and accept the shifting events, the varying success of the struggles for power, as a promiscuous agglomeration of happenings. To him, history will seem a medley of the actions and deaths of peoples, of grasping and losing, of triumph and misery, a meaningless hodge-podge to which the mind of man, time and again, gives an unreliable and unsubstantial semblance of meaning. Or he may view history dogmatically, derive laws from the past sequences of events, and calculate future sequences, as though the "main lines" were already traced on some roll which need merely unroll; as though history were not the vital living, growing, of time, constantly moving from decision to decision, of time into which my time and my decisions stream full force. He regards history as a stark, ever-present, inescapable space.

Both of these approaches are a misinterpretation of historic destiny, which is neither chance nor fatality. According to the biblical insight, historic destiny is the secret correlation inhering in the current moment. When we are aware of origin and goal, there is no meaningless drift; we are carried along by a meaning we could never think up for ourselves, a meaning we are to live—not to formulate. And that living takes place in the awful and splendid moment of decision—your moment and mine no less than Alexander's or Caesar's. And yet your moment is not yours, but rather the moment of your encounter.

The man of today knows of no beginning. As far as he is concerned, history ripples toward him from some prehistorical cosmic age. He knows of no end; history sweeps him on into a posthistorical cosmic age. What a violent and foolish episode this time between the prehistorical and the posthistorical has become! Man no longer recognizes an origin or a goal, because he no longer wants to recognize the midpoint. Creation and redemption are true only on the premise that revelation is a present experience. Man of today resists the Scriptures because he cannot endure revelation. To endure revelation is to endure this moment full of possible decisions, to respond to and to be responsible for every moment. Man of today resists the Scriptures because he does not want any longer to accept responsibility. He thinks he is venturing a great deal, yet he industriously evades the one real venture, that of responsibility.

Insight into the reality of the Bible begins with drawing a distinction between creation, revelation, and redemption.[112] Christianity withdrew from such insight—and thus from the grounds of the "Old Testament"—in its earliest theology which fused the essentials of revelation with the essentials of redemption in the Christ. It was entirely logical for Marcion to dispute the value of a creation which from this point of view was bound to seem nothing but a premise, and to brand it as the blunder of another, inferior god. With that act, the essence of time which was closely allied to the essence of our spirit, was abandoned, time which distinguishes between past, present, and future—structures which in the Bible reach their most concrete expression in the three structures of creation, revelation, and redemption. The only gate which leads to the Bible as a reality is the faithful distinction between the three, not as hypostases or manifestations of God, but as stages, actions, and events in the course of his intercourse with the world, and thus also as the main directions of his movement toward the world. But such distinction must not be exaggerated to mean separation. From the point of view of the Bible, revelation is, as it were, focused in the "middle," creation in the "beginning," and redemption in the "end." But the living truth is that they actually coincide, that "God every day renews the work of the beginning," but also every day anticipates the work of the end. Certainly, both creation and redemption are true only on the premise that revelation is a present experience. But if I did not feel creation as well as redemption happening to myself, I could never understand what creation and redemption are.

This fact must be the starting point for the recurring question, if and how the chasm between man of today and the Scriptures can be bridged. We have already answered the question whether the man of today can believe, by saying that while he is denied the certainty of faith, he has the power to hold himself open to faith. But is not the strangeness of biblical concepts a stumblingblock to his readiness to do so? Has he not lost the reality of creation in his concept of "evolution," that of revelation in the theory of the "unconscious," and that of redemption in the setting up of social or national goals?

We must wholly understand the very substantial quality of this strangeness, before we can even attempt to show that there is still an approach, or rather *the* approach.

And again we must begin with the center.

What meaning are we intended to find in the words that

God came down in fire, to the sound of thunder and trumpet, to the mountain which smoked like a furnace, and spoke to his people? It can mean, I think, one of three things. Either it is figurative language used to express a "spiritual" process; but if biblical history does not recall actual events, but is metaphor and allegory, then it is no longer biblical, and deserves no better fate than to be surrendered to the approaches of modern man, the historical, aesthetic, and similar approaches. Or it is the report of a "supernatural" event, one that severs the intelligible sequence of happenings we term natural by interposing something unintelligible. If that were the case, the man of today in deciding to accept the Bible would have to make a sacrifice of intellect which would cut his life irreparably in two, provided he does not want to lapse into the habitual, lazy acceptance of something he does not really believe. In other words, what he is willing to accept would not be the Bible in its totality including all of life, but only religion abstracted from life.

But there is a third possibility: it could be the verbal trace of a natural event, that is, of an event which took place in the world of the senses common to all men, and fitted into connections which the senses can perceive. But the assemblage that experienced this event experienced it as revelation vouchsafed to them by God, and preserved it as such in the memory of generations, an enthusiastic, spontaneously formative memory. Experience undergone in this way is not self-delusion on the part of the assemblage; it is what they see, what they recognize and perceive with their reason, for natural events are the carriers of revelation, and revelation occurs when he who witnesses the event and sustains it experiences the revelation it contains. This means that he listens to that which the voice, sounding forth from this event, wishes to communicate to him, its witness, to his constitution, to his life, to his sense of duty. It is only when this is true that the man of today can find the approach to biblical reality. I, at any rate, believe that it is true.

Sometimes, we have a personal experience related to those recorded as revelations and capable of opening the way for them. We may unexpectedly grow aware of a certain apperception within ourselves, which was lacking but a moment ago, and whose origin we are unable to discover. The attempt to derive such apperception from the famous unconscious stems from the widespread superstition that the soul can do every-thing by itself, and it fundamentally means nothing but this: what you have just experienced always was in you. Such no-tions build up a temporary construction which is useful for psychological orientation, but collapses when I try to stand upon it. What occurred to me was "otherness," was the touch of the other. Nietzsche says it more honestly: "You take, you do not ask who it is that gives." But I think that as we take, it is of the utmost importance to know that someone is/giving. He who takes what is given him, and does not experience it as a gift, is not really receiving; and so the gift turns into theft. But when we do experience the giving, we find out that revela-tion exists. And we set foot on the path which will reveal our life and the life of the world as a sign communication. This path is the approach. It is on this path that we shall meet with the major experience that is of the same kind as our minor experience.

The perception of revelation is the basis for perceiving crea-tion and redemption. I begin to realize that in inquiring about my own origin and goal, I am inquiring about something other than myself, and something other than the world. But in this very realization, I begin to recognize the origin and goal of the world.

What meaning are we intended to find in the statement that God created the world in six days? Certainly not that he cre-ated it in six ages, and that "create" must mean "come into being"—the interpretation of those who try to contrive an ap-proach to the Bible by forcing it into harmony with current scientific views. But just as inadequate for our purposes is the mystic interpretation, according to which the acts of creation are not acts, but emanations. It is in keeping with the nature of mysticism to resist the idea that, for our sake, God assumed the lowly form of an acting person. But divest the Bible of the acting character of God, and it loses its significance, and the concepts of a Platonic or Heraclitean system—concepts born from the observation of reality—are far preferable to the ho-munculus-like principles of emanation in such an interpretation. What meaning, then, are we intended to find? Here there can be no question of verbal traces of an event, because there was none to witness it. Is then access barred to everyone who cannot believe that the biblical story of creation is the pure "word of God"? The saying of our sages (Bab. Talmud, Berakot 31b) to the effect that the Torah speaks the language of men hides a deeper seriousness than is commonly assumed. We must construe it to mean that what is unutterable *can* only be uttered, as it is here expressed, in the language of men. The biblical story of creation is a legitimate stammering account. Man cannot but stammer when he lines up what he knows of the universe into a chronological series of commands and "works" from the divine workshop. But this stammering of his was the only means of doing justice to the task of stating the mystery of how time springs from eternity, and world comes from that which is not world. Compared to this, every attempt to explain cosmogony "scientifically," to supply a logical foundation for the origin of all things, is bound to fail.

If then, the man of today can find the approach to the reality of revelation in the fact that it is our life which is being addressed, how can he find the approach to the reality of creation? His own individual life will not lead him straight to creation as it does to revelation, which he can find so readily because—as we have seen—every moment we live can in itself be its midpoint. Nevertheless, the reality of creation can be found, because every man knows that he is an individual and unique. Suppose it were possible for a man to make a psychophysical inventory of his own person, to break down his character into a sum of qualities; and now suppose it were possible for him to trace each separate quality, and the concurrence of all, back to the most primitive living creatures, and in this way make an uninterrupted genetic analysis of his individuality by determining its derivation and reference—then his form, his face, unprecedented, comparable to none, unique, his voice never heard before, his gestures never seen before, his body informed with spirit, would still exist as the untouched residue, underived and underivable, an entity which is simply present and nothing more. If after all this futile effort, such a man had the strength to repeat the question "whence," he would, in the final analysis, discover himself simply as something that was created. Because every man is unique, another first man enters the world whenever a child is born. By being alive, everyone groping like a child back to the origin of his own self, we may experience the fact that there is an origin, that there is creation.

And now to the third, the last, and the most difficult problem: how are we to understand the concept that "in the end of days" everything in the world will be resolved, that the world will be so perfectly redeemed that, as it is written, there will be "a new heaven and a new earth"? Here again, two opposite interpretations must be avoided. We must not regard the tidings in the light of another world to come. They mean that this our world will be purified to the state of the kingdom, that creation will be made perfect, but not that our world will be annulled for the sake of another world. But neither do the tidings refer to a more righteous order, but to "righteousness," not to mankind grown more peaceful, but to "peace."

Here, too, the voice we hear stammers legitimately. The prophet, who is overwhelmed by the divine word, can only speak in the words of men. He can speak only as one who is able to grasp from what and whence he is to be redeemed, but not for what and whither. And the man of today? Must not this he hears be strangest to him, exactly because it is closest to his fathomless yearning? He dreams of change, but does not know transformation. He hopes that if not tomorrow, then the next day things will be better, but the idea that truth will come means nothing to him. He is familiar with the idea of development and the overcoming of obstacles, but he can realize neither that a power wishes to redeem him and the world from contradiction, nor that because of the existence of this power it is demanded of him that he turn with the whole of his being. How can we mediate between this man and the biblical message? Where is the bridge?

This is the most difficult of all. The lived moment leads directly to the knowledge of revelation, and thinking about birth leads indirectly to the knowledge of creation. But in his personal life probably not one of us will taste the essence of redemption before his last hour. And yet here, too, there is an approach. It is dark and silent and cannot be indicated by any means, save by my asking you to recall your own dark and silent hours. I mean those hours in the lowest depths when our soul hovers over the frail trap door which, at the very next instant, may send us down into destruction, madness, and "suicide" at our own verdict. Indeed, we are astonished that it has not opened up until now. But suddenly we feel a touch as of a hand. It reaches down to us, it wishes to be grasped—and yet what incredible courage is needed to take the hand, to let it draw us up out of the darkness! This is redemption. We must realize the true nature of the experience proffered us: it is that our "redeemer liveth" (Job 19:18), that he wishes to redeem us—but only by our own acceptance of his redemption with the turning of our whole being.

Approach, I said. For all this still does not constitute a rootedness in biblical reality. But it is the approach to it. It is a beginning.

THE FAITH OF JUDAISM

The Way of Faith

My subject is not the religion but only the faith of Judaism. I do not wish to speak to you about cult, ritual, and moral-religious standards, but about faith, and faith taken in its strictest and most serious sense. Not the so-called faith which is a strange mingling of assumptions and cognitions, but that faith which means trust and loyalty. It follows that I do not start from a Jewish theology, but from the actual attitude of faithful Jews from the earliest days down to our own time. Even though I must of necessity use theological concepts when I speak of this realm of faith, I must not for a moment lose sight of the nontheological material from which I draw those concepts: popular literature, and my own impressions of Jewish life in eastern Europe—but there is nothing in the East of which something may not be found in the West, as well.

When I refer to this popular material, it often happens that people say to me, "You mean, I take it, Hasidism?" That is a question which is natural enough, only it is not primarily Hasidism which I have in mind. In Hasidism, I see merely a concentrated movement, the concentration of all those elements which are to be found in a less condensed form everywhere in Judaism, even in "rabbinic" Judaism. Only, in rabbinic Judaism this movement is not visible in the structure of the community, but holds sway over the inaccessible structure of personal life. What I am trying to formulate may be called the theologoumena of a popular religion.

It is impossible to trace any one of these theologoumena back to any one epoch; my intention is to present the unity to be found in the changing forms. Religious truths are generally of a dynamic kind; they are truths which cannot be understood on the basis of a cross section of history, but only when they are seen in the whole line of history, in their unfolding, in the dynamic of their changing forms. The most important testimony to the truth of this conception comes from the way in which these truths clarify and fulfil themselves, and from their struggle for purity. The truth of the history of religion is the growth of the image of God, the *way* of faith. Though my subject does not impose the historical form on me, it is still of the *way* of the Jewish faith that I have to speak.

The Dialogical Situation

The question has often been raised whether a Jewish dogmatics does or does not exist. The emphasis should rather fall on the question of the relative power of dogma in Judaism. There is no need to prove that there are dogmas, in view of the incorporation of Maimonides' thirteen articles of faith into the liturgy. But dogma remains of secondary importance. In the religious life of Judaism, primary importance is not given to dogma, but to the remembrance and the expectation of a concrete situation: the encounter of God and man. Dogma can arise only in a situation where detachment is the prevailing attitude to the concrete, lived moment—a state of detachment which easily becomes misunderstood in dogmatics as being superior to the lived moment itself. Whatever is enunciated *in abstracto* in the third person about the divine, on the thither side of the confrontation of I and Thou, is only a projection onto the conceptual construct plane, which, though indispensable, proves itself again and again to be unessential.

It is from this point of view that we must regard the problem of so-called monotheism. Israel's experience of the Thou in the direct relationship, the purely singular experience, is so overwhelmingly strong that any notion of a plurality of principles simply cannot arise. Over against this stands the "heathen," the man who does not recognize God in his manifestations. Or rather: a man is a heathen to the extent to which he does not recognize God in his manifestations.

The fundamental attitude of the Jews is characterized by the idea of the *yihud*, the "unification," a word which has been repeatedly misunderstood. *Yihud* involves the continually renewed confirmation of the unity of the divine in the manifold nature of its manifestations, understood in a quite practical way. Again and again, this recognition, acknowledgment, and reacknowledgment of the divine unity is brought about through human perception and confirmation (*Bewaehrung*) in the face of the monstrous contradictions of life, and especially in the face of that primal contradiction which shows itself in multitudinous ways, and which we call the duality of good and evil. But the unification is brought about not to spite these contradictions, but in a spirit of love and reconciliation; not by the mere profession of unification, but by the fulfilment of the profession. Therefore, the unification is contained in no pantheistic theorem, but in the reality of the impossible, in translating the image into actuality, in the *imitatio Dei*. The mystery behind this fact is fulfilled in martyrdom, in the death with the cry of unity on one's lips, the "Hear, O Israel," which at this point becomes testimony in the most vital sense.

A wise man of the Middle Ages said: "My God, where can I find you, but where can I not find you?" The East European Jewish beggar of today softly and unfalteringly whispers his *Gotenyu* in the trembling and dread of his harshest hour; the term of endearment is untranslatable, naive, but in its saying it becomes rich in meanings. In both, there is the same recognition, the same reacknowledgment of the One.

It is the dialogical situation in which the human being stands that here finds its sublime or childlike expression.

Judaism regards speech as an event which grasps beyond the existence of mankind and the world. In contradiction to the static of the idea of Logos, the Word appears here in its complete dynamic as "that which happens." God's act of creation is speech, but the same is true of each lived moment. The world is given to the human beings who perceive it, and the life of man is itself a giving and receiving. The events that occur to human beings are the great and small, untranslatable but unmistakable signs of their being addressed; what they do and fail to do can be an answer or a failure to answer. Thus, the whole history of the world, the hidden, real world history, is a dialogue between God and his creature, a dialogue in which man is a true, legitimate partner, who is entitled and empowered to speak his own independent word out of his own being.

I am far from wishing to contend that the conception and

experience of the dialogical situation are confined to Judaism. But I am certain that no other community of human beings has entered with such strength and fervor into this experience as have the Jews.

The Human Action

What is presupposed when one is serious about the lived dialogue, regarding the moment as word and answer, is, of course, that one is serious about the appointment of man to the earth.

In strongest contrast to the Iranian conception with all its later ramifications, the Jewish conception is that the happenings of this world take place not in the sphere between two principles, light and darkness, good and evil, but in the sphere between God and men, these mortal, brittle human beings who yet are able to face God and withstand his word.

So-called evil is fully and, as a primary element, included in the power of God, who "forms the light and creates darkness" (Is. 45:7). The divine sway is not answered by anything which is evil in itself, but by individual human beings, through whom alone so-called evil, directionless power, can become real evil. Human choice is not a psychological phenomenon but utter reality, which is taken up into the mystery of the One who is. Man is truly free to choose God or to reject him, and to do so not in a relationship of faith which is empty of the content of this world, but in one which contains the full content of the everyday. The "fall" did not happen once and for all, and become an inevitable fate, but it continually happens here and now in all its reality. In spite of all past history, in spite of all his inheritance, every man stands in the naked situation of Adam: to each, the decision is given. It is true that this does not imply that further events are deducible from that decision; it only implies that the human being's choice is that side of reality which concerns him as one called upon to act.

It is only when reality is turned into logic, and A and non-A dare no longer dwell together, that we get determinism and indeterminism, a doctrine of predestination and a doctrine of freedom, each excluding the other. According to the logical conception of truth, only one of two contraries can be true; but in the reality of life as one lives it, they are inseparable. The person who makes a decision knows that his deciding is no self-delusion; the person who has acted knows that he was and is in the hand of God. The unity of the contraries is the mystery at the innermost core of the dialogue.

I said above that evil is to be taken only as a primary element —humanly speaking, as passion. Passion is only evil when it remains in the directionless state, when it refuses to be subject to direction, when it will not accept the direction that leads toward God—there is no other direction. In Judaism, there recurs again and again in many forms the insight that passion, the "evil urge," is simply the elemental force which is the sole origin of great human works, the holy included. The verse in the Scripture which says that at the end of the last day of creation God allowed himself to see his work "that it was very good" has been taken by tradition to refer to the so-called "evil urge." Of all the works of creation, it is passion which is the very good, without which man cannot serve God, or truly live. The words, "And thou shalt love the Lord thy God with all thy heart" (Deut. 6:5) are interpreted, "With both thy urges," with the evil, undirected, elemental urge, as well as the good, because directed, urge. It is of this so-called "evil urge" that God says to man: "You have made it evil."

Consequently, "inertia" is the root of all evil. The act of decision implies that man is not allowing himself any longer to be carried along on the undirected swirl of passion, but that his whole power is included in the move in the direction for which he has decided—and man can decide only for the direction of God. The evil, then, is only the "shell," the wrapping, the crust of the good, a shell that requires active piercing.

Some time ago, a Catholic theologian saw in this conception a "Jewish activism" to which grace is unknown. But it is not so. We are not less serious about grace because we are serious about the human power of deciding, and through decision the soul finds a way which will lead it to grace. Man is here given no complete power; rather, what is stressed is the ordered perspective of human action, an action which we may not limit in advance. It must experience limitation as well as grace in the very process of acting.

The great question which is more and more deeply agitating our age is this: How can we act? Is our action valid in the sight of God, or is its very foundation broken and unwarranted? The question is answered as far as Judaism is concerned by our being serious about the conception that man has been appointed to this world as an originator of events, as a real partner in the real dialogue with God.

This answer implies a refusal to have anything to do with all separate ethics, any concept of ethics as a separate sphere of life, a form of ethics which is all too familiar in the spiritual history of the West. Ethical life has entered into religious life, and cannot be extracted from it. There is no responsibility unless there is One to whom one is responsible, for there is no reply where there is no appeal. In the last resort, "religious life" means concreteness itself, the whole concreteness of life *without reduction*, grasped dialogically, included in the dialogue.

Thus, man has a real start in the dialogue over and over again. However mysteriously, something has been allotted to man, and that something is the beginning. Man cannot finish, and yet he must begin, in the most serious, actual way. This was once stated by a hasid in a somewhat paradoxical interpretation of the first verse of Genesis: " 'In the beginning'— that means *for the sake of the beginning;* for the sake of beginning did God create heaven and earth." For the sake of man's beginning, that there might be one who would and should begin to move in the direction of God.

At the end of the tractate of the Mishnah which deals with the Day of Atonement, there occurs a great saying, which must be understood in the same way as the hasid understood the words of Genesis. Here Rabbi Akiba is speaking to Israel: "Happy are ye, O Israel. Before whom do ye cleanse yourselves, and who is it who makes you clean? Your Father who is in heaven." Here both the reality and the insufficiency of man's action are clearly expressed, the reality of man's action and his dependence upon grace. And pregnant with meaning, the saying ends with words whose origin is a daring scriptural exegesis: "The Lord is the waters of immersion of Israel."

The Turning

This "beginning" by man manifests itself most strongly in the act of turning. It is usual to call it "repentance," but to do so is a misleading attempt to psychologize; it is better to take the word in its original, literal meaning. For what it refers to is not something which happens in the secret recesses of the soul, showing itself outwardly only in its "consequences" and "effects"; it is something which happens in the immediacy of the reality between man and God. The turning is as little a "psychic" event as is a man's birth or death; it comes upon the whole person, is carried out by the whole person, and does not occur as a man's self-intercourse, but as the plain reality of primal mutuality.

The turning is a human fact, but it is also a world-embracing power. We are told that when God contemplated creating the world, and sat tracing it on a stone, in much the same way as a master-builder draws his ground plan, he saw that the world would have no stability. He then created the turning, and the world had stability. For from that time on, whenever the world was lost in the abyss of its own self, far away from God, the gates of deliverance were open to it.

The turning is the greatest form of "beginning." When God tells man, "Open me the gate of the turning as narrow as the point of a needle, and I shall open it so wide that carriages can enter it," or when God tells Israel, "Turn to me, and I shall create you anew," the meaning of human beginning becomes clear as never before. By turning, man arises anew as God's child.

When we consider that turning means something so mighty, we can understand the legend that Adam learned the power to turn from Cain. We can understand the saying, which is reminiscent of a New Testament text, but which is quite independent of it, "In the place where those who have turned stand, the perfectly righteous cannot stand" (Bab. Talmud, Berakot 34b).

Again we see that there is no separate sphere of ethics in Judaism. This, the highest "ethical" moment, is fully received into the dialogical life existing between God and man. The turning is not a return to an earlier "sinless" state; it is the revolution of the whole being, in the course of which man is projected onto the way of God. This, *hē hodos tou theou,* however, does not merely indicate a way which God enjoins man to follow. It indicates that he, God himself, walks in the person of his *Shekinah,* his "indwelling," through the history of the world; he takes the way, the fate of the world upon himself. The man who turns finds himself standing in the traces of the living God.

When we remember this, we understand the full, pregnant meaning of the word with which first the Baptist, then Jesus, then the disciples begin their preaching, the word which is falsely rendered by the Greek *metanoeite* referring to a spiritual *process,* but which in the original Hebrew or Aramaic idiom cannot have been anything else than that cry of the prophets of old: "Turn ye!" And when we remember this, we can also understand how the following sentence is linked to that beginning of the sermon: "For *hē basileia ton ouranōn* is at hand," which, according to the Hebrew or Aramaic usage of the time cannot have meant the "kingdom of heaven" in the sense of "another world," for *shamayim,* Heaven, was at that time one of the paraphrases for the name of God; *malkut shamayim, hē basileia tōn ouranōn,* does not mean the kingdom of heaven, but the kingdom of God, which wills to fulfil itself in the whole of creation, and wills thus to complete creation. The kingdom of God is at the hand of man, it wills him to grasp and realize it, not through any theurgical act of "violence," but through the turning of the whole being; and not as if he were capable of accomplishing anything through so doing, but because the world was created for the sake of his "beginning."

Against Gnosis and Magic

The two spiritual powers of gnosis and magic, masquerading under the cloak of religion, threaten more than any other powers the insight into the religious reality, into man's dialogical situation. They do not attack religion from the outside; they penetrate into religion, and once inside it, pretend to be its essence. Because Judaism has always had to hold them at bay and to keep separate from them, its struggle has been largely internal. This struggle has often been misunderstood as a fight against myth. But only an abstract-theological monotheism can do without myth, and may even see it as its enemy; living monotheism needs myth, as all religious life needs it, as the specific form in which its central events can be kept safe and lastingly remembered and incorporated.

Israel first confronted gnosis and magic in its two great neighboring cultures: gnosis, the perception of the knowable mystery, in the Babylonian teaching about the stars whose power holds all earthly destinies in control, a teaching which was later to reach its full development in the Iranian doctrine concerning the world-soul imprisoned in the cosmos; and magic, the perception of the masterable mystery, in the Egyptian doctrine that death can be conquered and everlasting salvation attained by the performance of prescribed formulas and gestures.

The tribes of Jacob could only become Israel by disentangling themselves from both gnosis and magic. He who imagines that he knows and holds the mystery fast can no longer face it as his "Thou"; and he who thinks that he can conjure and utilize it, is unfit for the venture of true mutuality.

The gnostic temptation is answered by the Instruction, the Torah, with the truly fundamental cry: "The secret things belong unto the Lord our God; but the things that are revealed belong unto us and to our children for ever, that we may do all the words of this instruction" (Deut. 29:28). Revelation does not deal with the mystery of God, but with the life of man. And it deals with the life of man as that which can and should be lived in the face of the mystery of God, and turning toward that mystery, even more, the life of man *is* so lived when it is his true life.

The magical temptation is confronted with the word of God from out of the burning bush. Moses expected the people in their distress to ask him what was the name of the god as whose messenger he spoke (not what was the name of the "God of their fathers"! [cf. Ex. 3:13]). For according to the usage common to primitive peoples, once they seized the secret of the name, they could conjure the god, and thus coerce him to manifest himself to them and save them. But when Moses voices his scruple as to what reply he should give to the people, God answers him by revealing the sense of the name, for he says explicitly in the first person that which is hidden in the name in the third. Not "I am that I am" as alleged by the metaphysicians—God does not make theological statements—but the answer which his creatures need, and which benefits them: "I shall be there as I there shall be" (Ex. 3:14). That is: you need not conjure me, for I am here, I am with you; but you cannot conjure me, for I am with you time and again in the form in which I choose to be with you time and again; I myself do not anticipate any of my manifestations; you cannot learn to meet me; you meet me, when *you* meet me, "It is not in heaven, that thou shouldst say: 'Who shall go up for us to heaven, and bring it unto us, and make us to hear it that we may do it . . .' Yea, the word is very nigh unto thee, in thy mouth, and in thy heart, that thou mayest do it" (Deut. 30:12, 14).

It is also in the light of its own inner battle against the infiltration of gnosis and magic that the dynamic of later Judaism must be understood, and especially that vexatious Talmud. We can only grasp some of its apparently abstract discussions when we keep in mind this constant double threat to the religious reality, the threat from gnosis taking the form of the late-Iranian teaching of the two principles and the intermediary substances, and the threat from magic taking the form of the Hellenistic practice of theurgy. Both of these amalgamated inside Judaism and became the Kabbalah, that uncannily powerful undertaking by the Jew to wrest himself free of the concreteness of the dialogical situation.

The Kabbalah was overcome because it was taken just as it was into the primal Jewish conception of the dialogical life. This overcoming of the Kabbalah is the significant work of Hasidism. Hasidism caused all intermediary substances to fade before the relationship between God's transcendence, to be named only "The Unlimited," with the suspension of all limited being, and his immanence, his "indwelling." The mystery of this relationship is rendered, however, no longer knowable; it is applied directly to the pulsating heart of the human person as the *yihud,* the unification which man must profess and confirm (*bewaehren*) in every moment of his life, and in his relationship to all the things of the world. On the other hand, Hasidism drains theurgy of its poison, not by attempting to deny the influence of humanity on deity, but by proclaiming that far above and beyond all formulas and gestures, above all exercises, penances, preparations, and premeditated actions, the hallowing of the whole of the everyday is the one true bearer of the human influence. Thus, it dissolves the technique of theurgy, and leaves no "practicable," specific means behind, no means which are valid once and for all and applicable everywhere. In this way, Hasidism renews the insight into the mutuality where the whole of life is put unreservedly at stake; the insight into the dialogical relationship of the undivided human being to the undivided God in the fulness of this earthly present, with its unforeseeable, ever changing and ever new situations; the insight into that differentiation between "secret" and "revelation," and the union of both in that unknowable. but ever to be experienced "I shall be there"; the insight into the reality of the divine-human meeting.

Gnosis misunderstands that meeting; magic offends it. The meaning of revelation is that it is to be prepared; Hasidism affirms that revelation is to be prepared in the whole reality of human life.

The Triad of World Time

The insight which Judaism has with regard to the,dialogical situation, or rather the fact that it is completely imbued with the dialogical situation, gives Judaism its indestructible knowledge of the threefold chord in the triad of time: creation, revelation, redemption.

Within early Christianity, the Gospel according to John was the first to try to substitute a dyad for the triad by weaving revelation and redemption into one. The light which shone in darkness and was not received by the darkness, the light enlightening the whole man, which comes into the world—that light is at the same time revelation and redemption; by his coming into the world, God reveals himself, and the soul is redeemed. The Old Testament shrinks into a prologue to the New Testament.

Marcion went further: he tried to substitute a monad for the dyad by banishing creation from religious reality; he tore God the Creator away from God the Redeemer, and declared that the former was not worthy of being adored. The "alien" God, who reveals himself in redeeming the world, redeems the soul from the cosmos and simultaneously from the builder of the cosmos, who becomes the merely "righteous"—not the "good" —God of the Jews, the demiurge, the lawgiver, the sham god of this aeon. The Old Testament is rejected as being anti-God.

Marcion's work has not been accepted by the Church, which has indeed fought a great battle against it. The extent to which Marcion's influence has persisted in Christian thought, however, is shown by Adolf von Harnack's Marcionizing thesis, which is only one of many evidences. In his thesis, Harnack stamps the "preservation" of the Old Testament in Protestantism as a canonical document as "the consequence of religious and ecclesiastical paralysis." But more would be gained with the victory of this thesis than the separation of two books, and the profanation of one for Christendom: man would be cut off from his origin, the world would lose its history of creation, and with that its creaturely character; or creation would itself become the fall. Existence would be divided not only cosmologically, but in the last resort it would be divided religiously beyond possibility of redress into a "world" of matter and moral law, and an "overworld" of spirit and love. Here the Iranian teaching of two principles reaches its Western completion, and the duality of man, estranged from his natural, vitally trustful faith, finds its theological sanction. No longer does redemption crown the work of creation; redemption vanquishes creation. The world *as such* can no longer become the kingdom of God. "The Unknown" who is worshipped at this point is the spirit of *reduction*.

For the Western peoples, such an issue would have meant only a threat of disintegration; for Judaism, it would have meant certain dissolution. What saved Judaism is not, as the Marcionites imagine, the fact that it failed to experience the "tragedy," the contradiction in the world's process, deeply enough; but rather that it experienced that "tragedy" in the dialogical situation, which means that it experienced *the contradiction as theophany*. This very world, this very contradiction, unabridged, unmitigated, unsmoothed, unsimplified, unreduced, this world shall be—not overcome—but consummated. It shall be consummated in the kingdom, for it is that world, and no other, with all its contrariety, in which the kingdom is a latency such that every reduction would only hinder its consummation, while every unification of contraries would prepare it. It is a redemption not from evil, but of evil, as the power which God created for his service and for the performance of his work.

If it is true that the whole world, all the world process, the whole time of the world, unsubtracted, stands in the dialogical situation; if it is true that the history of the world is a real dialogue between God and his creature, then the triad, in which that history is perceived, becomes not a man-made device for his own orientation, but actual reality itself. What comes to us out of the abyss of origin, and into the sphere of our uncomprehending grasp and our stammering narrative, is God's cry of creation into the void. Silence still lies brooding before him, but soon things begin to rise and give answer—their very coming into existence is answer. When God blesses his creatures and gives them their appointed work, revelation has begun, for revelation is nothing else but the relation between giving and receiving, which means that it is also the relation between desiring to give and failing to receive. Revelation lasts until the turning creature answers, and his answer is accepted by God's redeeming grace. Then the unity emerges, formed out of the very elements of contrariety, to establish amidst all the undiminished multiplicity and manifoldness the communion of creatures in the name of God and before his face.

Just as God's cry of creation does not call to the soul, but to the wholeness of things, as revelation does not empower and require the soul, but all of the human being, so it is not the soul, but the whole of the world, which is meant to be redeemed in the redemption. Man stands created, a whole body, ensouled by his relation to the created, enspirited by his relation to the Creator. It is to the whole man, in this unity of body, soul, and spirit, that the Lord of Revelation comes, and upon whom he lays his message. So it is not only with his thought and his feelings, but with the sole of his foot and the tip of his finger as well, that he may receive the sign-language of the reality taking place. The redemption must take place in the whole corporeal life. God the Creator wills to consummate nothing less than the whole of his creation; God the Revealer wills to actualize nothing less than the whole of his revelation; God the Redeemer wills to draw into his arms nothing less than the all in need of redemption.

2

THE TWO FOCI OF THE JEWISH SOUL

You have asked me to speak to you about the soul of Judaism.
I have complied with this request, although I am against the
cause for which you hold your conference, and I am against
it not "just as a Jew," but also truly as a Jew, that is, as one
who waits for the kingdom of God, the kingdom of unification,
and who regards all such "missions" as yours as springing from
a misunderstanding of the nature of that kingdom, and as a
hindrance to its coming. If in spite of this, I have accepted your
invitation, it is because I believe that when one is invited to
share one's knowledge, one should not ask, "Why have you invited me?", but should share what one knows as well as one
can—and that is my intention.

There is, however, one essential branch of Judaism about
which I do not feel myself called upon to speak before you,
and that is "the law." My point of view with regard to this
subject diverges from the traditional one; it is not a-nomistic,
but neither is it entirely nomistic. For that reason, I ought
attempt neither to represent tradition, nor to substitute my own
personal standpoint for the information you have desired of
me. Besides, the problem of the law does not seem to me to
belong at all to the subject with which I have to deal. It would
be a different matter were it my duty to present the teaching
of Judaism. For the teaching of Judaism comes from Sinai; it
is Moses' teaching. But the *soul* of Judaism is pre-Sinaitic; it is
the soul which approached Sinai, and there received what it did
receive. It is older than Moses; it is patriarchal, Abraham's

soul, or more truly, since it concerns the *product* of a primordial age, it is Jacob's soul. The law put on the soul, and the soul can never again be understood outside of the law; yet the soul itself is not of the law. If one wishes to speak of the soul of Judaism, one must consider all the transformations it underwent through the ages till this very day; but one must never forget that in every one of its stages the soul has remained the same, and gone on in the same way.

This qualification, however, only makes the task more difficult. "I should wish to show you Judaism from the inside," wrote Franz Rosenzweig in 1916 to a Christian friend of Jewish descent, "in the same 'hymnal' way as you can show Christianity to me, the outsider; but the very reasons which make it possible for you to do so make it impossible for me. The soul of Christianity may be found in its outward expressions; Judaism wears a hard protective outer shell, and one can speak about its soul only if one is within Judaism." [1] If, therefore, I still venture here to speak about the soul of Judaism from the outside, it is only because I do not intend to give an account of that soul, but only some indication of its fundamental attitude.

It is not necessary for me to labor the point that this fundamental attitude is nothing else than the attitude of faith, viewed from its human side. "Faith," however, should not be taken in the sense given to it in the Epistle to the Hebrews, as faith that God exists. That has never been doubted by Jacob's soul. In proclaiming its faith, its *emunah*, the soul only proclaimed that it put its trust in the everlasting God, *that he would be present* to the soul, as had been the experience of the patriarchs, and that it was entrusting itself to him, who was present. The German romantic philosopher Franz Baader did justice to the depth of Israel's faith relationship when he defined faith as "a pledge of faith,[2] that is, as a tying of oneself, a betrothing of oneself, an entering into a covenant."

The fealty of the Jew is the substance of his soul. The living God to whom he has pledged himself appears in infinite manifestations in the infinite variety of things and events; and this acts both as an incentive and as a steadying influence upon those who owe him allegiance. In the abundance of his manifestations, they can ever and again recognize the One to whom they have entrusted themselves and pledged their faith. The crucial word which God himself spoke of this rediscovery of his presence was spoken to Moses from the midst of the burning bush: "I shall be there as I there shall be" (Exod. 3:14). He is ever present to his creature, but always in the form peculiar to that moment, so that the spirit of man cannot foretell in the garment of what existence and what situation God will manifest himself. It is for man to recognize him in each of his garments. I cannot straightaway call any man a pagan; I know only of the pagan in man. But insofar as there is any paganism, it does not consist in not discerning God, but in not recognizing him as ever the same; the Jewish in man, on the contrary, seems to me to be the ever renewed rediscernment of God.

I shall, therefore, speak to you about the Jewish soul by making a few references to its fundamental attitude; I shall regard it as being the concretion of this human element in a national form, and consider it as the nation-shaped instrument of such a fealty and rediscernment.

I see the soul of Judaism as elliptically turning round two centers.

One center of the Jewish soul is the primeval experience that God is wholly raised above man, that he is beyond the grasp of man, and yet that he is present in an immediate relationship with these human beings who are absolutely incommensurable with him, and that he faces them. To know both these things at the same time, so that they cannot be separated, constitutes the living core of every believing Jewish soul: to know both, "God in heaven," that is, in complete hiddenness, and man "on earth," that is, in the fragmentation of the world of his senses and his understanding; God in the perfection and incomprehensibility of his being, and man in the abysmal contradiction of this strange existence from birth to death—and between both, immediacy!

The pious Jews of pre-Christian times called their God "Father"; and when the naively pious Jew in Eastern Europe uses that name today, he does not repeat something which he has learned, but he expresses a realization which he has come upon himself of the fatherhood of God and the sonship of man. It is not as though these men did not know that God is also utterly distant; it is rather that they know at the same time that however far away God is, he is never unrelated to them, and that even the man who is farthest away from God cannot cut himself off from the mutual relationship. In spite of the complete distance between God and man, they know that when God created man, he set the mark of his image upon man's brow, and embedded it in man's nature, and that however faint God's mark may become, it can never be entirely wiped out.

According to Hasidic legend, when the Baal Shem conjured up the demon Sammael, he showed him this mark on the forehead of his disciples, and when the master bade the conquered demon begone, the latter prayed, "Sons of the living God, permit me to remain a little while to look at the mark of the image of God on your faces." God's real commandment to man is to realize this image.

"Fear of God," accordingly, never means to the Jews that they ought to be afraid of God, but that, trembling, they ought to be aware of his incomprehensibility. The fear of God is the creaturely knowledge of the darkness to which none of our spiritual powers can reach, and out of which God reveals himself. Therefore, "the fear of God" is rightly called "the beginning of knowledge" (Ps. 111:10). It is the dark gate through which man must pass if he is to enter into the love of God. He who wishes to avoid passing through this gate, he who begins to provide himself with a comprehensible God, constructed thus and not otherwise, runs the risk of having to despair of God in view of the actualities of history and life, or of falling into inner falsehood. Only through the fear of God does man enter so deep into the love of God that he cannot again be cast out of it.

But fear of God is just a gate; it is not a house in which one can comfortably settle down—he who should want to live in it in adoration would neglect the performance of the essential commandment. God is incomprehensible, but he can be known through a bond of mutual relationship. God cannot be fathomed by knowledge, but he can be imitated. The life of man, who is unlike God, can yet be an *imitatio Dei*. "The likeness" is not closed to the "unlike." This is exactly what is meant when the Scripture instructs man to walk in God's way and in his footsteps. Man cannot by his own strength complete any way or any piece of the way, but he can enter on the path, he can take that first step, and again and again that first step. Man cannot "be like unto God," but with all the inadequacy of each of his days, he can follow God at all times, using the capacity he has on that particular day—and if he has used the capacity of that day to the full, he has done enough. This is not a mere act of faith; it is an entering into the life that has to be lived on that day with all the active fulness of a created person. This activity is within man's capacity; uncurtailed and not to be curtailed, the capacity is present through all the generations. God concedes the might to abridge this central property of decision to no primordial "fall," however far-reaching in its effects, for the intention of God the Creator is mightier than the sin of men. The Jew knows from his knowledge of creation and of creatureliness that there may be burdens inherited from prehistoric and historic times, but that there is no overpowering "original sin" which could prevent the late-comer from deciding as freely as did Adam; as freely as Adam let God's hand go, the late-comer can clasp it. We are dependent on grace; but we do not do God's will when we take it upon ourselves to begin with grace instead of beginning with ourselves. Only our beginning, our having begun, poor as it is, leads us to grace. God made no tools for himself, he needs none; he created for himself a partner in the dialogue of time, and one who is capable of holding converse.

In this dialogue, God speaks to every man through the life which he gives him again and again. Therefore man can only answer God with the whole of life—with the way in which he lives this given life. The Jewish teaching of the wholeness of life is the other side of the Jewish teaching of the unity of God. Because God bestows not only spirit on man, but the whole of his existence, from its "lowest" to its "highest" levels, man can fulfil the obligations of his partnership with God by no spiritual attitude, by no worship, on no sacred upper story; the whole of life is required, every one of its areas and every one of its circumstances. There is no true human share of holiness without the hallowing of the everyday. Whilst Judaism unfolds itself through the history of its faith, and so long as it does unfold itself through that history, it holds out against that "religion" which is an attempt to assign a circumscribed part to God, in order to satisfy him who bespeaks and lays claim to the whole. But this unfolding of Judaism is really an unfolding, and not a metamorphosis.

To clarify our meaning, we take the sacrificial cultus as an example. One of the two fundamental elements in biblical animal sacrifice is the sacralization of the natural life: he who slaughters an animal consecrates a part of it to God, and so doing hallows his eating of it. The second fundamental element is the sacramentalization of the complete surrender of life. To this element belong those types of sacrifice in which the person who offers the sacrifice puts his hands on the head of the animal in order to identify himself with it; in doing so he gives physical expression to the thought that he is bringing himself to be sacrificed in the person of the animal. He who performs these sacrifices without having this intention in his soul makes the cult meaningless, yes, absurd; it was against him that the prophets directed their attack upon the sacrificial service which had been emptied of its core. In the Judaism of the Diaspora, prayer takes the place of sacrifice; but prayer is also offered for the reinstatement of the cult, that is, for the return of the holy unity of body and spirit. And in that consummation of Diaspora Judaism which we call Hasidic piety, both fundamental elements unite into a new conception which fulfils the original meaning of the cult. When the purified and sanctified man, in purity and holiness, takes food into himself, eating becomes a sacrifice, the table an altar, and man consecrates himself to the Deity. At that point, there is no longer a gulf between the natural and the sacral; at that point, there is no longer the need for a substitute; at that point, the natural event itself becomes a sacrament.

The holy strives to include within itself the whole of life. The law differentiates between the holy and the profane, but the law desires to lead the way toward the messianic removal of the differentiation, to the all-sanctification. Hasidic piety no longer recognizes anything as simply and irreparably profane; "the profane" is for Hasidism only a designation for the not-yet-sanctified, for that which is to be sanctified. Everything physical, all drives and urges and desires, everything creaturely, is material for sanctification. From the very same passionate powers which, undirected, give rise to evil, when they are turned toward God, the good arises. One does not serve God with the spirit only, but with the whole of his nature, without any subtractions. There is not one realm of the spirit and another of nature; there is only the growing realm of God. God is not spirit, but what we call spirit and what we call nature hail equally from the God who is beyond and equally conditioned by both, and whose kingdom reaches its fulness in the complete unity of spirit and nature.

The second focus of the Jewish soul is the basic consciousness that God's redeeming power is at work everywhere and at all times, but that a state of redemption exists nowhere and at no time. The Jew experiences as a person what every open-hearted human being experiences as a person: the experience, in the hour when he is most utterly forsaken, of a breath from above, the nearness, the touch, the mysterious intimacy of light out of darkness; and the Jew, as part of the world, experiences, perhaps more intensely than any other part, the world's lack of redemption. He feels this lack of redemption against his skin, he tastes it on his tongue, the burden of the unredeemed world lies on him. Because of this almost physical knowledge of his, he *cannot* concede that the redemption has taken place; he knows that it has not. It is true that he can discover prefigurations of redemption in past history, but he always discovers only that mysterious intimacy of light out of darkness which is at work everywhere and at all times; no redemption which is different in kind, none which by its nature would be unique, which would be conclusive for future ages, and which had but to be consummated. Most of all, only through a denial of his own meaning and his own mission would it be possible for him to acknowledge that in a world which still remains unredeemed, an anticipation of the redemption had been effected by which the human soul—or rather merely the souls of men who in a specific sense are believers—had been redeemed.

With a strength which original grace has given him, and which none of his historic trials has ever wrested from him, the Jew resists the radical division of soul and world which forms the basis of this conception; he resists the conception of a divine splitting of existence; he resists most passionately the awful notion of a *massa perditionis*. The God in whom he believes has not created the totality in order to let it split apart into one blessed and one damned half. God's eternity is not to be conceived by man; but—and this we Jews know to the moment of our death—there can be no eternity in which *everything* will not be accepted into God's atonement, when God has drawn time back into eternity. Should there, however, be a stage in the redemption of the world in which redemption is first fulfilled in one *part* of the world, we would derive no claim to redemption from our faith, much less from any other source. "If you do not yet wish to redeem Israel, at any rate redeem the *goyim*," the Rabbi of Koznitz used to pray.

It is possible to argue against me that there has been after all another eschatology in Judaism than that which I have indicated, that the apocalyptic stands beside the prophetic eschatology. It is actually important to make clear to oneself where the difference between the two lies. The prophetic belief about the end of time is in all essentials autochthonous; the apocalyptic belief is in all essentials built up of elements from Iranian dualism. Accordingly, the prophetic belief promises a consummation of creation, the apocalyptic its abrogation and supersession by another world, completely different in nature; the prophetic allows the "evil" to find the direction that leads toward God, and to enter into the good, the apocalyptic sees good and evil severed forever at the end of days, the good redeemed, the evil unredeemable for all eternity; the prophetic believes that the earth shall be hallowed, the apocalyptic despairs of an earth which it considers to be hopelessly doomed; the prophetic allows God's creative original will to be fulfilled completely, the apocalyptic allows the unfaithful creature power over the Creator, in that the creature's actions force God to abandon nature. There was a time when it must have seemed uncertain whether the current apocalyptic teaching might not be victorious over the traditional prophetic messianism; if that had happened, it is to be assumed that Judaism would not have outlived its central faith—explicitly or imperceptibly, it would have merged with Christianity, which is so strongly influenced by that dualism. During an epoch in which the prophetic was lacking, the tannaim, early Talmudic masters, helped prophetic messianism to triumph over the apocalyptic conception, and in doing so saved Judaism .

Still another important difference separates the two forms of Jewish belief about the end of days. The apocalyptists wished to predict an unalterable immovable future event; they were following Iranian conceptions in this point as well. For, according to the Iranians, history is divided into equal cycles of thousands of years, and the end of the world, the final victory of good over evil, can be predetermined with mathematical accuracy. Not so the prophets of Israel. They prophesy "for the sake of those who turn" (Bab. Talmud, Berakot 34b). That is, they do not warn of something which will happen in any case, but of that which will happen if those who are called upon to turn do not turn.

The Book of Jonah is a clear example of what is meant by prophecy. After Jonah has tried in vain to flee from the task God has given him, he is sent to Nineveh to prophesy its downfall. But Nineveh turns—and God changes its destiny. Jonah is vexed that the word for whose sake the Lord had broken his resistance had been rendered void; if one is forced to prophesy, one's prophecy ought to stand. But God is of a different opinion; he will employ no soothsayers, but messengers to the souls of men—the souls that are able to decide which way to go, and whose decision is allowed to contribute to the forging of the world's fate. Those who turn cooperate in the redemption of the world.

Man's partnership in the great dialogue finds its highest form of reality at this point. It is not as though any definite act of man could draw grace down from heaven; yet grace answers deed in unpredictable ways, grace unattainable, yet not self-withholding. It is not as though man has to do this or that "to hasten" the redemption of the world—"he that believeth shall not make haste" (Is. 28:16); yet those who turn cooperate in the redemption of the world. The extent and nature of the participation assigned to the creature remains secret. "Does that mean that God cannot redeem his world without the help of his creatures?" "It means that God does not will to be able to do it." "Has God need of man for his work?" "He wills to have need of man."

He who speaks of activism in this connection misunderstands the mystery. The act is no outward gesture. "The ram's horn, which God will blow on that day," so runs an haggadic saying, "will have been made from the right horn of the ram which once took Isaac's place as a sacrifice." The "servant" whom God made "a polished shaft" to hide apparently unused in his quiver (Is. 49:2), the man who is condemned to live in hiding —or rather, not one man, but the type of man to whom this happens generation after generation—the man who is hidden in the shadow of God's hand, who does not "cause his voice to be heard in the street" (Is. 42:2), he who in darkness suffers for God's sake (*ibid.*)—he it is who has been given as a light for the peoples of the world, that God's "salvation may be unto the end of the earth" (Is. 49:6).

The mystery of the act, of the human part in preparing the redemption, passes through the darkness of the ages as a mystery of concealment, as a concealment within the person's relation to himself as well, until one day it will come into the open. To the question why according to tradition, the Messiah was born on the anniversary of the day of the destruction of Jerusalem, a Hasidic rabbi answered: "The power cannot rise, unless it has dwelt in the great concealment. . . . In the shell of oblivion grows the power of remembrance. That is the power of redemption. On the day of the Destruction, the power will be lying at the bottom of the depths and growing. That is why on this day we sit on the ground; that is why on this day we visit the graves; that is why on this day was born the Messiah."

Though robbed of their real names, these two foci of the Jewish soul continue to exist for the "secularized" Jew too, insofar as he has not lost his soul. They are, first, the immediate relationship to the Existent One, and second, the power of atonement at work in an unatoned world. In other words, first, the *non-incarnation* of God who reveals himself to the "flesh" and is present to it in a mutual relationship, and second, the unbroken continuity of human history, which turns toward fulfilment and decision. These two centers constitute the ultimate division between Judaism and Christianity.

We "unify" God, when living and dying we profess his unity; we do not unite ourselves with him. The God in whom we believe, to whom we are pledged, does not unite with human substance on earth. But the very fact that we do not imagine that we can unite with him enables us the more ardently to demand "that the world shall be perfected under the kingship of the Mighty One."

We feel salvation happening, and we feel the unsaved world. No savior with whom a new redeemed history began has appeared to us at any definite point in history. Because we have not been stilled by anything which has happened, we are wholly directed toward the coming of that which is to come.

Thus, though divided from you, we have been attached to you. As Franz Rosenzweig wrote in the letter which I have already quoted: "You who live in an *ecclesia triumphans* need a silent servant to cry to you whenever you believe you *have partaken* of God in bread and wine, 'Lord, remember the last things.' "

What have you and we in common? If we take the question literally, a book and an expectation.

To you, the book is a forecourt; to us, it is the sanctuary. But in this place, we can dwell together, and together listen to the voice that speaks here. That means that we can work together to evoke the buried speech of that voice; together, we can redeem the imprisoned living word.

Your expectation is directed toward a second coming, ours to a coming which has not been anticipated by a first. To you the phrasing of world history is determined by one absolute midpoint, the year one; to us, it is an unbroken flow of tones following each other without a pause from their origin to their consummation. But we can wait for the advent of the One together, and there are moments when we may prepare the way before him together.

Pre-messianically, our destinies are divided. Now to the Christian, the Jew is the incomprehensibly obdurate man, who declines to see what has happened; and to the Jew, the Christian is the incomprehensibly daring man, who affirms in an unredeemed world that its redemption has been accomplished. This is a gulf which no human power can bridge. But it does not prevent the common watch for a unity to come to us from God, which, soaring above all of your imagination and all of ours, affirms and denies, denies and affirms, what you hold and what we hold, and which replaces all the creedal truths of earth by the ontological truth of heaven which is one.

It behooves both you and us to hold inviolably fast to our own true faith, that is to our own deepest relationship to truth. It behooves both of us to show a religious respect for the true faith of the other. This is not what is called "tolerance"; our task is not to tolerate each other's waywardness, but to acknowledge the real relationship in which both stand to the truth. Whenever we both, Christian and Jew, care more for God himself than for our images of God, we are united in the feeling that our Father's house is differently constructed than all our human models take it to be.

3

NATIONALISM

Judaism is not merely being a nation. It is being a nation, but because of its own peculiar connection with the quality of being a community of faith, it is more than that. Since Jewry has a character of its own, and a life of its own, just like any other nation, it is entitled to claim the rights and privileges of a nation. But we must never forget that it is, nevertheless, a *res sui generis*, which, in one very vital respect, goes beyond the classification it is supposed to fit into.

A great event in their history molded the Jews into a people. It was when the Jewish tribes were freed from the bondage of Egypt. But it required a great inner transformation to make them into a nation. In the course of this inner change, the concept of the government of God took on a political form, final for the time being, that of the "anointed" kingdom, that is, the kingdom as the representative of God.

From the very beginning of the Diaspora, the uniqueness of Judaism became apparent in a very special way. In other nations, the national powers in themselves vouch for the survival of the people. In Judaism, this guarantee is given by another power which, as I have said, makes the Jews more than a nation: the membership in a community of faith. From the French Revolution on, this inner bond grew more and more insecure. Jewish religion was uprooted, and this is at the core of the disease indicated by the rise of Jewish nationalism around the middle of the nineteenth century. Over and over again, this nationalism lapses into trends toward "secularization," and thus mistakes its purpose. For Israel cannot be healed, and its welfare cannot be achieved, by severing the concepts of people and community of faith, but only by setting up a new order including both as organic and renewed parts.

A Jewish national community in Palestine, a desideratum toward which Jewish nationalism must logically strive, is a station in this healing process. We must not, however, forget that in the thousands of years of its exile, Jewry yearned for the Land of Israel, not as a nation like others, but as Judaism (*res sui generis*), and with motives and intentions which cannot be derived wholly from the category "nation." That original yearning is back of all the disguises which modern national Judaism has borrowed from the modern nationalism of the West. To forget one's own peculiar character, and accept the slogans and watchwords of a nationalism that has nothing to do with the category of faith, means national assimilation.

When Jewish nationalism holds aloof from such procedure, which is alien to it, it is legitimate in an especially clear and lofty sense. It is the nationalism of a people without land of its own, a people which has lost its country. Now, in an hour rife with decision, it wants to offset the deficiency it realized with merciless clarity only when its faith became rootless; it wants to regain its natural holy life.

Here the question may arise as to what the idea of the election of Israel has to do with all this. This idea does not indicate a feeling of superiority, but a sense of destiny. It does not spring from a comparison with others, but from the concentrated devotion to a task, to the task which molded the people into a nation when they attempted to accomplish it in their earlier history. The prophets formulated that task and never ceased uttering their warning: if you boast of being chosen instead of living up to it, if you turn election into a static object instead of obeying it as a command, you will forfeit it!

And what part does Jewish nationalism play at the present time? We—and by that I mean the group of persons I have belonged to since my youth, that group which has tried, and will continue to try, to do its share in educating the people—we have summoned the people to a turning, and not to conceit, to be healed, and not to self-righteousness. We have equipped Jewish nationalism with an armor we did not weld, with the awareness of a unique history, a unique situation, a unique obligation, which can be conceived only from the supernational standpoint and which—whenever it is taken seriously—must point to a supernational sphere.

In this way, we hoped to save Jewish nationalism from the error of making an idol of the people. We have not succeeded. Jewish nationalism is largely concerned with being "like unto all the nations," with affirming itself in the face of the world without affirming the world's reciprocal power. It too has frequently yielded to the delusion of regarding the horizon visible from one's own station as the whole sky. It too is guilty of offending against the words of that table of laws that has been set up above all nations: that all sovereignty becomes false and vain when in the struggle for power it fails to remain subject to the Sovereign of the world, who is the Sovereign of my rival, and my enemy's Sovereign, as well as mine. It forgets to lift its gaze from the shoals of "healthy egoism" to the Lord who "brought the children of Israel out of the land of Egypt, and the Philistines from Caphtor, and Aram from Kir" (Amos 9:7).

Jewish nationalism bases its spurious ideology on a "formal nationalistic theory which—in this critical hour—should be called to account. This theory is justified in denying that the acceptance of certain principles by a people should be a criterion for membership in that people. It is justified in suggesting that such a criterion must spring from formal common characteristics, such as language and civilization. But it is not justified in denying to those principles a central normative meaning, in denying that they involve the task—posed in time immemorial—to which the inner life of this people is bound, and together with the inner, the outer life as well.

I repeat: this task cannot be defined, but it can be sensed, pointed out, and presented. Those who stand for that religious "reform" which—most unfortunate among the misfortunes of the period of emancipation!—became a substitute for a reformation of Judaism which did not come, certainly did all they could to discredit that task by trying to cram it into a concept. But to deny the task its focal position on such grounds is equivalent to throwing out the child along with the bath water. The supernational task of the Jewish nation cannot be properly accomplished unless, under its aegis, natural life is reconquered. In that formal nationalism disclaims the nation's being based on and conditioned by this more than national task; in that it has grown overconscious, and dares to disengage Judaism from its connection with the world and to isolate it; in that it proclaims the nation as an end in itself, instead of comprehending that it is an element, formal nationalism sanctions a group egoism which disclaims responsibility.

It is true that in the face of these results, attempts have been made from within the nationalistic movement to limit this expanding group egoism from without, and to humanize it on the basis of abstract moral or social postulates rather than on that of the character of the people itself, but all such efforts are bound to be futile. A foundation on which the nation is regarded as an end in itself has no room for supernational ethical demands because it does not permit the nation to act from a sense of true supernational responsibility. If the depth of faith, which is decisive in limiting national action, is robbed of its content of faith, then inorganic ethics cannot fill the void, and the emptiness will persist until the day of the turning.

We, who call upon you, are weighed down with deep concern lest this turning come too late. The nationalistic crisis in Judaism stands in sharp, perhaps too sharp, relief in the pattern of the nationalistic crises of current world history. In our case, more clearly than in any other, the decision between life and death has assumed the form of deciding between legitimate and arbitrary nationalism.

4

THE LAND AND ITS POSSESSORS:
AN ANSWER TO GANDHI

A land which a sacred book describes to the children of that land is never merely in their hearts; a land can never become a mere symbol. It is in their hearts because it is in the world; it is a symbol because it is a reality. Zion is the prophetic image of a promise to mankind; but it would be a poor metaphor if Mount Zion did not actually exist. This land is called "holy"; but it is not the holiness of an idea, it is the holiness of a piece of earth. That which is merely an idea and nothing more can not become holy; but a piece of earth can become holy.

Dispersion is bearable; it can even be purposeful, if there is somewhere an ingathering, a growing home center, a piece of earth where one is in the midst of an ingathering and not in dispersion, and whence the spirit of ingathering may work its way into all the places of the dispersion. When there is this, there is also a striving common life, the life of a community which dares to live today because it may hope to live tomorrow. But when this growing center, this ceaseless process of ingathering is lacking, dispersion becomes dismemberment. From this point of view, the question of our Jewish destiny is indissolubly bound up with the possibility of ingathering, and that is bound up with Palestine.

You ask: "Why should they not, like the other nations of the earth, make that country their national home where they are born and where they earn their livelihood?" Because their destiny is different from that of all the other nations of the earth; it is a destiny, in truth and justice, which no nation on earth would accept. Because their destiny is dispersion—not the dispersion of a fraction and the preservation of the main substance as in the case of other nations—it is dispersion without the living heart and center; and because every nation has a right to demand the possession of a living heart. It is different, because a hundred adopted homes without one that is original and natural make a nation sick and miserable. It is different, because although the well-being and the achievement of the individual may flourish on stepmotherly soil, the nation as such must languish. And just as you, Mahatma, wish not only that all Indians should be able to live and work, but also that Indian substance, Indian wisdom, and Indian truth should prosper and be fruitful, we wish the same for the Jews. For you there is no need of the awareness that the Indian substance could not prosper without the Indian's attachment to the mother soil and without his ingathering therein. But we know what is essential; we know it because it is denied us, or was so at least up to the generation which has just begun to work at the redemption of the mother soil.

But painfully urgent as it is, this is not all; for us, for the Jews who think as I do, it is indeed not the decisive factor. You say, Mahatma Gandhi, that to support the cry for a national home which "does not much appeal to you," a sanction is "sought in the Bible." No, that is not so. We do not open the Bible and seek a sanction in it; rather the opposite is true: the promises of return, of reestablishment, which have nourished the yearning hope of hundreds of generations, give those of today an elemental stimulus, recognized by few in its full meaning, but effective in the lives of many who do not believe in the message of the Bible. Still this, too, is not the determining factor for us who, although we do not see divine revelation in every sentence of Holy Scripture, yet trust in the spirit which inspired those who uttered them. What is decisive for us is not the promise of the land, but the demand, whose fulfilment is bound up with the land, with the existence of a free Jewish community in this country. For the Bible tells us, and our inmost knowledge testifies to it, that once, more than three thousand years ago, our entry into this land took place with the consciousness of a mission from above to set up a just way of life through the generations of our people, a way of life that cannot be realized by individuals in the sphere of their private existence, but only by a nation in the establishment of its so-

ciety: communal ownership of the land (Lev. 25:23), regularly
recurrent leveling of social distinctions (Lev. 25:13), guarantee
of the independence of each individual (Exod. 21:2), mutual
aid (Exod. 23:4f.), a general Sabbath embracing serf and beast
as beings with an equal claim to rest (Exod. 23:12), a sabbatical year in which the soil is allowed to rest and everybody
is admitted to the free enjoyment of its fruits (Lev. 25:2-7).
These are not practical laws thought out by wise men; they are
measures which the leaders of the nation, apparently themselves
taken by surprise and overpowered, have found to be the set
task and condition for taking possession of the land. No other
nation has ever been faced at the beginning of its career with
such a mission. Here is something which there is no forgetting, and from which there is no release. At that time, we did
not carry out that which was imposed upon us; we went into
exile with our task unperformed; but the command remained
with us, and it has become more urgent than ever. We need
our own soil in order to fulfil it; we need the freedom to order
our own life—no attempt can be made on foreign soil and under foreign statute. It cannot be that the soil and the freedom
for fulfilment are denied us. We are not covetous, Mahatma:
our one desire is that at last we may be able to obey.

Now you may well ask whether I speak for the Jewish people when I say "we." No, I speak only for those who feel themselves entrusted with the commission of fulfilling the command
of justice given to Israel in the Bible. Were it but a handful,
these constitute the pith of the people, and the future of the
people depends on them; for the ancient mission of the people
lives in them as the cotyledon in the core of the fruit. In this
connection, I must tell you that you are mistaken when you
assume that in general the Jews of today believe in God and
derive from their faith guidance for their conduct. Contemporary Jewry is in the throes of a serious religious crisis. It seems
to me that the lack of faith of present-day humanity, its inability truly to believe in God, finds its concentrated expression in
this crisis of Jewry; here all is darker, more fraught with danger, more fateful than anywhere else in the world. Nor is this
crisis resolved here in Palestine; indeed, we recognize its sever-
ity here even more than elsewhere among Jews. But at the
same time, we realize that here alone it can be resolved. There
is no solution to be found in the lives of isolated and abandoned individuals, although one may hope that the spark of
faith will be kindled in their great need. The true solution can

only issue from the life of a community which begins to carry out the will of God, often without being aware of doing so, without believing that God exists and that this is his will. It may issue from the life of the community, if believing people support it who neither direct nor demand, neither urge nor preach, but who share the common life, who help, wait, and are ready for the moment when it will be their turn to give the true answer to the inquirers. This is the innermost truth of the Jewish life in the land; perhaps it may be of significance for the solution of this crisis of faith not only for Jewry but for all humanity. The contact of this people with this land is not only a matter of sacred ancient history; we sense here a secret still more hidden. You, Mahatma Gandhi, who know of the connection between tradition and future, should not associate yourself with those who pass over our cause without understanding or sympathy.

But you say—and I consider it to be the most significant of all the things you tell us—that Palestine belongs to the Arabs, and that it is therefore "wrong and inhuman to impose the Jews on the Arabs."

Here I must add a personal note in order to make clear to you on what premises I desire to consider your thesis.

I belong to a group of people who, from the time Britain conquered Palestine, have not ceased to strive for the concluding of a genuine peace between Jew and Arab.

By a genuine peace, we implied, and still imply, that both peoples together should develop the land without the one imposing its will on the other. In view of the international usages of our generation, this appeared to us to be very difficult, but not impossible. We were, and still are, well aware that in this unusual—yes, unprecedented—case, it is a question of seeking new ways of understanding and cordial agreement between the nations. Here again we stood, and still stand, under the sway of a commandment.

We considered it a fundamental point that in this case two vital claims oppose each other, two claims of a different nature and a different origin which cannot objectively be pitted against one another and between which no objective decision can be made as to which is just, which unjust. We considered, and still consider, it our duty to understand and to honor the claim which is opposed to ours, and to endeavor to reconcile both claims. We could not and cannot renounce the Jewish claim; something even higher than the life of our people is bound up with this land, namely, its work, its divine mission. But we have been and still are convinced that it must be possible to find some compromise between this claim and the other, for we love this land and we believe in its future; since such love and such faith are surely present on the other side as well, a union in the common service of the land must be within the range of possibility. Where there is faith and love, a solution may be found even to what appears to be a tragic opposition.

In order to carry out a task of such extreme difficulty—in the recognition of which we have to overcome an internal resistance on the Jewish side too, as foolish as it is natural—we were in need of the support of well-meaning persons of all nations, and hoped to receive it. But now you come and settle the whole existential dilemma with the simple formula: "Palestine belongs to the Arabs."

What do you mean by saying that a land belongs to a population? Evidently you do not intend only to describe a state of affairs by your formula, but to declare a certain right. You obviously mean to say that a people, being settled on the land, has so absolute a claim to that land that whoever settles on it without the permission of this people has committed a robbery. But by what means did the Arabs attain to the right of ownership in Palestine? Surely by conquest, and in fact a conquest with intent to settle. You therefore insist that as a result their settlement gives them exclusive right of possession, whereas the subsequent conquests of the Mamelukes and the Turks, which were conquests with a view to domination, not to settlement, do not constitute such a right in your opinion, but leave the earlier conquerors in rightful ownership. Thus, settlement by conquest justifies for you a right of ownership of Palestine, whereas a settlement such as the Jewish—the methods of which, it is true, though not always doing full justice to Arab ways of life, were even in the most objectionable cases far removed from those of conquest—do not justify in your opinion any participation in this right of possession. These are the consequences which result from your axiomatic statement that a land belongs to its population. In an epoch when nations are migrating, you would first support the right of ownership of the nation that is threatened with dispossession or extermination; but were this once achieved, you would be compelled, not at once, but after a suitable number of generations had elapsed, to admit that the land "belongs" to the usurper. . . .

It seems to me that God does not give any one portion of

the earth away, so that the owner may say as God says in the Bible: "For all the earth is mine" (Exod. 19:5). The conquered land is, in my opinion, only lent even to the conqueror who has settled on it—and God waits to see what he will make of it.

I am told, however, I should not respect the cultivated soil and despise the desert. The desert, I am told, is willing to wait for the work of her children; she no longer recognizes us, burdened with civilization, as her children. The desert inspires me with awe, but I do not believe in her absolute resistance, for I believe in the great marriage between man (*adam*) and earth (*adamah*). This land recognizes us, for it is fruitful through us; and precisely because it bears fruit for us, it recognizes us. Our settlers do not come here, as do the colonists from the Occident, to have natives do their work for them; they themselves set their shoulders to the plow, and they spend their strength and their blood to make the land fruitful. But it is not only for ourselves that we desire its fertility. The Jewish farmers have begun to teach their brothers, the Arab farmers, to cultivate the land more intensively; we desire to teach them further. Together with them, we want to cultivate the land—to "serve" it, as the Hebrew has it. The more fertile this soil becomes, the more space there will be for us and for them. We have no desire to dispossess them; we want to live with them. We do not want to dominate them, we want to serve with them. . . .

5

ON NATIONAL EDUCATION

Ideologies, programs, or political orientation are not the true response of a generation to the situation it finds itself in, of a generation which, at long last, wishes to respond to that situation. Such a response must express itself in life, in the language of active life, and in the break-through of this live answer, it begets the new type of man. The halutz, the Palestinian pioneer, is the most striking example of the new Jewish type, and the most distinct goal of national education. In him, we see how the supernational task has been converted into a living urge, into a vital personal endeavor and creative power, even though the individual is frequently unaware of the supernational character of what he is doing.

We cannot understand the true halutz unless we learn to recognize him as a personification of the union of national and social elements. The social element is evinced by the very fact that he wants to participate in the rebirth of his people in the home of his people, and through his own labors. He wants to devote his entire self to physical labor, for he wishes to participate as a worker, and only as a worker—not as one who directs the work of others. And this personal ambition is closely connected with his ambition in regard to his objective: the goal of both ambitions is the "working society in Palestine," that is, the social synthesis of people, land, and labor. But here there is more in the connotation of the word "society" than society per se. It implies the will to realize the human community in a formal society, that is, a union of persons living together, a union founded on the direct and just relations of all to all.

The halutz does not draw this will to realize this ideal out of himself, or out of his era, or out of the Western world; nor does he derive it from the occidental socialism of his century. Whether or not he knows it, whether or not he likes it, he is animated by the age-old Jewish longing to incorporate social truth in the life of individuals living with one another, the longing to translate the idea of a true community into reality. The new type is a result of the development of very early traits. What we call "Israel" is not merely the result of biological and historical development; it is the product of a decision made long ago, the decision in favor of a God of justice and against a god of instinctive egoism. It was a decision in favor of a God who leads his people into the land in order to prepare it for its messianic work in the world, and against a god who dwells in various spots in the land of Canaan, lurking in brooks and trees, and whispering to all comers: "Take possession and enjoy!" It was a decision for the true God and against Baal. Nowhere else was the destiny of a people so bound up with its original choice and the attempts at realization of that choice. The unsuccessful function of the prophets was to remind the people of this ancient bond.

Hasidism was the one great attempt in the history of the Diaspora to make a reality of the original choice and to found a true and just community based on religious principles. This attempt failed for a number of reasons, among others because it did not aim for the independence, for the self-determination of the people; or to state it differently, because its connections with Palestine were only sporadic and not influenced by the desire for national liberation. The political corruption which invaded the Hasidic movement was the result of this deficiency. For in order to get the state to grant it religious self-determination, Hasidism sacrificed the wholeness and purity of its life, and so its integrity was corroded. This tragi-comical end of a great social and religious venture was followed by a period of theorizing on the task of translating ideal into reality. But finally the Jewish national movement, either consciously or unconsciously, took up the age-old social message, and impelled by it, set up as the goal of national education the pattern of the new type of man, of the man who can translate ideas into life, who along with the national idea will satisfy the longing for a just communal life.

In the meantime, however, Judaism has had to face a grave crisis of faith, perhaps the most ominous development in the religious crisis of the man of today. In most instances, the halutz has become estranged from the much deteriorated structure of Jewish religion. He even rebels against it. He takes over the ambition to realize the ideal of a society, but in a secular form, without the bond of faith. If he is at all aware of the religious bond, he usually rejects it, separates it from the social will, and makes that will autonomous. But this means that at a certain point of his consciousness, which is of basic importance for the national movement, the new type of man has no connection with the earliest tradition of his people, that is, with the original choice of Israel.

I say "of his consciousness," and not "of his existence." For we have seen that certain traditional forces influence the character and life of the halutz, even though he may be unaware of it. But in consciously severing himself from his earliest tradition, he is resisting these forces and working counter to them.

The relation to tradition is a vital problem in all national movements and in every kind of national education. The greatest virtue of a national movement and of national education is that the generations which are growing up are made conscious of the great spiritual values whose source is the origin of their people, and that these values are deliberately woven into the design of their lives. Such values may be compared to waters gathered in a vast basin and thence distributed through thousands of pipes to drench the thirsty fields. The most profound meaning of the concept "national *movement*" is that a people's truth and ethos which, as abstract qualities, are, one might say, enthroned high above life, now become movement, life in motion. And so the destiny of a national movement depends on whether, and to what extent, it acknowledges the national tradition.

National movements can have three possible relationships to tradition. The first is positive. The adherents of the movement open their hearts to the tide of the elements, absorb, and transform what they have absorbed, in response to the demands of the hour. They allow the forces inherent in the beginnings to shape present-day life in accordance with present-day needs.

The second form of relationship is negative. The impact of the age-old tidings is warded off as neither credible, nor usable, nor timely.

The third approach I should call the fictitious. Those who follow it exalt the works and values of national tradition, regard them as the subject of pride and piety, and point to them with the air of collectors and owners, as though they were coronation robes in a museum, not, of course, suitable apparel for a living sovereign. While they boast of their tradition, they do not believe in it. They teach it in school, but not with the purpose of seriously integrating it into actual life. All that seems necessary to them is to "have" it. Unfortunately, the relationship of our national movement and national education to tradition is mainly a mixture of the second and third forms.

No mere good intentions can work a thoroughgoing change in the status quo. The power to transform life must spring from life itself. Already the halutz and his communes, the kibbutzim, are beginning to feel that something is lacking in the structure of their existence. Somewhere in the life of the week, there is a dead end; somewhere in the web of the work, there is a hole. No one knows just what it is, and certainly no one will name it. There is silence on that score, silence and suffering. I am under the impression that this suffering will increase in the course of the next decade and penetrate consciousness until it breaks the silence.

I do not believe that it is important for the halutz, or the national type of which he is the best representative, to accept en bloc either a ready-made tradition, or one or another part of it. Any such acceptance would be purely arbitrary and would share the fate of all arbitrary actions; it would be wholly unfruitful. One project, in particular, which is bruited about in the country, seems to me quite hopeless: the project of reviving religious forms without their religious content. Forms in themselves are nothing. What value they have accrues to them only through that which has been expressed in them, what has pervaded them as the soul pervades the body. The secret of their origin is the secret of their effectiveness. Once they have grown empty, one cannot fill them with a new, timely content; they will not hold it. Once they have decayed, they cannot be resuscitated by infusion with a spirit other than their own. They will seem only as lifelike as dolls. All such attempts are dilettantish, devoid of reverence and vigor; they are unblessed. A Passover seder which is held to celebrate the national liberation as such will always be lacking in the essential, and that essential can only be gained when we feel that self-liberation enfolds the redemption of man and the world through a redeeming power as the husk enfolds the kernel. The Feast of Weeks is, of course, a nature festival, a festival in honor of a season and its abundance, the festival of the farmer who time and again experiences the miracle that earth gives him so much more than he has given her. But one cannot do justice to this festival by explaining it as a nature symbol. One must also know that nature herself is a symbol, that man can attain to true life only by surrendering himself to the unknown, and that the reward, the manifold harvest, is called revelation. No matter how devotedly the Sabbath is kept, the rite will be threadbare if the joy in a day of rest for everybody is not filled with the divination of a cosmic mystery of work and rest which is reflected in that day. This mystery is figuratively expressed with a childlike ingenuousness—in the idea that the Creator of heaven and earth "draws breath" after his labors on that day just as well as the "son of thy handmaid." Thus, the breath of relaxation which we draw merges with the breath of the world.

But what shall we do when a generation, like that of today, has become alienated from the religious content of the forms?

We must provide them with a truly national education, and this means that we must convey the primordial utterances of their people to their ears and their hearts. We must surmount the prejudice of this era which claims that those utterances can have interest for us only as literary history, as cultural history, religious history, etc., and that instruction should treat them only as the chief literary creation of the nation, as the source for the study of its ancient culture and the oldest document of its religious beginnings. We must surmount the superstition of the era which seems to hold that the world of faith to which those utterances bear witness is the subject of our knowledge only, and not a reality which makes life worth living. We must keep the younger generation free from the bias that says: "We know all about ourselves and the world, and in any event these utterances can no longer exert an authoritative influence on our lives." This generation must be taught to despise the inflexible self-assurance which says: "I am well prepared. Nothing can happen to change me fundamentally and transform the world before my eyes. I know what I know; I am what I am; tomorrow can be no different than today." This generation must be made receptive to the Unforeseen, which upsets all logical arrangements. Their ears and hearts must be opened to the voice of the mystery which speaks in those utterances. And we should do all this not with the purpose of preparing them to repeat the teachings and perform prescribed rites, but so that they may acquire the power to make the original choice, that —listening to the voice with that power—they may hear the message it has for their hour and their work; that they may learn to trust the voice, and through this trust, come to faith, to a faith of their own.

6

HEBREW HUMANISM

In his essay on the origin of humanism, Konrad Burdach eluci-
dates his subject by quoting from Dante's *Convivio:* "The
greatest desire Nature has implanted in every thing from its
beginning is the desire to return to its origin." Burdach accordingly believes that the goal of humanism is "to return to the
human origin, not by way of speculative thought, but by way
of a *concrete transformation* of the whole of inner life." The
Zionist movement was also moved by the drive to return to
the origin of our nature through the concrete transformation of
our life. By "return" neither Burdach nor the Zionist movement meant the restoration of bygone forms of life. So romantic an ideal is as alien to our humanism as it was to the earlier.
In this connotation, return means reestablishing the original
foundation to which we want to return with the material of a
fundamentally different world of man, under set conditions of
our contemporary existence as a people, with reference to the
tasks the present situation imposes on us, and in accordance
with the possibilities we are given here and now. As we consider these points, we may well speak of a similarity between
European and Hebrew humanism. But on another point, we
must reach for a farther goal than European humanism. The
concrete transformation of our whole inner life is not sufficient
for us. We must strive for nothing less than the concrete transformation of our life as a whole. The process of transforming
our inner lives must be expressed in the transformation of our
outer life, of the life of the individual as well as that of the

community. And the effect must be reciprocal: the change in the external arrangements of our life must be reflected in and renew our inner life time and again. Up to now, Zionist theory has not adequately realized the importance of this mutual influence. The power of external transformation has frequently been overestimated. Such overestimation cannot, of course, be counteracted by confronting it simply with faith in the power of the spirit. Only he who commends himself to both spirit and earth at the same time is in league with eternity.

Zionist thinking in its current forms has failed to grasp the principle that the transformation of life must spring from the return to the origin of our nature. It is true that every thoughtful Zionist realizes that our character is distorted in many ways, that we are out of joint, and expects the new life in our own land, the bond to the soil and to work, to set us straight and make us whole once more. But what a great many overlook is that the powers released by this renewed bond to the soil do not suffice to accomplish a true and complete transformation. Another factor, the factor of spiritual power, that same return to our origin, must accompany the material factor. But it cannot be achieved by any spiritual power save the primordial spirit of Israel, the spirit which made us such as we are, and to which we must continually account for the extent to which our character has remained steadfast in the face of our destiny. This spirit has not vanished. The way to it is still open; it is still possible for us to encounter it. The Book still lies before us, and the voice speaks forth from it as on the first day. But we must not dictate what it should and what it should not tell us. If we require it to confine itself to instructing us about our great literary productions, our glorious history, and our national pride, we shall only succeed in silencing it. For that is not what it has to tell us. What it does have to tell us, and what no other voice in the world can teach us with such simple power, is that there is truth and there are lies, and that human life cannot persist or have meaning save in the decision in behalf of truth and against lies; that there is right and wrong, and that the salvation of man depends on choosing what is right and rejecting what is wrong; and that it spells the destruction of our existence to divide our life up into areas where the discrimination between truth and lies, right and wrong holds, and others where it does not hold, so that in private life, for example, we feel obligated to be truthful, but can permit ourselves lies in public, or that we act justly in man-to-man relationships, but can and even should practice injustice in national relationships. The *humanitas* which speaks from this Book today, as it has always done, is the unity of human life under one divine direction which divides right from wrong and truth from lies as unconditionally as the words of the Creator divided light from darkness. It is true that we are not able to live in perfect justice, and in order to preserve the community of man, we are often compelled to accept wrongs in decisions concerning the community. But what matters is that in every hour of decision we are aware of our responsibility and summon our conscience to weigh exactly how much is necessary to preserve the community, and accept just so much and no more; that we do not interpret the demands of a will-to-power as demands made by life itself; that we do not make a practice of setting aside a certain sphere in which God's command does not hold, but regard those actions as against his command, forced on us by the exigencies of the hour as painful sacrifices; that we do not salve, or let others salve, our conscience when we make decisions concerning public life, but struggle with destiny in fear and trembling lest it burden us with greater guilt than we are compelled to assume. This trembling of the magnetic needle which points the direction notwithstanding—this is biblical *humanitas*. The men in the Bible are sinners like ourselves, but there is one sin they do not commit, our arch-sin: they do not dare confine God to a circumscribed space or division of life, to "religion." They have not the insolence to draw boundaries around God's commandments and say to him: "Up to this point, you are sovereign, but beyond these bounds begins the sovereignty of science, or society, or the state." When they are forced to obey another power, every nerve in their body bears and suffers the load which is imposed upon them; they do not act lightheartedly nor toss their heads frivolously. He who has been reared in our Hebrew biblical humanism goes as far as he must in the hour of gravest responsibility, and not a step further. He resists patriotic bombast, which clouds the gulf between the demand of life and the desire of the will-to-power. He resists the whisperings of false popularity, which is the opposite of true service to the people. He is not taken in by the hoax of modern national egoism, according to which everything which can be of benefit to one's people must be true and right. He knows that a primordial decision has been made concerning right and wrong, between truth and lies, and that it confronts the existence of the people. He knows that, in the final analysis, the only thing that can help his people is what is true and right in the light of that age-old decision. But if, in an emergency, he cannot obey this recognition of the "final analysis," but responds to the nation's cry for help, he sins like the men in the Bible and, like them, prostrates himself before his Judge. That is the meaning in contemporary language of the return to the origins of our being. Let us hope that the language of tomorrow will be different, that to the best of our ability it will be the language of a positive realization of truth and right, in both the internal and external aspects of the structure of our entire community life.

I am setting up Hebrew humanism in opposition to that Jewish nationalism which regards Israel as a nation like unto other nations, and recognizes no task for Israel save that of preserving and asserting itself. But no nation in the world has this as its only task, for just as an individual who wishes merely to preserve and assert himself leads an unjustified and meaningless existence, so a nation with no other aim deserves to pass away.

By opposing Hebrew humanism to a nationalism which is nothing but empty self-assertion, I wish to indicate that, at this juncture, the Zionist movement must decide either for national egoism or national humanism. If it decides in favor of national egoism, it too will suffer the fate which will soon befall all shallow nationalism, that is, nationalism which does not set the nation a true supernational task. If it decides in favor of Hebrew humanism, it will be strong and effective long after shallow nationalism has lost all meaning and justification, for it will have something to say and to bring to mankind.

Israel is not a nation like other nations, no matter how much its representatives may have wished it during certain eras. Israel is a people like no other, for it is the only people in the world which, from its earliest beginnings, has been both a nation and a religious community. In the historical hour in which its tribes grew together to form a people, it became the carrier of a revelation. The covenant which the tribes made with one another and through which they became "Israel" takes the form of a common covenant with the God of Israel. The song of Deborah, that great document of our heroic age, expresses a fundamental reality by repeatedly alternating the name of this God with the name of Israel, like a refrain. Subsequently, when the people desire a dynasty so that they may be "like unto all the *nations*" (I Sam. 8:20), the Scriptures have the man who, a generation later, really did found a dynasty, speak words which sound as though they were uttered to counterbalance that desire: "And who is like thy people Israel, a *nation* one in the earth" (I Sam. 7:23). And these words, regardless of what epoch they hail from, express the same profound reality as those earlier words of Deborah. Israel was and is a people and a religious community in one, and it is this unity which enabled it to survive in an exile no other nation had to suffer, an exile which lasted much longer than the period of its independence. He who severs this bond severs the life of Israel.

One defense against this recognition is to call it a "theological interpretation," and, in this way, debase it into a private affair concerning only such persons as have interest in so unfruitful a subject as theology. But this is nothing but shrewd polemics. For we are, in reality, dealing with a fundamental historical recognition without which Israel as an historical factor and fact could not be understood. An attempt has been made to refute this allegedly "theological interpretation" by a "religious interpretation," the claim being made that it has nothing whatsoever to do with the Judaism of a series of eminent men, as the last of whom Rabbi Akiba is cited, the first being none other than Moses. Remarkable, to what lengths polemic enthusiasm will go! As a matter of fact, it is just as impossible to construct an historical Moses who did not realize the uniqueness of Israel as an historical Akiba who was not aware of it. Snatch from Rabbi Akiba his phrase about "special love" which God has for Israel (Pirke Abot 3:18), and you snatch the heart from his body. Try to delete the words, "You shall be mine own treasure from among all peoples" (Exod. 19:5) from the account of the coming of Israel to the wilderness of Sinai, and the whole story collapses. If such comments as these about Moses have any foundation at all, I do not know on what hypotheses of Bible criticism they are based; they are certainly not supported by anything in the Scriptures.

There is still another popular device for evading the recognition of Israel's uniqueness. It is asserted that every great people regards itself as the chosen people; in other words, awareness of peculiarity is interpreted as a function of nationalism in general. Did not the National Socialists believe that Destiny had elected the German people to rule the entire world? According to this view, the very fact that we say, "Thou hast chosen us," would prove that we are like other nations. But the weak arguments which venture to put, "It shall be said unto them: You are the children of the living God" (cf. Hos. 2:1), on a par with "The German essence will make the whole world well," are in opposition to the basic recognition we glean from history. The point is not whether we feel or do not feel that we are chosen. The point is that our role in history is actually unique. There is even more to it. The nature of our doctrine of election is entirely different from that of the theories of election of the other nations, even though these frequently depend on our doctrine. What they took over was never the essential part. Our doctrine is distinguished from their theories, in that our election is completely a demand. This is not the mythical shape of a people's wishful dreams. This is not an unconditional promise of greatness and might to a people. This is a stern demand, and the entire future existence of the people is made dependent on whether or not this demand is met. This is not a God speaking whom the people created in their own image, as their sublimation. He confronts the people and opposes them. He demands and judges. And he does so not only in the age of the prophets at a later stage of historical development, but from time immemorial; and no hypothesis of Bible criticism can ever deny this. What he demands he calls "truth" and "righteousness," and he does not demand these for certain isolated spheres of life, but for the whole life of man, for the whole life of the people. He wants the individual and the people to be "wholehearted" with him. Israel is chosen to enable it to ascend from the biological law of power, which the nations glorify in their wishful thinking, to the sphere of truth and righteousness. God wishes man whom he has created to become man in the truest sense of the word, and wishes this to happen not only in sporadic instances, as it happens among other nations, but in the life of an entire people, thus providing an order of life for a future mankind, for all the peoples combined into one people. Israel was chosen to become a true people, and that means God's people.

Biblical man is man facing and recognizing such election and such a demand. He accepts it or rejects it. He fulfils it as best he can, or he rebels against it. He violates it and then repents. He fends it off, and surrenders. But there is one thing he does not do: he does not pretend that it does not exist, or that its claim is limited. And classical biblical man absorbs this demand for righteousness so wholly with his flesh and blood that, from Abraham to Job, he dares to remind God of it. And God, who knows that human mind and spirit cannot grasp the ways of his justice, takes delight in the man who calls him to account, because that man has absorbed the demand for righteousness with his very flesh and blood. He calls Job his servant and Abraham his beloved. He tempted both; both called him to account, and both resisted temptation. That is Hebrew humanity.

7

ZION AND THE OTHER NATIONAL CONCEPTS

It is impossible to appreciate the real meaning of "Zion" so long as one regards it as simply one of many other national concepts. We speak of a "national concept" when a people makes its unity, spiritual coherence, historical character, traditions, origins and evolution, destiny and vocation the objects of its conscious life and the motive power behind its actions. In this sense, the Zion concept of the Jewish people can be called a national concept. But its essential quality lies precisely in that which differentiates it from all other national concepts.

It is significant that this national concept was named after a place and not, like the others, after a people, which indicates that it is not so much a question of a particular people as such, but of its association with a particular land. Moreover, the idea was not named after one of the usual descriptions of this land —Canaan or Palestine or Eretz-Yisrael—but after the old stronghold of the Jebusites, which David made his residence, and whose name was applied by poets and prophets to the whole city of Jerusalem, not so much as the seat of the royal fort, however, but as the place of the sanctuary. . . . Zion is "the city of the great King" (Ps. 48:3), that is, of God as the king of Israel. The name has retained this sacred character ever since. In their prayers and songs, the mourning and yearning of the people in exile was bound up with it; the holiness of the land was concentrated in it; in the Kabbalah, it is equated with an emanation of God himself. When the Jewish people adopted this name for their national concept, all these associations were contained in it.

This was inevitable, for in contrast to the national concepts of other peoples, the one described by this name was no new invention, not the product of the social and political changes manifested by the French Revolution, but merely a continuation, the restatement of an age-old religious and popular reality adapted to the universal form of the national movements of the nineteenth century. This reality was the holy marriage of a "holy" people with a "holy" land, the point of location of which was named Zion.

It has been one of the disastrous errors of modern biblical criticism to attribute this category of the Holy, as applied in the Scriptures to the people and the land, to the sacerdotalism of a later age, for which the claims of public worship were all-important. On the contrary, it belongs rather to the *primitive* conception of the Holy as we find it in tribes living close to nature, who think of the two main supports of national life, man and the earth, as endowed with sacred powers. In the tribes which united to form "Israel," this concept developed and became transformed in a special way: holiness is no longer a sign of power, a magic fluid that can dwell in places and regions as well as in people and groups of people, but a quality bestowed on this particular people and this particular land because God "elects" both in order to lead his chosen people into his chosen land and to join them to each other. It is his election that sanctifies the chosen people as his immediate attendants, and the land as his royal throne, and which makes them dependent on each other. This is more a political, a theopolitical, than a strictly religious concept of holiness: the outward form of worship is merely a concentrated expression of the sovereignty of God. Abraham builds altars where God has appeared to him, but he does so not as a priest but as a herald of the Lord by whom he has been sent; and when he calls on the name of his Lord above the altar, he thereby proclaims his Lord's royal claim to possession of the surrounding land. This is not the transforming interpretation of a later age, but has its roots in primitive language, analogies of which are to be found among other early peoples, but nowhere in such historical concreteness as here. Here "holiness" still means to belong to God not merely through religious symbols and in the times and places consecrated to public worship, but as a people and a land, in the all-embracing range and reality of public life. It is only later that the category of the Holy becomes restricted to public worship, a process which advances the more the sphere of public life is withdrawn from the sovereign rule of God.

That it is God who joins this people to this land is not a subsequent historical interpretation of events; the wandering tribes themselves were inspired again and again by the promise made to their forefathers, and the most enthusiastic among them saw God himself leading his people into the promised land. It is impossible to imagine a historical Israel as existing at any time without belief in its God or previously to such belief: it is precisely the message of the common Leader that unites the tribes into a people. It is no less impossible to imagine this belief as existing before and outside Israel: it is an absolutely historical belief, the belief in a God leading first the fathers and then the whole people into the promised land at historically determined times for divinely historical purposes. Here is no "nation" as such and no "religion" as such, but only a people interpreting its historical experiences as the actions of its God.

This belief in divine leadership is, however, at the same time the belief in a mission. However much of the legislation that has come down to us in the Bible may be attributed to later literary accretions, there is no doubt at all that the exodus from Egypt was bound up with the imposing of a law that was taken to be a divine charter, and the positive nucleus of all later developments was essentially the instruction to establish a "holy" community in the promised land. For these tribes, divine leadership certainly implied an ordinance concerning the future in the land, and from this basis a tradition and a doctrine were evolved. The story of Abraham, which connects the gift of Canaan with the command to be a blessing, is a most concise résumé of the fact that the association of this people with this land signifies a mission. The people came to the land to fulfil the mission; even by each new revolt against it they recognized its continuing validity; the prophets were appointed to interpret the past and future destiny of the people on the basis of the people's failure as yet to achieve the righteous city of God for the establishment of which it had been led into the land. This land was at no time in the history of Israel simply the property of the people; it was always at the same time a challenge to make of it what God intended to have made of it.

Thus, from the very beginning, the unique association between this people and this land was characterized by what was to be, by the intention that was to be realized. It was a consummation that could not be achieved either by the people or by the land alone, but only by the faithful cooperation of the two together; and it was an association in which the land appeared not as a dead, passive object, but as a living and active partner. Just as to achieve fullness of life, the people needed the land, so the land needed the people, and the end which both were called upon to realize could only be reached by a living partnership. Since the living land shared the great work with the living people, it was to be both the work of history and the work of nature. Just as nature and history were united in the creation of man, so these two spheres, which have become separated in the human mind, were to unite in the task in which the chosen land and the chosen people were called upon to cooperate. The holy marriage of land and people was intended to bring about the union of the two separated spheres of being.

This is the theme, relating to a small and despised part of the human race and a small and desolate part of the earth, yet world-wide in its significance, that lies hidden in the name of Zion. It is not simply a special case among the national concepts and national movements; the exceptional quality that is here added to the universal makes it a unique category extending far beyond the frontier of national problems and touching the domain of the universally human, the cosmic, and even of Being itself. In other respects, the people of Israel may be regarded as one of the many peoples on earth, and the land of Israel as one land among other lands; but in their mutual relationship and in their common task, they are unique and incomparable. And in spite of all the names and historical events that have come down to us, what has come to pass, what is coming and shall come to pass between them, is and remains a mystery. From generation to generation the Jewish people have never ceased to meditate on this mystery.

When the national movement of this people inherited the mystery, a powerful desire to dissolve it arose in spite of the protests of the movement's most important spiritual leaders. It seemed to belong to the purely "religious" sphere, and religion had become discredited for two reasons: in the West, because of its attempt to denationalize itself in the age of Emancipation; in the East, because of its resistance to the Europeanization of the Jewish people on which the national movement wanted to base itself. The secularizing trend in Zionsism was directed against the mystery of Zion too. A people like other peoples, a land like other lands, a national movement like other national movements—this was and still is proclaimed as the postulate of common sense against every kind of "mysticism." And from this standpoint, the age-long belief that the successful reunion of this people with this land is inseparably bound up with a command and a condition was attacked. No more is necessary—so the watchword runs—than that the Jewish people should be granted the free development of all its powers in its own country like any other people; that, in fact, is what is meant by "regeneration."

The certainty of the generations of Israel testifies that this view is inadequate. The idea of Zion is rooted in deeper regions of the earth and rises into loftier regions of the air, and neither its deep roots nor its lofty heights, neither its memory of the past nor its ideal for the future, both of the selfsame texture, may be repudiated. If Israel renounces the mystery, it renounces the heart of reality itself. National forms without the eternal purpose from which they have arisen signify the end of Israel's specific fruitfulness. The free development of the latent power of the nation without a supreme value to give it purpose and direction does not mean regeneration, but the mere sport of a common self-deception behind which spiritual death lurks in ambush. If Israel desires less than it is intended to fulfil, then it will even fail to achieve the lesser goal.

With every new encounter of this people with this land, the task is set afresh, but every time it is rooted in the historical situation and its problems. If it is not mastered, what has already been achieved will fall into ruin. Once it is really mastered, this may become the beginning of a new kind of human society. To be sure, the problem proves to be more difficult every time it is tackled. It is more difficult to set up an order based on justice in the land if one is under the jurisdiction of a foreign power, as after the return from Babylon, than if one is comparatively free to determine one's own way of life, as after the first appropriation of the land; and it is still more difficult if one has to reckon with the coexistence of another people in the same country, of cognate origin and language but mainly foreign in tradition, structure, and outlook, and if this vital fact has to be regarded as an essential part of the problem. On the other hand, there seems to be a high purpose behind the increasing difficulty of the task. Even in the life of the individual, what has once been neglected can never be made up for in the same sphere and under the same conditions; but one is sometimes allowed to make amends for lost opportunities in a quite different situation, in a quite different form, and it is significant that the new situation is more contradictory and the new form more difficult to realize than the old, and that each fresh attempt demands an even greater exertion to fulfil the task—for such is the hard but not ungracious way of life itself. The same process seems to be true of the life of Israel.

8

THE SILENT QUESTION:
ON HENRI BERGSON AND SIMONE WEIL

From time to time, I seem to hear a question echoing out of the depths of stillness. But he who asks it does not know that he is asking it, and he to whom the question is addressed is not aware that he is being questioned. It is the question which the world of today, in utter unawareness, puts to religion. This is the question: "Art thou, perhaps, the power that can help me? Canst thou teach me to believe? Not in phantasmagoria and mystagogy, not in ideologies or in party programs, nor in cleverly thought-out and skillfully presented sophisms which appear true only while they are successful or have prospects of success, but in the Absolute and Irrefragable. Teach me to have faith in reality, in the verities of existence, so that life will afford some aim for me and existence will have some meaning. Who, indeed, can help me if thou canst not?"

We can take it for granted that the world of today will vehemently deny wishing to ask or even being capable of asking such a question. This world will passionately maintain that religion is an illusion—perhaps not even a beautiful one—and will support this contention with a clear conscience, for such is the assuredness of its conviction. In the innermost recesses of the heart, however, there where despair abides, the same question surges timidly upward again and again, only to be immediately repressed. But it will grow in strength; it will become strong.

The question is addressed to religion generally, to religion as such. But where is religion to be found? The question cannot be addressed to the isolated religious individual, for how can he measure up to such a claim at such a moment? It is only to the historic religions—or to some of them—that such a question can literally be addressed. But it is neither in their dogma nor in their ritual that the answer may lie; not in the one because its purpose is to formulate beliefs which are beyond conceptual thinking into conceptual propositions, not in the other because its object is to express the relation to the Unlimited by means of steadfast and regular performance. Both have their specific spheres of influence, but neither is capable of helping the modern world to find faith. The only element in the historic religions which the world is justified in calling upon is that intrinsic reality of faith which is beyond all attempts at formulation and expression but exists in truth; it is *that* which constantly renews the fullness of its presence from the flow of personal life itself. This is the one thing that matters: the personal existence, which gives actuality to the essence of a religion and thus attests to its living force.

Whosoever listens closely to the question of which I speak observes that it is also addressed to Judaism, and indeed that Judaism is included in the foremost ranks of those religions to which the appeal is made. I have recently received communications from many parts of the world from which it can be sensed that clarification and leadership are expected of Judaism. It can be sensed, too, that many of these correspondents are speaking for the many more who remain silent. That the world expects something from Judaism is in itself a new phenomenon. For centuries, the deeper spiritual content of Judaism was either unknown or given scant attention, for the reason perhaps that, during the period of the ghetto, the underlying reality of Jewish life was hardly glimpsed by the outside world, while during the emancipation period, Jews only—not Judaism—appeared upon the open scene.

A change seems to be taking place. Why? Is it because of the massacre of millions of Jews? That does not explain it. Or is it because of the establishment of a Jewish State? That does not explain it either. And yet both of these events are basically part of the reason why the real content of Judaism is beginning to become more perceptible. These astounding phenomena of dying and living have at last brought before the world the fact of the existence of Jewry as a fact of particular significance, and from this point Judaism itself begins to be seen. Now the world has gradually begun to perceive that within Judaism there is something which has its special contribution to make, in a special way, to the spiritual needs of the present time. It is only possible to realize this if Judaism is regarded in its entirety, in its whole way, from the Decalogue to Hasidism, in the course of which its peculiar tendencies have evolved in an increasingly comprehensive manner.

This "entireness," these fundamental tendencies and their evolution, are, for the most part, still unrecognized even by the Jews themselves, even by those who are earnestly seeking the pathway of truth. This becomes manifest when we consider those amongst our spiritually representative Jewish contemporaries whose religious needs have remained unsatisfied by Judaism. It is highly characteristic that, in the springtime of modern society, spiritually significant Jews turned to Christianity not for the sake of Christian religion but for the sake of Christian culture, whereas today the sympathies worth noting that spiritual Jews feel for Christianity are rooted rather in a sense of religious lack and a feeling of religious longing.

Let us consider two examples which will make my meaning clear and which will plunge us deeper into our purpose of examining the religious significance of Judaism for the world of today. The one example is afforded by Bergson, the thinker who, like Nietzsche, built up his philosophy on the affirmation of life, but in contrast to Nietzsche, regardèd not power, but participation in creation, as the essence of life. Consequently, again in contrast to Nietzsche, he did not fight against religion but extolled it as the peak of human life. The other example is to be found in Simone Weil, who died young, and the legacy of whose writings expresses a strong and theologically far-reaching negation of life, leading to the negation of the individual as well as of society as a whole. Both Bergson and Simone Weil were Jews. Both were convinced that in Christian mysticism they had found the religious truth they were seeking. Bergson still saw in the prophets of Israel the forerunners of Christianity, whereas Simone Weil simply cast aside both Israel and Judaism. Neither was converted to Christianity— Bergson probably because it went against the grain to leave the community of the oppressed and persecuted; Simone Weil for reasons arising from her concept of religion which, apparently, led her to believe that the Church was still far too Jewish.

Let us examine how Judaism appeared to each of these and

how the Judaism which they saw relates to the actuality of the Jewish faith, to that "entireness" which has developed in the course of time and of which, as I have already pointed out, most Jews today still remain ignorant.

The image of Judaism conceived by Bergson is the conventional Christian one, the origin of which lies in the endeavor to depict the new religion as a release from the yoke of the older one. This picture is of a God of justice who exercised justice essentially on his own people, Israel, being followed by a God of love, of love for humanity as a whole. For Bergson, therefore, Christianity represents a human conscience rather than a social conscience, a dynamic code as opposed to a static code, and the ethics of the open soul as opposed to the ethics of the closed soul.

Simone Weil takes the same line but goes much further. She reproaches Israel with idolatry, with the only idolatry she considers a real one, the service of the collectivity, which she, utilizing a simile of Plato, calls the "Great Beast." Gregariousness is the realm of Satan, for the collectivity arrogates to itself the right to dictate to the individual what is good and what is evil. It interposes itself between God and the soul; it even supplants God and sets itself up in God's place. In ancient Rome, Simone Weil sees the "Great Beast" as the atheistic materialist who worships only himself. Israel, however, is to her the "Great Beast" in religious disguise, and its god the god it deserved, a ponderous god, a god "of the flesh," a tribal god— ultimately, nothing but the deification of the nation. The Pharisees, whom Simone Weil obviously came to know only through the controversies of the New Testament, are defined by her as a group "who were virtuous only out of obedience to the Great Beast." Everything that was hateful to her in more recent history, such as capitalism and Marxism, the intolerance of the Church, and modern nationalism, was ascribed by her to the influence of what she called the "totalitarianism" of Israel.

Bergson accepted the principle of social life as a transition stage; for Simone Weil, who, by the way, was, for a while, actively associated with the extreme Left, it was the great obstacle. For both, Israel was its embodiment, and both strove to surmount it through Christianity, in which Bergson found the purely human element, Simone Weil, on the other hand, the supernatural.

Seldom has it been so evident as in this instance how a half-truth can be more misleading than a total error. (As far as Simone Weil is concerned, it is, indeed, scarcely a quarter-truth.)

The real definition of the social principle of the religion of Israel is something considerably different from Bergson's conception and something entirely different from Simone Weil's.

It is true, the group which is welded together out of families and tribes under the influence of a common belief in God and becomes a people is understood in Israel as a religious category. But this is not the actual people, not that which the prophet who harangues the people sees assembled around him. The religious character of the people consists emphatically in that something different is intended for it from what it is now, that it is destined for something different—that it should become a true people, the "People of God." Precisely in the religion of Israel is it impossible to make an idol of the people as a whole, for the religious attitude to the community is inherently critical and postulative. Whoever ascribes to the nation or to the community the attributes of the absolute and of self-sufficiency betrays the religion of Israel.

What, however, does it mean to become a "people of God?" A common belief in God and service to his name do not constitute a people of God. Becoming a people of God means rather that the attributes of God revealed to it, justice and love, are to be made effective in its own life, in the lives of its members with one another; justice materialized in the indirect mutual relationships of these individuals; love in their direct mutual relationships rooted in their personal existence. Of the two, however, love is the higher, the transcending principle. This becomes unequivocally clear from the fact that man cannot be just to God; he can, however, and should, love God. And it is the love of God which transfers itself to man: "God loves the stranger," we are told, "so thou too shalt love him." The man who loves God loves also him whom God loves.

It is not true that the God of the Bible has, as Simone Weil expresses it, "never until the Exile spoken to the soul of man." He has always spoken to the soul of the individual, even in the time of the Decalogue; to whom else, if not to the soul of the individual, can the injunction be given not to covet, that is to say, not to be envious of what is another's? But God speaks to individuals according to their real existence, and this means, in the pre-exilic period, as members of the people into which they are incorporated and from which they are undetachable. The

Ten Commandments are not addressed to the collective "You," but all of them to a single "Thou"; this "Thou" means every individual, and as every individual is yet thoroughly embedded in the people, he is thus addressed as a part of it. It is only in the degree to which the individual, in the course of historic reality, discovers himself and becomes aware of himself that God speaks to him as such. But even in the most highly individualized times that "Thou" still concerns every single individual so long as he does not intentionally shut himself away from it.

Bergson's conventional differentiation between Jewish particularism and Christian universalism is equally unfounded. According to Amos, the earliest of the "literary" prophets, who significantly takes as his example the arch enemies of Israel, the wanderings of all peoples are directed by God himself. The prophet states that, not as something new but as something generally known. This is, indeed, a universalism not of individuals but of nations, through which it reaches out to individuals. Within this universalism, however, there is a particularization of vocation: Israel shall begin the work of the materialization of God's justice and love on earth; Israel shall be "the first-fruits of his harvest."

It is not true that Israel has not accorded to spiritual inwardness its rightful place; rather, it has not contented itself with it. Its teachings contest the self-sufficiency of the soul: inward truth must become real life, otherwise it does not remain truth. A drop of messianic consummation must be mingled with every hour; otherwise the hour is godless, despite all piety and devoutness.

Accordingly, what may be called the social principle of Israel's religion is fundamentally dissimilar from any "Great Beast." It is concerned with social humanity, for human society is here legitimate only if built upon real relationships between its members; and humanity is taken in its religious meaning, because real relationship to God cannot be achieved on earth if real relationships to the world and to mankind are lacking. Both love of the Creator and love of that which he has created are finally one and the same.

In order to achieve this unity, man must indeed accept creation from God's hands, not in order to possess it, but lovingly to take part in the still uncompleted work of creation. Creation is incomplete because discord still reigns within it, and peace can only emerge from the created. That is why, in Jewish tradition, he who brings about peace is called the companion of God in the work of creation. This concept of man's vocation as a co-worker with God is emphasized by Bergson as the goal of that mysticism which he glorifies and which he does not find in Judaism; it is, however, a fundamentally Jewish concept.

Both Bergson and Simone Weil turned away from a Judaism they did not know; in actual fact, they turned aside from a conventional conception of Judaism created by Christianity. But while Bergson was close to true Judaism which he did not know, Simone Weil was remote from it. When she referred to the God of Israel as a "natural" God and to that of Christianity as a "supernatural" God, she failed entirely to understand the character of the former inasmuch as he is not "natural" but is the God of nature as well as the God of spirit—and is superior to both nature and spirit alike. But even if Simone Weil had known the true God of Israel, she would not have been satisfied, for he turns toward nature, which he dominates, whereas Simone Weil sought flight from nature as well as from society: reality had become intolerable to her, and for her, God was the power which led her away from it. But that is definitely not the way of the God of Israel; such a way would be the very opposite of his relation toward his creation and his creatures. He has placed man in the center of reality in order that he should face up to it. Simone Weil's idea was to serve mankind, and so she again and again took to heavy manual labor on the land, but her soul was always put to flight by reality. And she began with her own reality: she contested the "I"; it was one's duty, she thought, to slay the "I" in onself. "We possess nothing in this world," she wrote, "other than the power to say I. This is what we should yield up to God, and that is what we should destroy." Such a basic orientation is, indeed, diametrically opposed to Judaism; for the real relationship taught by Judaism is a bridge which spans across two firm pillars, man's "I" and the "I" of his eternal partner. It is thus the relation between man and God, thus also the relation between man and man. Judaism rejects the "I" that connotes selfishness and pride, but it welcomes and affirms the "I" of the real relationship, the "I" of the partnership between I and Thou, the "I" of love. For love does not invalidate the "I"; on the contrary, it binds the "I" more closely to the "Thou." It does not say: "Thou art loved" but "I love thee." The same applies to the "We," about which Simone Weil said: "One should not be I and even less should one be We." Judaism rejects the "We" of group egotism, of national conceit and party exclusiveness, but it postulates that "We" which arises from the real relationships of its components and which maintains genuine relations with other groups, the "We" which may say in truth: "*Our* Father."

Simone Weil knew neither the old religion of Israel nor its later way, in which the changed conditions of history brought about a new display of its basic elements. Bergson knew the prophets of Israel, yet without realizing how in their messages the principle of justice which he found in them was complemented by the principle of love; but he knew not the road taken by the Jewish religion, and consequently he did not consider the prophets in connection with the whole of Jewish religious history. The prophets protest against the religious failure of Israel, against the fact that God's demand to create a place on earth for his justice and his love has not been sufficiently complied with—neither by the people nor by the individuals within it—at least not in the measure compatible with the strength available and under the prevailing conditions. And the seed of the prophets is springing up; though late, it is sprouting into stronger and stronger growth. In the Diaspora, it is true, a comprehensive realization of the principle of justice could not be aspired to, since that would have required an autonomous national entity, autonomous national institutions, which could only be hoped for with the return to the Holy Land; but the higher, the decisive principle which alone can knit together the relationship to God and the relationship to man—the principle of love—requires neither organizations nor institutions but can be given effect at any time, at any place. The will to realization was not, however, confined to the individual. Within the communal form of life adopted in the place of a state—that is, the local communities—active love in the guise of mutual help recurs as a basic social element. This structure found its perfection about two centuries ago in Hasidism, which was built on little communities bound together by brotherly love. An inner religious development of the highest significance corresponds to that tendency, the striving to bridge the gulf between love of God and love of man. Again the Hasidic movement succeeded in giving full effect to this striving. It teaches that the true meaning of love of one's neighbor is not that it is a command from God which we are to fulfill, but that through it and in it we meet God. This is shown by the interpretation of this command. It is not just written: "Love thy neighbor as thyself," as though the sentence ended there, but it goes on: "Love thy neighbor as thyself, I am the Lord." The grammatical construction of the original text shows quite clearly that the meaning is: You shall deal lovingly with your "neighbor," that is, with everyone you meet along life's road, and you shall deal with him as with one equal to yourself. The second part, however, adds: "I am the Lord"—and here the Hasidic interpretation comes in: "You think I am far away from you, but in your love for your neighbor you will find me; not in his love for you but in yours for him." He who loves brings God and the world together.

The Hasidic teaching is the consummation of Judaism. And this is its message to all: *You yourself must begin*. Existence will remain meaningless for you if you yourself do not penetrate into it with active love and if you do not in this way discover its meaning for yourself. Everything is waiting to be hallowed by you; it is waiting to be disclosed in its meaning and to be realized in it by you. For the sake of this your beginning, God created the world. He has drawn it out of himself so that you may bring it closer to him. Meet the world with the fullness of your being and you shall meet him. That he himself accepts from your hands what you have to give to the world is his mercy. If you wish to believe, love!

Bergson speaks of an "active mysticism." Where is this to be found, if not here? Nowhere else is man's essential doing so closely bound up with the mystery of being. And for this very reason the answer to the silent question asked by the modern world is found herein. Will the world perceive it? But will Jewry itself perceive that its very existence depends upon the revival of its religious existence? The Jewish State may assure the future of a nation of Jews, even one with a culture of its own; Judaism will live only if it brings to life again the primeval Jewish relationship to God, the world, and mankind.

PART V: *Of Teaching and Learning*

1. Teaching and Deed

TEACHING AND DEED

Among all peoples, two kinds and lines of propagation exist side by side, for quite as continuous as the biological line, and parallel to it, is—in the words of the philosopher Rudolf Pannwitz—the line of the "propagation of values." Just as organic life is transmitted from parents to children and guarantees the survival of the community, so the transmission and reception, the new begetting and new birth of the spirit, goes on uninterruptedly. The life of the spirit of a people is renewed whenever a teaching generation transmits it to a learning generation, which, in turn, growing into teachers, transmits the spirit through the lips of new teachers to the ears of new pupils. This process of education involves the person as a whole, just as does physical propagation.

In Judaism, this cycle of propagation involves another and peculiar factor. In Israel of old, the propagation of values itself assumed an organic character and penetrated the natural life of the people. It is true that it does not imitate biological reproduction in guaranteeing the survival of the community as such; it only guarantees its survival as Israel. But can we drown out the voice which tells us that if our life as Israel were to come to an end, we could not go on living as one of the nations? We, and we only, once received both life and the teachings together, and in the selfsame hour became a nation and a religious community. Since then, the transmission of life and the transmission of the teachings have been bound together, and we consider the spiritual transmission as vital as bodily propagation.

317

The talmudic sages say: "He who teaches the tradition to his fellow-man is regarded as though he had formed and made him, and brought him into the world. As it is said (Jer. 15:19): 'And if thou bring forth the precious out of the vile, thou shalt be as my mouth.'" In this quotation from the Bible, God summons the prophet, who has just begged for help to wreak vengeance on his foes, to the turning, to the conquest of his own hatred and repugnance, and promises him that if he turns, he will be allowed adequately to fulfil a divine action. And the "forming" and the "making" of the child in the womb (Jer. 1:5; Ps. 139:15) is counted among such divine action. The influence of the teacher upon the pupil, of the right teacher upon the right pupil, is not merely compared to, but even set on a par with, divine works which are linked with the human maternal act of giving birth. The inner turning of the prophet is an actual rebirth, and the educator, who brings the precious ore in the soul of his pupil to light and frees it from dross, affords him a second birth, birth into a loftier life. Spirit begets and gives birth; spirit is begotten and born; spirit becomes body.

Even today, in spite of all deterioration, the spiritual life of Jewry is not merely a superstructure, a nonobligatory transfiguration, an object of pride which imposes no duties. Rather, it is a binding and obligatory power, but one which attains to earthly, bodily reality only through that which it binds to the obligations of Jewish spiritual life. So profoundly is the spirit here merged with the physical life that even the survival of the community in time can be guaranteed only by both operating together.

But if we are serious about the simile of generation, we must realize that in spiritual as well as in physical propagation, it is not the same thing that is passed on, but something which acquires newness in the very act of transmission. For tradition does not consist in letting contents and forms pass on, finished and inflexible, from generation to generation. The values live on in the host who receives them by becoming part of his very flesh, for they choose and assume his body as the new form which suits the function of the new generation. A child does not represent the sum total of his parents; it is something that has never been before, something quite unpredictable. Similarly, a generation can only receive the teachings in the sense that it renews them. We do not take unless we also give. In the living tradition, it is not possible to draw a line between preserving and producing. The work of embodiment takes place spontaneously; and that person is honest and faithful who utters words he has never heard as though they had come to him, for it is thus—and not as if he had "created" them—that such words live within him. Everyone is convinced that he is doing no more than further advancing that which has advanced him to this point; yet nonetheless he may be the originator of a new movement.

That this holds for Jewry is due to the intensity which time and again characterizes the encounters between generations, involving mutual and radical interactions and bringing forth changes in values as though they were not changes at all. In these recurring encounters between a generation which has reached its full development and one which is still developing, the ultimate aim is not to transmit a separable something. What matters is that time and again an older generation, staking its entire existence on that act, comes to a younger with the desire to teach, waken, and shape it; then the holy spark leaps across the gap. Transmitted content and form are subordinate to the tradition of existence as such, and become valid only because of it. The total, living, Jewish human being is the transmitting agent; total, living, Jewish humanity is transmitted. Tradition is concentrated in the existence of the Jew himself. He lives it, and it is he who approaches the new generation and influences it by producing the blend of the old and the new. Israel is inherent in these human beings; they are Israel. Israel is renewed, not by what they say, but by the totality of their existence.

We have already indicated that in our case teaching is inseparably bound up with doing. Here, if anywhere, it is impossible to teach or to learn without living. The teachings must not be treated as a collection of knowable material; they resist such treatment. Either the teachings live in the life of a responsible human being, or they are not alive at all. The teachings do not center in themselves; they do not exist for their own sake. They refer to, they are directed toward, the deed. In this connection, the concept of "deed" does not, of course, connote "activism," but life that realizes the teachings in the changing potentialities of every hour.

Among all the peoples in the world, Israel is probably the only one in which wisdom that does not lead directly to the unity of knowledge and deed is meaningless. This becomes most evident when we compare the biblical concept of *hokmah* with the Greek concept of *sophia.* The latter specifies a closed realm of thought, knowledge for its own sake. This is totally alien to *hokmah,* which regards such a delimitation of an independent spiritual sphere, governed by its own laws, as the misconstruction of meaning, the violation of continuity, the severance of thought from reality.

The supreme command of *hokmah* is the unity of teaching and life, for only through this unity can we recognize and avow the all-embracing unity of God. In the light of our doctrine, he who gives life and gives that life meaning is wronged by a teaching which is satisfied with and delights in itself, which rears structures, however monumental, above life, and yet does not succeed in wresting even a shred of realization out of all the outer and inner obstacles we must struggle with in every precarious hour of our lives. For our God makes only one demand upon us. He does not expect a humanly unattainable completeness and perfection, but only the willingness to do as much as we possibly can at every single instant.

Man is a creature able to make spirit independent of physical life, and his great danger is that he may tolerate and even sanction existence on two different levels: one, up above and fervently adored, the habitation of the spirit; the other, down below, the dwelling of urges and petty concerns, equipped with a fairly good conscience acquired in hours of meditation on the upper level.

The teachings do not rely on the hope that he who knows them will also observe them. Socratic man believes that all virtue is cognition, and that all that is needed to do what is right is to know what is right. This does not hold for Mosaic man, who is informed with the profound experience that cognition is never enough, that the deepest part of him must be seized by the teachings, that for realization to take place his elemental totality must submit to the spirit as clay to the potter.

Here dualism is fought with the utmost vigor. "He who studies with an intent other than to act," says the Talmud, "it would have been more fitting for him never to have been created" (Pal. Talmud, Shabbat 3b). It is bad to have teaching without the deed, worse when the teaching is one of action. Living in the detached spirit is evil, and worse when the spirit is one of ethos. Again and again, from the Sayings of the Fathers down to the definitive formulation of Hasidism, the simple man who acts is given preference over the scholar whose knowledge is not expressed in deeds. "He whose deeds exceed his widsom, his wisdom shall endure; but he whose wisdom exceeds his deeds, his wisdom shall not endure." And in the same vein: "He whose wisdom exceeds his deeds, what does he resemble? A tree with many boughs and few roots. A wind, springing up, uproots it, and overturns it. But he whose deeds exceed his wisdom, what does he resemble? A tree with few boughs, but many roots. Though all the winds in the world come and blow upon it, it cannot be moved." What counts is not the extent of spiritual possessions, not the thoroughness of knowledge, nor the keenness of thought, but to know what one knows, and to believe what one believes, so directly that it can be translated into the life one lives.

I repeat that in Judaism the true value of the deed has nothing to do with "activism." Nothing is more remote from Judaism than the glorification of self-confident virtue. But Judaism knows that *true* autonomy is one with true theonomy: God wants man to fulfil his commands as a human being, and with the quality peculiar to human beings. The law is not thrust upon man; it rests deep within him, to waken when the call comes. The word which thundered down from Sinai was echoed by the word that is "in thy mouth and in thy heart" (Deut. 30:14). Again and again, man tries to evade the two notes that are one chord; he denies his heart and rejects the call. But it has been promised that a time will come when the Torah will be manifest as the Scripture present in the hearts of all living men, and the word will fulfil itself in the harmony of heaven and earth. In Jewry, the way which leads to that promised time, the way of man's contribution to ultimate fulfilment, is trodden whenever one generation encounters the next, whenever the generation which has reached its full development transmits the teachings to the generation which is still in the process of developing, so that the teachings spontaneously waken to new life in the new generation.

We live in an age when deeds tend to assert their superiority over the teachings. The present generation universally believes more and more unreservedly that it can get along without the teachings and rely on a mode of action which—in its own opinion—is correct. In an address I delivered years ago at a Zionist congress, in memory of our teacher Ahad Haam, I drew attention to the fact that "it is not only the official state politics that is freeing itself from spiritual teachings—that has, on occasion, happened before—but the internal popular movements, and national groupings, are also stressing their independence from spiritual teachings, and even regard independence as a warrant of success. And," I went on to say, "they are not entirely mistaken. The conduct of life without the teachings is successful: something is achieved. But the something thus achieved is quite different, and at times the very caricature, of what one is striving for at the bottom of one's heart, where the true goal is divined. And what then? As long as the goal was a pure goal, yearning and hope were dominant. But if in the course of being achieved, the goal is distorted, what then?"

The implied warning I intended for Jewry passed them by almost unnoticed—as was to be expected. Although we are less able to get along without the teachings than any other community, a widespread assimilation of the errors of the other nations has been rampant among us for a long time. It is not my office to discuss what may happen to other nations because of their denial of the spirit. But I know that we, who believe that there can be no teaching apart from doing, will be destroyed when our doing becomes independent of the teachings.

A Jewish house of study—that is a declaration of war upon all those who imagine they can be Jews and live a Jewish life outside of the teachings, who think by cutting off the propagation of values to accomplish something salutary for Jewry. A truly Jewish communal life cannot develop in Palestine if the continuity of Judaism is interrupted. Let me reiterate that such continuity does not imply the preservation of the old, but the ceaseless begetting and giving birth to the same single spirit, and its continuous integration into life. Do not let us delude ourselves: once we are content to perpetuate biological substance and a "civilization" springing from it, we shall not be able to maintain even such a civilization. For the land and the language in themselves will not support our body and soul on earth—only land and language when linked to the holy origin and the holy destination. Moreover, in this crisis of humanity in which we stand at the most exposed point, the Diaspora cannot preserve its vital connection, which has so long defied history's attempt at severance, without recognizing and renewing the power the teachings possess, a power strong enough to overcome all corroding forces. For all that which is merely social, merely national, merely religious, and therefore lacking the fiery breath of the teachings, is involved in the abysmal problematic of the hour and does not suffice to ward off decay.

Only the teachings truly rejuvenated can liberate us from limitations and bind us to the unconditional, so that spiritualized and spirited, united within the circle of eternal union, we may recognize one another and ourselves and, empowered by the fathomless laws of history, hold out against the powers moving on the surface of history.

Concerning the words of Isaac the patriarch, "The voice is the voice of Jacob, but the hands are the hands of Esau" (Gen. 27:22), the Midrash tells this story. Delegates of the other nations were once dispatched to a Greek sage to ask him how the Jews could be subjugated. This is what he said to them: "Go and walk past their houses of prayer and of study . . . So long as the voice of Jacob rings from their houses of prayer and study, they will not be surrendered into the hands of Esau. But if not, the hands are Esau's and you will overcome them" (Gen. Rabbah, on 27:22).

The teachings cannot be severed from the deed, but neither can the deed be severed from the teachings! Our tradition assigned quite as much importance to the one danger as to the other. The Talmud tells us that at a gathering of sages the question arose as to which was greater, deeds or teachings. And one of them, who seemed to share our point of view, said that deeds were greater. But Rabbi Akiba said: "The teachings are greater!" And all agreed, saying: "The teachings are greater, for the teachings beget the deed" (Bab. Talmud, Kiddushin 40b). This sounds like a contradiction of the assertions of the importance of action. But after we have more deeply pondered these assertions, we comprehend that the teachings are central, and that they are the gate through which we must pass to enter life. It is true that simple souls can live the true life without learning, provided they are linked to God. But this is possible for them only because the teachings, which represent just such a link to God, have, although they are unaware of it, become the very foundation of their existence. To do the right thing in the right way, the deed must spring from the bond with him who commands us. Our link with him is the beginning, and the function of the teachings is to make us aware of our bond and make it fruitful.

Again we are confronted with the concepts of continuity and spontaneity, the bond of transmission and begetting. The teachings themselves are the way. Their full content is not comprehended in any book, in any code, in any formulation. Nothing that has ever existed is broad enough to show what they are.

In order that they may live and bring forth life, generations must continue to meet, and the teachings assume the form of a human link, awakening and activating our common bond with our Father. The spark that leaps from him who teaches to him who learns rekindles a spark of that fire which lifted the mountain of revelation "to the very heart of heaven."

SOURCES

BIBLIOGRAPHY

NOTES

SOURCES

Part I *I and Thou*

I AND THOU

The selections are from *I and Thou,* translated from the German by Ronald Gregor Smith (Edinburgh: T. and T. Clark, 1937; New York: Charles Scribner's Sons), pp. 3-4, 11-17, 22-23, 28-34, 75-81, 104-106, 109-112. *Ich und Du* first appeared in 1923 (Leipzig: Insel-Verlag).

THE QUESTION TO THE SINGLE ONE

The selections are from "The Question to the Single One," *Between Man and Man,* translated from the German by Ronald Gregor Smith (London: Routledge and Kegan Paul, 1947; New York: Macmillan Company, 1948), pp. 40-61, 65, 69-71, 79-82. *Die Frage an den Einzelnen* first appeared in 1936 (Berlin: Schocken Verlag).

GOOD AND EVIL

These selections constitute chapters III and IV of Part Three of "Images of Good and Evil" (pp. 125-138) in *Good and Evil: Two Interpretations* (New York: Charles Scribner's Sons, 1953). The German, *Bilder von Gut und Bose,* appeared in 1952 (Cologne: Jakob Hegner).

THE LOVE OF GOD AND THE IDEA OF DEITY

This selection constitutes chapter IV, "The Love of God and the Idea of Deity," in *Eclipse of God: Studies in the Relation Between Religion and Philosophy* (New York: Harper and Brothers, 1952), pp. 67-84. It first appeared in Hebrew in *Kenesset,* 5703 (1943), and was translated by I. M. Lask. It is also to be found in *Israel and the World: Essays in a Time of Crisis* (New York: Schocken Books, 1948), pp. 53-65.

GOD AND THE SPIRIT OF MAN

This selection constitutes chapter VIII, "God and the Spirit of Man," in *Eclipse of God: Studies in the Relation Between Religion and Philosophy* (New York: Harper and Brothers, 1952). It is substantially one of the lectures delivered by Martin Buber at a number of American universities in November and December, 1951, and was translated from the German by Maurice S. Friedman.

Part II   *Of Social Life*

THE IDEA; IN THE MIDST OF CRISIS;
AN EXPERIMENT THAT DID NOT FAIL
These selections are chapters from *Paths in Utopia,* translated
from the German by R. F. C. Hull (New York: Macmillan
Company, 1950): chapter I, "The Idea," pp. 1-6; chapter X,
"In the Midst of Crisis," pp. 129-138; and "Epilogue—An Ex-
periment That Did Not Fail," pp. 139-149. The German edi-
tion, *Pfade in Utopia,* appeared in 1950 (Heidelberg: Verlag
Lambert Schneider).

"AND IF NOT NOW, WHEN?"
The selection included constitutes a chapter from *Israel and
the World: Essays in a Time of Crisis* (New York: Schocken
Books, 1948), pp. 234-239, and was translated from the German
by Olga Marx. It is an address delivered at a Jewish youth con-
vention in Antwerp in 1932, and was first published in *Kampf
um Israel: Reden und Schriften 1921-1932* (Berlin: Schocken
Verlag, 1932).

Part III   *Of Biblical Faith*

SAGA AND HISTORY
The selection included constitutes a chapter from *Moses*
(Oxford: East and West Library, 1946), pp. 13-19. The German edition is *Mose* (Heidelberg: Verlag Lambert Schneider,
1952).

HOLY EVENT
This selection constitutes chapter V, "Holy Event," in *The
Prophetic Faith,* translated from the Hebrew by Carlyle Witton-
Davies (New York: Macmillan Company, 1949), pp. 43-59.
Der Glaube der Propheten was published in 1950 (Zurich:
Manesse Verlag).

"UPON EAGLES' WINGS"; THE WORDS ON THE
TABLETS; THE ZEALOUS GOD;
THE CONTRADICTION
The selections included are chapters from *Moses* (Oxford:
East and West Library, 1946): " 'Upon Eagles' Wings,' " pp.

101-109; "The Words on the Tablets," pp. 119-140; "The Zealous God," pp. 141-146; "The Contradiction," pp. 182-190.

BIBLICAL LEADERSHIP; PLATO AND ISAIAH; THE MAN OF TODAY AND THE JEWISH BIBLE

These selections are chapters from *Israel and the World: Essays in a Time of Crisis* (New York: Schocken Books, 1948). "Biblical Leadership" (pp. 119-133) was a lecture delivered in Munich in 1928, and was first published in *Kampf um Israel: Reden und Schriften 1921-1932* (Berlin: Schocken Verlag, 1933); the translation is by Greta Hort. "Plato and Isaiah" (pp. 103-112) is an introductory lecture delivered at the Hebrew University in Jerusalem, and published by the University in 1938; the translation is by Olga Marx. "The Man of Today and the Jewish Bible" (pp. 89-102) is from a series of lectures delivered in 1926, and published in *Die Schrift und ihre Verdeutschung*, by Martin Buber and Franz Rosenzweig (Berlin: Schocken Verlag, 1936); the translation is by Olga Marx.

Part IV *Of Jewish Destiny*

THE FAITH OF JUDAISM; THE TWO FOCI OF THE JEWISH SOUL; NATIONALISM; OF THE LAND AND ITS POSSESSORS; ON NATIONAL EDUCATION; HEBREW HUMANISM

The selections included are chapters from *Israel and the World: Essays in a Time of Crisis* (New York: Schocken Books, 1948). "The Faith of Judaism" (pp. 13-27) was first prepared in 1928 as a lecture for a political science institute in Reichenhall, and was delivered at the Weltwirtschaftliches Institut in Kiel. It was first published in *Kampf um Israel: Reden und Schriften 1921-1932* (Berlin: Schocken Verlag, 1933); the translation is by Greta Hort. "The Two Foci of the Jewish Soul" (pp. 28-40) is an address delivered at an institute held by four German-language missions to Jews at Stuttgart in March 1930, and published in *Kampf um Israel;* the translation is by Greta Hort. "Nationalism" (pp. 222-226; only part of the essay is presented here) is an address delivered at the twelfth Zionist congress at Karlsbad, on September 5, 1921, and published in *Kampf um Israel;* the translation is by Olga Marx. "The Land and Its Possessors" (pp. 227-233) is from an open letter addressed to Gandhi in 1939; it first appeared in *The Bond,*

Jerusalem, 1939. "On National Education" (pp. 157-163; only part of the essay is presented here) is an address delivered at the national conference of the Palestinian Teachers Association held at Tel Aviv in 1939; it appeared in *Ha-Ruah veha-Metziut* (Tel Aviv, 1942). "Hebrew Humanism" (pp. 241-254; only part of the essay is presented here) appeared in *Ha-Ruah veha-Metziut*, and was translated by Olga Marx.

ZION AND THE OTHER NATIONAL CONCEPTS
The selection included constitutes the introductory chapter of *Israel and Palestine: The History of an Idea*, translated from the German by Stanley Godman (London: East and West Library, 1952), pp. ix-xiv. A Hebrew edition appeared in 1944. The German edition is *Israel und Palästina: Zur Geschichte einer Idee* (Zurich: Artemis-Verlag, 1950).

THE SILENT QUESTION
The selection included is from *At the Turning: Three Addresses on Judaism* (New York: Farrar, Straus, and Young, 1952), pp. 29-44. It is an address delivered at the Jewish Theological Seminary in November 1951.

Part V   *Of Teaching and Learning*

The selection included is a chapter from *Israel and the World: Essays in a Time of Crisis* (New York: Schocken Books, 1948), pp. 137-145. It is an address delivered at the Freies Jüdisches Lehrhaus in Frankfort on the Main in 1934, and was published in *Die Stunde und die Erkenntnis: Reden und Aufsätze 1933-1935* (Berlin: Schocken Verlag, 1936); the translation is by Olga Marx.

BIBLIOGRAPHY

A full bibliography of writings by, about, and relating to Martin Buber will be found in Maurice S. Friedman, *Martin Buber: The Life of Dialogue* (see below), pp. 283-298. The following list includes only Buber's major works available in English, as well as a few outstanding studies of Buber's life and thought.

WORKS BY MARTIN BUBER AVAILABLE IN ENGLISH

At the Turning: Three Addresses on Judaism. New York: Farrar, Straus, and Young, 1952.

Between Man and Man. Translated by Ronald Gregor Smith. New York: Macmillan Company, 1948.

"Distance and Relation." Translated by Ronald Gregor Smith. *The Hibbert Journal*, Vol. XLIX, January 1951.

Eclipse of God: Studies in the Relation Between Religion and Philosophy. Translated by Maurice S. Friedman, et al. New York: Harper and Brothers, 1952.

For the Sake of Heaven. Translated by Ludwig Lewisohn. 2nd ed. New York: Harper and Brothers, 1953.

Good and Evil: Two Interpretations. New York: Charles Scribner's Sons, 1953.

Hasidism. New York: Philosophical Library, 1948.

"Hope for This Hour." Translated by Maurice S. Friedman. *World Review*, December 1952.

I and Thou. Translated by Ronald Gregor Smith. Edinburgh:
T. and T. Clark; New York: Charles Scribner's Sons, 1937.

Israel and Palestine: The History of an Idea. Translated by
Stanley Godman. London: East and West Library, 1952.

Israel and the World: Essays in a Time of Crisis. New York:
Schocken Books, 1948.

The Legend of the Baal-Shem. Translated by Maurice S. Friedman. Harper and Brothers, 1955.

Mamre: Essays in Religion. Translated by Greta Hort. Melbourne: Melbourne University Press, 1946.

Moses. Oxford: East and West Library, 1946.

Paths in Utopia. Translated by R. F. C. Hull. London: Routledge and Kegan Paul, 1949.

Pointing the Way: Collected Essays. Translated by Maurice S.
Friedman. New York: Harper and Brothers, 1956.

The Prophetic Faith. Translated by Carlyle Witton-Davies.
New York: Macmillan Company, 1949.

"Remarks on Goethe's Concept of Humanity," *Goethe and the
Modern Age.* Edited by Arnold Bergstraesser. Chicago:
Henry Regnery, 1950.

Right and Wrong: An Interpretation of Some Psalms. Translated by Ronald Gregor Smith. London: S.C.M. Press, 1952.

"Society and the State." *World Review,* New Series 27, May
1951.

Tales of the Hasidim: The Early Masters. Translated by Olga
Marx. New York: Schocken Books, 1947.

Tales of the Hasidim: The Later Masters. Translated by Olga
Marx. New York: Schocken Books, 1948.

Ten Rungs: Hasidic Sayings. Translated by Olga Marx. New
York: Schocken Books, 1947.

Two Letters to Gandhi. With Judah Magnes. (Pamphlets of
The Bond.) Jerusalem: Rubin Mass, 1939.

Two Types of Faith. Translated by Norman P. Goldhawk.
London: Routledge and Kegan Paul, 1951. New York:
Macmillan Company, 1952.

The Way of Man, According to the Teachings of Hasidism.
London: Routledge and Kegan Paul, 1950.

WORKS ABOUT MARTIN BUBER

Agus, Jacob B., *Modern Philosophies of Judaism.* New York:
Behrman's Jewish Book House, 1941.

Friedman, Maurice S., *Martin Buber: The Life of Dialogue.*
Chicago: University of Chicago Press, 1955.

Kohn, Hans, *Martin Buber, Sein Werk und Seine Zeit: Ein Versuch über Religion und Politik.* Hellerau: Jakob Hegner Verlag, 1930.

Pfuetze, Paul E., *The Social Self.* New York: Bookman Associates, 1954.

Introduction by WILL HERBERG

[1] J. H. Oldham, *Real Life Is Meeting* (London: Sheldon Press, 1942), p. 28.

[2] Such testimony will be found cited in Maurice S. Friedman, *Martin Buber: The Life of Dialogue* (Chicago: University of Chicago, 1955); see esp. the introductory chapter, "The Narrow Ridge," the chapters on education and psychology, and the chapter on "Buber and Christianity." For Buber's influence on Christian thought, see Paul Tillich, "Jewish Influence on Contemporary Christian Theology," *Cross Currents*, Vol. II, No. 3, Spring 1952, and "Martin Buber and Christian Thought," *Commentary*, Vol. V, No. 6, June 1948.

[3] See Martin Buber, *Between Man and Man*, translated by Ronald Gregor Smith (London: Kegan Paul, 1947; New York: Macmillan, 1948), "Dialogue," pp. 13-14. The essays in this volume contain other fragments of autobiographical disclosure.

[4] Martin Buber, *Daniel: Gespräche von der Verwirklichung* (Leipzig: Insel-Verlag, 1913).

[5] Buber did, however, by the time of *Daniel*, decisively reject the impersonalist, absorptionist type or aspect of mysticism. Criticisms of this kind of mysticism abound in his later writings. "All doctrine of absorption is based on the colossal illusion of the human spirit bent back on itself . . ." (*I and Thou*, translated by Ronald Gregor Smith [Edinburgh: T. and T. Clark, 1937], p. 93). "It [mysticism] too lets man be alone before God, but not as a Single One. The relation to God which it thinks of is the absorption of the I, and the Single One ceases to exist if he cannot—even in devoting himself—say I. As mysticism will not permit God to assume the servant's form of speaking and acting person, . . . so it prohibits man, as the Single One persisting as such, from really praying and serving and loving, such as is possible only by an I to a Thou" (*Be-*

tween Man and Man, "The Question to the Single One," p. 43).
"But in the actuality of lived life, the man in such a moment [of
mystical experience] is not above but beneath the creaturely situation . . . He is not above but beneath dialogue" (*Between Man
and Man,* "Dialogue," p. 25). A. Steinberg is quite justified in his
assertion: "If at first, he [Buber] regarded himself as a mystic, he
later came to the conclusion that mysticism, which seeks through
'nearness to God,' to submerge and efface man's individual character, is essentially anti-religious, and therefore non-Jewish" (A. Steinberg, "The History of Jewish Religious Thought," in *The Jewish
People Past and Present,* Vol. I [New York: Jewish Encyclopedic
Handbooks, Central Yiddish Culture Organization, 1946], p. 505a).

[6] Martin Buber in cooperation with Franz Rosenzweig, *Die Schrift,*
15 vols. (Berlin: Schocken Verlag, 1927-37); see also Martin Buber
and Franz Rosenzweig, *Die Schrift und ihrer Verdeutschung* (Berlin: Schocken Verlag, 1936).

[7] "All real living is meeting" (*I and Thou,* p. 11).

[8] "The more perfect and more eternal aspect of the universe is represented in our religions as having a personal form. The universe is
no longer a mere *It* to us, but a *Thou,* if we are religious; and any
relation that may be possible from person to person might be possible here . . ." (William James, *Essays in Pragmatism,* ed. by
Alburey Castell [New York: Hafner, 1949], "The Will to Believe,"
p. 106). The "Will to Believe" was first published in 1897.

[9] Buber asserts that even hate is possible only with part of one's
being and that "only a part of a being can be hated." "Yet the
man who straightforwardly hates is nearer to relation than the
man without hate or love" (*I and Thou,* p. 16).

[10] *I and Thou,* p. 3.

[11] *I and Thou,* p. 33.

[12] Maurice S. Friedman, *Martin Buber: The Life of Dialogue,* pp. 164,
186.

[13] The term is Reinhold Niebuhr's, in *The Self and the Dramas of
History* (New York: Scribner's, 1955). Niebuhr makes specific acknowledgment to Buber in defining his understanding of life and
history in terms of the "dramatic" elaboration of personal encounter: "I acknowledge my indebtedness to the great Jewish philosopher, Martin Buber, whose book *I and Thou* first instructed me
and many others on the uniqueness of human selfhood and on the
religious dimension of the person" (p. ix). Buber would not seem
to fit in exactly into either of the two categories which I employ
in interpreting Niebuhr's thinking—the *ontological* (Tillich) and
the *historical* (Niebuhr)—but in the end he is definitely closer to
Niebuhr's approach (see Will Herberg, "The Three Dialogues of
Man," *New Republic,* May 16, 1955, esp. pp. 30-31).

[14] See Paul E. Pfuetze, *The Social Self* (New York: Bookman, 1954),
pp. 281, 346-47.

[15] *I and Thou,* p. 28.

[16] See Pfuetze, *The Social Self.*

[17] Buber calls this "the soul's adventures in doubling roles . . . , [which] can never become *ontically* true, just as the 'one and one in one' of mysticism can never be ontically true" (*Between Man and Man*, "The Question to the Single One," p. 50).

[18] *Between Man and Man*, "The Question to the Single One," pp. 48, 43.

[19] Martin Buber, *At the Turning: Three Addresses on Judaism* (New York: Farrar, Straus, and Young, 1952), "The Silent Question," p. 39.

[20] *Between Man and Man*, "The Question to the Single One," p. 50.

[21] For the discussion with Kierkegaard, see *Between Man and Man*, "The Question to the Single One," esp. pp. 40-65.

[22] *I and Thou*, p. 78.

[23] *I and Thou*, p. 75.

[24] *Between Man and Man*, "What Is Man?," pp. 168, 167.

[25] *I and Thou*, pp. 34, 11.

[26] *Between Man and Man*, "The Question to the Single One," p. 43.

[27] Martin Buber, *Israel and the World: Essays in a Time of Crisis* (New York: Schocken, 1948), "Teaching and Deed," p. 142.

[28] Martin Buber, *Hasidism* (New York: Philosophical Library, 1948), "Spinoza," p. 99. Jacob B. Agus has well summarized Buber's teaching: "To be religious is to be 'actual,' to live in perpetual conversation with God—a conversation which, coming from God to us, is expressed in the needs of the situation as understood by man, . . . and which, returning from us to God, is concretized in the form of deed performed to meet those needs" (Jacob B. Agus, *Modern Philosophies of Judaism* [New York: Behrman's, 1941], p. 269).

[29] *Israel and the World*, "Biblical Leadership," pp. 131-32.

[30] *Israel and the World*, "The Two Foci of the Jewish Soul," p. 33.

[31] *I and Thou*, p. 51.

[32] Friedman, *Martin Buber*, p. 107. See also Martin Buber, *Good and Evil: Two Interpretations* (New York: Scribner's, 1953), pp. 107-113.

[33] *Between Man and Man*, "What Is Man?," p. 166. Ferdinand Ebner has traced mental disturbance to this same "remaining with oneself;" he sees insanity as the end product of *Icheinsamkeit* ("I-aloneness") and *Dulosigkeit* ("Thou-less-ness"), the isolation of the I from the Thou (Ferdinand Ebner, *Das Wort und die geistigen Realitäten* [Innsbruck: Brenner-Verlag, 1921]; Friedman, *Martin Buber*, p. 185).

[34] Martin Buber, *Two Types of Faith*, translated by Norman P. Goldhawk (New York: Macmillan, 1952), p. 84.

[35] *Good and Evil*, p. 140.

[36] Some confusion in Buber's discussion of the problem of evil is on occasion introduced by his use of a familiar rabbinic saying that man must serve God not simply with his good *yetzer,* but with his *yetzer ha-ra* ("evil impulse;" better, "inclination to evil") as well.

This would seem to imply that the *yetzer ha-ra* is not "really" evil, but that something else (what?) makes it evil. What Buber is attempting to say here is that man must serve God not only with his "spirit," but with his "passions" as well. "From the same passionate powers, which undirected give rise to evil, when they are turned toward God, the good arises. One does not serve God with the spirit only, but with the whole of his nature, without any subtractions" (*Israel. and the World*, "The Two Foci of the Jewish Soul," p. 34). But despite frequent rabbinic precedents, it seems wrong to identify the *yetzer ha-ra* with the "passions," as though there was something evil in them. In the classic rabbinic passage, the *yetzer ha-ra* is understood as something very different. "Were it not for the *yetzer ha-ra*," we are told, "a man would not build a house or take a wife or beget a child or engage in business, as it is said: 'All labor and work comes of a man's rivalry with his neighbor'" (Gen. R. ix.7). Here the *yetzer ha-ra* is not the "passions," but "rivalry with one's neighbor," Buber's "false self-asserting instinct."

[37] *Good and Evil*, p. 60.

[38] *I and Thou*, p. 80.

[39] Buber thus characterizes the two ways of philosophy and mysticism, and the third way of the dialogic "meeting" with God in the world: "If you explore the life of things and of conditioned being [as in philosophy], you come to the unfathomable [the *Urgrund*, the "primal ground" of being]; if you deny the life of things and of conditioned being [as in mysticism], you stand before nothingness [the *Ungrund*, the "no-ground" of being]; if you hallow this life, you meet the living God" (*I and Thou*, p. 79).

[40] *I and Thou*, p. 81.

[41] Martin Buber, *Der heilige Weg: Ein Antwort an die Juden und die Völker* (Frankfort: Literarische Anstalt Rütten und Loening, 1920), pp. 67-68.

[42] *I and Thou*, p. 106.

[43] *Between Man and Man*, "The Question to the Single One," p. 81.

[44] *Israel and the World*, "What Are We To Do About the Ten Commandments?," p. 86.

[45] *Between Man and Man*, "The Question to the Single One," p. 82.

[46] Martin Buber, "Remarks on Goethe's Concept of Humanity," in Arnold Bergstraesser, ed., *Goethe and the Modern Age* (Chicago: Regnery, 1950), pp. 232-33.

[47] *Between Man and Man*, "Dialogue," p. 16.

[48] *Between Man and Man*, "The Question to the Single One," p. 45.

[49] *At the Turning*, "The Dialogue between Heaven and Earth," p. 56.

[50] *Between Man and Man*, "The Education of Character," p. 114.

[51] *Between Man and Man*, "What is Man?," pp. 203, 176.

[52] *I and Thou*, p. 45.

[53] *Between Man and Man*, "What Is Man?," p. 200.

[54] *Good and Evil*, p. 136. See also Martin Buber, "Distance and Rela-

tion," translated by Ronald Gregor Smith, *The Hibbert Journal,* Vol. XLIX, January 1951.

[55] Martin Buber, "Hope for This Hour," *World Review,* December 1952.

[56] See Martin Buber, *Paths in Utopia,* translated by R. F. C. Hull (Macmillan, 1949), epilogue.

[57] Ben Halpern, in a perceptive article on the new problems of the Israeli commune, notes that to the more recent immigrants from Eastern and Central Europe, "kibbutz collectivism is repellantly reminiscent of the concentration camp, the kolkhoz, or the DP camp" (Ben Halpern, "The Israeli Commune: Privacy and the Collective Life," *Modern Review,* Summer 1949). Mr. Halpern believes the kibbutz to be a valuable and enduring part of the Israeli social system, but asserts that it needs greater flexibility and adaptiveness to meet pressing new problems.

[58] *Paths in Utopia,* p. 145.

[59] Martin Buber, "Society and the State," *World Review,* New Series 27, May 1951. This contrast of the "social" and "political" principles reminds one of the social philosophy of eighteenth and nineteenth century liberalism. It was Tom Paine who declared: "Society in every state is a blessing, but government, even in its best state, is but a necessary evil; in its worst state, an intolerable evil" (*Common Sense,* chap. i). In the nineteenth century, the "social" principle became the "economic" principle, the "political" principle remaining the *bête noir* of the liberal.

[60] *Paths in Utopia,* p. 104.

[61] *Israel and the World,* " 'And If Not Now, When?' ", p. 238.

[62] *Israel and the World,* "Hebrew Humanism," p. 246.

[63] Martin Buber and Judah L. Magnes, *Two Letters to Gandhi* (Jerusalem: Rubin Mass, 1939), pp. 20-21.

[64] *Israel and the World,* "Hebrew Humanism," p. 246.

[65] Ernst Simon, "Martin Buber: His Way Between Thought and Deed," *Jewish Frontier,* Vol. XV, No. 2, February 1948.

[66] Martin Buber, *For the Sake of Heaven,* translated from the German by Ludwig Lewisohn, 2nd. ed. (New York: Harper, 1953), foreword, p. x.

[67] *Between Man and Man,* "The Question to the Single One," p. 77.

[68] See esp. Reinhold Niebuhr, *The Children of Light and the Children of Darkness: A Vindication of Democracy and a Critique of Its Traditional Defense* (New York: Scribner's, 1944). In an address on October 16, 1854, Abraham Lincoln stated: "What I do say is that no man is good enough to govern another without that other's consent. I say this is the leading principle, the sheet anchor, of American republicanism" (T. Harry Williams, ed., *Abraham Lincoln: Selected Writings and Speeches* (Chicago: Packard, 1943), pp. 36-37. See also Will Herberg, "The Biblical Basis of American Democracy," *Thought,* Vol. XXX, No. 116, Spring 1955.

[69] *Between Man and Man,* "What Is Man?," p. 201.

[70] *Between Man and Man*, "The Education of Character," p. 111.

[71] *Between Man and Man*, "The Question to the Single One," pp. 80-81.

[72] Martin Buber, *The Prophetic Faith*, translated from the Hebrew by Carlyle Witton-Davies (New York: Macmillan, 1949), p. 54.

[73] *Israel and the World*, "The Man of Today and the Jewish Bible," p. 89.

[74] *At the Turning*, "The Dialogue between Heaven and Earth," p. 48.

[75] Martin Buber, *Moses* (Oxford and London: East and West Library, 1946); *The Prophetic Faith*, as above. (Buber's basic work on biblical faith, *Königtum Gottes* [Berlin: Schocken Verlag, 1932; 2nd edition, 1936] has unfortunately not yet appeared in English). Buber describes his method as the "intuitively scientific method," and holds to "tradition criticism" as distinct from "source criticism," and presumably "form criticism" as well (*The Prophetic Faith*, pp. 6-7).

[76] *The Prophetic Faith*, p. 70.

[77] *I and Thou*, p. 79.

[78] Emil Fackenheim, "In the Here and Now" (review of Buber's *The Prophetic Faith*), *Commentary*, Vol. IX, No. 4, April 1950.

[79] *Eclipse of God*, "Religion and Ethics," p. 127.

[80] *Israel and the World*, "The Faith of Judaism," p. 27.

[81] *The Prophetic Faith*, p. 54.

[82] *Moses*, p. 131.

[83] *At the Turning*, "The Dialogue between Heaven and Earth," pp. 47-48.

[84] *Eclipse of God*, "Religion and Philosophy," p. 51.

[85] Friedman, *Martin Buber*, p. 253.

[86] *At the Turning*, "The Silent Question," p. 37.

[87] *The Prophetic Faith*, p. 146.

[88] *Moses*, p. 145. Cp. the celebrated rabbinic saying: " 'Unto me are the children of Israel slaves' (Lev. 25:55)—not slaves unto slaves." (Bab. Talmud, Baba Metzia 10a [Kiddushin 22a]).

[89] *Israel and the World*, "The Faith of Israel," p. 17.

[90] *At the Turning*, "The Dialogue between Heaven and Earth," p. 56.

[91] *Israel and the World*, "The Man of Today and the Jewish Bible," p. 102.

[92] *The Prophetic Faith*, p. 52.

[93] *Israel and the World*, "The Faith of Judaism," p. 17.

[94] *Israel and the World*, "The Faith of Judaism," p. 20.

[95] *The Prophetic Faith*, p. 195.

[96] *At the Turning*, "The Silent Question," p. 39.

[97] *I and Thou*, p. 110.

[98] Emil Brunner, *Wahrheit als Begegnung: Sechs Vorlesungen über das christliche Wahrheitsverständnis* (Berlin: Furche-Verlag, 1938); the English translation of this book is entitled *The Divine-Human Encounter*, translated from the German by Amandus W. Loos (Philadelphia: Westminster, 1943).

[99] Buber distinguishes between revelation through nature and revelation through history. The former is "continuous" and continuously proclaims "that one, though all-inclusive something, that which the psalm calls the glory of God." Revelation through history, on the other hand, is discontinuous and varied: "times of great utterance, when the mark of divine direction is recognizable in the conjunction of events, alternate with, as it were, mute times, when everything that occurs in the human world and pretends to historical significance appears to us empty of God." Moreover, in revelation through nature man is only the receiver; in revelation through history, on the other hand, "mankind, being placed in freedom, cooperates incessantly in shaping its [history's] course" (*At the Turning*, "The Dialogue between Heaven and Earth," pp. 57-58). These distinctions are important, but are they ultimate? In a great natural catastrophe, destroying men and communities, does nature speak so obviously and unequivocally the same word of revelation of the glory of God?

[100] *Israel and the World*, "The Man of Today and the Jewish Bible," p. 94.

[101] Oscar Cullmann, *Christ and Time: The Primitive Christian Conception of Time and History*, translated from the German by Floyd V. Filson (Philadelphia: Westminster, 1951), pp. 81ff., 90, 101, 124, 167, 211, and passim.

[102] "The Exodus was basic in the consciousness of Israel . . . [It] was of existential significance . . . For Israel, reality was laid bare in that bit of history. God revealed himself in it. It is the normative event . . . Yahweh redeemed Israel . . . This is the people by which he will fulfill his intention for all mankind . . . This is the perspective in terms of which the Exodus becomes the formative and guiding 'event' in Israel's religious tradition. When we read on to the end of the Old Testament, we find that all of it—with the possible exception of such items as Proverbs and Ecclesiastes, which omit reference to our historical locus of revelation—is written as testimony to this perspective that emerges from the Exodus event" (J. Coert Rylaarsdam, "Preface to Hermeneutics," *The Journal of Religion*, Vol. XXX, No. 2, April 1950).

[103] *Israel and the World*, "The Faith of Judaism," p. 27.

[104] *Israel and the World*, "The Two Foci of the Jewish Soul," p. 36.

[105] *Israel and the World*, "The Two Foci of the Jewish Soul," p. 34.

[106] Quoted by Ernst Simon, "Martin Buber: His Way Between Thought and Deed," *Jewish Frontier*, Vol. XV, No. 26, January 1948.

[107] Martin Buber, "Der Preis," *Der Jude*, October 1917.

[108] Friedman, *Martin Buber*, p. 252.

[109] *Israel and the World*, "Biblical Leadership," p. 131.

[110] *At the Turning*, "The Silent Question," p. 39.

[111] *Israel and the World*, "The Two Foci of the Jewish Soul," p. 29. Here, and especially in *Two Types of Faith*, Buber attempts to

contrast faith as *emunah* with the New Testament *pistis*, which he asserts means faith in the sense of believing some proposition about God or Christ. While *pistis* does occasionally bear this meaning in the N. T. (e.g., Heb. 11:6), its general usage is indistinguishable from *emunah*. "In the vast majority of cases, the meaning [of 'faith' in the New Testament] goes back to a Hebrew concept . . . The core of this Hebrew concept is firmness, reliability, or steadfastness . . . Usually, it is a person rather than a statement which is believed, and in the context of men's relation to God, the verb always implies personal conviction and trust arising within direct personal relationship . . . The NT Greek reflects this point by introducing a preposition ('believe in . . .') in almost every instance where more is intended than mere credence. If a person 'holds sure to God,' he may be said to 'have faith' . . . It is the act by which he lays hold of God's proffered resources, becomes obedient to what God prescribes, and abandoning all self-interest and self-reliance, trusts God completely. This is the meaning which the noun 'faith' receives in St. Paul's writing . . . To believe, in the technical Christian sense, is to be related to God in trust via those historical events [the 'Christ-events']" (W. A. Whitehouse, "Faith," in Alan Richardson, ed., *A Theological Word Book of the Bible* [Macmillan, 1951], pp. 75-76).

[112] *I and Thou*, p. 106.

[113] *Eclipse of God*, "God and the Spirit of Man," p. 162.

[114] *Eclipse of God*, "God and the Spirit of Man," p. 163.

[115] *The Prophetic Faith*, p. 170.

[116] *Hasidism*, "Hasidism in Religion," p. 199.

[117] *The Prophetic Faith*, p. 88. G. Ernest Wright subtitles his *God Who Acts* with "Biblical Theology as Recital" (Chicago: Regnery, 1952).

[118] "In the biblical religion, which is a history religion, . . . there is no nature in the Greek, the Chinese, or the modern Occidental sense. What is shown us of nature is stamped with history" (*Moses*, pp. 78-79). The messianic vision of Israel, Baron points out, is the vision of an age in which, through divine action, " 'history' will finally vanquish 'nature,' even changing its course, for in that day, 'the wolf shall dwell with the lamb' (Is. 11:6) and . . . nature will be transformed into a community" (Salo W. Baron, *A Social and Religious History of the Jews* [New York: Columbia, 1937], Vol. I. p. 7).

[119] *Moses*, p. 131.

[120] *Israel and the World*, "Biblical Leadership," pp. 127-28.

[121] "The individual Israelite approaches God in virtue of his membership in the holy people . . . In the whole of the Bible, . . . there is no such thing as a private personal relationship between the individual and God apart from his membership in the cove

nant folk" (Alan Richardson, "Instrument of God," *Interpretation*, Vol. III, No. 3, July 1949).

[122] "The collectivity cannot enter instead of the person into the dialogue of the ages which the Godhead conducts with mankind" (*Between Man and Man*, "The Question to the Single One," p. 80).

[123] *At the Turning*, "The Silent Question," p. 36.

[124] *Moses*, pp. 189-90.

[125] See Martin Buber, *Die Schriften über das dialogische Prinzip* (Heidelberg: Verlag Lambert Schneider, 1954), "Nachwort," p. 296.

[126] *Israel and the World*, "In the Midst of History," pp. 81-82. Emil Brunner has said of Buber's *Königtum Gottes* (Berlin: Schocken Verlag, 1932) that it is "a book which shows what history is better than any philosophy of history" (Emil Brunner, *Man in Revolt* [Philadelphia: Westminster, 1947], p. 448, note 2).

[127] Martin Buber, *Drei Reden über das Judentum* (Frankfort: Literarische Anstalt Rütten und Loening, 1911).

[128] *Drei Reden über das Judentum*, p. 70.

[129] *Drei Reden über das Judentum*, p. 71.

[130] *Drei Reden über das Judentum*, p. 75-91, esp. p. 90.

[131] Franz Rosenzweig, in an essay published in 1914, branded Buber's views, without mentioning him by name, as "atheistic theology." "The will to unity, this most Jewish of all concepts, these new theologians of ours see as the crowning of their Jewish folk picture. Here they stray most consciously from tradition. For whereas traditional Judaism assigns the Jew the task of unity on the ground of the revealed unity of God, and regards the acknowledgment of the coming kingdom of God as involving the assumption of the God-bidden way of life, these new theologians make this relation between man and his God into an historical corollary of the yearning for the unity of life that has informed the Jewish folk character in all ages" (Franz Rosenzweig, "Atheistische Theologie," *Kleinere Schriften* [Berlin: Schocken Verlag, 1937], p. 286).

[132] *Drei Reden über das Judentum*, p. 101.

[133] *Israel and the World*, "The Faith of Judaism," p. 13.

[134] This distinction between the two strains in Hasidism has been made by J. G. Weiss, "Contemplative Mysticism and 'Faith' in Hasidic Piety," *The Journal of Jewish Studies* (London), Vol. IV, No. 1, 1953. Weiss writes: "The entire Hasidic literature, as far as theory is concerned, may be divided into two clear-cut types—the mystical, contemplative Hasidism, . . . with an idealistic and semi-pantheistic outlook . . . , and the Hasidism of faith, . . . which lives in an atmosphere of 'existentialism'" (pp. 20, 29).

[135] *Israel and the World*, "On National Education," p. 159.

[136] *At the Turning*, "The Silent Question," p. 43.

[137] *Israel and the World*, "On National Education," p. 159.

[138] *Israel and the World*, "The Land and Its Possessors," pp. 229-30

[139] *At the Turning*, "The Silent Question," p. 42.

[140] Rosenzweig's view of Judaism and Christianity may be found briefly described in Nahum N. Glatzer, "Franz Rosenzweig," *Yivo Annual of Jewish Social Science I* (1946), and Nahum N. Glatzer, ed., *Franz Rosenzweig: His Life and Thought* (New York: Schocken, 1953), esp. pp. xxv-xxvi, 341-48. See also Will Herberg, "Judaism and Christianity: Their Unity and Difference," *The Journal of Bible and Religion,* Vol. XXI, No. 2, April 1953.

[141] The phrase is Jacques Maritain's; see his *A Christian Looks at the Jewish Question* (New York: Longmans Green, 1939), p. 29.

[142] *Israel and the World,* "The Two Foci of the Jewish Soul," p. 35.

[143] *Israel and the World,* "The Two Foci of the Jewish Soul," pp. 39-40.

[144] "To Buber Zionism represents the opportunity of the people to continue its ancient existence on the land which was interrupted by the generation of exile. This implies that Jewish existence in the Diaspora from the time of the exile to the present cannot be understood as Judaism in the full sense of the word" (Friedman, *Martin Buber,* p. 262).

[145] *Israel and the World,* "The Two Foci of the Jewish Soul," pp. 28-29.

[146] *Moses,* p. 188.

[147] *Two Types of Faith,* p. 57.

[148] *Der heilige Weg,* p. 53.

[149] Franz Rosenzweig, "Die Bauleute," *Kleinere Schriften;* Buber's and Rosenzweig's exchange of letters will be found in Franz Rosenzweig, *On Jewish Learning,* ed. by N. N. Glatzer (New York: Schocken, 1955), pp. 109-24.

[150] *At the Turning,* "The Silent Question," p. 44.

[151] *At the Turning,* "The Silent Question," p. 44.

OF HUMAN EXISTENCE

[1] *The Question to the Single One.* The German which I have rendered by the cumbrous and none too clear phrase "the Single One" is *der Einzelne,* which is a fairly precise rendering of Kierkegaard's *hiin Enkelte.* It is a pity that in the English translations of Kierkegaard no effort seems to have been made by the translators to avoid the use of the word "individual," which is highly misleading. For every man is *individuum,* but not everyone is an *Einzelner* or *Enkelte.* In fact, the whole course of Kierkegaard's life, and the whole force of his teaching, is directed toward "becoming a Single One," and this is not a natural or biological category, but, as Kierkegaard reiterates, it is "the spirit's category," and a rare thing. The reader's complaisance is invited, therefore, as it was decided better to make the English a little odd rather than customary and misleading. [Translator]

[2] All Kierkegaard's works, and a selection of the Journals, are now available in English. An English translation of Stirner's book, by S. C. Byington, was published under the title *The Ego and His Own*, London (A. C. Fifield) and New York (E. C. Walker), 1913. [Translator]

[3] "Love your neighbour as one like yourself": this departure from the customary rendering of the Authorized Version is again an effort to render the original more precisely (in this case the Hebrew of Lev. 19:18) in order to keep before the reader the stark objectivity of the command—the other whom you are required to "love" being one with a real life of his own, and not one whom you are invited to "acquire." [Translator]

OF SOCIAL LIFE

[1] The minutes appeared in Zurich in 1929 under the title "Sozialismus aus dem Glauben" (*Socialism from Faith*).

[2] Of course, I am not dealing here with the otherwise successful "socio-economic organizations, used by governmental or semi-governmental agencies to improve rural conditions" (Infield, *Cooperative Communities at Work*, p. 63).

[3] Cf. Julien Benda, *The Treason of the Intellectuals* (New York, 1928).

OF BIBLICAL FAITH

[1] Usener, "Der Stoff des griechischen Epos," *Sitzungsberichte der Wiener Akademie der Wissenschaften, philologisch-historische Klasse*, Vol. CXXXVII (1897), pp. 4f. (reprinted in Usener, *Kleine Schriften*, Vol. IV, pp. 201f.).

[2] Herzfeld, "Mythos und Geschichte," *Archaeologische Mitteilungen aus Iran*, Vol. VI (1933), pp. 102ff.

[3] Jacob Grimm, "Gedanken ueber Mythos, Epos und Geschichte," *Deutsches Museum* (1813), Vol. III, p. 53 (reprinted in Jacob Grimm, *Kleinere Schriften*, Vol. IV, p. 74).

[4] Sachsse, *Die Bedeutung des Namens Israel* (1922), p. 91; cf. Noth, *Das System der Zwoelf Staemme*, pp. 90ff.

[5] Noth, *Die israelitischen Personennamen* (1929), p. 207f. Buber, *Koenigtum Gottes*, pp. 193, 252f.; *Moses*, pp. 113f.

[6] Volz, *Mose*, p. 88.

[7] Cf. Buber, *Koenigtum Gottes*, pp. 119ff. (against Mowinckel, *Psalmenstudien* II).

[8] Cf. Buber, *Moses*, pp. 74ff.

[9] The view connecting these words with the Schechem assembly is without foundation; nothing in the Joshua story fits this hymn of a great theophany.

[10] Sellin, *Einleitung in das Alte Testament* (1935), p. 22. The view that this is a late psalm (so e.g., H. Schmidt, "Das Meerlied," *Zeitschrift fuer alttestamentliche Wissenschaft,* Neue Folge, Vol. VIII (1931), pp. 59ff.) cannot be supported from the fact that there is hardly any more mention in it of the dividing of the Red Sea than in other psalms; no other psalm is so built upon the one event and its effects.

[11] Cf. *Moses,* pp. 101ff.

[12] The saying is later elaborated many times homiletically (cf. Deut. 4:20; 7:6; 14:2; 26:19; I Kgs. 8:53); but it differs completely from these in its concentrated style. Its presentation of the deity, to whom the whole earth belongs and who can choose to himself one people out of all, is *earlier* in the history of faith than the universal liberator deity of Amos.

[13] Cf. Eerdmans, *De godsdienst van Israel* (1930), Vol. I, pp. 56ff.; Volz, *Mose,* pp. 100ff.; Klamroth, *Lade und Tempel* (1933), pp. 30ff.; Sellin, *Alttestamentliche Theologie* (1933), Vol. I, pp. 30ff.; Buber, *Koenigtum Gottes,* pp. 228ff., *Moses,* pp. 147ff.

[14] Cf. M. Dibelius, *Die Lade Jahves* (1906).

[15] Cf. especially Pedersen, "Passahfest und Passahlegende," *Zeitschrift fuer alttestamentliche Wissenschaft,* Neue Folge, Vol. XI (1934), pp. 161ff.; and Buber, *Moses,* pp. 69ff.

[16] Pedersen, *op. cit.,* p. 168.

[17] Hempel, *Das Ethos des Alten Testaments* (1938), p. 43.

[18] Volz, *Das Daemonische in Jahwe* (1924), and Buber, *Moses,* pp. 56ff.

[19] Cf. *Moses,* pp. 8off.

[20] Oesterley and Robinson, *A History of Israel,* Vol. I (1932), p. 96; and Buber, *Moses,* pp. 119ff.

[21] Alt, *Die Urspruenge des israelitischen Rechts* (1934), p. 52.

[22] R. Kittel, *Geschichte des Volkes Israel,* Vol. I, Supplement I.

[23] Alt, *op. cit.,* p. 69. For an examination of the types of ordinance style, cf. Jirku, *Das weltliche Recht im Alten Testament* (1927).

[24] Alt, *op. cit.,* p. 47.

[25] *Ibid.,* p. 70.

[26] Jirku, *Das israelitische Jobeljahr* (Seeberg-Festschrift, 1929), p. 178. Cf. Alt, *op. cit.,* pp. 65f.; but Alt ascribes only the statutes about the Sabbatical year to an early age, and conjectures that in this year there was a completely new allotment of field plots to families, somewhat like that which is to be found amongst semi-nomads in our time; cf. also Kennett, *Ancient Hebrew Social Life and Custom* (1933), p. 77.

[27] Cf. *Koenigtum Gottes,* pp. 56ff.

[28] Cf. Eerdmans, *Alttestamentliche Studien,* Vol. IV (1912), pp. 121ff.; Kugler, *Von Moses bis Paulus* (1922), pp. 49ff.; Ramsay, *Asianic Elements in Greek Civilization* (1927), pp. 49f.

[29] Alt, *op. cit.,* p. 47.

[30] Such an addition is to be seen in the mention of the two kinds of sacrifice in verse 24.

[81] Cf. *Koenigtum Gottes*, pp. 143ff.

[82] Cf. Rost, *Die Vorstufen von Kirche und Synagoge im Alten Testament* (1938), pp. 7f.

[83] Cf. *Koenigtum Gottes*, pp. 157f., 287f.

[84] *Ibid.*, pp. 3ff.

[85] Volz, *Mose*, 2nd ed. (1932), p. 84; cf. also Staerk, "Zum alttestamentlichen Erwaehlungsglauben," *Zeitschrift fuer die alttestamentliche Wissenschaft*, New Series, Vol. XIV (1937), p. 8, and von Rad, *Das formgeschichtliche Problem des Hexateuchs*, p. 36.

[86] Buber, *Koenigtum Gottes*, p. 112ff.; cf. also Quell, article *diathéke* in Kittel, *Theologisches Woerterbuch zum Neuen Testament*, Vol. II (1935), p. 123.

[87] Gressmann, "Die Anfaenge Israels," *Die Schriften des Alten Testaments*, I, 2, 2nd ed. (1922), p. 60; cf. Gressmann, *Mose*, p. 185.

[88] Eissfeldt, *Einleitung in das Alte Testament* (1934), p. 260.

[89] Cf. Buber, *Koenigtum Gottes*, pp. 126ff. Regarding the interpretation in detail, cf. Staerk, *Zum alttestamentlichen Erwaehlungsglauben*, pp. 8ff.

[40] Cf. the excellent exposition in Baudissin, *Kyrios als Gottesname im Judentum*, Vol. III (1927), pp. 379ff.; see pp. 398ff. in particular for the attribute of justice.

[41] Cf. Buber, *Koenigtum Gottes*, pp. 140ff.

[42] *Ibid.*, pp. 132ff., 273ff.; cf. also Gunkel, *Einleitung in die Psalmen* (1933), p. 208.

[43] Eichrodt, *Theologie des Alten Testaments*, Vol. I, p. 96.

[44] Cf. Buber, *Koenigtum Gottes*, pp. 69f., 93ff., 211ff.

[45] On Gideon see *ibid.*, pp. 3ff. I have demonstrated the unity of nucleus of the Samuel story in my as yet unpublished work, "The Anointed" (passages from which have appeared in the Hebrew historical quarterly *Zion*, Vol. IV (1939), pp. 1ff.).

[46] Buresch, *Klaros* (1899), pp. 89ff.; the passage on the Decalogue is found on p. 116.

[47] Wellhausen, "Skizzen und Vorarbeiten I," *Die Composition des Hexateuchs*, p. 96.

[48] Alt, *Die Urspruenge des israelitischen Rechts* (1929), p. 52; cf. Rudolph, *Der "Elohist" von Exodus bis Josua*, p. 59: "a conglomerate of little value from the Book of the Covenant, which is in no way source material."

[49] B. Duhm, *Israels Propheten* (1916), p. 38.

[50] Beer, *Exodus*, p. 162.

[51] Hoelscher, *Geschichte der israelitischen und juedischen Religion* (1922), p. 129.

[52] Steuernagel, *Einleitung in das Alte Testament* (1912), p. 260.

[53] Beer, *op. cit.*, p. 103.

[54] Budde, *Religion of Israel to the Exile*, p. 33: "both superfluous and impossible."

[55] Mowinckel, *Le Décalogue* (1927), p. 102, is of the opinion that unlike the decalogue the moral elements "seem to be lost within a

long series of ritual and cultic commandments"; but a glance at the text shows that the ritual and cultic commandments constitute less than half in the Egyptian, and only a small fraction in the Babylonian.

[56] Bruno Gutmann, *Die Stammeslehren der Dschagga,* 3 vols. (1932).

[57] Mowinckel, *op. cit.,* p. 101.

[58] Nowack, *Der erste Dekalog* (Baudissin-Festschrift, 1917), p. 395.

[59] Beer, *Mose und sein Werk* (1912), p. 26.

[60] Cf. J. Kaufmann, *History of the Religion of Israel,* II/1, p. 77; he connects Aaron with these influences.

[61] With regard to the powerful influence exerted on Goethe particularly by the "Faustian" element in the Moses saga, cf. the fine essay by Burdach, "Faust und Mose," *Sitzungsberichte der Koeniglich Preussischen Akademie der Wissenschaften, philosophisch-historische Klasse,* 1912.

[62] Mowinckel, *op. cit.,* p. 75.

[63] Wellhausen, *Reste arabischen Heidentums,* p. 102.

[64] Lehmann, "Erscheinungs und Ideenwelt der Religion," in Chantepie de la Saussaye, *Lehrbuch der Religionsgeschichte,* 4th ed. (1925), Vol. I, p. 89.

[65] Thus, e.g., Edvard Lehmann, *ibid.* Vol. I, p. 33; cf. also K. Florenz, "Die Japaner," *ibid.* Vol. I, p. 294; Hempel, *Politische Absicht und politische Wirkung im biblischen Schrifttum* (1938), p. 14; also Gressmann, *Mose,* pp. 203, 207, 211. In my book *The Prophetic Faith,* I have dealt with the matter in detail in the chapter, "The God of the Fathers"; cf. also *Koenigtum Gottes,* pp. 73ff.

[66] Lagrange, *Études sur les religions sémitiques,* 2nd ed. (1905), p. 507; cf. Février, *La Religion des Palmyréens* (1931), p. 37; cf. also Rostovtzeff, "The Caravan-gods of Palmyra," *Journal of Roman Studies,* Vol. XXII (1932), pp. 111f.

[67] Schrader, *Die Keilinschriften und das Alte Testament,* 3rd ed. (1903), p. 29.

[68] Haller, *Religion, Recht und Sitte in den Genesissagen,* p. 23, is of the opinion, to be sure, that YHVH "detached himself from stone, tree, and spring and linked himself with the person of the shepherd," but also remarks: "Or is the process to be regarded as reversed, so that Yahve was originally a protective spirit that wandered with the shepherds and gradually, as the nomads began to settle, became established at a fixed habitation?" Gunkel noted in his copy of Haller's book that stationary god and settled worshipers as Canaanite are faced by "wandering god and wandering nomads as Israelite." It must, however, be added that this god does not sleep in the tents of the nomads like the *teraphim* fetishes, but from time to time withdraws to the spacious heavens, which are inaccessible to men; Jacob's vision of the gate of Heaven is a primordial constituent of the tradition. (That it is therefore impossible to "have" this god may hence have been one of the chief

reasons for the women of the tribe to take the *teraphim* about with them.)

[69] According to Lods, *Israel,* p. 531, the people imagined YHVH with an aerial and therefore invisible body, "susceptible d'apparaître sous des formes diverses."

[70] For the relation between imagelessness and invisibility cf. Max Weber, *Gesammelte Aufsaetze zur Religionssoziologie* (1921), Vol. III, p. 170, who sees the relation otherwise but as no less close: "A god whose cult has been imageless since immemorial time had to be normally invisible as well, and also had to nourish his specific dignity and uncanny quality by means of that invisibility."

[71] Mowinckel, *op. cit.,* p. 103.

[72] Mowinckel, *op. cit.,* p. 60.

[73] Mowinckel, *Psalmenstudien II* (1922), p. 224.

[74] Mowinckel, *Le Décalogue,* p. 100.

[75] Eissfeldt, *Hexateuch-Synopse* (1922), p. 275*.

[76] Cf. Koehler, *Theologie des Alten Testaments,* p. 238: "The fact that in the biblical decalogue any such commandment as 'Thou shalt not lie' is absent awakens all kinds of thoughts."

[77] Gunkel, "Die israelitische Literatur," *Die Kultur der Gegenwart,* I/7 (1906), p. 73.

[78] Gressmann, *Mose,* p. 477.

[79] Cf. Buber-Rosenzweig, *Die Schrift und ihre Verdeutschung,* pp. 176ff.; Staples, "The Third Commandment," *Journal of Biblical Literature,* Vol. LVIII (1939), pp. 325ff.

[80] Cf. Procksch, *Der Staatsgedanke in der Prophetie* (1933), p. 5.

[81] J. M. Powis Smith, *The Origin and History of Hebrew Law* (1931), pp. 8f.

[82] Hempel, *Das Ethos des Alten Testaments* (1938), p. 183.

[83] Volz, *Mose,* 2nd ed., p. 25.

[84] Volz, *Mose,* 1st ed. (1907), pp. 93f.

[85] Caspari, *Die Gottesgemeinde von Sinai,* p. 159.

[86] Sellin, *Geschichte des israelitisch-juedischen Volkes,* Vol. I, p. 72.

[87] Volz, *Mose,* 2nd ed., p. 78.

[88] L. Koehler, "Der Dekalog," *Theologische Rundschau,* Vol. I (1929), p. 184.

[89] Rudolph, *Der "Elohist,"* p. 47.

[90] Cf. Ganszyniec, *Der Ursprung der Zehngebotetafeln* (1920), p. 18. (This little study contains interesting material, from which, however, unwarrantable conclusions are drawn.)

[91] Cf. Eerdmans, *Alttestamentliche Studien III,* pp. 69f.

[92] Morgenstern, *The Book of the Covenant I* (1928), p. 34, argues against the originality of the tradition of the Tables that the description "tables of witness" is late, and is only found in the Priestly Code. But Exodus 32:15, in general, is not attributed to P.

[93] Morgenstern, *loc. cit.,* adduces the absence of any such tradition as his chief argument against the witness character of the tables. But

it seems reasonable to assume that Solomon, with his cult policy which aimed at immobilizing the ark and its contents in order to withdraw political coloration from the *melek* character of YHVH, would have no objection to ordering the removal of all traces of such a tradition (cf. Klamroth, *Lade und Tempel* (1933), p. 60; Buber, *The Prophetic Faith*, pp. 78f.).

[94] Hans Schmidt, *Mose und der Dekalog* (Gunkel-Festschrift), p. 90.

[95] L. Koehler, *Der Dekalog*, p. 179.

[96] Wellhausen (*Die Composition des Hexateuchs*, p. 89), followed by many others, has regarded the word as "most strikingly" Deuteronomic, but this can have a meaning only if the end of the Song of Deborah is mutilated—which has been done by some for no other reason than the use of this word. The turns of phrase which it is customary to regard as Deuteronomic, and hence as late, derive naturally from the history sermon (cf. Koehler, *Der Dekalog*, p. 169), which collected its basic phrases from verbal and written tradition, while admittedly depriving them of their original weight by incorporating them into the rhetorical sequence. The fact that Exodus 34:7 does not mention the haters and the lovers does not prove anything, since here almost half of the sentence, including the entire positive section, has been omitted. This appears to be an extract from the decalogue section, introduced for elucidatory purposes.

[97] A. Klostermann, *Der Pentateuch II* (1907), p. 515.

[98] Jepsen, *Untersuchungen zum Bundesbuch* (1927), p. 25; cf. S. A. Cook, *The Laws of Moses and the Code of Hammurabi* (1903), p. 155.

[99] Cf. Ring, *Israels Rechtsleben im Lichte der neuentdeckten assyrischen und hethitischen Gesetzesurkunden* (1926), p. 148.

[100] Schmoekel, *Das angewandte Recht im Alten Testament*, p. 65.

[101] Cf. *inter alia* Baudissin, *Die Geschichte des alttestamentlichen Priestertums*, p. 35.

[102] Thus Gressmann, *Mose*, pp. 261f.

[103] Cf. Gray, *Sacrifice in the Old Testament*, pp. 249f.

[104] The article "Levi" by Hoelscher, in Pauly-Wissowa's *Real-Enzyklopaedie des klassischen Altertums*, Vol. XII, pp. 2155ff., is most comprehensively based, but is nevertheless an unsuccessful attempt to view the Levites as the ancient priestly order of Kadesh, by whom Moses was supported. Cf. Gray, *Sacrifice in the Old Testament*, pp. 239ff., on the complexity of the problem. Albright's assumption, in *Archaeology and the Religion of Israel* (1942), p. 109, that the Levites were "a class or tribe" which as such exercised sacral functions (even in pre-Mosaic times), and which increased both naturally as well as through children who were dedicated to the service of YHVH, is satisfactory in certain respects, but still does not offer any adequate solution of the problem. And that Moses as well as Aaron were Levites "by virtue of

their priestly function" presupposes a professional priesthood on the part of Moses, which must be questioned.

[105] Cf. Rost, *Die Vorstufen von Kirche und Synagoge im Alten Testament*, pp. 7ff., 32ff.; on Numbers 16f., pp. 10, 14, 90. The double sense of *edah* in our section is not given consideration here.

[106] Cf. Buber and Rosenzweig, *Die Schrift und ihre Verdeutschung*, pp. 217ff.

[107] The latest attempt of which I am aware to prove that Moses was a priest, in Gray's *Sacrifice in the Old Testament*, pp. 198ff., is one that I likewise cannot regard as successful.

[108] This is *inter alia* the thesis of J. Kaufmann, *History of the Religion of Israel*, II/1, pp. 342ff.

[109] Thus, e.g., Bacon, *The Triple Tradition of the Exodus*, p. 190: "Certain prominent individuals aspire to the priesthood and raise rebellion against Moses."

[110] To complete what follows cf. Buber, *Koenigtum Gottes*, pp. 140ff.

[111] Lorenz von Stein, *System der Staatswissenschaft* (Stuttgart, 1856), Vol. II, p. 384.

[112] Franz Rosenzweig, in his *Stern der Erloesung*, has the great merit of having shown this to our era in a new light.

OF JEWISH DESTINY

[1] Franz Rosenzweig, "Judentum und Christentum," appendix to *Briefe*, Berlin 1935.

[2] Baader assumes that the German *Glaube* (faith) is derived from *geloben* (to pledge).

Martin Buber

Martin Buber was born in Vienna in 1878 and was educated at the Universities of Vienna, Berlin, Leipzig, and Zurich. Co-founder of the Judischer Verlag in Germany, he also edited *Der Jude* from 1916 to 1924. With Franz Rosenzweig, he published a German translation of a number of books of the Hebrew Bible in a version considered by many to be comparable to that of Martin Luther. For a time before leaving Germany, he taught at the University of Frankfurt. In 1938 he joined the faculty of the Hebrew University in Jerusalem, retiring from his post after fifteen years to continue his translation of the Bible. His numerous published works cover wide aspects of contemporary philosophy and religious thought, and include studies in Hasidic literature, which have served to revive interest in this Jewish religious movement. In 1954 he received the Goethe Prize in Hamburg. He died in 1956.